C000172656

Yesterday's EXMOOR

Hazel Eardley-Wilmot

EXMOOR BOOKS

Published in association with Exmoor National Park Authority

First published in Great Britain in 1990 by Exmoor Books

ISBN: 0 86183–173–X

British Library Cataloguing-in-Publication Data
Eardley-Wilmot, Hazel
  Yesterday's Exmoor.
  1. England. Exmoor, history
  I. Title
  942.385

Printed and bound in Great Britain by BPCC Wheatons Ltd, Exeter.

EXMOOR BOOKS
Official Publisher to Exmoor National Park Authority
An imprint of Wheaton Publishers Ltd
A member of the Maxwell Communication Corporation plc

Wheaton Publishers Ltd
Hennock Road, Exeter, Devon EX2 8RP
Tel: 0392 74121; Telex: 42794 (WHEATN G)

SALES
Direct sales enquiries to Exmoor Books at the address above

LIST OF SUBSCRIBERS

Mr David R. J. Ackland, *46 Roundfield Road, Minehead, Somerset.*
Gina Ackland, *33 Glenmore Road, Minehead, Somerset.*
Tracy Ackland, *2 Meadow Terrace, Hopcott Road, Minehead, Somerset.*
Mr & Mrs John Adnitt, *Rockford Lodge, Brendon, North Devon.*
Revd Ian Ainsworth-Smith, *Knutsford Cottage, North Street, Milverton, Taunton, Somerset.*
Mrs V. Anand, *53 Melrose Avenue, Mitcham, Surrey.*
Isabel Arkle, *Treetops, Northdown Road, Bideford, Devon.*
Neil Arnold, *30 Alcombe Road, Minehead, Somerset.*

Miss Annabel G. Bain, *27 Duchess of Bedford House, Campden Hill, London.*
N. W. Baker, *Benham Water Farm, Newingreen, Hythe, Kent.*
Rachel J. Bale, *117 Fern Way, Ilfracombe, North Devon.*
Donald R. Barber, *Craigwell, 10 Coulsdon Road, Sidmouth, Devon.*
D. L. Bayley, *10 Tarnwell, Upper Stanton Drew, Nr. Bristol.*
Dr Roger B. Beck, FGS, MIGeol, *1 Walreddon Cottages, Whitchurch, Tavistock, Devonshire.*
Noel Beer, *13 Nelson Road, Rayleigh, Essex.*
F. Bennett, *Newton Ferrers, Devon.*
June Bennett, *106 Bishops Mansions, Bishops Park Road, London.*
Mr J. B. Bentley, *5 Compass Hill, Taunton, Somerset.*
Mr H. H. Betts, *Parkway, 3 Benford Road, Hoddesdon, Herts.*
Mr Courtney Bickey, *59 Canada Road, Heath, Cardiff.*
Blundells School Library, *Tiverton, Devon.*
Anne Born, MA, BLitt, *Oversteps, Froude Road, Salcombe, South Devon.*
C. H. Bowden, *'Rushmere', High Bank, Porlock, Minehead, Somerset.*
Christopher Brewer, *77 Ridgeview Road, London.*
Mrs R. L. B. Brockington, *2 Barton Close, Charlton Kings, Cheltenham, Glos.*
Mr & Mrs J. E. Brown, *'Marham', 14 Shepherds Way, Saffron Walden, Essex.*
John F. Brown, *14 Rylands Lane, Weymouth, Dorset.*
Mrs D. Buckingham, *6 Churchill Crescent, South Molton, Devon.*
M. R. Bull, *Verlands, Pond Road, Hook Heath, Woking, Surrey.*
Mr & Mrs W. R. Bullen, *3 Windsor Close, Minehead, Somerset.*
R. J. Burrough, *6 Overlands, Ruishton, Taunton, Somerset.*
K. J. Burrow, *Bucks Cross, Devon.*
Mr & Mrs J. W. Burt, *Dan-Y-Parc, 93 Parkhouse Road, Minehead, Somerset.*
Roger & Ann Butcher, *Rock Cottage, Brompton Regis, Dulverton, Somerset.*

Mrs B. M. Cameron, *Meadows, Ware Lane, Lyme Regis, Dorset.*
Mrs J. Catchpole, *9 Bishops Avenue, Northwood, Middlesex.*
Peter F. Chapman, *The Castle Hotel, Castle Green, Taunton.*
Sally Chilcott & Family, *8 Almond Grove, Trowbridge, Wiltshire.*
Kevin Chown, *16 Kirkcroft Drive, Killamarsh, Sheffield.*
Brian Gordon Coe, *4 Lawrence Close, Kettering, Northants.*
David Condon, OBE, *Rose Cottaqe, Weir, Dulverton, Somerset.*

Russ & Kath Constant, *7 Park Street, Lynton, North Devon.*
Charles Coombes, *Church Cottage, 164 Slade Road, Portishead, Bristol.*
Mr J. S. & Mrs N. M. Cotton, *15 Back Lane, Cerne Abbas, Dorset.*
Mr S. R. Curtis, *Stable Flat, Simonsbath, Minehead, Somerset.*

C. A. & W. T. David, *8 King Edward Road, Minehead, Somerset.*
Dr Russell M. Davies, *Radworthy, 68 Romsey Road, Winchester, Hants.*
Rowland P. Dell, *Little Close, Wootton Courtenay, Minehead, Somerset.*
F. Dibble, *Quantock Cottage, Triscombe, Bishops Lydeard, Taunton.*
Nigel Dobbins, *Chamberlains Farm, Whitnage, Tiverton, Devon.*

Charles & Sheila Eardley-Wilmot, *Thornbury, Avon.*
Mr & Mrs S. G. Earley, *Little Orchard, Monmouth Road, Staunton, Coleford, Glos.*
John L. Edwards, *Westermill, Exford, Minehead, Somerset.*
Jonathan Wynne Evans, *Knowstone Mill, Knowstone, South Molton.*
The Exmoor Society, Parish Rooms, *Dulverton.*

Ann Feldberg, *Hope Cottage, The Holloway, Minehead, Somerset.*
Dr R. J. Ferrar, *The Cleeve, Lynton, Devon.*
Michael C. Fitter, *'Greensleeves', 6 Avon Road, Keynsham, Bristol.*
Andrew Fleming, *5 Clifford Road, Sheffield.*
T. W. Forster, *South Hill, Shirwell, Barnstaple, Devon.*
The Lady Margaret Fortescue.
Dr M. J. F. Fowler, *60 Harrow Down, Badger Farm, Winchester, Hants.*
Mrs J. R. Frazer, *1 Chantry Place, Rosemary Lane, Colyton, Devon.*
Mrs D. E. Friendship-Taylor, BA, *Toad Hall, 86 Main Road, Hackleton, Northampton.*

Lady Gass, *Fairfield, Stogursey, Near Bridgwater, Somerset.*
R. Gee FCCA, IPFA, *15 St David's Road, Green Lane, Tavistock, Devon.*
Keith Gilfoy, *16 Wordsworth Drive, Taunton, Somerset.*
Mr P. H. Gill, *The Old Cottage, Church Road South, Portishead, Bristol.*
Captain & Mrs W. E. B. Godsal, *Edbrooke House, Winsford, Minehead, Somerset.*
Mr & Mrs S. J. Godsell, *4 Fielden Road, RAF, Benson, Oxfordshire.*
Mr & Mrs Ernst Goldschmidt, *33 place Georges Brugmann, 1060 Brussels, Belgium.*
Miss N. D. Goodwin, *Bugford Cottage, East Down, Barnstaple, N. Devon.*
Wesley & Margaret Gould, *43 Conygar View, Dunster, Minehead, Somerset.*
Dr Alison Grant, *Mimosa, Instow.*
Ian Peter Green, *66 Eastland Road, Yeovil, Somerset.*

David Hall, *The Old Vicarage, Elm Grove, Taunton, Somerset.*
Mr & Mrs Ben Halliday, *Ashton, Countisbury, Lynton, Devon.*
R. O. Hancock, *Staple Cross Cottage, Hockworthy, Wellington, Somerset.*
A. G. Ham, *Hillside Farm, Clewer, Wedmore, Somerset.*
Mr J. E. Hamilton, *9 Jackson Road, Bromley, Kent.*
D. & M. J. Hamlin, *30 Sandhurst Road, Yeovil, Somerset.*
John & Gretha Harding, *Chulmleigh, North Devon.*
Miss M. Hatch-Barnwell, *'The New House', The Parks, Minehead, Somerset.*
Graham Hawkins, *Jordans, West Monkton, Taunton, Somerset.*
Michael Lynton Haycraft, *9 Meadow View, Swinderby, Lincoln.*
Audrey Heckels, *8 Ridgewood, Knoll Hill, Sneyd Park, Bristol.*

A. P. Hill, *7 Shire Close, Cowplain, Hampshire.*
Joseph S. Hines, *11 Fairlawn Grove, Banstead, Surrey.*
Mr J. S. & Mrs K. M. Hobbs, *3 Stepstone Lane, Knowle, Braunton, North Devon.*
L. M. Hubbard, *1 Magnolia Villas, Brixton Street, Bampton, Tiverton, Devon.*
Mr A. G. Huxtable, *The Firs, 1 Maclins Close, South Molton, North Devon.*

Audrey Jane Jenkins.
F. A. Jones, *'Kingswood', Barton Road, Alcombe, Minehead.*

Lt Cdr P. R. Kenyon-Bell, RN, *Broadoaks, Buzzacott Lane, Combe Martin, Ilfracombe, North Devon.*
Gwendolen M. Kirby, *Brackenfield, Winsford, Minehead, Somerset.*
C. J. Kitchener, *Horsacott Bungalow, Lydacott, Newton Tracey, Barnstaple.*
Mr & Mrs I. C. Knifton, *15 Newlands Avenue, Bexhill-on-Sea, East Sussex.*

F. A. Leach, *Westaway, West Street, Bampton.*
Michael Leat, *57 Trelawney Road, Cotham, Bristol.*
Dr Michael A. Leonard, *10 Dukes Orchard, Bradninch, Exeter, Devon.*
Stephen Paul Leworthy, *2 Bradford Cottages, Fore Street, North Molton, Devon.*
George H. Lidstone, *7 Edenhurst Court, Park Hill Road, Torquay, Devon.*
C. J. N. Lindsey, *Ickleton Place, Ickleton, Cambridgeshire.*
Georgina Longthorne, *2 Lower Wilbury Farm, Stotford Road, Letchworth, Herts.*
John Holland Lovett, *Helena, Littlemoor Road, Mark, Near Highbridge, Somerset.*

Mrs M. H. Mackender, *9 Hopcott Close, Minehead, Somerset.*
Mr David Machin, *4 South Square, Gray's Inn, London.*
Ronald Maggs, *Pendower House, Hillcommon, Taunton, Somerset.*
Mr & Mrs Edward Mattocks, *Goose Cottage, 12 Spring Lane, Colden Common, Winchester, Hants.*
Derek Maude, *Bridge End Cottage, Ockham Lane, Ockham, Woking, Surrey.*
G. L. McCracken, *Gray Gables, Cheriton Fitzpaine, Crediton, Devon.*
G. C. Merrifield, *Ash Court, 5 Stanway Close, Taunton, Somerset.*
Brian Le Messurier, *11 Landsdowne, Woodwater Lane, Exeter.*
Roger Miles, *Collipriest House, Tiverton, Devon.*
Mrs Olive Moody, *Westcott, Parkhouse Road, Minehead, Somerset.*
S. A. Mucklejohn, *Wigston Magna, Leicestershire.*

P. A. Osmond, *London.*
Mrs E. L. Overstall, *6 Marlingdene Close, Hampton, Middlesex.*
Mr K. G. & Mrs D. I. Owen, *4 King Street, Tavistock, Devon.*
Alistair Ozanne, FRMetS, *Venniford, Tivington, Minehead.*

Anna Parry-Jones, *Brunswick Place, Bath, Avon.*
Mr Gerald Passmore, *31 Paganel Road, Minehead, Somerset.*
Mr J. W. Passmore, *Huntspill, The Parks, Minehead, Somerset.*
Mrs H. A. Peacock, *Burrowlea, Exeter Road, Rewe, Exeter.*
C. D. Pike, OBE, DL, *Dunderdale Lawn, Penshurst Road, Newton Abbot, Devon.*
D. B. Post, *Lower Sellicks, Roadwater, Watchet, Somerset.*

Henrietta & Norman Quinnell, *9 Thornton Hill, Exeter.*

J. E. Rawle, *1 Queen Edith's Way, Cambridge.*
Paul Rendell, *20 Rolston Close, Southway, Plymouth, Devonshire.*
D. B. Richards, *5 Wychwood Close, Earley, Reading, Berks.*
J. K. Ridler, MBE, *West Wind, Wootton Courtenay, Minehead, Somerset.*
Dr J. W. Rodgers, *Combe Bank Cottage, Brayford, Barnstaple, Devon.*
Captain R. F. B. Roe, RN, *Seafin, Charlton Adam, Somerton, Somerset.*
F. C. Rose, *Flitton Mill, North Molton, Devon.*
Mr B. Rowe, *31 Harepark Terrace, Alcombe, Minehead, Somerset.*
Eric E. Rowlands, *Luccombe, Minehead, Somerset.*

J. A. Samuel, *Salisbury House, Heasley Mill, South Molton, Devon.*
Ian Segar, *Amberley, The Parks, Minehead, Somerset.*
Misses M. J. & M. Shapland, *Pilton, Barnstaple, Devon.*
Tim & Caroline Shipsey, *Little Court Cottage, Grib Lane, Blagdon, Avon.*
Dennis & Maud Sims, *28 Long Park, Chesham Bois, Amersham, Bucks.*
J. H. Skinner, *60, North Brink, Wisbech, Cambridgeshire.*
Miss Sally Ann Smith, *76 Parkhouse Road, Minehead, Somerset.*
S. Smith, *Oxfordshire.*
M. A. Storr, *Saddlers Cottage, Westleigh, Tiverton, Devon.*
Bertram H. Sweetman, *'Kelfield', 24 Parkhouse Road, Minehead, Somerset.*

Hugh Thomas, *Elm House, Bishops Tawton, Barnstaple, Devon.*
Mrs G. M. Thomson, *The Dormer House, 8 North Avenue, Leicester.*
Mrs E. Thorne, *Bowchurch Farm, Molland, South Molton, Devon.*
Jeremy N. Trood, *27 Ashburnham Place, Greenwich, London.*
Neil B. Trood, *Blackdown Cottage, Curland, Taunton, Somerset.*
Timothy B. Trood, *Forest Cottage, Curland, Taunton, Somerset.*
Mrs J. G. Trouton, *North Wheddon Farm, Wheddon Cross, Minehead, Somerset.*
R. E. Tudball, *4 Chertsey Close, Woolavington, Bridgwater, Somerset.*
Dr A. J. Tugwell, *10 Sandringham Road, Newton Abbot, Devon.*
Mr K. G. Tyers, *17 Rosebarn Lane, Exeter, Devon.*

John Usmar, *Engine Park, Witheridge, Tiverton.*

F. H. Waight, *Tyn Rhos, Treuddyn, Mold, Clwyd.*
Mrs J. M. R. Walpole, *Seloplaw, Drews Pond Lane, Devizes, Wiltshire.*
Mrs Ethel L. West, *4 Tanyard Lane, Carhampton, Minehead, Somerset.*
Mrs Mary White, *Warrs Farm, Luckwell Bridge, Wheddon Cross, Near Minehead, Somerset.*
D. S. Whitelegge, *Westport Lodge, Cricket St Thomas, Chard, Somerset.*
G. W. G. Whybrow, *Buzon 166, Mijas la Nueva 44, Mijas (Malaga), Spain.*
Mr S. M. Wide, *56 First Avenue, Worthing, West Sussex.*
John & Patricia Woodburne, *4 Prospect Cottages, Blackmore's Path, Lynton, North Devon.*
Reginald A. Woodley, *50 Poundfield Road, Minehead, Somerset.*

FOREWORD

Towards 1970 two Exmoor farmers were pondering the changes
of the previous two decades. They had known the moor all their
lives, and the small farms they rented were Saxon holdings named
in Domesday Book. One summed up their talk: 'There isn't going
to *be* any Exmoor, is there, not as we knew it, by the time our
children are grown up?' The other agreed. A yesterday many
centuries old had ended somewhere about 1950. This book is for
remembrance.

It could not have been written without the help and
encouragement of many people over many years. Some of
them are named in its pages; the reader, like the writer, is
indebted to them all.

HAZEL EARDLEY-WILMOT
NORTH MOLTON, 1989

To
Ernest Mold

CONTENTS

ACKNOWLEDGEMENTS

The jacket illustration of Lyn Gorge in 1884 is by an Irish artist, J. A. H. Jameson, who worked on the popular coastal fringe of Exmoor for some years. (The figures in blue are his wife and two of their children.) The painting was lent by the artist's great-granddaughter, Mrs Quinn.

No. 33 was provided by the owner, Mr Samuel Josefowitz, and no. 22 by Dr E. Mold. Nos 8, 9, 17 and 24 are from Chadwyck Healey's *History of part of West Somerset* and no. 16 from Savage's *History of the Hundred of Carhampton*, all reproduced from copies in the West Country Studies Library. No. 20 is from Page's *Exploration of Exmoor* and 26 from N. Allen's microstudy *Churches and Chapels of Exmoor*. No. 5 was drawn especially for this book.

No. 6 is from the Occleve MS in the British Library, 14 from the National Maritime Museum, 15 and 23 from the National Portrait Gallery, 19 from the Ashmolean Museum and 35 from the Press Association. No. 21, from Molland church archive, was photographed by M. Deering, and 25 by courtesy of Somerset Record Office.

Nos 31 and 32 are photographs of old picture-postcards, lent by Alan Buckingham and Susan Proctor respectively. No. 34 is from an unidentified Lynton donor. No. 30 and the more recent 7 and 13 are from Exmoor National Park, and 18 from the Royal Commission on the Historical Monuments of England. The rest were given by the friends named in the captions.

All maps were devised by the author and drawn by Ian Foulis & Associates. Information on Map 3 is from MacDermot's *History of the Forest of Exmoor*. Map 4 records new work.

LIST OF ILLUSTRATIONS

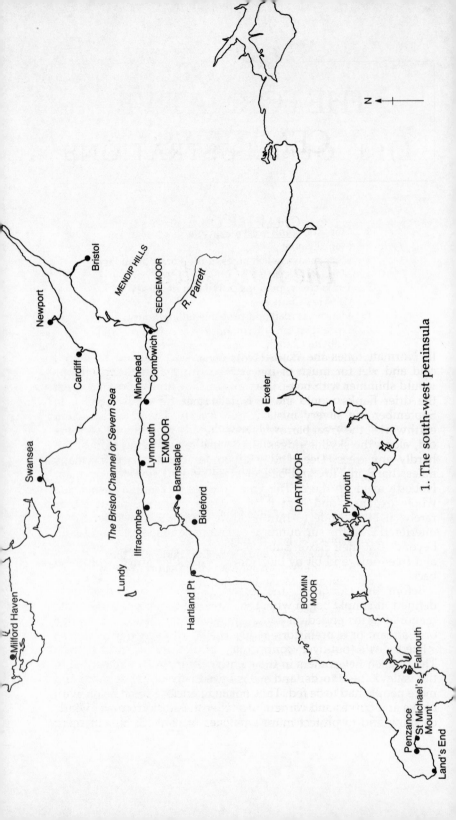

1. The south-west peninsula

PART I

THE FORMATIVE CENTURIES

CHAPTER ONE

The King's deer

In Norman times the Forest of Exmoor was untilled highland, cold and wet for much of the year. In June the sodden hilltops would shimmer with bog-cotton in sunshine and wind; in August the drier flanks would glow with heather for a few weeks; in September the silvery mists would return. There were ancient earthworks, the great barrow graves, already more than 2000 years old, along the skyline ridges, and a few tall standing stones, but hardly any trees. Deer and wild ponies roamed free for many miles, hare and fox and badger were seldom troubled by man. Nobody lived up there. The French kings in London owned the whole expanse, and kept it as a game preserve, though they rarely, if ever, came to hunt. Through rapacious wardens they interfered with the surrounding commons, and even the farmland beyond. But their Saxon subjects remembered former boundaries and freedoms, and bit by bit, from century to century, won them back.

Before the Conquest, the Forest had been only negatively defined. It simply began where the unfenced rough pasture of the manorial farms ended, at some convenient landmark like a ridge or a stream or a prehistoric road. The word *forest* meant *outland* – like today's 'out-over' contrasted with the 'in-bye' near home.[1] The English newcomers in the eighth century A.D. had settled in the valleys, near fords, and spread gradually uphill as more and more people had to be fed. They began to enclose small fields, with banks and curves and corners to shelter the stock from wet winds or snow and to protect minute patches of corn. Each settlement

1

was part of a manor, and the lord would allow his cottagers to graze their few cows or pigs or goats on his waste land, and to cut themselves furze and peat. Gradually these concessions came to be seen as rights of common, stubbornly guarded, and the outer edge of the common became also the edge of the parish. The difficult moorland higher up was merely an unclaimed part of England, rather vaguely belonging to the king.

Some of the Saxons had come westward from the rich farmland round North Petherton – all royal country, from the beginning – and cultivated the fertile land along the coast; Carhampton was one of the estates King Alfred left to his eldest son. They had suffered heavily from raiding Norsemen, who could beach their ships anywhere between Watchet and Porlock and harry inland. But from the great hill-fort *Cynuit*, on Wind Hill at Countisbury, the Devon Saxons so crushed a large invading force that the King, beleaguered in the Somerset marshes, was able to rally an army there, fortify Athelney, and soon afterwards, on the Wiltshire border, defeat Guthrum's Danes and make a peace whereby all Wessex became secure. Alfred built up his defences with a network of forts – including one at Pilton and one at Watchet – and an effective navy (he himself designed a long ship which could outmanoeuvre the Viking 'dragons'),[2] and meanwhile set about civilizing his demoralized people. He educated the hardly literate clergy by inviting bishops and scholars from abroad, he initiated the national chronicle which the monasteries continued for some three centuries, he himself translated important religious and philosophical books from Latin into English, collected and edited the old and newer laws, sifted and stimulated slack judges, and listened to explorers and recorded what they told. Amidst all this, says his friend and biographer Bishop Asser, he pursued all manner of hunting and gave instruction to all his goldsmiths and craftsmen as well as to his falconers, hawk-trainers, and dog-keepers. He sent a pair of fine wolf-hounds as a gift to the Archbishop of Rheims, and he went hunting in Cornwall. Whether he chased the Exmoor deer is not known, but it would be surprising if he did not.

The Danish raids and the strengthening of Christianity both touched the moor. Bishop Asser saw and described *Arx Cynuit*, and it is tempting to surmise that Countisbury church, looking across to the hillfort, had been built as a thank-offering for the victory, and that he was on a pastoral visit. The tiny church of Culbone, founded earlier by a Celtic saint, is not alone in having traces of Saxon masonry.

But the chief activity of the West Saxon farmers round the moor must always have been taming the ground and winning food from it. A century and a half elapsed between the death of English Alfred and the coming of Norman William, and it was a period of miserable disasters. The Danish raids were renewed and intensified (at Porlock and at Watchet again, as elsewhere). The raiders harried and conquered more and more of the country, until resistance ended and for nearly thirty years all England was ruled by Danish kings. When Alfred's line was restored, there was conflict between the King, Edward the Confessor, and his chief minister, Godwin, who was outlawed for a time, together with two of his sons – one of them the future King Harold. Godwin sailed, plundering, along the south coast from Kent to Portland; Harold brought soldiers in nine ships from Ireland to Porlock, marched them overland to join his father, and returned eastward with him to attack London. Yet most of the hill-farms which encircle the true Forest today were carved out of the rough land before Domesday, and Saxon kings were taking a rent for summer grazing up on the Forest itself. (One such rent accompanied the tenure of the royal manor of Molland which Earl Harold held under King Edward.) There is nothing to show whether the later English kings hunted the Forest, but certainly the lords of the neighbouring manor-farms must have killed – and eaten – deer which ravaged their crops.

Domesday Book records three Saxons – Dodo, Almar and Godric – holding land in the parish of Withypool until King Edward's death, and describes them as *forestarii*. The French-Latin word used by the Norman clerks, translating the sworn information of local Saxons, may or may not have meant that Exmoor was already a hunting forest. The three men lived near the outland, and close to the steep woods of the Barle valley, always full of deer. Dodo also held land near Dulverton, not specified by name in Domesday but lately identified as probably Hawkridge.[3] That too has ancient woodland beside the Barle.

The Conqueror evicted them at once, and gave the tenancies in both parishes to Robert de Auberville or Osburville: this French follower also held part of the crown estate of South Petherton with the duty of 'keeping' the five Somerset forests – Mendip, Selwood, Neroche, Petherton and Exmoor. The link was to become important. Robert soon acquired other estates, including Exton, and when his last descendant died, a century later, his whole 'barony' was leased with the wardenship of the forests. Withypool, Hawkridge and Exton were then all part of the royal manor of North Petherton or Newton (where the Alfred Jewel was found). Consequently their farmers, unlike any others on the moor, were tenants of the warden and sub-tenants of the King, and the duties and privileges stemming from this special position lasted for more than four centuries.

The Norman kings, with their passion for the chase, claimed nearly seventy royal forests. Exmoor had a disadvantage for them – it lacked trees. The wooded combes where the deer could harbour and breed were for the most part in the manorial land surrounding it. So all the adjacent country, and sometimes much more, was declared 'purlieu', subject to the oversight of the King's officers and the inflexible Forest Law. The Normans had brought this with them. It was full of foreign words and concepts – purpresture and assart, venison and vert, chiminage and pannage.[4] The essence of it was that all wild deer were the King's animals. They must be neither killed nor in any way inconvenienced, and there must be no interference with the 'vert' – the young greenery on which they browsed. Hunting, then and long afterwards, involved archery as well as pursuit; horsemen and hounds drove the deer towards well-placed marksmen. (In the thirteenth and fourteenth centuries some manors were held of the King by a duty laid on the tenant to provide him with three barbed arrows whenever he might come to Exmoor.) This way of stag-hunting was still customary in the sixteenth and early seventeenth centuries; Shakespeare, in a little scene in *Love's Labour's Lost* (IV. i.) showed a visiting princess, the King's guest, waiting with bow and arrow at the edge of a coppice, to shoot at driven deer, and later, in *As You Like It* (II. i.), he described the miserable suffering of a stag which had been wounded but not killed. So the mediaeval law decreed that nobody might have 'bows or arrows, or dogs or greyhounds' in the Forest or purlieus without special warrant. Any mastiff, and later any dog too big to be drawn through a stirrup, must be lamed and kept lame. No woodland might be felled, no fresh ground enclosed for cultivation. Penalties for offences against the venison were pitiless – mutilation, long imprisonment, banishment or death. It was said to be safer to be a beast than a Christian man, where Forest Law prevailed.

An English chronicler who lived through the Conqueror's reign weighed the good and bad when it ended. He praised the establishment of peace and good order; nobody dared break the law; a man could ride across the kingdom carrying gold, without fear of robbery. The country had been surveyed, cathedrals built, monks encouraged. But the evil was heavier. The King's castles burdened the neighbouring poor; taxation was extortionate; 'assuredly in his time men suffered grievous oppression and manifold injuries'. The prose gives way to bitter and ironical verse:

A bad man was the king...
He was sunk in greed and utterly given up to avarice.
He set apart a vast deer preserve and imposed laws concerning it.
Whoever slew a hart or a hind was to be blinded.
He forbade the killing of boars even as the killing of harts,

4

For he loved the stags as dearly as though he had been their
   father.
Hares, also, he decreed should go unmolested.
The rich complained and the poor lamented,
But he was indifferent to his people's hatred,
And those who wished to keep their lands and goods and his
   favour
Had to submit entirely to his will.

After his death, the peace and order did not last, and oppression
grew steadily worse; within fifty years there was total anarchy,
under the spineless King Stephen and the unbridled tyranny of
his barons. A monk recorded the miseries: 'Men said openly that
Christ and his holy ones were asleep.' Remoteness and poverty
may have saved Exmoor from the worst troubles of that time, but
when national order was restored, under Henry II, and the towns
were gaining their charters, life in and near the outlands grew
more difficult than ever. Henry and his two sons Richard I and
John annexed more and more land around the royal forests, and
strengthened the savage decrees. King John enlarged his Exmoor
domain right out to Wootton Courtenay and Dulverton. Here,
as elsewhere, his greed helped to unite Normans and English
against him, until in 1215 at Runnymede they compelled him to
sign Magna Carta.
   As a result of this, all the recent extensions were annulled, the
boundaries of all forests to be as they were on the day of Henry
II's coronation. In fact only King John's encroachments were
disafforested at once, his father's and his brother's being deferred
for full enquiry. Shortly afterwards King John died, and was
succeeded by the boy-king Henry III; a perambulation of Exmoor
made for him shows an interim boundary at the north-east corner
of the Forest – running from County Gate along the coast road
to Hawkcombe Head, and thence to Alderman's Barrow. This
freed Culbone, but left a big loop of Porlock parish within the
Forest, as well as much of Oare. In 1217 a new Forest Charter
was issued in the name of the young king, moderating stern
practices and known abuses: 'Henceforth let no man lose life or
members for our venison.' But the promises were not kept, the
grievances accumulated again, and in 1225 a reissue of the charter
had to be bought by a capital levy of 'the fifteenth part of all the
(movable) goods of the men of England'. In 1258 a petition from
the barons in Parliament complained that in spite of this the king
(still Henry III) had 'reafforested at his will'. In 1279 a statement of
the grievances of the people of Somerset pointed to reafforestation
and oppression of many kinds, 'contrary to the charter'. By 1301
Edward I was in such need of money that he reluctantly agreed to
honour the old boundaries, though he demanded another 'grant'

of one-fifteenth from 'the community of our kingdom'. Four years later he persuaded the Pope to overrule this concession. (The Papal power to excommunicate offenders was a formidable weapon, putting the victim right outside the shelter of society – an outlaw, in soul as well as body.) Soon afterwards the King added his own revocation.

Nonetheless, Parliament was slowly winning. At the accession of Edward III as a minor, the complaints were renewed, and in 1327 the bounds recognized in 1301 – which freed the remaining loop of Porlock Common, and Hawkcombe Head – became statutory. Results were not immediate, but by the end of the century the three-hundred-year-old tyranny had lost most of its force. Though the deer remained royal property, nearly all borderers had the full use of their land. From 1508, under the first of the Tudors, the Forest of Exmoor itself, not merely the wardenship, was leased, usually for three lives, and except briefly under the Commonwealth this system lasted until the Crown land was sold in 1819. The King retained no hunting rights, and Forest Law was at an end.

The charters and the complaints show what was happening in all the seventy royal forests, under greedy foresters, during those bad centuries. In addition, E. T. MacDermot, tireless historian of the Forest of Exmoor, scrutinizing every known record with a lawyer's sharp eye, found specific local evidence. Surprisingly, he was able to show, in his *History*, that very few deer were killed, even for their royal owners. The profit of the Forest was not in venison, but in fines and extortion, and income from the summer grazing. Now and again the King issued a warrant for one stag, or one hind, to be allowed to an eminent landowner living nearby. In 1237 the lord of North Molton was given two stags, by special royal command; on another occasion the lord of Dunster Castle was authorized to kill four. Once Edward II sent huntsmen and hounds to take twenty stags to be salted for his larder: fresh venison might be too high at the end of a long journey, roads being what they were. Travelling archbishops or bishops, earls or barons, were entitled to kill one or two deer as they passed through any royal forest, provided they blew their horns as they hunted, to notify the foresters, but there is no record, nor much likelihood, of such an occasion on Exmoor. The Warden had permission to take one or two a year, his foresters apparently none; perhaps they were allowed a hare from time to time. Poachers were hunted down, imprisoned until judgement if they were caught, and outlawed or banished if they were identified but not arrested. There is no knowing, of course, how many took the risk and ate the good meat and were never detected.

The aim of the borderers had always been to perpetuate, if they could, the limits of the true Forest, recognized as royal land,

and try to retain some of their old rights in the 'purlieus', the surrounding parishes, where Forest Law was an encroachment. The boundary was an invisible line across wild moorland, and knowledge of it depended on the countryman's long memory, in days when few could read and very little was written down. Since the commons reached to the boundary, even the poorest labourers had a stake in this. Every few years the Forest was 'perambulated' – ridden round, from landmark to landmark, by foresters together with farmers – and besides that each bordering parish beat its own bounds every spring. So everyone knew where the ancient line ran, and if the King was brandishing his power far beyond it, countrymen would remember carefully, and bide their time. Exact information would be handed down from father to son. If there was a serious wrong to be righted, local knowledge might run back two or three centuries, and it was respected in the courts.

The boundary which was agreed in 1301, revoked soon afterwards, and then legalized in 1327, surrounded the present parish of Exmoor, or Simonsbath, with Oare joined to it. Oare was not royal property, and its inclusion is odd. Its landowners ranked as 'Suitors at Large', as did those of all parishes bordering the moor (except Withypool and Hawkridge).[5] This meant only that they must attend the Swainmote courts held twice a year, and in return they were allowed to graze their stock on the Crown land at less than full fee. By the time of the 1632 perambulation Oare was recognized as outside the Forest. Perhaps it had fallen away quietly in 1508, when the King could not lease land which did not belong to him.

Another curiosity is that the disafforestation of Withypool and Hawkridge in 1327 made little real difference. They were part of the royal manor of North Petherton which every Warden held, and the first incumbent, Robert de Auberville, made clever use of this. He had to 'keep' all the five Somerset forests, controlling the agistment (the rented grazing) of stock and enforcing the harsh new laws. For Exmoor alone the task was immense. Paid foresters were resented; later the authorized number was only three – one on horseback and two afoot – for the whole moor. It would only be possible if he could enlist local help. Exton was inconveniently far away, but Hawkridge and Withypool, farmed by fifty-two of his own tenants, had commons adjoining the Forest. He offered them the system of the 'Free Suitors', which proved thoroughly satisfactory to both sides.

In return for duties undertaken, the fifty-two farmers were given valuable privileges. They had free grazing for a specified number of animals, though only by day. They were allowed to cut as much turf, heather and bracken as they could use in their own homesteads, and to fish the rivers inside the Forest, and the

Barle outside it where it flowed through the two parishes – again, only for themselves. (They might not fish in the week preceding a Swainmote Court, when it would have been tempting to give or trade a fine salmon away.) They were exempt from jury service outside the Forest, and were entitled to buy or sell tax-free at any fair or market in the realm. Their duties included driving the Forest for horses, cattle or sheep, when summoned by the Warden, up to nine times a year, and riding the whole boundary with him when required (once in seven years at the least). They were to serve on the coroner's jury for any dead body found in the Forest, and to attend the two Swainmote Courts held annually, one at Lanacre, in the 'Court Hams', on the day after Ascension Day, and the other a fortnight later in Hawkridge churchyard. These dealt with minor offences or disputes, not with deer-stealing. That was a very serious crime, taken to a higher court, the Forest Eyre, held in a Somerset town when the Justice of all the forests south of Trent came on circuit. The Exmoor Warden and his officers would be present, with a jury of 'twelve good and free men' drawn from any part of the county. Free Suitors or Suitors at Large might be called to give evidence if the theft had occurred in their parish. It was a long ride to Ilchester, Somerton or Wells, and absence was penalized. Yet, disproportionate as it all seems now, it was due legal process instead of arbitrary punishment. It tended to draw Saxon and Norman together to see that the law, however harsh, was upheld. There is no sign that the fifty-two Suitors disliked their role, and when their two parishes were disafforested 'the King's farmers' went on fulfilling their obligations and claiming their privileges exactly as before.

All this explains why there was no manor-house in Withypool or Hawkridge. (Lanacre was not the manor until much later.) The Wardens, with all the Somerset forests to superintend, would hardly choose to live at this high western extremity when at North Petherton they had a comfortable home in the smiling lowland country of the Saxon kings. Only two of them left any trace on Exmoor – both at Hawkridge. They were William Brewer and William de Plessy, a hunting warden and a warden indulgent to poachers. It is not clear where either of them lodged.

The last de Auberville had been succeeded by an able servant of the Crown, William de Wrotham, and his descendants. During the minority of the third of that line, King John seems to have appointed two or three temporary wardens at the same time; it was the year after Magna Carta, and each would pay him a useful fee. The longest-lasting of them, William Briwer or Brewer, was tenant 'during pleasure' for nine years (1216–25). He was an influential man. In 1204 he had been one of the nine – a bishop and four earls among them – who witnessed King John's charter disafforesting Devon. In the same year he was awarded the royal manor of Axminster, and in 1207 became Sheriff of Somerset for two years. On appointing him to look after the Somerset forests the king notified the sheriff then in office, adding 'and therefore we command you that you lay not your hand on Exton, Hawkridge and Withypool or the rest which pertain to the aforesaid Manor of Niwentone' (Newton, part of Petherton). Perhaps Brewer had his eye on the wooded valleys of Exe and Barle and insisted on this? In the following year he obtained special royal licence to hunt stags in the Somerset forests. His brief tenure covered the 1219 perambulation when the furthest encroachments were annulled, and the shortened boundary ran along Winsford Hill and down between the two Ashways to the Barle, 'and along the water of Barle to where Danesbrook falls into Barle'.[6] West of this the Danesbrook was – and still is – the county boundary, and the Devon side was outside the Forest. Above the confluence, on the last spur of Hawk Ridge, stood the small prehistoric earthwork now called Brewer's Castle, commanding river, stream, woods and ford.

After the perambulation – in which he took no recorded part – William Brewer was commissioned to find out, in association with the Bishops of Bath and Salisbury and the Earl of Salisbury or his deputy, which encroachments in Wiltshire, Dorset and Somerset were made by King John, and which by his brother or father. The bishops would gather information from the parish clergy, but to answer for Exmoor, which was outside all the parishes, Brewer must have needed close understanding of the country and its people. Had he already acquired this through hunting? Was he trusted by his tenants as well as by Hubert de Burgh and the Council of Regency, so that Exmoor people remembered his name when they forgot the de Aubervilles and de Wrothams, wardens for much longer? And why was his name attached to the ancient fort?

It can only be conjecture. He would hardly have built a castle, or seriously restored the old one, when no fighting was required. An elaborate house would be inappropriate, since his appointment was only 'during pleasure', and his visits to this westernmost forest are likely to have been short. But he would need some kind of hunting-lodge. The wooded hillside overlooking river and stream would be an ideal place for that. Did he convert the old earthwork? Or perhaps have something smaller built in a less conspicuous position? A few years ago an exploratory visit in spring to consider these questions led to an interesting find.

About half-way downhill between the old fort and Castle Bridge the slope broadens into a flat apron-like shelf before curving steeply down again, and there, in a slight clearing among tall beeches, are the remains of a small rectangular building, not shown on the Ordnance Survey maps. Three stretches of sandstone walling, little more than a foot high, define the shape, and very low banks, disturbed now by the roots of beech trees in one corner, complete it. In summer, long straggling grass-blades veil it all.

The ruin is some nine paces long and eight across, and runs almost north–south. The hill shelters it from north and west, and on the exposed east side the wall is twice as strong as elsewhere – about 4 ft thick and made of a *double* row of boulders. The outer ones are squared (or very carefully selected) and fit close together. A big slab of stone lies on the surface within the northern end, and on the south, outside the wall, is what might be a sunny platform or might be only debris. The whole thing, with the walls at their full height and a well-thatched roof, would have been weather-proof and snug, and beautifully situated for watching the deer go down to drink.

It does not suggest a shepherd's cot, either in structure or position. Moreover there stands, lower down to eastward on the valley floor, the ruin of 'Castle Farm' – a three-roomed longhouse with adjacent walled enclosures as though for garden, pens and in-fields. Owners are recorded in the mid-eighteenth century, but it was uninhabited by the 1840s, and is shown on the Tithe Map as a ruin. (A chimney stood for nearly a century more.) The building of longhouses persisted far into mediaeval and even modern times, so they are seldom datable. This one might be coeval with the walled rectangle higher up, and if so would have made unnecessary a shepherd's cot so near; or it might be later, made partly with stones rolled downhill from the other site. Perhaps the little farmstead, or a timber-built forerunner of it, provided food for the Warden and his huntsman or keeper, up in their lodge with bows and arrows to hand? A haunch of venison now and then would be a welcome recompense.

Whether the hillside ruin was indeed Brewer's hunting-lodge may never be known. But until there is proof to the contrary, one can continue to wonder.

The permission to hunt in the King's Forest was granted personally to Brewer. Richard de Wrotham, who succeeded him in 1225, was unpopular. He reafforested, and the Sheriff was ordered to support his foresters by arresting and imprisoning poachers who had escaped over the boundary. Carhampton farmers complained that he was grazing their commons. After twenty-five years he died without issue, leaving four married sisters, and the wardenship passed to William de Plessy, son of the eldest, at the annual rent of fourteen heifers and one young bull, or ten pence for each.

This first de Plessy warden may have lived somewhere in Hawkridge for a time, and died there. In the church is a stone tomb-lid, carved with a simple and gracefully decorated cross, and a surrounding Latin and French inscription, not fully deciphered, to a 'William de...' who might be de Plessy. Style and lettering are thought to suit the decade of his death in 1274. (Some forty years later a Robert de Plecy was rector of the parish.) During repair-work in 1877 the slab was found built into the wall, near the pulpit. The coffin has not survived.

Hawkridge, tiny nowadays, took precedence of Withypool at that time. The parish church was here, and St Andrew's at Withypool was only a Chapel of Ease. The Hawkridge font, made from a single lopsided boulder of tawny Hangman Grits (not immediately local) is touchingly primitive. The Norman doorway has simple dignity, as of country masons doing their best with an unfamiliar design. The congregation cannot have been large, but in 1270 a dozen Hawkridge men were charged with 'offences against the vert', and others for clearing woodland or heath to grow corn. Did the fine deer-coverts, near the little town of Dulverton which could be reached from the outer world by several long roads, attract de Plessis as well as Brewer? If he brought a retinue, more cottages would be needed, more firewood and more food, so more wild land would have to be tamed.

William de Plessy, a shadowy figure now, only to be glimpsed from a few brief records, was obviously less than satisfactory to his masters. Two thirteenth-century records of Somerset Eyres are a stiff reminder that the Justice of all the forests south of Trent, and not the Warden, represented the King. The Justice received reports made shortly before each Eyre by 'regarders' chosen for him by the Sheriff. In 1257 they said that John, the parson of Hawkridge, had cleared several acres of woodland and sown them with corn for four years. In 1270 he did worse than that.[7] Two Molland poachers had lately shot a hind, chased her out of the Forest and killed her near their Devon home; it was alleged that they 'were wont often to enter the aforesaid forest with intent to do evil to the venison, and they were harboured in the house of John then the chaplain of Hawkridge, who consented to their evil deeds'. They lived outside the Forest, out of reach, but he was detained in prison. He was, however, 'pardoned for the sake of the King's soul'.

There is no mention of de Plessy or his foresters in this connection, but he had trouble enough at the same Eyre. An Anstey man, and one from 'Cridilaunde' (Kidland?), 'with many other evil doers, whose names are to be discovered, entered the forest' (on 22nd July, 1269) 'with bows and arrows with intent to do evil to the venison of the Lord King, and remained there for three days following'. Like the Molland poachers, they escaped, and were reported to the Sheriff of Devon, who was ordered to bring them to justice. 'And because the aforesaid evil doers were there for so long a time and William de Plesset the forester in fee neither took them nor raised hue and cry, nor his foresters,

11

therefore to judgement with him and his foresters.' The sequel is not known, but within four years of this, shortly before de Plessy died, jurors at Carhampton said that the Lord King's Justice of the Forest had lately dismissed him from the stewardship, 'but they know not whether he was ejected by sentence of law or not'. The hereditary wardenship passed to his nephew, Richard, and if the tomb-lid is indeed his, William was buried at Hawkridge. Perhaps John the chaplain took the funeral, and poachers attended, for the sake of *his* soul?

The law allowed no fences round the Forest, because they would hinder the movement of the deer. Sometimes this made poaching easier, sometimes more difficult. The Devon boundary with the Hawkridge woods was very convenient, not only for the Anstey and Molland neighbours but even for a hunting party from Tawstock. Normans as well as Saxons were killing the royal deer; in 1270 several members of the de Regny family of Hele were in trouble, and Simon the Miller of Bampton was described as 'an habitual evil-doer to the venison of the Lord King'. In the fourteenth century, when the surviving records are more frequent (until they peter out in the 1370s) the offences against the deer begin to look different. Many take place outside the reduced Forest, though within reach of Forest Law. In 1338 a Molland farmer was charged with killing a stag which he found in his rye, 'two leagues and more outside the said forest'.

In 1364 Sir Robert Cornu and his men surrounded Burrow Wood in Winsford and killed a specially protected stag, and another such, two years later, when he was fox-hunting near Dulverton. Even the Abbot of Athelney and his brother were said to have 'beset' a wood one Michaelmas and taken a calf. In 1364, too, James de Audele of North Molton was accused of having his park badly enclosed (meaning that the deer could get in but perhaps not out). He may have been within his rights – the decisions of these later eyres are not on record. Four years later he killed a stag inside the Forest. The old brutal punishments were past, and a man who could afford the fine might not grudge it, to have the day's excitement and the venison at the end of it, and perhaps to settle a score with the gamekeepers.

Meanwhile, offences concerned with land and herbage were increasing. In 1270 there had been a few: seven men of Withypool and Exford were fined a shilling each for cutting turf, and a great many from the neighbourhood of Dulverton for interfering with the vert – perhaps cutting saplings or ash-stakes, or taking away firewood. Their names are descriptive – William le Petit of Huckham, William le Lung of Mousehanger, Thomas Bullock, William the Stodhurd of Hawkridge, Richard the miller and Robert the Miller from further away, and – interesting evidence of early cloth-making – William le Combère and Robert le Fulur, both of Dulverton. There had been graver trouble too, from the Lanacre farmers who in the 1250s and 1260s persistently enclosed land and sowed it with oats and winter corn. By the 1330s misdeeds varied. The lord of Oare and his tenants were cutting peat without warrant, the rector was felling oak saplings and carrying them away at will, though the accusers insisted that Oare was within the Forest. Perhaps the lord and the rector thought, with reason, that it should have been disafforested in 1327. At Lucott 100 acres of heath were swaled by accident, when the fire leapt a path, and near North Molton three men burnt 1000 acres deliberately. The climax came, from all sides at once, in 1335, when the grazing restrictions were triumphantly flouted.

The Warden, Mathew Pecche, together with two 'foresters on foot', a verderer, the independent 'regarders' and 'twelve good and free men' declared on oath that some twenty-eight owners of bordering land, including two abbots, the lord of Dunster (who owned Cutcombe), Hugh de Courtenay (lord of Wootton), Robert Beaupel (of Knowstone) the lords of Molland and Champsons and (North) Molton, High Bray and Gratton, the lady of Challacombe Ralegh, the lords of Parracombe and Lyn, Brendon and Oare, Porlock, Almsworthy and Exford, Winsford and Exton and the Ashways, in a great encirclement, were all 'with their men and tenants', entering the Forest (not only once) to graze their stock 'on the herbage of the deer of the Lord King'. Nobody mentioned collusion – or needed to. The defence, if any, is not recorded, nor is the ruling of the Justice in Eyre, nor how it was enforced. Were all those influential borderers fined? Did the offence continue? Exton – listed among the trespassers – was no longer part of the Warden's own manor, but were the fifty-two Free Suitors of Hawkridge and Withypool summoned to help the two or three foresters drive out all those intruders, man and beast? Mathew Pecche had not been Warden long – he was a stranger, a younger brother who succeeded unexpectedly at the death of an infant nephew – and he was the last to inherit from William de Wrotham. A few years after this embarrassing episode he sold all his hereditary rights and went away.

The wardenship – always with the manor of North Petherton – then changed hands several times before passing to the Mortimers, Earls of March. Four times in their seventy-five years' tenure temporary appointments were made because an earl had died young and his heir was a minor. These were troubled and dangerous years, with war at home and abroad, the deposition of Richard II, and then a rebellion against his usurping cousin Henry IV, and the Mortimers were too eminent to be safe. Meanwhile, one of the interruptions in their succession brought to North Petherton, and almost certainly to Exmoor, a quiet little man who has been a delight ever since, one of the greatest of all poets, Geoffrey Chaucer.

In 1390, towards the end of his very active life (as a diplomatic envoy to France and Italy, as Controller of Customs for wool and hides in the port of London, and then as Clerk of the King's Works, responsible for the Tower, the palaces, and other royal estates) Chaucer had charge of the repair of St George's Chapel, Windsor, which was on the point of falling down. The Constable of Windsor, Sir Peter Courtenay, a younger son of the Earl of Devon, was at this time holding the custody of the Somerset Forests during the minority of the fourth Earl of March. He, too, was engaged on repairs at Windsor, and he saw the worth of this widely experienced civil servant.[8] So he made him his deputy at North Petherton, and Geoffrey Chaucer remained Forester in charge of that estate and 'park' for at least eight years. His national appointment ended, and he probably spent much of his time in Somerset. Now Chaucer is not an obscure or remote figure; he moves unobtrusively in full daylight, and everything we know about him makes it inconceivable that he would not ride over, now and then, to the outlying villages on the Barle, Hawkridge and Withypool, to meet the tenants and to see for himself what was going on. And he would miss nothing and would relish all that he saw.

If only he had come while he was still writing *The Canterbury Tales*! Then one of his pilgrims might have told some story of the Forest pound at Withypool to match that of the thieving miller of Trumpington, who untied the students' palfrey and sent it galloping after wild mares in the fen, but was richly paid out before they left. No matter. That random company riding from London to Canterbury in the spring sunshine is drawn from all over England. Alongside the Knight just home from a Crusade, the elegant sentimental Prioress, the Monk ('a manly man', fit to be an abbot) and the irrepressible Wife of Bath, there are minor characters who would certainly have been recognized on Exmoor. One is a yeoman, a forester, dressed in green; he is neatly built and brown as a berry, carrying (even on pilgrimage!) a mighty bow, a sheaf of bright peacock-arrows, and a hunting-horn. Another is a country landowner, white-haired and rosy-cheeked, who has been a sheriff, understands good food and wine, and keeps open house – as it might have been at Selworthy or Timberscombe. A weaver and a dyer, prospering in the cloth-trade, travel with three other craftsmen. They all wear the livery of the same great guild, and bid fair to become aldermen (which, says the poet, their wives would certainly approve, for it is very pleasant to be called 'Madam' and walk at the head of a procession). And there is a competent and piratical merchant seaman from Dartmouth, who has no scruples of conscience:

If that he fought and had the higher hand,
By water he sent them home to every land.

He is not unlike John Hawley, a leading citizen and benefactor of that town, and later its Mayor. Chaucer had visited the port on business, and he may have heard Hawley make some such rough boast.

'The web of our life is of a mingled yarn, good and ill together.' Chaucer knew the darkness of the fourteenth century very well, but he saw the human comedy too, caught it on the wing and kept it fresh for ever in his own wit and irony and delicious sense of fun.

Much of the 1327 boundary of Exmoor Forest, final except for its inclusion of Oare, can still be traced on the ground. From the southernmost point, Upper Willingford Bridge, it ran clockwise along the county boundary for nearly 20 miles, up Litton Water, along Fyldon Ridge, across from Moles Chamber to Woodbarrow and over to the Saddle Stone, then eastward to the head of Badgworthy Water and north to County Gate. From here, at that date, it went east along the coastal ridge almost exactly on the line of the modern A39 past the Five Stones and as far as the head of Lillycombe, then down the stream to cross Oare Water near Robber's Bridge, and up over Mill Hill to Black Barrow, whence it can be followed along unchanged parish boundaries all the way back to Willingford Bridge.

Some of its landmarks were there long before the Forest was defined – streams or ridges, Bronze Age barrows, or big longstones known by name. Some of these – Hooked Stone and the Sandyway Longstone for instance – have disappeared, but like Horsehead Stone and Lewcombe Stone and the lost Five Stones, each stood where two Saxon parishes met against the Forest border and marked the division between manor 'wastes'. Those at a stream head, like Horsehead and Lewcombe stones, may have been set up by prehistoric hill-men in reverence to the life-giving water. Several other important tall stones on the moor, far from boundaries but similarly pointing down combes, hint at stream-worship in the Bronze Age,[9] and down in the foothills the same belief, shrewdly adapted by the Christian clergy, lasted on, in Holy Wells and Lady Wells, until very recently indeed.

Where no natural or ancient landmark saved them labour, mediaeval and later farmers set up small boundary stones, 'lesser meare-stones', sandstone slabs about knee-high, pointing the direction between the greater ones.[10] Some of these still show the way across Roosthitchen to the Edgerley Stone (in the road-bank at the county boundary west of Simonsbath) and others lead uphill from there to Woodbarrow. A good line runs eastward from Saddle Stone to Gammon's Corner, crossing open

15

moorland, considerably north of the wall which John Knight built, later on, to enclose his part of the old Forest; one stone was placed on the small cairn of a Bronze Age ring-barrow, on Furzehill, to be seen more easily. This stretch must have been typical of much of the old boundary – clear enough for those who knew the general direction, but costing no more work than was necessary. Another surviving line, set up after the 1301/1327 contraction of the boundary, runs from Black Barrow to Alderman's Barrow, over rushy wet ground; it is more difficult to follow, but the O.S. 1:25 000 maps – the old 2½ inch – show seven visible stones.

About a quarter of a mile east of Gammon's Corner, where the Knight wall returns to the true boundary, stands a three-parish mark of a different kind – the lonely tree at Hoar Oak Water, the latest in a long succession, planted where the stream named after them separates Lynton from Brendon. The earliest Hoar Oak on record died 'of very age and rottenness' in the middle of the seventeenth century. The stream comes down quickly from the Chains, and can flood violently in the steep-sided combe. A tree may have seemed a more secure mark here than a stone, and visible from further away, but the present oak, planted about seventy years ago, testifies to the struggle each in turn has had against wind and weather. For a long time this and the vanished Kite Oak were the only trees recorded on the whole Forest, except for a few hawthorns.

Big stones are scarcer here than on the granite moors, and obviously more difficult than timber to carry and erect, but they last much longer in the mist and rain. Only one wooden post is recorded as a Forest boundary mark – at Coles Cross, on the ridge road between Sandyway and Two Barrows – and that rotted or fell in the seventeenth century. The site is shown on the Inclosure Map of 1819, at the point where now a long hedge-bank leaves the boundary road to run straight to a ford of the Barle below Picked Stones, and then, at a slightly changed angle, on again to Honeymead Cross. It is on a crest, looking ahead to Two Barrows, and in 1678 a man of sixty, Thomas Pearse of Withypool, said in evidence that he remembered an oaken post at this place – implying that it was no longer there. In the final perambulation before enclosure the reference is to a boundary stone *near* 'a landmark called Coles Cross' and that stone, a big handsome slab drilled as for a gate-hinge and incised with an O.S. bench-mark, can still be seen leaning against the hedge beside a gateway in the dip of the road, about a hundred yards south-east of the crest. The long hedge-bank, built after 1819, follows the line drawn on the Inclosure Map to separate John Knight's purchase from the land allotted to the Free Suitors. The field south-east of it, adjoining the road, is called Coles Cross Common now, but cannot have been common land in Forest days.

The name has been a puzzle – what lane or track made even a three-ways cross with the ridge road here, and who or what was Cole? A clue found recently seems to answer both questions. In the early part of the seventeenth century a Mr John Cole lived at South Radworthy – a manor since before Domesday, with a fourteenth-century Chapel of Ease. (At one time it had belonged to William Brewer, the Warden.) In 1609 he was one of six paying 'the King's rate' there; in 1624 he is recorded as owning land in North Molton; in 1627 he was churchwarden.[11] He was clearly a man of some importance in the neighbourhood. From near South Radworthy a broad track still runs down north-eastward to a ford over the Mole. It points towards Coles Cross, and about half-way along the hillside of rough pasture between the ford and the ridge a stretch of footway or bridleway – narrow, but not a sheep-path – follows the 1000 ft contour for nearly a quarter of a mile in the same direction. It is difficult not to conclude that this was John Cole's way into Somerset. Perhaps there had been an earlier name; the perambulations before that century are no help, as they all state only that from the Danesbrook to County Gate the Forest and county boundaries were identical, and no landmarks are mentioned. But John Cole's dates correspond well with the deposition of Thomas Pearse, who went on the perambulation for the first time in 1632, when he was 'about 13 or 14 years of age'.

Again and again the mediaeval boundary-riders made use of what was already there. The ridge road past Coles Cross is prehistoric; so is the old northern boundary along the coast road, which has been a highway for about 4000 years. East of County Gate the territory so long disputed in the twelfth and thirteenth centuries stretched far into Somerset, but the first few miles of the boundary were always the same, except under King John. He claimed the land as far as the cliffs and sea, but had to retreat after Magna Carta. Otherwise the northern edge of the Forest was always, until Tudor times, along part of the ancient highway. In 1219, pending full investigation, the boundary followed it eastward and then swung away south to Hawkcombe Head and thence to Alderman's Barrow. After the 1301/1327 contraction of the Forest, it turned south sooner; after passing the 'Fifstones' it went down Lillycombe, up to Black Barrow, and to Alderman's Barrow from there.

The mark called 'Fifstones' may have been among the earliest man-made monuments on the moor, but it is another puzzle. The stones are lost, and nobody knows for certain what they were. *Where* they were was well-known until the end of the nineteenth century. The 1301 and 1327 records show that they were between County Gate and the head of Lillycombe. They were already missing when John Fortescue wrote his *Stag-hunting on Exmoor* (1887) but he said they had been where the Culbone/Oare

17

boundary crossed the main road, 'where Deddycombe cot stood'. Rawle, in his *Annals of the Ancient Royal Forest of Exmoor* (1893), showed the Five Stones at this point on his map, exactly at the grassy hard shoulder where a car or two can pull in now, and so did MacDermot in 1911. The civil boundary between the two parishes was moved further east in 1933, but a long straight fence still follows the old one, north and south of the road. The crossing is on Windwhistle, the worst place on the whole road in time of snow, and the ruin of Deddycombe Cot – now called Rook's Cottage after its last inhabitant – can be recognized by a clump of beech trees, once hedges which enclosed its little garden.

When there were no trees or hedges a group of stones standing here on the false crest of Windwhistle would have been plain to boundary-riders coming from the east. It would also have been in the kind of position prehistoric people often chose for their religious sites. A very early Bronze Age burial in a stone coffin, with a beaker beside the skeleton – the Culbone cist, now in Taunton Museum – was found nine years after the publication of Fortescue's book, in a quarry slightly to the east, and on the higher side of the road, at the head of the combe; and names like Deddycombe sometimes imply skeletons. There may have been others.

The earliest perambulation record, made in 1219 when the Forest extended to Hawkcombe Head, referred to the Five Stones as 'Whiteston'. In recent years this has caused confusion with the two Whitstones on Porlock Common, still further east, and not in the right place for any Forest boundary line, early or late. Applied to Windwhistle, the older name is another hint that the stones may have been a prehistoric group. 'White stone' *need* not mean quartz – the Porlock Whitstones are pale sandstone – but it often does, and early peoples in Britain used the shining white rock for important monuments if they could, just as the Greeks used glistening Pentelic marble. There is an outcrop of big boulders, sandstone with veins of quartz, further up the old parish boundary north of the road. The tallest could have been brought downhill quite easily to build a monument associated with the Beaker burial, on a track which went on eastward past round barrows and the stone row on Culbone Hill. Two which might have been taken uphill again are now high gateposts in the north-going fence, and there are one or two others nearby, perhaps adopted by farmers or roadmakers shortly before Fortescue wrote. And a tantalising scrap of information from the early fourteenth century may just possibly be relevant. At Brendon one of the seventeen contributors to Edward III's subsidy for the Calais and Crécy expedition was called Robert de Whitering. Where did he live?[12]

When the 1327 demarcation became law, and still after 1508 when the Crown land was leased, and the deer belonged neither to the King nor to the Warden if they were outside the Forest, the perambulations continued. Exact knowledge of the boundary was useful against trespass, poaching and the straying of stock, and it proved its worth again when the Civil War was followed by a last attempt to include the commons in the Forest.

The procedure had not been altered. Once in seven years, if not more often, the Warden would appoint a day and summon the Free Suitors and the Suitors at Large to meet him on the boundary. The round often began and ended at the Hooked Stone, where Hawkridge and Withypool commons converged. The Warden or one or two of his foresters, and the fifty-two Free Suitors or their deputies, would ride round the entire Forest, the Suitors at Large only along their own border, joining the company at one parish boundary mark and leaving it at the next. Quite distinct from this, but useful corroboration at a crisis, was the annual church ceremony at Rogationtide, when the clergy and congregation of each parish went in procession round their own bounds, to invoke a blessing on crops or animals. Surely they had the Commination service in mind too? The Mosaic 'Cursed be he that removeth his neighbour's landmark' was read at least once a year in every village church. On parish as on Forest perambulations the men often took boys with them, to make sure the knowledge was carried forward. It was a wise precaution.

Under Cromwell, all Crown land was appropriated by Parliament, and after survey and assessment, sold. Exmoor was bought by a London merchant of Dutch origin, James Boevey. He was a thrusting little man, perpetually busy, and much given to law-suits, 'in which,' wrote Aubrey, 'he always overcame.' Pepys met him at dinner in London, and described him as a 'Sir Positive' – a Mr Know-all in a contemporary play. Being owner, not tenant, he immediately built himself a mansion at Simonsbath, and from this lonely centre he began suing his neighbours, disputing their ancient rights, making himself thoroughly disliked, and – if his own account is to be believed – provoking various knavish tricks in retaliation. These were staunchly denied, but Boevey prevailed at law.

So when the monarchy was restored in 1660, and the Forest became royal property again, a petition from 'many hundreds of your Majesty's subjects inhabiting near Exmoor in the counties of Devon and Somerset' was sent to Charles II, to complain that Boevey had 'much vexed and troubled your poor petitioners' and to beg for the restoration of *their* rights. This had no effect. Boevey had lost the freehold but acquired the tenancy – the wardenship – on long lease, and continued his quarrels and litigation. The most important was his outrageous claim, in 1675,

19

that all the surrounding commons were part of the Forest and that in consequence he was entitled to tithes on the wool of all sheep pastured there and on all crops grown by the commoners in their little temporary fields.

His claim went to the Court of Exchequer, where it was very carefully examined; the case lasted nearly four years. The defendants naturally included the rectors who had always received these tithes, the big landowners – a Courtney (sic) of Molland, a Parker of North Molton – and smaller farmers from the edges of the disputed common land. In 1678 depositions were taken, in Dunster, Dulverton, Taunton and Barnstaple, from thirty-three witnesses for the defence, mostly yeomen and husbandmen who had known the moor all their lives.

One after another made it crystal clear that the boundary had not changed, and that it had always separated Forest from commons. Thomas Pearse of Withypool had gone round with the Free Suitors on his father's behalf in 1632, and twice since. Peter Houndell had acted for his father, another Free Suitor, in 1623. Both emphasized that the bounds were always the same. John Baker of Withypool, aged 80, had been on two perambulations, the first in 1613. The longest date came from William Gregory of Exford, aged 79, who had beaten the bounds of Exford parish, 'with the Parson and a great number of the inhabitants' in 1606, when he was seven years old. On that occasion 'an inhabitant', Richard Edbrooke, had tricked the child into putting his finger on a meare stone, telling him it was scalding hot, and then wrung the finger very hard, exhorting him to remember that this was a boundary stone of the parish of Exford.

As plaintiff, Boevey called seventy-three witnesses, many of them from the Devon parishes, especially North Molton, High Bray, and Challacombe, but they distinguished between Forest and commons as confidently as the defence did. Some said they had always understood that the Forest lay in Somerset; this, if true, destroyed Boevey's claim to any Devon tithes – and it had been true for many centuries. A Challacombe man who had been employed by the Warden's agent to claim tithes from two Lynton farmers, David and Thomas Dyer, reported that they set out their tithe wool and said whoever had a right to it might take it – and the Rector's agent did so. Witness added that several Challacombe parishioners had in recent years paid tithes to the Warden *and* to their Rector, 'to avoid law suits'.

Strong evidence came, too, from those who remembered men being found dead in different parts of the moor. The crux was who had been responsible for burying them. Henry Fray of Challacombe said that 'Fifty years ago an unknown person was found dead on Challacombe Common, and was buried in Challacombe churchyard at the cost of the parish.' Charles Lock of North Molton believed that the common west of Sandyway Longstone lay in North Molton parish, because 'about thirty years previous a friend being found dead upon the said common was buried in North Molton churchyard, at which time it was said that the then agent for the King's farmer of the said Forest' (i.e. the Warden) 'had refused to take care for any inquisition upon his death, therefore the inhabitants of North Molton procured the coroner to enquire of the same at the said place.' This evidence he gave as *plaintiff's* witness, adding that no tithe on the said common had been known to be paid to anyone but Edmund Parker, the lord of North Molton. He had also spoken as a defence witness, and referred to what must surely have been the same death, naming the 'friend' as Richard Land of Withypool, found dead in the road near Sandyway Longstone; the inquest had been held by the Devon coroner. Anthony Mole of High Bray said that 'thirty years ago' he and another 'were sent into the Forest, on the information of two travellers, to save a person's life, who was then dying in the Forest; when they reached the dying man, finding him frozen to the ground and past hope of recovery, they left him. He was afterwards buried by the Forester in Withypool Churchyard.'

Deliberate and careful, speaking of what they knew, qualifying what they only believed to be true, or 'had heard many very aged persons say', these countrymen, chosen because they had no direct stake in the outcome, built up an impregnable defence against the testy little Dutchman. He lost his case. He had over-reached himself, and thenceforward spent far less time in his fine house at Simonsbath. From away in Surrey 'Sir Positive' would still, from time to time, sue or threaten some Exmoor farmer, but without success.

The shape of the Forest was not challenged again.

CHAPTER TWO

The farmer's sheep

During the Norman centuries the well-being of the King's deer had over-ridden all else. The farmers had merely held their ground as best they could, and rented some Forest grazing from the Warden. After 1508, when the whole Forest was leased and the deer were no longer 'royal animals', paramountcy passed to their distant cousins the domesticated sheep. Sixteenth- and seventeenth-century litigation shows the difference; the proceedings are about commons and grazing, not 'offences against the vert'.

The country was too high and wet to grow much corn, but there was plenty of grass and rough pasture. Sheep were, time out of mind, the mainstay of the hill-farms, of the cottages where the wool was spun, and of the neighbouring market towns where it was woven into cloth. All through the Middle Ages care of the flocks had been determining the sites for farmhouses and villages, and the routes for packhorse tracks leading off the moor. The resulting pattern was quite different from that of the arable lowlands, with their big farmsteads, granaries and tithe barns close to village and roads, and cornfields stretching away into the distance. A hill-farmer wanted his flock near at hand, especially when snow was falling or at lambing-time, and this was easiest if the farmhouse was in the middle of his fields. So the farms were out in the combes or on sheltered hillsides, a mile or two from each other and probably a little further from the village, which in turn was somewhere in the middle of the parish, easy of access, usually near a ford, and where the stream was strong enough to drive the water-mill.

Forest, common, farm and village together sustained the sheep-farming from which everyone's livelihood stemmed.

The sheep agisted on the unfenced Forest might stray from it and browse on a strange common. A witness against Boevey in 1678 said that that was usual in spring on the southern commons, North Molton and others, when warmer soil and earlier grass attracted them down; he thought the commoners seldom bothered to drive them back. Another said there was little shepherding on the Forest. But earlier, in 1641, in a lawsuit about a proposed increase in grazing charges, several farmers, including a septuagenarian from North Molton, William Thorne, affirmed that shepherding was needed against the dangers of loss by 'stealing, killing, and drowning or stifling in the snow'. A South Molton owner, William Squire, for that reason 'always kept a man to herd his sheep in the Forest'. A shepherd was normally paid 3s.4d. a score, for the year. A sixty-five-year-old husbandman from East Buckland said that if agisters did not have someone to look after their sheep on the Forest 'they must see to them themselves two or three times a week'. All these three emphasized that close grazing improved the value of the preponderant sedge or coarse grass, which should not be left to grow hard. 'The lower the sedge grass is eaten in the spring, the pasture will be sweeter all the year and the sheep prove the better.' (This was to counter the forester's argument that because some farmers were withdrawing their flocks, the remaining sheep would have more feed, so their owners should pay more.) Some of the flocks came from 15 or 20 miles away, and would have to be left untended. Sheep will generally stay together unless they see greener grass elsewhere; the distant farmers must have relied on this, and resigned themselves to the occasional theft or accidental death of one or two ewes.

Flocks were taken up in spring and left until June, when they were brought down for shearing; some were returned for another two or three months before the nights grew cold in autumn. Normally, a farmer would rent the same pasture year after year – Pinkery, Horsen, Larkbarrow, from which the new farms were named in the nineteenth century; Madacombe, Winaway, Benjamy, which still describe areas of the open moor – and the sheep would graze happily again on the land they knew.

It sounds simple, but for the nearer farms there were complications. Some borderers had daytime rights only, others paid for 'night-learing' to save much time and trouble. Commoners' sheep or cattle might be found grazing just inside the Forest – or so it might be alleged, when there was no independent witness. Farmers might sometimes 'forget' to bring the flock down at dusk. Or there might be dishonesty about numbers – never difficult with sheep. The fifty-two Suitors of Withypool and Hawkridge had free pasture by day on the Forest for up to 140 sheep each, but had to fold them on the commons at night. Sometimes the forester or his deputies suspected that too many were spending the day on Crown land, and would count them 'in the King's highways as they came from the fold'. (The King's highways would be well-worn tracks, no more. Possibly the Withypool sheep were driven up Kitridge Lane to Braddimoor, folded there, and taken each morning by Gipsy Lane to the Honeymead corner of the Forest. Gipsy Lane is as broad as a drove-road and may have been where the foresters made their count.) On other borders the Suitors at Large sometimes cheated by taking in a neighbour's sheep for a fee and turning them out on to the Forest among their own, but this would be detected before long, since their own had to be clearly branded and the 'stood-iron' (or stud-brand) shown to the foresters.

Another kind of misdemeanour is recorded of one Anthony Jennings. On a June day in 1677 John Sloley of High Bray was with Boevey's agent at the top of Melcombe Hill, near Moles Chamber and just outside the boundary, 'in the King's highway leading from the Forest to South Molton' (from Lynton) when he met Jennings 'with other persons unknown' driving a large flock of sheep. The agent tried to stop the sheep so that Sloley could count them, and 'notwithstanding interruption by the said persons, this deponent told 16 score and upwards. What became of them afterwards or where they were shorn, he knows not, but has heard they came from Woolhanger.' It was supposed that Jennings was trying to avoid paying for their summer keep in the north of the Forest.

So methods had been evolved to check abuses. Eight or nine times a year the whole Forest was driven – five drifts for ponies, either two or three for cattle, and one for sheep – and any animal which should not have been there was impounded at Withypool, or in later years at Simonsbath, to be redeemed by payment of a fine to the Warden. All the Free Suitors had to take part in these drifts or preys (from which Preyway Head is named) and they began very early in the morning – five or six o'clock for sheep, one o'clock for cattle, so as to catch any beasts wrongfully 'night-leared'. Now and then the foresters were accused of malpractice; a Stoke Pero man testifying in 1622 said he had often known of cattle and ponies which had been 'sitting quietly upon the said commons late in the evening after sunset a mile from the said Forest' and were taken in the early morning drift and impounded at Withypool. Perhaps the most important thing is that they *were* accused and brought before the courts. A Porlock farmer sued an unscrupulous forester and his men for removing forty-five sheep in this way – a Culbone farmer had seen them doing it. The case was heard in the Exchequer Court and judgement went against the foresters, who were ordered to pay compensation to the farmer.

The drift for sheep was made only once a year, just after they should all have been taken down past the telling-houses where they were counted, and away home to be shorn. Soon after sunrise on a June morning the Free Suitors and the Forester's men, mounted on good ponies, would meet at Wincombe Head on the Lanacre side of Braddimoor, and they had generally driven the prey to Withypool pound by noon.

The Free Suitors took away their own sheep, and the rest were shorn for the Forester, to whom the wool was forfeit. Meanwhile, the other borderers were driving their commons, and similarly confiscated the fleeces of any trespassing sheep, which might include strays from the Forest. All these were only at large now through negligence, and the round-up ensured that shearing was finished while days and nights were warm for the suddenly naked animals, and before their coats were too heavy in July heat.

The telling-houses are interesting, and may have been peculiar to Exmoor. The Forest remained a royal estate, under single control, for more than 700 years, and from earliest Norman and even late Saxon times sheep and other stock from neighbouring farms had been grazed there. It must always have been necessary to count them off and reckon what fee was due. (The word 'count' was a Norman import; shepherds used the native English 'tell'.) When there were no fences or gates, it would be easiest to count them where the track narrowed or deepened and could be closed by hurdles. At the same places every year the tellers, paid by the Warden but chosen in agreement with the farmers, checked them out in June, and at some of these sites little huts were built. In one of the Forest Books – 1719 – lately found and studied by Roger Burton, the number of tellers was given as four. The number of telling-houses is not known.

In the eighteenth century, and probably much earlier, a very high proportion of the sheep came from south-west of the moor – great sheep-rearing country to this day. In 1736 there were more than 30 000 sheep in the Forest, a quarter of them from the parish of North Molton alone. In addition nearly 3000 had come up from Swimbridge, over 1300 from Landkey, 1100 from Bishop's Tawton, and smaller flocks from nearly a dozen other parishes in the same direction. The count on this side took nearly all June, and it looks as if a substantial shelter was built for the teller.

In 1657 a Swimbridge farmer said he used formerly to drive his sheep in and out of the Forest at 'a place called the Spanne' where the teller made a note of them. Confusingly, there are two or three places called Span Head, as well as a Span Wood, Span Lane and Span Bottom, all on the former Span Common, which stretched down southward from the Forest boundary and was not enclosed until 1853. The 1809 O.S. map (often inexact) shows 'Telling Ho' at the foot of the common, and recent study of the ground confirms this, as an approximation. Two old roads off the hills intersected there, a little to the north of the present Yard Down Cross. One was the Lynton–South Molton track coming from Moles Chamber; part of its course is sometimes perceptible on the slope, but southward most of the line is now lost in farmland or under the modern road. The other, recorded by Leland as his route from Dunster to Barnstaple in 1540, came down from Kinsford Cross. It ran a little way east of its mid-nineteenth-century replacement. In 1864 it was still officially called 'the old road' and was sometimes used for carts.[1] In 1986 it was a well-defined hollow way across the last three fields downhill, and again behind The Poltimore Arms on the way to Brayford. The track curves slightly with the contour, and has been deepened by surface water after heavy storms. As it reaches level ground it changes course a little, and here a tall conical mound, grass-covered but stony, projects into it from the west bank, leaving only a narrow passage. This may well be the remnant of a telling-house. It is almost a mile from the Forest boundary but near the ancient border between commons and farmland, and it is where the flocks would part to go west or south. Before the enclosure hedges were made the sheep would have come tranquilly down Span Common by the sunken track, and any attempt at cheating could have been seen afar. It would be much more comfortable for the teller than Kinsford Cross, at the true head of the common, where the old road spanned the ridge and left the Forest, and where, at 1500 feet above sea-level, a west wind sweeping up with rain from the Atlantic can be wintry cold even in June.[2]

Day and Masters, mapping Somerset in 1782, showed another telling-house beside the Barnstaple bridle-path which entered the Forest at Moles Chamber and crossed the Barle at Driver on its way to Exe Head and Porlock (see p.53). This one seemed lost. MacDermot in 1911 spoke of it as only a vague tradition, but a north Devon farmer recently recalled that his father had spoken of sheep being parted 'somewhere near Moles Chamber'. Long search for it failed, until Roger Burton, doing field-work for his *Heritage of Exmoor* (1989), found a convincing little ruin much further along the path towards Driver than anyone had supposed, on a ridge where the hill begins to drop towards the Barle valley, and opens a wide view of the southern slope of the Chains. The grass-grown footing – of stone like the nearby outcrop – is interrupted by an entrance facing north-east, the direction from which agisted sheep would come homeward for shearing. The position is ideal.

It is well inside the Forest – two-thirds of the distance from Moles Chamber to Driver along the footpath which is still shown on the O.S. maps, and that is exactly where Day and Masters placed it. Two factors had delayed rediscovery. One was that those very good cartographers, meticulous in tracing rough 'roads' across the moor, were oddly inexact about the little tributaries near the head of Lewcombe Water. (Was this perhaps a clerical error, unnoticed?) Consequently their telling-house seemed to be on low ground at a ford, where the view is restricted. They marked a fork a little way to the north-east of the building, with one track leading to Exe Head and the other to Simonsbath. The disappearance of

26

the latter under plough and tarmac was a second impediment to recognition, especially as sheep have made several paths down to the running water at the tiny ford. But this is less than half-way to Driver, not two-thirds. The ruin now identified stands about 80 yards south-west of a gateway which lets the bridle-path through a wire fence. It seems very likely that this was where the former ways parted, and the tellers could oversee them both.

These two telling-houses would account for all the flocks from the south and south-west, the great majority of the agisted sheep. Two others are rumoured, north and east, where the numbers were much smaller, and where according to the newly found Forest Books most farmers kept their stock in the home fields or on their own commons until after shearing. It would not take long to count the Lynton and Exford sheep – perhaps not long enough to justify building a shelter – but there are hints at Gammon's Corner, and somewhere west of Exford.

Until a few decades ago a small ruin stood at Gammon's Corner, where the old Lynton road from Exe Head leaves the Forest at a ford, and it was locally reputed to have been a telling-house. All that remained in the 1980s was a low grass-covered heap of stones just outside the Forest gate, but even then, more than thirty years after the Lynmouth flood, one could see, a little further upstream, how the water rushing down from the Chains scoured the steep sides of the combe on that dreadful August night. A disused rough-built hut would be overwhelmed at once.

There has been talk of another at Redstone – once an important mearestone where the Forest boundary made a sharp corner with the parish of Exford. But Richard Locke, usually very reliable, who helped Billingsley with information for his review of Somerset agriculture in 1794, said there was a telling-house 'in Exford, half a mile west of the church' – much further from the boundary. He made no mention of the one near Moles Chamber. The Somerset map by John Cary, 1787, which Billingsley used as frontispiece, names a telling-house at Moles Chamber, but no other (Yard Down being in Devon). J. K. Ridler, a very careful local historian, has lately taken characteristic pains to extract this information from the documents, but he finds nothing relevant in the Exford tithe map and nothing conclusive on the ground.

There seem to have been other telling-houses, outside the Forest and no part of its economy, and perhaps the enigmatic sites at Gammon's Corner and near Exford were among these. The position of another survives in the name 'Telling-House field', at Yelland Cross, west of Challacombe. Blackmore, introducing his *Tales from the Telling-house* (the title is only a pun) spoke of neighbouring farmers gathering at one of them near Charles, in his boyhood, to separate the flocks they had brought down from the hills in autumn. He suggested another in *Lorna Doone*.

27

His John Fry, bringing Jan Ridd home from Tiverton by way of Dulverton and the Brendons, staves off the boy's questions by saying his father is busy about the farm but will meet them at the telling-house – presumably a few miles south-east of Oare. This is not topographical evidence; Blackmore was not mapping the moor for posterity. He merely drew on his memory of local detail, transposing it at will, to enrich his romance. He seems to have liked these little buildings as part of the moorland scene, and perhaps wished to record them before they vanished for ever.

While the Forest pasture was useful to farmers who could afford it, and to the fifty-two Free Suitors who had their special entitlement, the commons helped nearly everybody. They provided every commoner, rich or poor, with free grazing – for a cow or two, so many sheep, so many geese – and also with free fuel for his own use. Furze for a quick blaze, peat for steady warmth, and the darkest cottage would hold a little comfort in winter gales and snow, and in the rain which sent labourers home drenched to the skin. Besides peat, this right of turbary included heather and rush; both could be used for thatching, and rush lights must have been the poor man's candles for a great many centuries. Moreover, an enterprising commoner could, by arrangement, enclose a piece of moorland and till it for a few years. The soil was thin, and two or three crops of oats or rye would exhaust it. After that it was left to 'go back'.

This practice was widespread for a very long time. It explains many field-banks which are still recognizable in winter sunlight or after swaling, though they can seldom be dated. Walkers or riders notice them momentarily as a slight obstacle underfoot and forget them because there are so many. Some – on Braddimoor for example, on Moorhouse Ridge above the Danesbrook, and on Middle Hill, Brendon – are fairly high and may be no more than one or two hundred years old. Others, worn very low but built of stone and earth – on Ilkerton Ridge, on Wilmersham Common, and on Lucott Great Hill north of Chetsford Water – seem prehistoric. Sometimes, as on Codsend Moor, old and new survive together: a good sunny slope is perennially attractive, and may be criss-crossed by the work of farmers ages apart in time.

Neither ploughing nor building could go unobserved in open hill country, and on the Forest proper it would have been very difficult indeed to enclose even a tiny field at any time between 1066 and 1819. Even during the eleven Commonwealth years, when Boevey made a farmstead round his new house, he would not have tolerated any hedging by anyone else. Except on his home farm at Simonsbath, any traces of ploughing or building must be pre-Conquest, or post-1819.

Outside the Forest, in the old purlieus, opportunities were

greater, and attitudes perhaps rather different. The arrival of the Norman landlords had dispossessed the Saxons, but not banished them. Though they were demoted, their knowledge of the difficult country and its quick changes of weather were needed, and very often they were the men and women really working the land – and remembering it as their own. They knew it intimately enough to poach the deer in spite of the foresters, and the thirteenth and fourteenth-century records show that the farmers of Lanacre and a parson of Hawkridge did not scruple to carve themselves fields from land the French king had annexed.

Yet long after Withypool and Hawkridge were disafforested, and even when the Royal Forest was leased to a subject, from 1508 onwards, the Free Suitors continued to regard themselves as 'the king's farmers'. Some Tudor 'presentments' by the Swainmote Courts seem to be anachronistic, but their eloquence, in a mixture of debased Latin and clumsy English, is that of the righteously indignant. MacDermot transcribes long extracts, in his *Appendix 2*, but makes no comment.

In the first one, in Henry VIII's reign, the Justices of the Forest with some of the fifty-two Suitors affirmed that although Withypool Common had not, in living memory, been used for anything but pasture, and that only for the commoners' stock or for beasts impounded at the preys and drifts, yet six husbandmen of Withypool had recently 'upon the said Common and waste ground ... entered, and then and there seven acres parcel thereof with ox and plough turned and put to tillage, and the same enclosed ... as well to the disinheritance of our said Sovereign Lord as to the loss and damage of his Grace's Farmers for the time being'.

A few years later, under Edward VI, the rolls record another enquiry, and now two of the former evil-doers were among the virtuous signatories. This report states that whereas the late King Henry VIII and all his farmers on his behalf had been peacefully taking the profit of all cattle and sheep grazing the Halscombes, as part of the royal revenue from the Forest, yet now two husbandmen, John Edbrooke of Winsford and John Thomas of Nymett Bishop, 'the right of our said Sovereign Lord nothing regarding, upon the aforesaid ground called the Halsecombes entered, and all the Cattle Beasts and sheep there found wrongfully took, and them from the said ground drove, and in Hawkridge them there did impound, and in pound did retain by a long time, not only to the great damage of the owners thereof, but to the disinheritance of the King's rights and contrary to the peace of our Sovereign Lord'. This John Thomas of Bishop's Nympton was a persistent offender: a few years later he drove away animals grazing on Withypool Common and shut them into a pound of his own at Hawkridge, and in Queen Mary's reign he made a similar raid with the help of four Hawkridge men and another, and again kept the animals a long time.

The final offence in the series is the most blatant. As soon as Elizabeth I became Queen, the Swainmote held an enquiry, ostensibly on her behalf, because in the last three years of the short reign of 'our Sovereign Lord and Lady King Philip and Queen Mary' twenty-two named husbandmen of Withypool and two from Winsford had 'entered upon' Withypool Common, 'and there twenty acres thereof with ox and plough turned and put to tillage and the same then enclosed'. Twenty acres for three years is a considerable encroachment, but no retribution seems to have followed.

John Thomas's raids were barefaced roguery, damaging to the owners and contrary to the Queen's peace, but in none of the offences is it easy to see infringement of royal rights. Technically there were none left, by now. The Warden, paying rent to the Crown, reimbursed himself by charging for the pasture. Tillage of the commons, once an offence against the vert, had long ceased to matter to the Crown. Unauthorized cultivation would limit the commoners' pasture, and this was the Swainmote's proper concern. But were these sanctimonious references to royal loss a delusion, or an attempt to delude? And were the husbandmen calling the Swainmote's bluff? How was it settled?

Just over a century later Thomas Pearse of Withypool, testifying against Boevey, said: 'At certain times parts of Withypool and Hawkridge Commons have been ploughed and tilled by those holding the right of common there; 6d an acre being due to the lord of the soil from all commoners who were not his tenants, while tenants paid 4d an acre. The said payment never known to be denied, nor anyone without right of common to plough any part of the said common except by licence from the lord or his bailiff.'

The custom continued. Early in the present century a boy growing up at Knighton farm, on the edge of this same common, asked his uncle what the ridges on the sunny slope were. 'The rye-beds, boy!' snapped Uncle, as though even a child should know that without being told. He did not date them, but the nephew, telling the anecdote forty years later, said that the old method had been to plough the patch and then raise a contour bank below it, so that heavy rain would not wash the topsoil away. The implication was that it was nineteenth-century work.

Withypool and Hawkridge are well documented, because of their special relationship with the Forest, but use and abuse of the commons must have been much the same in all the purlieus, right round the moor.

Round the commons was an outer ring of farmsteads, each

surrounded by its small in-fields, the 'in-bye' to which the ewes were brought for lambing, and bigger ones, further away, for the 'early bite' in spring and for hay and small domestic corn crops later in the year. The farmed land was separated from the commons by very strong hedge-banks, and each farmer had his own 'moorgate' for taking his flocks out to the common, or beyond it to the unfenced Forest.

The boundary banks had to be strong, high and stockproof, to keep the home sheep in and the other commoners' animals out, and as a defence against sagacious wild ponies or great leaping stags. Here and there stretches of these ramparts against the wilderness can still be seen. There is a fine length where the old road from Dunster ran down towards Brayford, between the tongue of Saxon wood and farmland, Beara, and the waste of Yard Down; still, after a storm, rain-water lies on the flat surface outside the big hedge, where the ground was trodden hard by innumerable flocks and herds during countless years.

Another, even more impressive, divides Spangate Land, in Wootton Courtenay, from the wastes of Dunkery and Cutcombe. The track is still gated at the boundary, and the beech trees in the embankments are old and well-grown, sheltered from stunting westerlies by the bulk of Dunkery Hill. It has long outlived its farmstead, which was last recorded early in the fourteenth century, and may have been a ruin ever since the Black Death ravaged Cutcombe, in 1348–9. (There are no mortality figures, but in that winter there were three rectors of the little parish in quick succession.) Later generations farming the land must have repaired the wall from time to time, but without taking or yielding an inch more ground than they must. Jealous eyes would be watching.

Sometimes the pattern of lanes is a clue to the old boundary. Above Lower Fyldon, alone among its fields a mile north of Heasley Mill, a hollow lane runs uphill between strong earth-and-stone hedge-banks on which grow ash and oak, blackthorn and holly, willow and elder, wild rose and bramble, all rampant together. Where the lane is deepest, the eastern bank is some 10 feet high. Suddenly, at a corner named Moorgate, the old walls turn away. Then the lane straightens and continues at field level, lined by uniform beech-hedges about a century old, and climbing to what was until lately Fyldon Common. The straightness is evidence that the lower part of the common was enclosed in the middle of the nineteenth century; the geometrical field shapes hereabout were designed with map and ruler in offices far away from the hills. The gate – like London's Moorgate, which gave on to the marshes east of Fenchurch and Finsbury – has gone now, but it must have been weather-battered, mended and replaced again and again.

There were moorgates wherever a borderer used his right of common. Cloutsham Gate survived until, not long ago, it was replaced by one of the new cattle grids, convenient for motorists but ugly, alien to the moor and sometimes cruel to its wild creatures. Comer's Gate and Dunkery Gate, Scobhill Gate north of Brendon Common, Greystone Gate south-east of Withypool Hill, Blackmoor Gate, not quite at the present crossroads but a little to the south, opposite the turning to Loxhore – all these are only names now, but their old purpose can be recognized by a massive hedge-bank or by an abrupt change from farmland to heath.

They are quite distinct from the later forest gates, which barred, in the 1820s, the gaps John Knight had to leave in his long boundary wall to let the old roads through – at Kinsford Cross, Moles Chamber, Saddle Gate, Gammon's Corner, Brendon Two Gates, Honeymead Two Gates.[3] Indeed there were no forest gates until technically there was no Forest.

Many of the hill-farms were Saxon, listed in Domesday Book because the Conqueror wished to know exactly what his new kingdom contained. The first farmhouses and cottages, made of cob[4] and timber, and thatched, must have tumbled down a great while ago, in the wind and the rain, but they would be rebuilt in the same place, to the same ancient longhouse design – two or three small rooms in a row, on a slight slope, with a passage between the dwelling-house, uphill, and the cowshed at the lower end.

Some, like Spangate farmhouse, crumbled in the late Middle Ages and were not rebuilt. Out on the moor, or in land long ploughed, there are still traces of old farmsteads, hamlets and in-fields, perhaps abandoned in the fourteenth century when so many people died of plague, and too few were left to work the land. One of the saddest of these is the group of fallen longhouses by a stream, with a smaller ruin on a hillock beside them, where Hoccombe Combe runs into Badgworthy. In the twelfth century the 'land of the hermits of Baga Wordia', some 800 acres of enclosed ground just outside the Forest, was given by its overlord to the Brethren of the Hospital of Jerusalem. In the thirteenth century there was mention of several tenements and a chapel; a recent suggestion that the ruin on the eastern hillock was the chapel is pleasantly persuasive.[5] By 1400 A.D. the whole site had passed, untenanted, to the manor of Brendon, and the dates suggest that the Black Death had silenced that little community. The tenements may have been reinhabited, centuries later, by petty thieves, sheep-stealers and such. The name 'Doone Valley' derives only from Blackmore's romance. Perhaps if he had known about the hermits he would not have glorified their humble home into a stronghold for his fictitious villains.

Nobody would go back to the plague-stricken sites, but there were plenty of others. Moorland air was healthy, sheep could graze undisturbed and wool was in steady demand. It was easy to keep a few cows near home and pigs in the oak-woods and combes. By the sixteenth century the remote hill-farms must have been fairly prosperous. Many farmhouses were enlarged at this time, with thick cob walls, oak beams, and slate-flagged floors. Down towards the foothills, some were developed into comfortable manor-houses, each with its own mill and forge, cartwright and wheelwright. The smaller farmers would do most of their work themselves, but needed a miller and a blacksmith in the nearest hamlet or village. They did not require carts or wheels up on the moor, for there were no fit roads; they managed very well with ponies and oxen and trackamucks (sledges dragged through the muck).[6] The range of everyday life was not wide – witness the recurrence of simple descriptive names for places only a few parishes apart, North Hill or South Common, Upcot, Nethercot, Twitchen and Combeshead.

The villages were small. Besides the mill and the forge there might be only a cluster of tiny cottages near the ford, always at risk from floods. The church stood further uphill, where it could be seen from distant farmhouses, and the sound of its bells carried far out over the parish. High Bray church, for instance, is splendidly sited in the old compact hamlet, far above the straggling riverside village of Brayford. This was not the easy country of villages built round sunlit greens with great trees for shade; in many there would hardly be enough level ground for a game of bowls. On great occasions like the annual parish revel a field could be borrowed and everybody would come down for the day, but at other times, when the sackful of corn had been ground or the smith had finished the job, when the church service was over and churchyard gossip was exhausted, most people would want to be getting homeward by the muddy lanes and footpaths before rain or darkness set in.

Friendliness was at its best out on the farms, when neighbours gathered to help each other with hay-harvest or shearing, and relaxed afterwards over the best fare the farmer's wife could provide. 'Fie, daughter!' said the Shepherd to Perdita, at the shearing-feast in *The Winter's Tale*:

> 'Fie, daughter! When my old wife lived, upon
> This day she was both pantler, butler, cook;
> Both dame and servant, welcomed all, served all,
> Would sing her song and dance her turn, now here,
> At upper end o' th' table, now i' th' middle';

33

On his shoulder, and his, her face afire
With labour and the thing she took to quench it
She would to each one sip.'

Shakespeare placed the scene in Bohemia, but knew it from the big Cotswold sheep-farms. It would not be very different on Exmoor, except in scale. Shearing was the culmination of the year's work, like corn-harvest elsewhere, and the shearer's feast was its appropriate happy ending.

The wool was spun at home; the weavers worked in the small towns. Wild plants and lichens were used for dyes, and somebody – perhaps the cottage children – had to gather them. The need increased, and some plants were carefully cultivated; Weld, or Dyer's Rocket, still grows near the old dye-house at Bury, east of Dulverton. Woad was an important crop in the lowlands – 'pipes of woad' were among the contributions in kind to the building of St Mary's Church, Taunton. By early Tudor times dye-stuffs were being imported at Bridgwater to supplement the local supply.

The farming cycle did not change, in bad times or good; lambing and weaning and shearing, selling off some of the sheep in autumn and keeping the rest of them fed all through the long winter. It is still so. For how much longer, in these days of synthetic fabrics? The meat is still needed, but there must be a generation growing up, in the towns, which hardly knows the feel of warm woollen cloth.

CHAPTER THREE

Early roads

'Roads' over the moor, in the sixteenth century and long afterwards, were only long-used tracks, miry and rutted. Loads were taken by strings of pack-ponies, for which, here and there, narrow bridges were built beside the fords, to keep the wool or cloth dry when streams were swollen. Farmers and their wives rode to market carrying their goods for sale in panniers or saddle-bags – in South Molton and Barnstaple the high halls like Victorian railway termini are still called pannier-markets, though now the fresh food comes from the country in cars or vans. Out beyond the farmland the unfenced moor stretched away, mile upon mile, crossed by a few grassy 'roads', and threaded by paths which had to be well known to be used safely. Moorland people, like their ponies, could distinguish bridle-ways from sheep-paths, avoid the squelchy ground near the hilltops, ford the rivers where they were shallow, and be safely indoors before dark; a stranger without a guide would do best to keep to the roads, such as they were.

Exmoor has been pastoral for so long that tracks of widely differing age remain. Animals may have trodden their banks down here and there, rain may have either washed them level or deepened them into runnels, peat may have covered them. But innumerable short stretches survive – not all comprehensible now. Their original purpose may have ended: the way by which the Free Suitors of Withypool took their sheep across Braddimoor to the Forest is now a bridle-path linking two farm lanes, and South Radworthy farmers no longer need John Cole's track to the boundary road. These can be partly seen, partly deduced from the records. Others led to farmhouses now derelict, or were made for the mining and lime traffic in the eighteenth and nineteenth centuries. Some of the recorded 'bridle-roads' can no longer be recognized on the ground with any certainty, while other tracks, wide enough for wheeled traffic, are so clear as they cross the pasture that they ought to be explicable, though no satisfactory explanation is available yet. One such slants down south-west across Fyldon Common from near a modern gravel-pit; it may or may not be the Barnstaple–Withypool road indicated in the 1819

Inclosure Map. It seems to reappear at the head of Lyddicombe, where a small rectangular ruin is perched on the left bank of a cleave. The stone footings of this suggest a shepherd's cot in a tiny enclosure; its wide gateway through a beech-topped hedge to the modern lane has been skilfully walled in to match the rest. It may be no more than about two centuries old; the tracks crossing that corner of the field may be older, or may not. At this height, 1300 feet, and facing the rainy south-westerlies, a simple building collapses very quickly once its roof has gone; and the neighbouring farms have changed hands so often that there seems to be no local memory of road or cottage, people or purpose.[1]

More than a dozen long-distance roads are clearly recognizable, though. Some are prehistoric, some mediaeval, and they fit the lie of the land so well that most of them have remained, all this time, the most convenient routes. The oldest – Bronze Age or earlier – are still the best. They follow the ridges, which would have been open and dry when valleys were uncleared swamps, and they surround the moor. The mediaeval ones supplement these by crossing it, going steeply uphill or down and serving Saxon farms or villages at the fords. (The roads are shown in Map 4.)

The oldest roads, trodden at least fifteen hundred years before the Roman invasion, run along the high ridges which enclose the Forest and the northern commons like ramparts. A long wide ridge is a good, but not infallible, clue to the antiquity of a road. It would always have been inviting, provided it led where travellers wanted to go. From the high ground they could see other ridges, converging or parting. Exmoor people need no map to show them Dartmoor on the southern horizon, Hartland and Lundy in the west, and northward the Severn Sea and Wales, with the channel narrowing north-east past Steep Holm and Flat Holm and Mendip.[2] So an early trader carrying copper or amber, tin, or Cornish greenstone axes would follow the upland path, the high way, only while it suited his purpose – perhaps until he could easily cross to another.

As early as the Bronze Age, too, great barrows on the skyline marked the way; they may have been royal burial-grounds for many generations. Often, but not always, they stood beside long ridgeways. An undulating line of more than twenty stretches from Setta Barrow through Five Barrows to Two Barrows in a fine arc, but the track (A on plan) used later as county and Forest boundary, goes straight along more level ground between the two ends, like the string of a bow. Similarly, it drops a little way down the southern slope after passing Two Barrows, and goes on easily by Coles Cross to Sandyway, while the ridge continues to One Barrow, at 1431 feet, and then plunges steeply to Sherdon Water. The Chapman line (C on plan) seems to end at Exe Head, as though the burials were spaced along a processional way. After Preyway Head – bare of monuments, as far as is known – the central ridge is lower for the next six miles, north of the Exe. When it rises again to 1500, 1600 and finally 1700 feet, a chain of impressive barrows culminates at Dunkery and continues along the north-eastern spur to Robin How and Joaney How. Like the Chapman line, it stretches for about four miles (**E2** on plan) and runs out eastward from an important north–south road, giving easy access to the great tombs. The highest sites were the places of greatest honour, visible from a very long way away. Winsford Hill was another (**F**). All three of these short stretches became incorporated in mediaeval roads, but were not necessarily thoroughfares from the beginning.

A third clue – also to be followed with caution – is offered by later boundaries, county or Forest or parish, between old commons and ancient 'waste', if they ran for a time along a ridge. That would provide a convenient natural divider – better than a river, which may alter course and carry a bit of one man's meadow across to another's bank. If an old boundary runs level, just below the watershed and often on the sunnier side of it – as between Setta Barrow and Sandyway – it is likely to have been the prehistoric road. The contour and the barrows and perhaps some ancient longstones would provide a recognizable line for mediaeval boundary-riders, and that in turn would perpetuate the road. (Leland, crossing this ridge in the sixteenth century, accepted a local mistake; he wrote that the Five Barrows were 'hillocks of earth cast up in ancient time for marks and limits between Somersetshire and Devonshire'. They had of course been standing for some two thousand years before the Saxons defined the shires.)

While the border of the Forest might hold the same direction along the ridge for many miles, a parish boundary would have to leave it soon, to encircle the parish and return to its starting-point; so if it swings suddenly away from the line of a long prehistoric road it is no longer evidential. And there may have been recent alterations; the Cutcombe–Winsford–Exford corner was adjusted in the nineteenth century, Culbone–Oare in the twentieth. But when the ridge road separates a whole series of parishes on the left from another series on the right, as does the highway along the Brendon Hills, the Harepath, it must have been there before them.

Unfortunately not even the combination of parish boundaries with Bronze Age monuments along a crest is incontrovertible proof; the Exford–Withypool boundary north of Braddimoor runs along a ridge, past two barrows, to the Forest boundary at Stone Crest (or Stone Chiste or Stone Christ) 'on the top of White Hill', yet it is probably no more than a short Saxon boundary using the topography and ancient landmarks. As a road, it would have to go steeply downhill at either end, cross the Barle or Pennycombe Water, and then climb again, with no obvious prehistoric reason in either direction.

The destination can seldom be more than careful conjecture, but it is always worth thinking about. There was trade along the ridgeways from very early times – stone axes from Cornwall have been found in Wiltshire, and amber from the North Sea in a burial near Heasley Mill. The tidal estuary of the Taw and the natural harbours along the north coast must always have been important to Exmoor. They were a way *in*, from the sea, as well as out – a way for explorers, missionaries, traders or piratical enemies. It looks as if all the long-distance roads, whether prehistoric or mediaeval, led to or from a seaport.

From ground evidence – with a wary eye on later history, and on the danger of confusing quite separate origins – it is possible to trace six or perhaps seven prehistoric roads, nearly all of them still in use. Taking them clockwise from Dulverton (**A to G** on plan) shows an interesting pattern. In early millennia Exmoor was virtually an island, bounded by sea to the north and west, marsh and scrub to the south, and eastward by the broad Parrett estuary, with Sedgemoor beyond. The oldest roads surround the moor, and lead away from it. Three head for the little port of Combwich on the Parrett, where a natural causeway once afforded passage at low tide.

A. The track along the south-western ridge, from Anstey Five Cross Ways to the similar five at Fullaford (and a meeting of so many roads, in open country, often signifies great age) had come up from Combwich together with **G**, as far as Brushford, where Exe and Barle could be forded separately, a mile above their confluence. Here the ways diverged. **A** went up north-west along a ridge where it is still a parish and then a field boundary, marked by strong hedges, on by Combe Farm lane, up past the only easy approach to Oldberry Castle, and so to Hinam's Cross and westward to the Anstey 'Five Crosses'.[3] From there it ran – and still runs – across Molland Common, then north along a watershed to White Post and north-west again past Twitchen barrows, Sandyway and Coles Cross, and along Fyldon ridge to the dip at Moles Chamber. From Sandyway it has been the Forest and county boundary, but here it swings 90° and runs south-westward, with the last spur of Exmoor proper, to Fullaford Five Cross Ways. It has been passing big skyline barrows all the way for fifteen miles, and the sequence continues after the Moles Chamber turn; one, seldom noticed, stands at a false crest just inside the left-hand hedge on the way up from the dip, with an old track straight through it and parallel with the metalled lane; further on, in ploughed land, a group which must once have been impressive marks the parting of the five ways.

As the road begins to drop, passing below the later encampment of Shoulsbury, it looks straight down to Barnstaple Bay – far ahead, but shining like a mirror in afternoon sunlight. It appears to be aiming for Pilton – a key port long afterwards, in King Alfred's time. From the crossways, the western track runs down to Fullaford, and over the Bray to Leworthy. From there the old way may well have gone on past Bratton Fleming and Chelfham to the Yeo valley and the Taw – and been reused many centuries later as the 'Barnstaple Bridle Road' (**3** on plan).

B. West of Leworthy, if this high road was making for the Taw estuary, it would cross the long north–south ridgeway over Bratton Down. This had climbed from somewhere between the Bucklands, skirted the row of three barrows on Stoodleigh Down, and run along the western flank of Mockham Down, which was later defended by an Iron Age fort. Northward to Blackmoor Gate it is the modern main road, passing near inconspicuous Bronze Age barrows at each gentle summit, and from there it crossed Kentisbury Down, where Stone Age hunters knapped their flints. From Coulsworthy the signs are that it went by the high lane along the ridge to Combe Martin. Lately this lane – or series of lanes – has been adopted, in the old practical way, as an obvious boundary line for the National Park. Three thousand years are as yesterday.

C. Just south of the modern crossroads called Blackmoor Gate the road from Loxhore meets the Bratton Down ridgeway at Blackmoor Gate Cross. Immediately opposite, a track runs eastward as far as a good standing stone – visible from the road – which seems to mark a division of ways. One goes down towards Parracombe, confirmed by a long hedge, a low barrow and a grassy sunken road. The other continues uphill to Holwell Barrow, and on near others to the great Chapman burial mounds. These are part of what must in antiquity have been a very holy place, stretching along the high ridge. The track ran past the tall Longstone (at the source of the Bray) to Woodbarrow, where there are groups of small standing stones, and very probably on to Chains Barrow and Exe Head. There it seems to end. There is no clear sign that it went on to Preyway Head. A suggested continuation north of Exe Cleeve by Rexy Barrow and Swap Hill would be very bad going. (*Rexy* is Old English for rushy, *Swap* was formerly *Snab*, meaning a marsh.) As a highway it was abandoned long ago – perhaps when it lost its religious significance, perhaps when the climate deteriorated. In bad weather the Chains (the *Chine*, or backbone, of the moor) are no place for a thoroughfare. But in a humbler way part of it continued to serve moorland travellers until less than two centuries ago (see 1, below).

D. The coast road eastward from Lynmouth, today's A39, has been in such continuous use since about 2000 B.C. that periods cannot easily be separated. Evidence of one illuminates another, and when its three stretches are considered together – the coastal ridgeway, the lowland road from Porlock to Dunster Steep, and the level eastern way past Carhampton and Watchet – it looks as though from very early times they provided for travel to, or from, the Parrett causeway at Combwich; and that in turn could lead to Glastonbury and the Midlands, or to Old Sarum and Salisbury Plain.

The five miles between County Gate and the Whitstones were clearly of great importance to Bronze Age people. The very early Culbone cist, in which the buried man had a beaker beside him for his journey into the unknown, was found beside the ridgeway; big barrows at intervals along the crest as far as Stent Hill seem contemporary with the imposing ones on other Exmoor skylines. The Five Stones at Deddycombe may have had religious significance, as the recently recognized stone row on Culbone Hill undoubtedly had, though nobody now knows what it meant. The two big sandstone slabs, the Whitstones, stand at the sharp angle on Porlock Common where perhaps the Harepath (**E**, below) joined the coast road. They are thought to have been set up in the Bronze Age or earlier. Had they something to do with the parting of important roads? Did some friendly little god of the crossways protect travellers, here as in ancient Greece?

The promontory fort at Countisbury, west of the Bronze Age concentration, was probably built in the early Iron Age, before the Roman conquerors made their look-out station at Old Barrow, above Glenthorne. As *Arx Cynuit* it was used again by the Devon Saxons, a stronghold against Hubba and his Danes. But before that, in the Dark Ages after the Romans left, Celtic missionaries landed on this coast. It is believed that one of them was the Welsh saint, Beuno (punisher, in legend, of a villainous Caradoc or Caratacus) and that he founded the tiny church, the *kil* or *cella* of *Beuno*, at Culbone, on the steep hillside between sea and moorland. At the top of the hill, near the ridgeway, was the stone row, probably still revered by the local pagans. Between that and the road a single sandstone slab is aligned towards the church. On its face is cut an oblique cross, an X in a circle, like a wheel with four spokes, one of them extended like the shaft of a Christian cross, also pointing downhill towards the hidden church. The encircled cross-head, as though a halo for the Crucified, was a familiar symbol in the Dark Ages, but the slant was unusual.

Questions abound. Did the stone always stand just here? If so, was it set up by heathens or by Christians? Was it there to guide Christian strangers down to the church? Did the saint have the cross carved to drive away pagan spirits from the long row which barred the way? And when did the church become a place of pilgrimage? In Tudor times it was a shrine; was that only coincidence, or had a tradition lasted for nine hundred years? In 1532 – just before the Reformation – James Hadley of Withycombe made his will, and having, he said, neglected to visit holy places, he bequeathed money to various shrines, including threepence to 'St Culbone' and five shillings to 'Our Blessed Lady of Cleeve'. Several were only recent shrines, and the Cleeve pilgrimage was a popular revival.[4] There is no written evidence of continuity; the Culbone shrine might have been recent too; from the Dark Ages to the sixteenth century is a very long time – but is it quite so long here as it would be in easier country? Saxons came, and in due course rebuilt the church; heathen Danes landed in Porlock Bay and harried inland; Normans arrived, and pitiless oppression was followed by near-anarchy. Might not the farmers and fishermen and their wives have clung to the memory of their saint through very harsh times, and spread word of his protective power?[5]

The prehistoric track served as mediaeval Forest boundary from County Gate to the head of Pittcombe, and then probably followed the ridge to its abrupt end above Porlock. Perhaps the Bronze Age people crossed the low ground and climbed again to the Bossington–Minehead ridge; a line of their barrows runs eastward from Selworthy Beacon. The mediaeval road kept to the lowland, past Allerford and Periton to Dunster; in 1425 the bailiff of Porlock manor went along it with a waggon and two men to fetch a load of wine.[6] Near Dunster, it met the Bridgwater road, by which, in 1540, Leland travelled along the coast and then diagonally across the moor to Barnstaple.

From the fertile Vale of Porlock eastward past Watchet to the 'redlands' beyond Quantock, memories of the Somerset Saxons are uppermost. Farm and village names are theirs, King Alfred had important estates at Carhampton and Cannington, Watchet was a stronghold in his defensive network against Danish raiders. The coastal road was an easy way to these from the royal lands beyond Bridgwater, and it may have been in use a long time before the Saxons built that bridge.

Lower down the Parrett, at Combwich, there was a natural causeway by which the wide estuary could be crossed at low tide. The Roman soldiers knew it, and built their port on the left bank; immediately opposite, their road started south-eastward, along the slight Polden ridge, past another river-port, Crandon Bridge (inland now, because the course of the Parrett has twice been artificially changed) and on to Ilchester and Dorchester. Early in the fifteenth century it was reported that the causeway had fallen into decay, and maintenance was becoming difficult. It must have been restored, for it took regular traffic in the eighteenth century. During the nineteenth century it was silting up, but was still used by local people. In the 1930s an old gentleman, Robert Guy Everard, who lived at Hill House on the left bank, told a young friend (who told me in 1985) that some fifty years earlier he had often taken his private pack of harriers across at low tide to hunt on the Pawlett Hams; he was proud of being the only person who remembered the firm way under the mud, and he would not tell his secret. But his own and his father's recollections of the ford were preserved by a local parson, the Rev. W. Greswell, who related in 1922, in his *Dumnonia and the Valley of the Parrett*, what he had learnt from them and other old parishioners. He was a Fellow of the Royal Geographical Society as well as an M.A., and he described the causeway as a natural hard of blue lias. (A vein of this runs up from Blue Anchor towards the Poldens; ships waiting off Watchet for the tide brought up their anchors coated with blue clay.)

When the silt was periodically cleared away, cattle and sheep could still be driven across safely at low tide, and it was the herdsmen's chief route to Glastonbury and Salisbury. They might have a long wait; besides the great rise and fall of the channel tides, a bore pushes upstream to Bridgwater (where it nearly capsized Oliver Cromwell's boat when he was reconnoitring to besiege the town). As time wore on a high-tide alternative shortened the delay; large ferries crossed from Combwich to the end of the White House road ('Combwich passage') directly opposite. They plied until after 1914; the skeleton of their wooden jetty on the left bank remains, and so does the ruin of the White House Inn on the right.

An old ferryman, born in the early 1830s, remembered waggons being driven across the hard now and then. Another very old man told Parson Greswell that Irish labourers formerly used 'the cassy' on their way to pick hops in Kent. He also recalled an occasion, in his youth, when a stag being hunted from the Quantocks had run down to the river and right across it. The tide was out; the huntsman and some of the field followed him over, killed on the Hams and celebrated at the Shoulder of Mutton near Pawlett church. They forgot the tide, which waits for no man.

Though nearly all this was in print, the causeway was lost for the greater part of the twentieth century. Either the mud thickened, or the water-table rose, or perhaps seekers were looking in the wrong place. But three people from beyond Exmoor, at the lowest tide of the spring equinox in 1987, had better fortune. The river was slightly swollen by overnight rain, but there was no mist, and not a breath of wind to ruffle the surface. About an hour and a half before the end of the ebb a shadow began to appear on the water, and became a stronger and stronger ripple, not straight across, as we had expected, but aslant in a long diagonal. More and more of this appeared, the bar growing longer at each end, and in the middle, where the veil of muddy water was thinnest, the ripple broke in tiny waves.

A deeper channel, not very wide, separated this reach from the left bank, now a long slope of mud on stone, with a few yards of outcrop jutting out into the water's edge, and a tree-trunk, washed bare, standing like a marker, its age and purpose unknown. One of the party, Ernest Mold of Lynton, waded out along the little promontory, probing until it ended in a sudden drop; another, the geologist Roger Beck, F.R.G.S., of the Open University, followed the river downstream till it turned slightly at the north-west end of the diagonal, and there he found a shelf of blue lias in the bank – plainly the beginning of the wide hard, to which the narrow outcrop may once have been a short cut.

This wide approach would have been easy for the waggons. Clear of the port, and directly east from Hill House, it would also have given the huntsman and harriers an unobtrusive way on to the ancient causeway – already superseded by the ferry, which would itself soon be discarded for the Bridgwater road.

The hard was used from Roman times until almost our own; so why not from much earlier? An animal from either side might have shown some primaeval hunter on the Hams the way across, and once known it would not be forgotten. Mesolithic nomads knapped their tiny flint weapons at Hawkcombe Head on Exmoor, and they had seasonal camps strung along the coast at Doniford, Williton and Watchet, as well as near North Petherton at the foot of the Quantocks. Had they paddled over the causeway from the marshes to hunt deer in the western hills, and found the sea-fish tasty and wild fruit plentiful and good, and returned with their families year after year – the first summer visitors, here for the hunting, nine or ten thousand years ago?

The slightly undulating lowland west of Combwich, as far as the five crossways near Kilve where the A39 (like its predecessor on older maps) turns sharply south, continued to be valued. It contains the early Bronze Age barrow of Wick and the Romano-British hillfort of Cannington; the northern way at the crossroads is from Kilton, another of King Alfred's manors, and the series of lanes leading directly to Combwich goes through Stogursey, site of a Benedictine priory built very soon after the Norman Conquest. Somewhere near here the coastal track would have converged with the very long prehistoric ridgeway (**G** and **A** on plan), coming down through Nether or Over Stowey towards the river-crossing.

E. At Pittcombe Head the contour swings south from the coast road

43

by a wide unmetalled track, shown on the Day and Masters map in 1782, to Hawkcombe Head, and for some two miles a hedge-bank defines the modern road across Porlock Common. Almost by chance, a detail of the thirteenth-century Forest boundary here lights up prehistory. In 1219 the temporary line, annulling King John's encroachments but leaving his father's and his brother's for later attention, followed the high ground through Hawkcombe Head and southward to the Stoke Pero parish boundary, just before Lucott Cross, where it turned south-west to Alderman's Barrow. Straight on southward is the modern Exford road, dividing next at Hillhead Cross. In the $3\frac{1}{2}$ miles from Pittcombe Head this high road dips only twice – first to cross the marshy source of Colley Water at Porlock Stone Circle, and then Chetsford Water near its head. At Chetsford[7] (a hybrid name, indicating that both Celts and Saxons knew the place) it runs between the enigmatic stone-setting on Almsworthy Common and the very old field-walls on Lucott Great Hill, and then passes near Bendel's Barrows. The Bronze Age monuments, the road using the watershed, and the half-Celtic name, are all significant, and so is the identity at the northern end with the 1219 boundary of the Forest. When a temporary but easily recognizable demarcation was needed it would be common sense to use an existing highway until it joined a known parish boundary.

Hillhead was formerly a full crossroads, with four branches. The fourth is now only a farm lane, but it prolongs the road from Hawkcombe Head and points straight to the top of Stone Down. A small damaged bowl-barrow, some 100 paces west of the impressive ring-bank with its one wind-swept beech tree, can be seen on the skyline ahead as one walks down the lane. From that summit, the same direction leads on across Kitnor Heath, through a bewildering network of nineteenth-century quarry tracks, into Langdon's Way (by a gate set aslant in the modern hedge, neatly confirming the putative line). Thorne Lane, almost opposite, keeps on south-east and east to cross the Quarme at Bushel Bridge and reach the modern turnpike at Harepath Cross. From there a very steep track goes up to Summerway Cross at the extreme north-western tip of the Brendons ridgeway, where, as the recognized Harepath, it runs through Heathpoult Cross, important for many centuries (see 7, below) and on for the whole length of the ridge, passing big isolated Bronze Age burial mounds, defended at the southern end by the Iron Age hillfort miscalled Elworthy Barrows, and lined by the boundaries of Saxon parishes.

At Bushel Bridge the Quarme is not wide, and in summer not deep, but it can be turbulent after heavy rain. A bad-weather variant may have been needed, perhaps later in prehistory, and this probably ran from Bendel's Barrows eastward past the Rowbarrows (E2) leaving the ridge before Dunkery summit, to go south-east to what is now Wheddon Cross on the turnpike, and then up to join the southerly route at Summerway Cross.[8] It is a longer and bleaker way but it avoids the whole course of the Quarme. When the river was fordable there was a highway almost direct from Elworthy Barrows to Pittcombe Head, 22 miles or more. I suggest that the whole of this, including the seasonal variation, was the Bronze Age trackway later called the Harepath. Apart from the stretch across Stone Down and Kitnor Heath, and the steep climb from Harepath Cross, the southern route is still used by traffic, and so is the northern one except where it crosses open moor between Dunkery Gate and Bendel's Barrows. Both the lost stretches appear (after a fashion) on the 1809 O.S. map, but now the mediaeval road (Leland's) from Blagdon Cross to Exford, modernized for fast cars, has superseded both.

This interpretation differs from what we have all been believing and repeating about the Harepath for years. Following Charles Whybrow, who knew Exmoor very well, we have accepted the German instead of the English meaning of the name *harepath*, have brought West Saxon fighters in by it, and assumed that they wanted to reach the Taw estuary. Grundy, writing a little earlier, took them there by a huge detour; but he owned to the handicap of not knowing the country and having to depend on maps.[9] He had, though, done careful work on Saxon charters and minor roads, and found many short ridgeways along low hills near Taunton, and larger ones elsewhere, called by variants of the word *harepath*. He concluded that it came to mean little more than a connecting road, or thoroughfare, along the higher and drier ground.

German *heer* is an army, but Old English *here* was a party of raiders (*harrying* the land). In the Laws of the early Saxon King Ine of Taunton it was defined as a band of robbers, not fewer than thirty-five. In the Anglo-Saxon Chronicle it always meant the Danish invaders, whereas the king's army was never anything but the *fyrd*. The Saxons of the ninth and tenth centuries are unlikely to have named such a good ridgeway after the hated foe. They may, indeed, have advanced along it earlier to harry British farmsteads, but they would hardly have applied King Ine's definition to themselves. Soldiers would always have preferred the dry ridge road, as would any other travellers; but there is no need to seek a military destination for the Brendons highway, which was prehistoric.

Grundy proposed the northern route from Summerway Cross via Dunkery Gate to Bendel's Barrows, but postulated a westward track from there along Swap Hill and the Chains, though he admitted there was no evidence. He thought it turned south at Woodbarrow while a branch ran westward via Blackmoor Gate to Berry Down, then south to Barnstaple.

Charles Whybrow, working carefully on the ground, set off on the southern route by Harepath Cross and Bushel Bridge, but two-thirds of the way along Thorne Lane he was seduced by a very alluring byway which, together with the parish boundary, swung away sharply to his left. It is broad enough for carts, and sheltered between good beech hedge-banks, the trees now overgrown and forming a fine overarching avenue. Alas, it deceived him! It led to a disused stone quarry and limekiln, on the steep spur east of Larcombe Brook near the modern Exford–Winsford road. The quarry and kiln were developed only in the nineteenth century, and the short lane does not appear on any early maps; the contours suggest that it was made for waggons bringing limestone and coal from Watchet. Moreover, the corner of three adjacent parish boundaries, Exford, Winsford and Cutcombe, was adjusted at about this time, and the new lane coincided with the new boundary.

Tracks go down the spur to the brook, and on to Exford. Workmen would have used them daily. But Charles went on westward by field paths across to the Exford–Simonsbath road, which was part of Leland's road from Dunster to Brayford (4 on plan) a fact he seems, strangely, to have overlooked. That road ran down through Birch Cleeve in Simonsbath, where it is still visible, to cross the Barle and climb the 'great moorish hill' opposite, but he believed the woodland track was part of the Harepath, forking in Simonsbath. He thought one branch went uphill and over by Brayford to Barnstaple, as the recorded mediaeval road did, and the other along the Barle and Bale Water to Driver, turning left there to go up to Moles Chamber by the well-known parallel ruts. He took these to be mediaeval reuse of a much older road going on over Bratton Down to Barnstaple.

But the ruts can also be interpreted as mediaeval only, part of the bridleway from Barnstaple to Porlock over Exe Head (3 on plan). No traces of prehistory are apparent anywhere between Moles Chamber and Thorne Lane, on the course proposed. It is sad work disagreeing with such a kindly mentor and friend after his death, but it does seem now that he combined three quite different roads and that neither Birch Cleeve nor Moles Chamber formed any part of the Harepath.

Topographically, Grundy's route leads through hilltop bogs, Whybrow's beside a quick-rising river in a valley which may have been thickly wooded.[10] The Bronze Age offered a shorter and easier way from the Brendons to the Taw estuary than either of these, along Haddon Hill and over Molland Common (A on plan). The high way (E) from Elworthy Barrows to Hawkcombe Head is convincingly prehistoric on the ground, and admirably direct. Whether travellers turned west along the coast road to Lynmouth, or swung eastward past the Whitstones and down to Porlock Bay, is perhaps unknowable; Porlock seems the likelier destination, with its good soil, good harbour, and seaways across to Wales.

F. A ridgeway along Winsford Hill, between Exe and Barle, passes close to Ernesbarrow on Road Hill, and further on, the Wambarrows, and the Caratacus Stone. Then the ground begins to drop, and the signs of great antiquity seem to end, but the five-mile stretch is guarded by hillforts, presumed to be of Iron Age date, at either end and on either flank – Road Castle above the Exe and Mounsey above the Barle. The ridgeway was probably a track (which still exists) running rather higher along the hill than the modern road, and passing east of the Wambarrows and the stone – in which case the name of Caratacus carved on the eastern face during the Dark Ages would have been easily visible to wayfarers. The stone itself may have been set up during the Bronze Age to mark the source of a stream and honour its deity. (The water-table has dropped, and the stream now appears first at the edge of the modern road.)

These few miles were another part of the temporary Forest boundary in the early thirteenth century; the men riding it, clockwise, went from the Exe to 'la Rode'[11] and thence to Ernesbarrow, along the ridge past the 'Langeston' to 'Magildesdene Heved' (taken to be Mounsey Hill Gate) and down to the Barle, very probably at Three Waters. The perambulation record calls this whole stretch 'the great way', the broad or well-trodden track. The boundary went on downstream, and up the Danesbrook, but after the Barle crossing there is no further mention of 'the great way'. Where that had come from before the riders joined it near Exford, and where it went when they left it, are unsolved puzzles. Perhaps it was an ancient long-distance road which the boundary used for a little way. A possibility is that it climbed straight up from Three Waters, over the descending spur of Hawk Ridge and down to Castle Bridge. From there the county boundary runs very steeply uphill to Anstey Five Cross Ways and down a long lane (5 on plan) to Oldways End (more properly Allways End). The lane continues to Tucker's Moor Cross, and that is on the ridgeway to Chulmleigh, running towards the Cornish hills in the far distance (G on plan). Charles Whybrow thought that north of Winsford Hill the ancient road probably 'found its way to the sea at Porlock by a route which still needs to be discovered'. On the new hypothesis of a northward Harepath, the 'great way' could have gone up from the Exe to join it at Hillhead Cross (part of the lane up from Exford is very deep, as though mediaeval at latest). If these surmises are right, it might have been part of a prehistoric route from Porlock Bay to St Michael's Mount, where Phoenician traders came in search of tin. A great way indeed.

G. The long road from Cornwall may have been part of one yet longer, crossing England diagonally to the Humber and the seaway to Denmark. South-west of Chulmleigh the line is conjectural, but it could have crossed the Taw at Eggesford, gone up through Winkleigh and eventually over Bradbury Down, where Bronze Age barrows stand at a ridgeway intersection with another very old road (Roman or earlier) and on to cross the Carey and the Tamar separately, just north of Launceston. From the border town the modern A30 leads straight on, through signs of Neolithic, Bronze Age, Iron Age and Roman occupation, right down to the sandy shore of Mounts Bay.

The section which skirts the south of Exmoor and cuts through a corner of it can be followed more exactly from Chulmleigh to Combwich. From Stone Moor Cross it is a ridgeway, twice passing near round barrows; on Beaple's Hill a shoulder-high longstone stood – until it was moved slightly away from the route of the new Link Road – just at the point where a much shorter road, Rattle Street, joined it from beyond Rose Ash. The stone is an irregular cylinder at base, but the upper part is roughly shaped (or chosen) to give three pointers indicating the direction of the three tracks. It seems more than coincidence that one leads on beyond Dulverton and Combwich to Glastonbury, one passes near the spring on Munson farm, Rose Ash, where the farmer found and saved a bronze bowl of Glastonbury type made just before the Roman invasion, and the south-westerly one has come up from Cornwall where a very similar bowl was unearthed at Warbstow, some eight miles north of the A30. More round barrows mark the line of the ridgeway across Knowstone Inner Moor, then it drops down Langaller Lane to Brushford below Dulverton, to cross the Barle and then the Exe at Perry, about a mile before they unite. It looks as though the ridgeway (**A**) from Anstey Five Crosses used the same two fords, the roads then going on north-eastward to Combwich as one. There were alternative possibilities, by valley or hill routes, to the barrows on Haddon Hill, and from there a high road still runs through Upton to the Brendons Harepath, which it joins above the source of the Tone; the old track may have struck the ridge a little further west, near the big meare-stone, the Naked Boy. Opposite Elworthy Barrows (more accurately burrows or bury) a modern road on the other side of the Doniford valley resumes the same general north-easterly direction from Crowcombe over the Quantocks to Over and Nether Stowey beside the coast road. From there, the lanes lead through Fiddington to Combwich Causeway. There was no need for ferry-boats.[12]

Once over the Parrett and on the Poldens, travellers had their choice of ways, south, east or north – and the timber tracks discovered lately under the peat show that even in Neolithic times the marshland round Glastonbury was no real barrier. Northward over Mendip, hill roads could lead to Bathford on the Avon, and from Bath the limestone ridge, the Jurassic Way, slanted across the Midlands to Lincolnshire and was a well-used road long before the Romans built the Fosse; it passes the Rollright Stones. Its last low spur, forking, carried the Roman Ermine Street to the Humber, and parallel with it was very probably an older track where a minor modern road runs along the eastern cliff of the Trent. Alkborough, the terminus of this, looks down over both rivers. On the far bank of the estuary, at North Ferriby, the remains of three large flat-bottomed boats dating from the Bronze Age lay hidden in the mud until the 1940s. It is considered possible that these plied across the North Sea and into the shallow Baltic.

On Exmoor there must always have been side tracks and short cuts, and perhaps other long roads, not now recognized, but except along the Chapman and Dunkery spurs these high ridge-roads seem to have been the prehistoric arteries. They all lead to or from sea-ports, and at least three of them to Combwich – where they leave the peninsula for the mainland. (So does 1, below, which was probably Saxon at latest.) This was the pattern which successive conquerors found and modified or supplemented but did not discard.

The Romans were based further south, at Ilchester and Exeter, but they had to guard against attack by sea from Wales. They held the mouth of the Parrett, with a port on each bank and the road from Ilchester serving both. They may also have had two valley roads from Exeter, one east and one west of the moor, for quick movement of legions. There are signs of a possible western route via Lapford, on the Yeo/Nymet, and down the Taw to its estuary; recent work at Bury Barton, overlooking the Nymet at Lapford, has revealed a fortified site which may have been their *Nemeto statio*.[13] East of the moor, they may have travelled up the Exe valley from Tiverton, then along the Batherm to Bampton, north to Morebath and the Dulverton Bury, up 'Miniard Lane' to Baron's Down (Barren Down on Day and Masters' Map, 1782) and over the hills on the old coach road (7 on plan) to Minehead, intersecting the Brendons Harepath at Heathpoult Cross. Again, recent excavations at Bolham, north of Tiverton, have uncovered a fort, and at Chawleigh on one route, Bury on the other, local antiquaries have from time to time found what they believed to be scraps of supporting evidence. These may or may not have been the routes used, but they would make good military sense. Similarly, the road along the north coast must have been important; Porlock especially would need to be guarded (and the defenders could reach it easily from Combwich or by the Harepath (E) from Heathpoult Cross). There were also, for a short time, the two fortlets on the cliffs, Old Burrow and Martinhoe, to be maintained.

Whether or not the Legions marched up this road from Tiverton to Minehead, the greater part of it was certainly important in the Middle Ages. It became a regular way for the packhorse trains taking Irish wool from the ships at Minehead to the looms in Bampton, when the demand for woollen cloth had outpaced the local supply of fleeces. From Bampton another packhorse route went to London – in the seventeenth century and probably much earlier.

Of the mediaeval roads (1 to 7) across the moor, the first two may have been developed during the Saxon centuries. Not all carry traffic along their whole length today, but the lost stretches can still be traced on the ground. The first has lately been rediscovered, after a lapse of nearly two centuries, and is particularly interesting.

1. The rediscovery began with an anecdote told by J. K. Ridler, of Selworthy. A relation of his, John Clarke, yeoman, of West Lynch, had in 1814 courted and married a young woman who lived at Smythapark near Loxhore, in the western foothills. After the wedding he had ridden home, some 35 miles across the moor, with his bride on the pillion behind him.

The lane up from Loxhore, which he would have joined, meets the Bratton Down ridgeway (**B**) at Blackmoor Gate Cross, just south of the modern crossroads and opposite the track to Chapman Barrows (**C**). In 1628 Hugh de Wichehalse, leaving Barnstaple for Lynton in time of plague, came up through Pilton, Shirwell, and Loxhore, and at that crossing had to decide between going on over 'the black moors' to Woodbarrow and thence down the old road to Lynton (**2** on plan) or taking what looked the easier way, downhill to Parracombe. He had a Lynton man as guide, but he chose wrong and paid for it, like a character in *Pilgrim's Progress*; after Parracombe he found no road at all. John Clarke, nearly 200 years later, knew better and took the high way past all the Bronze Age barrows to Exe Head. There another mediaeval track from Barnstaple (**3** on plan) came up from the Barle and crossed the ridge. He would turn north-east and follow it over the open moor to Hawkcombe Head and Porlock, and then home to Lynch along an easy level stretch, now the busy A39.

Not long afterwards the moorland track was abandoned, and then lost. It was shown by Day and Masters on their map of Somerset in 1782, but not on the first O.S. map in 1809 nor the 1819 Inclosure Map. (The 1809 surveyors are locally suspected of not having set foot on inner Exmoor, and the Inclosure Map drawn by His Majesty's Commissioners was chiefly concerned with boundaries and with the new roads which the buyer of the

Forest was to make.) Lately, careful search on the ground has revealed some two miles in the middle of its course, including a length of old rutted road and then a ditched pathway like a dry bank, out on West Pinford in the undrained land. The track from the ridge went down past Blackpits and kept along the contour, above the combeheads, to the site of the later Larkbarrow farmhouse. Then, probably crossing Chalk Water at Three Combes' Foot, it climbed to Black Barrow and went on by Periam's Way to join the old highway from the Brendons (E) at Hawkcombe Head. It served for a long time, but the peaty bogs indicated by all these *black* names, as well as *Rexy* and *Snab*, were a good reason for finding a firmer road when carts replaced pack-ponies and trackamucks.

So its history ended; but perhaps its finest hour was a thousand years earlier. It may have been the lifeline between two burghs, Pilton and Watchet, in King Alfred's system of defence against the piratical Danes. The old road up from Pilton by Shirwell and Loxhore ran past the fortifications of Roborough Camp, and that was ideally placed to repel any enemies who might sail up the estuary and attempt to land at the mouth of the Yeo. It may, like Wind Hill at Countisbury, have been an Iron Age fort which the West Saxons reused, or they may have built it themselves to meet the dire threat. Behind it lay the series of lanes and tracks which took Hugh de Wichehalse to Blackmoor Gate and John Clarke from there to Lynch, on the coastal way to Watchet. From Watchet the Saxons would have no difficulty in getting word to Lyng and Langport, the next burghs west of the Parrett, or across Combwich Causeway to Axbridge at the foot of Mendip.

And if Roborough Castle was Iron Age work, was it protecting some overland route which spared traders the risky sea-journey round Morte Point?

And further back still, the Mesolithic nomads who camped year after year at Hawkcombe Head made most of their little tools from beach pebbles that are believed to have come from Barnstaple Bay. Somebody must have found a way west – perhaps by Blackmoor Gate and Kentisbury to the long Atlantic beaches? – and trudged back laden with small stones in a bag made of scraped deerskin.

2. The old road from Lynton past Woodbarrow and Moles Chamber to South Molton provided a direct way across the moor, up and down from the coast over the northern and central ridges to the southern rampart, and then steadily downhill for eight miles or more to the market town of South Molton. Only parts of it are in use now, though for centuries it was 'the king's highway'. The five-mile stretch from Barbrook to Moles Chamber shows what all the roads were like until the nineteenth century – wide enough for droving, but very rough. This one begins as

a deep lane between hedges, and continues as a good farm-track over the common past Shallowford and up to the corner of the Forest and county at Saddle Gate, where the Saddle Stone is a three-parish meare-stone. It follows the combined Forest and county boundary up to Woodbarrow, the skyline landmark, and down southward past the Twizzlemark Stone – now immured in an enclosure bank – through Broadmead, where some of the lesser meare-stones which preceded the fence can still be seen. Then for a short distance road and boundary part, the road going west of the boundary and its marker, the Edgerley Stone, curving sharply round a stream-head (which both avoid) and climbing Roosthitchen to rejoin the boundary at Broadbarrow Stone. They continue downhill together, under the lee of Castle Common, to cross Lewcombe where an unimpressive but named meare-stone almost in the stream-bed is another three-parish boundary mark; together they climb again, along the side of the hill, to Moles Chamber. The undulation is noteworthy; this part of the road is nowhere a ridgeway, though it has been mistakenly called so. It defines the eastern limits of the Saxon parishes of Challacombe and High Bray; the waste land outside them was the king's land before the Conquest, and Royal Forest after Domesday. Legal references at the time of the disafforestation of most of Devon, in 1204, suggest that Forest and county boundary had been identical for at least a century before that.

It would seem that the Saxons set these parish boundaries as a north–south line, perhaps imaginary at first, between recognizable marks – big stones and a skyline barrow – where the ridges and streams were no help because they all ran east and west. Parish bounds had to be beaten, long before the Forest boundary was perambulated; there is no knowing when the line became a track, nor how long the landmarks had been there. Woodbarrow was prehistoric, of course, belonging to the great row along the central ridge, and the Lewcombe stone may denote pagan stream-worship. The others are probably undatable. The Saxons may have extended the parish boundary line north and south as their shortest and easiest way to and from the coast. Once clearly trodden, it would have been the obvious recognizable line for Normans defining the Forest – especially if it was already the boundary between the Saxon shires.

At Moles Chamber the road turned left, along the southern ridgeway, and climbed with it for a little way, but at the top of the steep, when the boundary went straight on up to Setta Barrow, the north–south road curved away to the right, along the sunny side of the hill. (Here or hereabout Anthony Jennings was caught driving his flock from Woolhanger, to escape grazing dues, in 1677.) After rounding the boggy stream-head east of Whitefield Down it swung south into Devon, down through

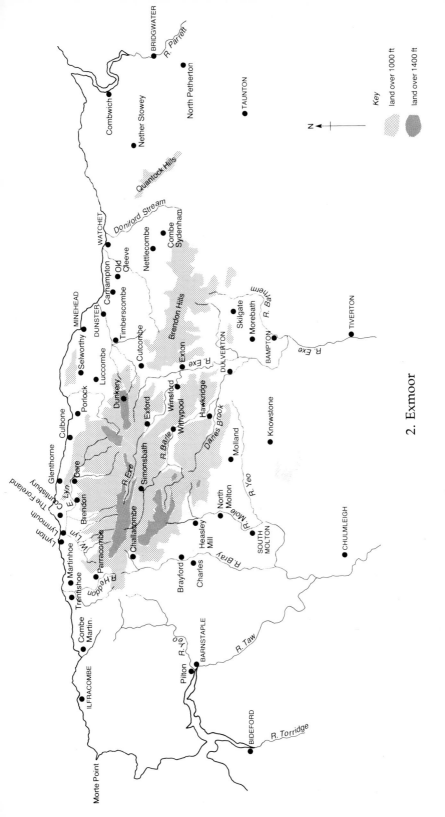

2. Exmoor

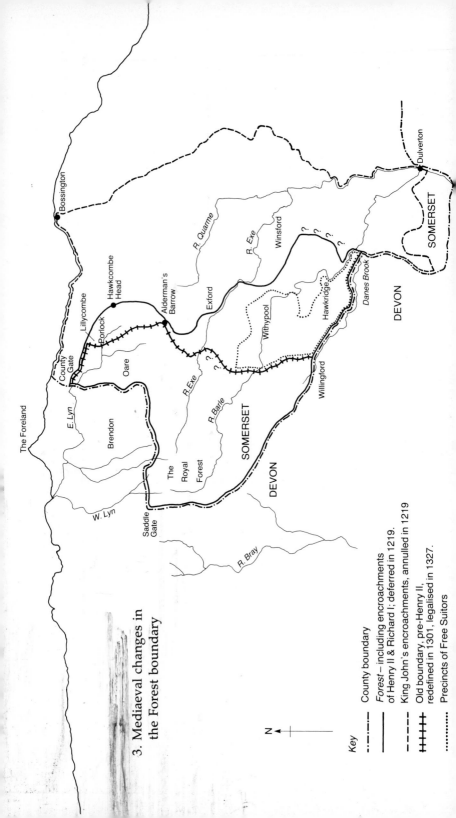

3. Mediaeval changes in the Forest boundary

Key

— · — · — County boundary

———— *Forest* – including encroachments
of Henry II & Richard I; deferred in 1219.

– – – – King John's encroachments, annulled in 1219

+++++ Old boundary, pre-Henry II,
redefined in 1301, legalised in 1327.

··········· Precincts of Free Suitors

N ←

Bossington
The Foreland
County Gate
E. Lyn
Lillycombe
Porlock
Hawkcombe Head
Alderman's Barrow
Oare
Brendon
W. Lyn
Saddle Gate
The Royal Forest
R. Exe
R. Barle
R. Exe
R. Quarme
R. Exe
Exford
Winsford
Withypool
Hawkridge
Danes Brook
Willingford
Dulverton
SOMERSET
DEVON
SOMERSET
DEVON
R. Bray

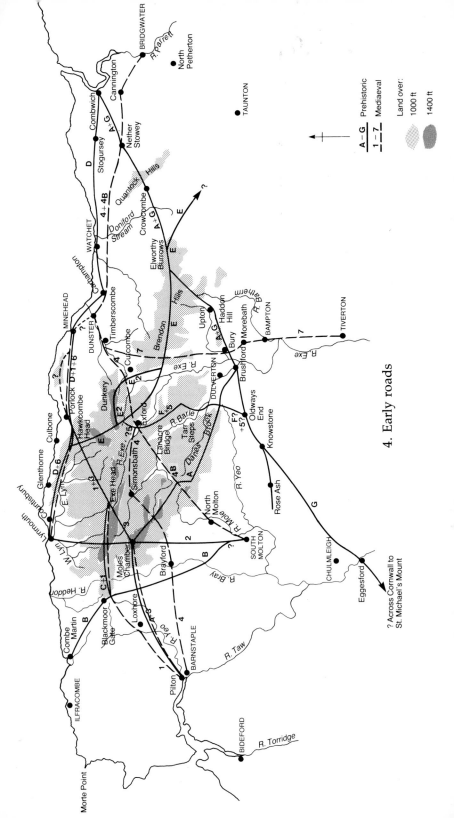

4. Early roads

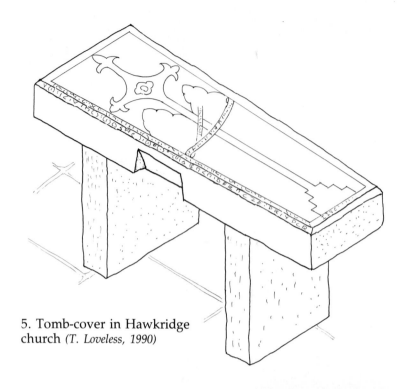

5. Tomb-cover in Hawkridge
church *(T. Loveless, 1990)*

6. Geoffrey Chaucer
(Anonymous miniature, c. 1410)

7. Mediaeval road and probable telling-house (*Exmoor National Park, 1990*)

9. Culbone church *(John Crowther, c. 1895)*

LEFT: 8. Lower Doverhay farmhouse *(John Crowther, c. 1895)*

10. Culbone wheeled-cross stone *(A. Phillips, 1982)*

pastures enclosed in the nineteenth century, and across another long mediaeval road (4) at Yard Down Cross near the Telling House. The ghost of it can still sometimes be seen on the slope, in slanting sunlight when the grass is short, and south of Molland Cross there are signs of the wider drove-way on either side of the modern South Molton road.

3. On the 1819 Inclosure Map this was called 'the Barnstaple Bridle Road' (entering the Forest at Moles Chamber) as far as Exe Head, where the Commissioners made it curve away north, to leave the Forest at what later became Brendon Two Gates. Day and Masters, in 1782, had shown the road running east and north-east to Black Barrow on its way to Porlock (1, above).

The whole road was mediaeval in character, going up and down diagonally across the moor, and incorporating lengths of the older ways along level ground whenever the opportunity arose. Most of it has already been described. From Barnstaple via Bratton Down to Fullaford Five Crosses it is conjecturally the western end of the long ridgeway (A); from there to Moles Chamber it is authenticated by Bronze Age barrows and the Iron Age camp, Shoulsbury. It bisected the most easterly barrow, which no longer commanded respect. For the same reason, farmers have lately ploughed the big ones near the Five Cross Ways flatter and flatter. The stretch from Moles Chamber down to the Barle and up through Driver to Exe Head would be a mediaeval innovation; comparative lateness may be why the tracks are still so plain. From Exe Head to Hawkcombe Head it is identical with (1). Day and Masters in 1782 showed it looping southward to avoid Blackpits bog. Out on the marshland the recently identified stretch of road, the ditched path (revetted here and there) and a few boulders like markers, are on the old line but may have been a nineteenth-century reinforcement. Had they anything to do with the siting of Larkbarrow farmhouse and the stell at Three Combes' Foot? Was the track used to get help out in bad weather from John Knight's Simonsbath–Brendon road? (3) and (1) continue together to Hawkcombe Head, with nothing to show which was the original. The ruts of (3) near the Barle must have been worn down by generations of shepherds with their flocks and packhorse men with their ponies, and this was probably where, some time in the 1640s, Anthony Mole of High Bray went out into the Forest on the prompting of two travellers, and found a dying man frozen to the ground. But if (1) was the line of communication for King Alfred's soldiers when Danes appeared off the coast, surely it must have been very much the older of the two?

4. This was the main diagonal road across Exmoor in the Middle Ages, passing south of the others. It was John Leland's route from

Bridgwater to Barnstaple in the early 1540s, and he described it in detail. It left the coast at Dunster, and from there it is still followed nearly all the way across the moor by modern roads and lanes. The road up the Avill forked at Timberscombe, where one branch (7) climbed over the Brendons via Heathpoult Cross for Bampton (the valley turnpike dates only from the 1820s) and the other, to Barnstaple, crossed the river and went up its left bank through Steart Lane (long known as Draper's Way[14] and now, for visitors, Snowdrop Valley) to Blagdon Cross. From here Leland would go by Luckwell Bridge and past Stone Cross to Exford, where 'a little timber bridge' took him over Exe brook, there only 'a small water'. Still heading westward, and along the Forest boundary for a mile or so, he would enter Crown land at Honeymead, on his way to Simonsbath. No house had yet been built there, and the origin of the name is still unknown, but it must have been familiar to graziers, like the descriptive words *Emmetts* (plateau), *Pinkery* (stony hill) and *Duredon* (animals' hill), used long before any farms were carved out of the Forest. Leland records: 'There runneth at this place called Simonsbath a river betwixt two great moorish hills in a deep bottom, and there is a bridge of wood over this water. The water in summer most commonly runneth flat upon stones easy to be passed over, but when rains come and storms of winter it rageth and is deep. Always this stream is a great deal bigger water than the Exe is at Exford, yet it resorteth into Exe river.' (Had he a guide over this wild part, who told him of the winter storms and the ever-regrettable affront to the Barle?) He went up one of the great moorish hills by a path now indistinguishable, then down gradually, with the Five Barrows on the skyline in front of him, over Kinsford Water, and up on the western side of the modern road to leave the Forest and Somerset at 'the Spanne' – Kinsford Cross, on the ridgeway. His road downhill from there is east of today's road; it is the hollow way past the Telling House, and onward behind the Poltimore Arms to the convergence of the massive Beara hedge with the modern highway to Brayford (which he thought 'a poor village'). Leaving it, he would continue on the line of the modern Barnstaple road until it enters the parish of Gunn. At Stone Cross (the name recurs – always near a Stone Farm) the most direct way to Barnstaple Bridge is the lane down to Sandick and thence through Harford to join the old highway from Taunton at Four Oak Cross, west of Landkey.

4B. A branch road from (4) was sufficiently important in the Middle Ages to need a stone bridge at Lanacre over the River Barle – strengthened by two lively tributaries since it left Simonsbath. An old lane between hedges leads straight up from Exford bridge, climbing steeply in the direction of Chibbet Cross;[15] from there a lane still used goes down past Chibbet farm, over Pennycombe Water, across Braddimoor and over Lanacre Bridge towards the Moltons in Devon. In 1610 this bridge was already old, and when, soon afterwards, it needed repair, the ratepayers of Carhampton and Williton had to bear much of the cost. By 1782 the road was joined at the top of the next hill – at Crooked Post, later called Litton Cross and now Withypool Cross – by a road from Withypool and Winsford, and they went on together as Sandy Way. This reached to the three-parish corner where Forest and county boundary were marked by the important Sandy Way longstone. (There were not, of course, any buildings here before the sale of the Forest in 1819; the Sportsman's Arms was first mentioned in a census in 1851.) The way down the long spur to North Molton curved south of the straight 'Mile Hill' which has replaced it, and would have gone on by the old hill road to South Molton; the 'New Road' along the valley is still recent.

From Exford to Lanacre the branch road crossing the valleys is recognizably mediaeval. Two old farmhouses stand conveniently close to it; the lane down past Chibbet is worn very deep. The ford used to be shallower until somebody dammed the upstream side, not long ago, to make an ornamental pond; on the lower side a little three-span clapper bridge at a cottage gate tells an older and more homely tale. North and south of Braddimoor the road was gated to prevent sheep from straying; where it descends past Lanacre farmhouse it is again very steep-sided, with another gate at the bottom, just before the double turn to cross the bridge for Withypool Common (the stone gateposts are still there). The fields north-east of this gateway are the 'Court Hams' where the Swainmote Court met once every summer, in the Forest centuries.

The purpose of this branch road – seemingly quite as important as Leland's – is obscure to us; perhaps it seemed to contemporaries too obvious to need mention. The charge upon Williton and Carhampton for the upkeep of a remote moorland bridge near the western edge of their county implies that this way into Devon was valuable to them. Was it to persuade the cloth-merchants of North and South Molton to send some of their goods down to the Severn ports instead of to Barnstaple or Exeter? And what did the packhorse trains take inland when they returned? Fresh or cured fish? Imported salt? We can only guess, until somebody finds relevant records of thirteenth- or fourteenth-century origin. But the importance of the road cannot be doubted.

5. This has already been considered, together with (F). The debate is whether it linked Bronze Age tracks to make the mediaeval 'Great Way' or whether the whole way from Porlock to Tucker's Moor was prehistoric.

6. The easy stretch from Porlock to the Dunster–Bridgwater coastal road, used for wheeled traffic in 1422, may have been a Saxon link – it would be part of the direct way between the hidal burghs of Pilton and Watchet – or it may first have been a Bronze Age alternative to the high road over North Hill.

7. This, too, has been discussed earlier (p. 49); it was certainly a mediaeval packhorse route, for the wool-trade, but may perhaps have been used by the Roman legions long before.

These were not all. There are unsolved puzzles – most notably, what road led across Tarr Steps. The great clapper bridge, the longest and most impressive in England, spans a shallow ford where the Barle, wide and strong, flows between steep wooded hillsides. In dry weather the ford would always have been easy, and refreshing for ponies, though the quick-flowing water and loose stones might keep a foot-traveller dependent on his stout stick. The huge slabs of the clapper are flat, not far above water-level but far enough for safe passage in any ordinary flood. Then – twice or thrice in a century perhaps – weeks of heavy rain followed by really bad storms, such as the one that broke on the Chains in August 1952, transform the river. Beginning to fill on the slopes of Pinkery, increasing in power and turbulence as swollen side-streams bring in more and more water, it enters the woods below Withypool able to uproot tall trees, and it piles them against the clapper with the weight of the torrent behind them, until at last the bridge gives way. Even then the massive stones are not carried many yards downstream. When the engineers come to replace them – each stone is now numbered and plotted - everybody marvels at the work of the original builders. Yet nobody knows who they were, nor when the bridge was built, nor why.

The design is ageless – an obvious sequel to the clammer, the single-span bridge first made by laying a tree-trunk across a stream. Here, seventeen spans carry the traveller some sixty paces from bank to bank, and the bridge is thought to be late mediaeval. It is not mentioned in the 1279 perambulation record, when the 'great way' ran down from Mounsey Hill 'between the two Ashways' and almost certainly crossed the Barle at Three Waters. The line of that road was probably the one marked now by a long straight hedge over the summit of Mounsey Hill, separating farmland from common, and this is roughly parallel with the lane from Winsford and Spire Cross down to the clapper, but less than a mile further downstream. Surely the boundary would have gone straight down from the Caratacus stone if the steps had been in existence, and surely such an unmistakable landmark would have been named in the record?

There is no sign of a drove-road. Packhorses would refuse to cross – all packhorse bridges have walls on either side so that ponies will not be frightened by the water running below. Nor would it have been a road to Dulverton, crossing the river twice, when there was an easy way down from Mounsey Hill Gate past Ashwick to Marsh Bridge, long before the turnpike over South Hill was made. Yet something must have justified the toil of building that long clapper, needed only in time of spate. One guess is that some change in the river's course near Slade, later than the 1279 perambulation, made the crossing at Three Waters impracticable, and so the clapper and a new road were made to replace that stretch of the great way. If so, this probably happened before 1349, when the Black Death terribly reduced the number of labourers on the land.

And there may be dateless puzzles not yet recognized, let alone solved. For instance, after a big flood some years ago two Exmoor people riding upstream from Marsh Bridge, on the Mounsey side, noticed paving in the river where a length of the bank had been washed away. They came from another part of the moor, but asked somebody local what this was, and the unhesitating answer was, 'The Salt Way'. Where from, where to, and when? The detective work is still waiting to be done.

Besides the long-distance roads, the arteries, there were countless local tracks linking farm and village and highway. Until half a century ago Winsford, with its river and brook, ford and little bridges, was the centre of a web of sunken lanes and half-lost ways through the woods. Anywhere on the moor a farm may still have a field named 'Church Path' – undatable – and there are lanes called Century or Sentry by which, once upon a time, fugitives ran to the church for sanctuary. If it had for door-knocker a great iron sanctuary-ring, as at Combe Martin and Molland still, a man with pursuers close on his heels could put himself under divine protection by grasping it, and only a very impious and daring man would harm him then.

There were drove-roads, short as well as long. Some can still be seen, wide green ways between fields or like firebreaks across the heather; unused now, they were trodden and fertilized by flocks for a great many years. Traces survive beside ancient ridgeways – broad grassy sidewalks left, in mercy to the animals, when the carriageway was hardened. These are very plain along the Brendons highway, and at intervals on the Chulmleigh ridge. Latterly, the roadmakers' habit has been to swallow up the friendly greensward and make more room for cars and coaches and huge delivery vans. Lanes are widened too – their banks made steeper and sheltering corners cut away. More often than not, now, sheep are moved in double-decker lorries; large milk-tankers hurry away from the farms to the distant main roads. Yet it is not a lifetime since these same lanes were stony and uneven, dusty in summer, muddy and slippery in winter, grooved and pitted by frost and flood, but quiet and wholesome, bordered with wild flowers and nuts and blackberries, happy places for dawdling on an autumn afternoon and exchanging pleasantries with the rare passers-by.

In the sixteenth century the moor was much wilder, of course, and there were few hedges and little shelter. Shakespeare describes the country roads of the time – ways foul in winter, 'fair enough' in summer. He has a stranger to Gloucestershire deploring the 'high wild hills and rough uneven ways'. A messenger who has ridden fast from the Scottish border to Westminster arrives 'stained with the variation of each soil' he has traversed; just so might a traveller crossing Exmoor be spattered with red mud or brown or black, and the ostler would deduce which way he had come.

Maintenance of the roads was a charge on the parish. In the Forest, which was still extra-parochial, the Warden, as leaseholder, was responsible, and made such repairs as were essential – a bog to be 'cut out' here, a roadside stone to be set up there. But the ancient pattern enabled a farmer to ride down to an inland market town or to a port which led away to the trackless Atlantic. He would bring home nuggets of up-country news and rumour, or wonderful tales from mariners about savages and sea-monsters in the New World. Tales and rumours would be sifted and weighed, discussed with neighbours, relished and effortlessly remembered for weeks and months and years.

PART II

EXMOOR IN A CHANGING ENGLAND

CHAPTER FOUR

The Reformation and the New World

Partly through the wool-merchants and their packhorse men, and partly from the great houses in the foothills, with lords and ladies and their retainers coming and going, news from the world outside would gradually reach the moor. Sir John Harrington of Porlock Manor, a friend of Henry V, may have fought with the King at Agincourt in 1415 ('We few, we happy few, we band of brothers') and certainly he came home to muster eighty-six archers and twenty-nine lancers for the second campaign, two years later. The archers had learnt their skill with the longbow in a field still called the Buttyard,[1] and they marched away from Porlock to Southampton to embark for France. Sir John did not return; his widow Lady Elizabeth – a Courtenay – inherited his manors of Porlock and Brendon. Her visits westward to the lonelier manor-house were great occasions, as the bailiff's accounts make clear: there was always a flurry of preparation – 'against the coming of the lady' – repairing and cleaning, stocking the woodpile and the larder, cutting rushes to be spread in the hall and the chamber, and providing straw for the lady's bed. The humblest farm-hand would know that the lord had been lost in King Henry's war in France. When the lady died, half a century later, she was buried beside the lord in the church of St Dubricius. Beautiful alabaster effigies of both lie on the tomb – his martial, a sword at his side and a crested helmet for pillow, hers like a portrait carved with loving respect. Her robed figure, waxen now, its colour long faded away, and the tranquil features, personal not conventional, speak of gracious wisdom, and make five hundred years seem not very long.

A Bottreaux of Molland, south of the moor, carried a lance at Agincourt too, and is unlikely to have gone alone. It was a far cry to Southampton, but rough though the roads were, people made these long journeys, on horseback or on foot. Pilgrims went to Canterbury from all over England; Chaucer rode from Greenwich to Dartmouth on the King's business in the fourteenth century, and Leland still further in 1540. News would be gathered and given at each night's halt. Bishops and abbots travelled with their retinue; there were mendicant friars on the roads, as well as pedlars and itinerant craftsmen. An enquiring young hill-farmer would not have to ride very far to pick up some kind of news.

And there was the north coast. While hills and hard climate were schooling the moorland farmers in endurance, the huge cliffs sheer to the water, rock-fringed, the few natural harbours, the narrow inlets, and the immense rise and fall of the tides were breeding fearless seamen. Long before any history was recorded in Britain, boats of some kind were out on the Severn Sea. How else was Lundy peopled in Neolithic times? Much later, Roman soldiers watched the channel against attack from Wales. Celtic missionaries came over; (some, it is said, brought their sisters with them, and one, at least, coaxed a cow into his little boat). Saxons invaded overland, but before long they had to defend their coast against Viking raiders. The sea was often a highway, seldom a barrier.

In the Middle Ages the easiest way to carry any awkward load between Ilfracombe and Minehead, in fair weather, must surely have been by boat. And the sea was full of good fish, which could be traded against meat or wool or hides; herrings were caught at sea and dried ashore, salmon were trapped on the foreshore in fish-weirs, stone walls like huge triangular snares, between the tide-lines. (One can still be seen clearly at Lynmouth.) There would be few men in the coastal hamlets unable to handle a boat in rough water, and still fewer who could not help in the ancillary work – building boats (out on the beaches), making sails and ropes (there were hemp-gardens at Porlock, Minehead and Combe Martin), tanning them with oak bark from the steep coastal woods, to protect them from rot, or maintaining the beacons and harbour-lights in their iron fire-baskets (one such crowns the Rhenish tower on Lynmouth jetty).[2]

It is not surprising, then, that when Edward III commandeered ships and seamen from every port in England to take an invading army to Normandy, Ilfracombe was able to provide (by one account) eight ships and sixty-two sailors. After its victory at Crécy, the army besieged Calais, where six notable burghers yielded themselves as prisoners, to win mercy for the rest of the town. Only the intercession of the pregnant Queen, kneeling to her husband in front of the whole gathering of knights and lords and captives, saved the burghers from King Edward's brutal anger. What a tale to be told when the soldiers returned to the ships, and retold by the sailors back in their home port!

Ilfracombe, a fine natural haven, at the outer end of the Bristol Channel, had long been valued; King John had ships assembled there – in *February* – to take his soldiers to Ireland. But the harbour-mouth was not easy, and sailors needed a light to guide them in. During the fourteenth century the Chapel of St Nicholas was built, probably by some sea-captain who had implored the saint's help during a bad storm; few such votive chapels survived the Reformation, but this one was described in Stuart times as a lighthouse with its flame always burning. In the fourteenth century, too, a fire-beacon at Embury Hill, Hartland, and a coastwise light dedicated to St Catherine, lessened the dangers of rounding 'Harty Point'. By then English and foreign ships were passing it regularly, plying between Bristol or Bridgwater and France, Portugal or Spain. Dunster had a harbour until the sea-level dropped. Minehead was developing one in the fourteenth century. In the middle of the sixteenth, Leland, passing through Porlock, noted that 'the rode commonly called Porlock Bay is a meatly good rode for shippes' (a very convenient harbour), while its fertile plain was producing 'great plenty' of beans, wheat and cattle. Porlockford Combe, running up towards the Whitstones and the old bridleway to Barnstaple, was known within living memory as Mariners' Combe.

So when the discovery of the New World, and of the way round Africa to the East, shifted interest away from the landlocked Baltic and Mediterranean, and the Pope assigned all rights of exploration and sovereignty in the eastern hemisphere to Portugal and in the western to Spain, south-west England had plenty of seamen accustomed to the open Atlantic and well able to challenge that arrogant decree.[3] They sailed south with Drake, capturing, whenever they could, Spanish treasure-ships homeward-bound from Peru and the River Plate. They went north-west with Sir Humphrey Gilbert, Raleigh's step-brother, to Newfoundland, where the cod fisheries became almost a monopoly for the 'Western Venturers'. They were in the Azores with Lord Howard's fleet, notably in Sir Richard Grenville's *Revenge*, when the fighting between Protestant England and Catholic Spain had become explicit. The expeditions and the indomitable leaders are famous; often the names of the ships are recorded, each with her tonnage and home port, and the name of her master. (A Minehead seaman, John Kerry, was master of the *Lion*, sailing to

61

Barbary under Thomas Wyndham in 1552.) The ordinary seamen are unnamed; but characteristically Drake, on his voyage round the world, told his crew that he 'must have the gentleman to haul and draw with the mariner and the mariner with the gentleman' – which was not how the great Spanish galleons were sailed.

In 1588, as King Philip's 'Invincible' Armada came slowly eastward, bound for the Netherlands where a Spanish army was waiting to be brought across, five ships of Grenville's, being fitted out at Bideford for the colonization of Virginia, were sent round by royal command to join Drake at Plymouth.[4] Their main task would be to ferry more and more ammunition out from the south coast ports to the fighting ships, in that long chase up-channel which ended so disastrously for Spain.

The defeat of the Armada, and its utter destruction in the ensuing storm, removed from the whole country two long-standing and closely associated threats – conquest by Spain, and the Counter-Reformation which the Spanish Inquisition would have enforced. King Philip was the richest and most powerful ruler in the western world; in northern Europe he still held the Netherlands, though they were in stubborn revolt; he was supporting the Catholic faction in divided France, had established and then lost a foothold in Catholic Ireland, and as the husband of Queen Elizabeth's half-sister, Mary Tudor, he laid claim to the English crown. Queen Mary had wrenched the country back from Protestantism to Catholicism, but not for long. Now the Pope formally 'deposed' Queen Elizabeth – considered illegitimate by those who did not accept her father's divorce. He thought to rally the English Catholics against her, and Philip hoped for their armed support. That hope foundered when the Armada reached English waters. The attack was long-expected, preparations were good – in spite of the Queen's parsimony – and morale was high. The beacon system was in working order – on Exmoor, North Molton beacon near Sandyway was to pick up the warning from Cornwall or Dartmoor and flash it to Dunkery, which would pass it to Wales and the Midlands. Grenville had organized the western defences against any attempt to land on the peninsula, the ships in the Channel were a shield behind which the eastern land forces were strategically gathered, and the sea-dogs were straining at the leash. They had old scores to settle with a regime they detested; they had witnessed its cruelty abroad, and had no intention of letting it prevail here.

Drake was a Puritan, delighted to 'singe his Catholic Majesty's beard'. John Hawkins of Plymouth, treasurer of the navy, was another. The Puritans were as yet a minority, but by now the temper of the country was Protestant, and for the most part tolerant; people were sickened by the years of religious persecution alternately from this side and that. It was two generations since Henry VIII's breach with Rome, and thirty years since Elizabeth's accession checked the violence, but the bad times were not out of mind. All Europe was splitting into two armed camps, and there was constant danger of another reversal of state religion. Queen Mary's attempts to extirpate heresy had been ruthless – daughter of Katherine of Aragon, she was herself half-Spanish. Protestant merchants and craftsmen from the Netherlands, migrating to London and East Anglia, recounted the brutalities of Spanish rule and the Inquisition. And though in England full civil war had been averted, there had been serious risings and rebellions by whichever party was undermost, and the punishment for failure was always venomously severe.

The cities saw the worst of all this – rebel lords publicly beheaded, bishops burnt at the stake, parish clergy and laymen herded to the fires and gibbets from which they could have saved themselves by recantation. But the country experienced it too. Reforms and counter-reforms were forced upon every parish in the land, and the remotest village felt the repercussions as the Pope was, was not, *was* again and finally *was not* head of the Church in England. Suddenly a country congregation would be told, from the pulpit, to believe something new and completely unfamiliar. Exmoor shepherds and their wives might not be much interested in the status of the Pope, but the question would come right home when – as happened at Exton in 1535 – their curate was imprisoned for refusing to disown him. When Barlynch Abbey was closed and destroyed, two years later, 13 tons of lead stripped from the roofs were sent to the Mayor of Bristol for the King. Relentlessly, for twenty years, the King's men worked at change. The reformed ideas and the protest against corruption had been gaining support for nearly two centuries – ever since Wyclif – but now ambitious politicians forced the issue, trampled upon the beliefs of simple people, made enemies and had to buy friends.

The removal of 'graven images' from inside the churches and from their outer walls could seem either a curb on idolatry or wanton sacrilege. Much that is commonly blamed on Oliver Cromwell's soldiers was the work of his pitiless namesake Thomas, Henry VIII's all-powerful minister, or of Protector Somerset who was regent for his young nephew Edward VI, and Cranmer his Archbishop of Canterbury. So it is difficult to know how long the niches have been empty, or how a few small statues escaped destruction. At Bishop's Nympton a fifteenth-century wooden image of St James survives – perhaps brought from Compostella when it was new; was it hidden away for safety, both at the Reformation and during the Civil War? North Molton church tower has a graceful Virgin and Child above the south porch; the tale told is that the villagers, ordered to remove it, said they could not find a ladder long enough. Perhaps the commissioners were satisfied with the removal of figures from the old pulpit; they did not damage those on the font. At Minehead, similarly, there are empty niches on either side of the west door of St Michael's, but on the tower stone images of the Trinity, and of the Virgin watching St Michael weigh souls, are unhurt. The tower is high; perhaps there was easier prey, the church's silver plate – nothing pre-Elizabethan has survived. The confiscation of vestments and silver went forward a step at a time; in 1551 Edward VI was said to need a great deal of money immediately, and commissioners were sent into every county to gather up 'such church plate as remaineth'. They may not have found everything. Nettlecombe saved its Communion plate, made by the Goldsmiths' Company in 1479. Morebath still has the church records maintained by rector and wardens all through the troubles, and they show that superficial conformity covered quiet resistance. Leading parishioners took vestments and books and images away to their farmhouses; a few years later the accession of the Catholic Queen Mary removed the danger of confiscation, and the 'true and faithful Christian people', John Williams of Bery, William Morsse at Lanton, the widow Jurdyn, and the rest, brought the treasures back to the church. It is sad that the recorder did not consider the Protestants true Christians.

The monasteries had been 'dissolved' in the late 1530s. Barlynch and Exford, on the moor, were small, but the great Cistercian Abbey of Cleeve, founded in the 'flowery valley' of Roadwater at the end of the twelfth century, had once been a fine centre, pastoral in two senses. Its flocks had sustained the Dunster cloth-making; its monks, in their white habits and cowls of Exmoor wool, were well-loved for their kindness to the poor and the Abbey's generous hospitality to strangers. Its closure was a bad loss.

Meanwhile, some laymen did well out of the changes. 'New' families basked in King Henry's favour and grew rich on their new estates – the former monastic lands. Pickings included the church bells, when towards 1550 their number was drastically reduced, and one or perhaps two in a parish had to suffice. (Some Exmoor towers still have one or two pre-Reformation bells with dedications engraved in Latin – Sancta Katerina and Sancta Thoma at Hawkridge, Sancta Barbara at Stoke Pero, Sante Peter Paule at Skilgate, Maria and Sancta Maria at Martinhoe.) Probably some were melted down and some hidden. In Barnstaple a curious list of church property restored in Queen Mary's reign notes that the Commissioners paid to John Courtenay, Esq. and Edward Ford, Gentleman, £2.13s.4d. 'for the clappers of the bells and other furniture of the bells'. The bells had presumably been taken down and kept – somebody arguing that their day might return.

No bells pealing, no silver chalice, no richly coloured vestments; shrines and rood and side-altars gone; new faces, new voices, new prayers; to the congregation of a little moorland church it must all have felt sadly alien and bleak. The innovations came from outside, from the new bishops and far-away London. Ironically, new prayers were, for some countrymen, the last straw – ironically because the finest reformers had long wanted uneducated people to be able to worship in their own language, not in the obscurity of Latin. But this was compulsion and was resented. In the name of Edward VI – still a minor – the English Prayer Book, with its Protestant communion service instead of the Roman mass, was to be used in all churches from Whit Sunday, 1549. On the next day, this was defied in Sampford Courtenay, north of Dartmoor; the parishioners forced their priest to put on his vestments and say mass. The defiance spread, and became 'the Prayer Book Commotion', a summer-long Western Rebellion intrepidly fought by farmers and husbandmen. Headed by a procession of priests in full robes, with cross and banners, pyx and incense, the Devon rebels marched to Crediton, where like-minded Cornishmen joined them, and together they besieged Protestant Exeter for more than a month. Then the siege was lifted, and the amateurs defeated, by a professional army under one of the new lords, using German and Italian mercenaries against the King's subjects on the King's behalf.

Four years later came the brief return to Catholicism and the grim Marian persecutions, then Protestantism again, under Queen Elizabeth I, who had no religious passion either way but wished to unite her kingdom and remain on the throne. She did both. Fanaticism subsided; the Church of England, independent of the Pope, was Protestant but not Calvinist. Catholic extremists had plotted treason on behalf of Mary, Queen of Scots, and she and they had paid for it. The moderates were not interested in the Spanish King's claim to the English throne, and fought beside their countrymen against his Armada. With that defeated, England could go her own way.

The villages must have felt a little of the ensuing relief. Gradually things relaxed – new church plate was made, new bells were cast. (Was this when the tales of the Knighton pixies began? The farm is hidden from Withypool by a curve of the Barle, and here, they said, the King of the Pixies and his family had lived happily for years, but then church bells began to ring, and all was over. He went to his friend the farmer and asked for the loan of pack-ponies and crooks so that he could move away; he could not bear the sound of the 'ding-dongs'.) Now the age-old feast-days, pagan before they were absorbed into Christianity, could be comfortably enjoyed again – Christmas at the winter solstice, Easter at the coming of spring, Midsummer which St John the Baptist never quite made his own, Hallowe'en when nights grew long and dark. The Puritans were not yet strong enough to spoil the boisterous fun and the nervously courted thrills.

Friendly and mischievous pixies were one side of the coin; on the reverse were dark fears and cruelty. Women suspected of practising black magic were tortured to make them confess. When Mary Stuart's son James, 'the wisest fool in Christendom', succeeded Elizabeth in 1603, the witch-hunt worsened. The new King had published a treatise called *Demonology* and Parliament subserviently decreed that all witches were to be killed. Perhaps on Exmoor there was more respect for the wise woman's power than that of the law; neighbours may have thought appeasement the better part of valour. Madam Joan Carne, born in Dunster and three times married, finally lived as a witch at Sandhill farm, near Withycombe, where she was thought to transform herself into a white hare and back again at will; she died a natural death in 1612, and was given not only Christian burial but the honour of a brass plate in the church; yet local belief in the malign power of her ghost, haunting Sandhill pond, lasted for nearly three centuries.

And the law's control was precarious. Not only were 'rogues and vagabonds' endangering the Queen's peace, but there were also people of substance enlisting them for private ends. The vagrants included soldiers discharged after foreign campaigns, and retainers whose masters had fallen from power. Shakespeare noted the shams among them, the 'swaggerers' whom Mistress Quickly dreaded; the Ensign (or 'Ancient') Pistol in *Henry IV* and *Henry V* was a stage caricature of these. Autolycus, in *The Winter's Tale*, had been dismissed – he said – from Prince Florizel's service, and now lived by cheating at country fairs or feasts. His type was not dangerous, but there were professionals too, and anybody, vagrant or not, might be armed, with sword or dagger, handbow or pistol, or the more homely bill-hook or axe or 'prangstaff,'[5] a kind of pitchfork. In such conditions, a quarrelsome landlord wanting an unscrupulous bodyguard could easily find recruits. His opponent would arm his own servants, and hire a few extras, and sooner or later the two gangs would come to blows.

Luccombe was either enlivened or frightened by a drama of this kind for several years during the early 1570s. The ownership of one of the manors was shared, and partly in trust; one claimant, John Bowyer from Cannington, was as aggressive and litigious as was Boevey at Simonsbath some ninety years later, and his methods were much cruder – it was said that during a fight Bowyer would shout to his men, 'Kill him! Kill him!' He was obviously a nuisance to the whole neighbourhood, but he took his case to Chancery, to the Lord Chief Justice, and to the Star Chamber, so there is full documentation of the charges, denials and counter-charges – though unfortunately the record of the Star Chamber judgement is lost. In his monumental work on Luccombe and neighbouring parishes, published in 1901, Sir Charles Chadwyck Healey, wise in local history and local ways, quotes at length from the depositions – everybody examined was indignantly innocent – and partly disentangles the story. The account is so rich in authentic detail that it should be read fully in his book; here it can only be told in short.

Bowyer pleaded that he was 'daily in danger to be murthered or to comytt murther', but he may have been rather timorous; a defendant whose servant had been badly wounded at Bowyer's 'setting on' said he happened to find the instigator afterwards in Horner Wood, and 'did give him two or three blowes with a little cudgell which he then had and there did carry in his hand'. The merest trifle? The cudgeller, Henry Hawley, foremost of the exasperated co-owners, stated that Bowyer had wrongly possessed himself of the disputed land, and ruined it by felling a great deal of good timber, which he left to rot on the ground; so Hawley had asked his tenants to help him, with their plough-horses and wains, and they and some of his servants 'did take, loade and carry away such timber, wodde, barke and haye' (as belonged to him) 'in very peaceable manner'. Equally peacefully, he had grazed some of his stock there, as, he said, he was entitled to do. Bowyer's version was that Henry Hawley with a band of fifty 'ryotous persons' including at least two swordsmen (fencers) and a number of vagrant strangers, variously accoutred, forced their way into the woods and fields and spoilt the meadow and the corn, 'ryotously' put in their own cattle, and 'in like Ryotous manner' carried away the felled timber. (With each repetition of 'riotous', he was alleging breach of the Queen's peace.)

The officers of the law did their best, but could not be everywhere; 'Clutsome Cleve' (Cloutsham now), for instance, was not very accessible. The fight most fully recorded was one at which the Sheriff's men were present. Bowyer's accusations had brought them to East Luccombe, headed by one William Burland, with authority to arrest four men, including Ned the fencer and John Selye. The affair stopped short of murder, but after it Bowyer appealed to the Star Chamber for the Queen's protection, and the whole matter was thoroughly investigated.

Plaintiff's and defendant's accounts are very differently coloured, but it seems that the officers, finding that the 'Ryotous persons' were numerous and well-armed, required Bowyer and several of his bailiffs to accompany them. Ned Harvey the fencer and Selye were arrested. The details do not tally: Bowyer alleged that they were allowed to keep their weapons and he protested to Burland; Harvey said that while he was disarmed and under arrest Bowyer shot him with his hand-gun and the bailiffs with bows and arrows, wounding him grievously, so that the Sheriff's men, shocked, returned Ned his sword, and told him to save himself as best he could. Selye's story was that when the officers approached he was on horseback 'in a very watery slough'; one of Bowyer's bailiffs attacked him and injured his horse, and he was then arrested; he said he gave up his dagger but that Burland later returned both men's weapons. After crossing a bridge they turned quickly and held it against pursuit, Harvey with his sword and Selye using a convenient heap of stones as ammunition. The climax was a vicious hand-to-hand struggle, which stopped abruptly when Selye wounded Bowyer from behind and the 'riotous persons' made off.

It is an unsavoury tale of violence and greed. Harvey was known for swaggering and bullying, in and about Porlock, and Bowyer had the reputation of 'a common barrator', an habitual trouble-maker and litigant. The neighbourhood would have been well rid of both.

Twenty years later an unruly episode at Skilgate was part of another Star Chamber case.[6] There had been a dispute about deer between the plaintiff, Roger Sydenham of North Quarme, ranger of the Forest, and another Sydenham with his cronies. The accused, wanting to raise money for the quarrel, organised an 'ale' to be held in the Church House, to begin during divine service on Thursday in Easter week. Roger Sydenham, himself one of the churchwardens, was unable to prevent them from breaking into the Church House ('in very riotous and disordered manner') and stocking it with three or four hundred gallons of ale. They spread word of their plan, and great companies of people arrived from Taunton and elsewhere, 'to the terror of the whole country', just as the curate was beginning to read the homily. Some of the organizers were inside the church, and they had posted a boy named Milton on a hill as lookout; when he saw the crowd approaching he rushed in, and called aloud to the leader, 'They'm come, they'm come, Mr Langham, ring out the bells'. Mr Langham ordered the curate to stop the service and have the bells rung. Bagpipes were blown, and out the congregation trooped, 'in this outrageous manner and lawless way' to meet the visitors and begin the rowdy 'ale'. Again, the depositions survive but the Star Chamber judgement does not.

Such things were not happening every day, nor in all the Exmoor parishes. Bad behaviour reaches the law-courts, while good slips quietly by. The buoyant vigour of the post-Armada years, the last fifteen of the Queen's long reign, and perhaps especially the great flowering of poetry and drama which reflected it, have earned the whole era the facile epithet of 'Merry England'. In fact, one generation at the most enjoyed an uneasy lull between the national upheavals just past and those which were still to come.

CHAPTER FIVE

Divided loyalties, 1600–1700

The seventeenth century brought a darkening of atmosphere, a sharpening of issues, in England as in most of Europe. The Pope and the Emperor – an Austrian Habsburg – were determined to counter the Reformation, and also to preserve their unfettered power. Heresy must be uprooted and the heretic nations subdued, at any cost.

The Protestant countries of northern and central Europe were on the defensive. In Bohemia the Hussites, Protestants for nearly three centuries already, fought as 'the warriors of God' and were utterly defeated by the 'Holy' Roman Emperor in 1625. Their culture and their language were suppressed, and their country subjected to Austria for the next three hundred years. Holland had won its Protestant independence from Spanish rule by a long and bitter struggle, but Belgium remained Catholic. In France, thousands of Protestants had been massacred on a single day – St Bartholomew's Day, 1572 – but the civil wars had ended in a pact, the famous Edict of Nantes, which left the strong Huguenot minority their religious freedom. A century later Louis XIV revoked the Edict, and launched a persecution which scattered countless Huguenots, skilled and industrious exiles, to Protestant lands.

The subjugation of Bohemia was followed by the ferocity and misery of the Thirty Years' War, Catholic against Lutheran and Calvinist, which involved half the continent's rulers in power-politics and greedy ambition, and made the German states a battlefield for three long decades. Both sides recognized that religious and political freedom were inseparable; the Protestant Dutch republic under the House of Orange could be seen as a shining example or as a danger-signal, according to standpoint.

England was Protestant, with Edward VI's prayer book and King James's Bible in every church; politically, Parliament was steadily growing stronger. But James was the son of Mary Queen of Scots, a Catholic, and French on her mother's side; he was Protestant by religion, but autocratic by temperament, and his declaration that kings ruled as the appointed agents of God did not commend itself

69

to the Commons of England. His son Charles I, Protestant and High Anglican, married a French Catholic princess, and later their elder son, Charles II, became a secret Papist, and the younger, James II, openly declared for Rome. By then, Spain was in decline and the Holy Roman Empire was exhausted by the Thirty Years' War and the Turkish attacks on its further provinces. The great Catholic power, rich and acquisitive, was now France. English Protestants saw the old threat recurring from very near at hand.

The Channel was a protection against the armies which were breaching land-frontiers on the Continent, but the Counter-Reformation had other resources, diplomatic and financial, and was using them to estrange King from people. It deployed, too, a highly disciplined fifth column, the 'Society of Jesus'. The Jesuits infiltrated the seminaries and the older religious orders, training young men in unflinching obedience, courage and casuistry. In England they tried to win a foothold in the universities, and they lived as chaplains in the big recusant families. The extent of their influence was not known, but much was suspected. (What, for instance, were villagers on the Brendon Hills to make of the Douai priest, Dom Philip Powel, who had a chapel at Leigh Barton, serving the Poyntz family and, discreetly, their Catholic neighbours?)[1]

As the rift widened, Charles I, convinced, like his father, of a divine right to govern as he wished, resented Parliament's control of funds. When the Commons refused to vote him supplies until he redressed their grievances he dissolved one parliament after another, and ruled despotically for eleven years, raising money in any way he could; one device, Ship Money, provoked especially bitter resentment, of which Hampden was the spokesman. Catholics were given more protection, Puritans less. When the fighting began, the Catholic families took up arms for the King, which should have embarrassed the Protestant Royalists. To the Parliamentarians, it seemed proof that their fears were well-founded. Dom Philip of Leigh Barton, like many another, was captured and executed as a traitor.

All over England, counties, towns, villages, even families were tragically divided on these religious and political principles. Some people were drawn naturally, by temperament and cast of mind or by long association, to one side or the other, but in both camps there were thoughtful moderates who, seeing the importance of the issues, were gravely worried, and felt it would be shameful to stand aside. These tried to curb their own party's excesses. Loyal clergymen, like the Royalist parson of Luccombe, Henry Byam, signed the 'Protestation' of 1641, drawn up by Parliament and vowing 'to maintain and defend...the true reformed Protestant Religion expressed in the Doctrine of the Church of England, against all Popery and Popish innovation within the realm' and to 'defend his Majesty's Royal Person, Honour and Estate. Also the Power and Privilege of Parliament, the Lawful Rights and Liberties of the Subjects, and every Person that shall make this Protestation.' Alas, within a few years these vows became incompatible, and free subjects had to choose between Charles and his Parliament. Civil war followed - then capture of the king, negotiation, intrigues and quarrels, royal escape, a second war, and recapture; the intricacies would be little known to the nation at large, though the trends must have been clear enough. Moderates were more and more unhappy. Fairfax, a seasoned young general in Cromwell's army, and a well-read and reflective man, was chosen as one of the judges at the trial of the King who had knighted him, and he tried to prevent the verdict; but enmity had grown far too bitter, and - despot or martyr - the royal captive was executed.

The poet Andrew Marvell, half a generation younger, a confirmed but temperate republican and Puritan, was tutor to Fairfax's daughter at Appleton House in Yorkshire in the next few years and there wrote some of his loveliest poetry, including the calm and lucid *Horatian Ode*. In that he extolled Cromwell's great achievement, honoured the King for his dignity on the scaffold where 'he nothing common did, or mean' and warned the victor, 'the War's and Fortune's son', that he would have to keep his sword drawn:

> Besides the force it has to fright
> The spirits of the shady night,
> The same arts that did gain
> A power, must it maintain.

Two decades later, in 1672, he looked back on it all, and wrote: 'Whether it be a war of religion or of liberty it is not worth the labour to enquire. Whatsoever was at the top, the other was at the bottom; but considering all, I think the cause was too good to have been fought for. Men ought to have trusted God - they ought to have trusted the King with the whole matter.' The last sentence comes strangely from him; one would have thought that his older friends, veterans of the protracted quarrel, would have taught him that it was worse than useless to rely on the King. Cromwell, badly tricked, in 1647, by King Charles's double-dealing and renewal of the war, had said, 'The King is a man of great parts and great understanding, but so great a dissembler and so false a man that he is not to be trusted.' The story was not over, though, when Marvell wrote in that conclusive way. The King's two sons were still to prove false - ready to sell English liberties, in secret, to the Catholic Louis XIV of France. The poet attacked Charles II and his ministers in satirical verse and pamphlets, privately circulated. He died ten years before the clamour for 'a free parliament and the Protestant religion' brought James II's Protestant daughter and

71

her Republican husband to the throne, and the long struggle to an end.

How much of all this touched Exmoor in the years when the clouds were gathering is difficult to assess. Evidence is sparse. Westminster was a long way from the sheep-farmers on the moor and the herring-fishermen working from the coastal villages; not quite so remote, though, from the merchants whose ships traded up and down the Bristol Channel and far overseas. One of these was Robert Blake of Bridgwater, several times M.P. for the port, who joined the Parliamentary army as soon as the fighting began, and became one of Cromwell's ablest commanders both by land and sea. News travelled overland, too. In South Molton, a thriving little cloth town where important roads met, an incident just as the war was beginning showed that the townspeople knew what was afoot.

An eye-witness reported it in a letter which survived. By now, the King had planned war but lacked money to arm his followers; Parliament had raised a new force, the Militia; Charles replied by sending out Commissions of Array to the Lords Lieutenant, who should raise troops, each man arming himself, in every county. King and Parliament were both acting illegally, because separately, but the Militia was apparently trusted and approved. In September 1642 one of the Commissioners, the Earl of Bath, sent to ask the Mayor of South Molton, a few days in advance, whether he would have peaceful entry into the town the following Tuesday to meet some gentlemen about some business; the Mayor said he should, provided 'the intent was for peace'.

The Earl and his gentlemen – a Chichester, a Pollard, a Sydenham, an Acland, a Giffard – arrived, and had a good lunch, provided at the Angel Inn by the Earl, who had sent venison, and his own cook to dress it.[2] The townspeople mistrusted this; they thought the Mayor had been incautious. They felt sure this distinguished company had come to read the Commission of Array, and swore that if they attempted any such thing 'they would beat them all down and kill them, if they were all hanged for it'. About a thousand people, men and women and children, gathered in the market-place (now Broad Street) with all sorts of improvised weapons as well as some loaded muskets. The women had filled all the steps of the old High Cross with big stones, and climbed up and sat on them 'swearing, if they did come there, they would brain them'.[3] One, a butcher's wife, 'came running with her lapfull of Ram's hornes for to throw at them'.

Some of the gentlemen came towards the Cross, as though to proclaim the Array. 'The people gave a shoute and did cry, they be come, at which they were all ready to stand against them.' The gentlemen withdrew, and after that neither they nor their servants dared show themselves in the street. The unknown eye-witness thought that 'if the town had not risen against them, they would not so soon have departed'.

The big landowners on the fringes of the moor had chosen their allegiances. Aclands and Pollards were Royalist, Bampfyldes and North Devon Fortescues were for Parliament. Two Catholic families which had kept their lands joined the King; in October 1642 a Puritan reported that a great quantity of 'substantial armour' had been found 'in Mr Chichester's house at Arlington, and Master Courtenay's house at Molland', and that 'at the searching of these two houses there were several wounded'.

The tenants of good landlords would either support them or else move away to follow their own conscience, but many a smallholder must have tried to keep clear of it all, until he was jolted out of neutrality by a troop of hungry soldiers riding in to his yard, or until one of his sons went away to fight and was killed. And when an armed fugitive, hotly pursued, came to the door of a lonely farmhouse imploring to be hidden, what was the farmer's wife to do? There was no time for hesitation.

Naturally, both armies wanted control of the main roads to south Devon and to Royalist Cornwall, so the bigger towns repeatedly changed hands. Taunton and Bridgwater declared for Parliament in 1642, but had to surrender to the Royalist general, Hopton, in the following year. Later, Blake recaptured Taunton and Cromwell besieged Bridgwater. Exeter, too, was Parliamentarian at first, surrendered to Prince Maurice in 1643, and was besieged and recaptured by Fairfax in 1646. Plymouth was staunchly Puritan and Parliamentarian throughout, as Drake and Hawkins would have wished. Thomas Luttrell defended Dunster Castle for Parliament at the beginning of the war, but when the King's cause was prospering Colonel Francis Wyndham was able to convert him to Royalism. Wyndham then became governor of the castle for three years, and was host in 1645 to the Prince of Wales, who paused there before crossing the moor (by Leland's road) to the safety of Barnstaple. Later that year the redoubtable Blake laid siege to the castle, and Wyndham held out for more than five months, yielding only when Fairfax sent reinforcements to Blake. Cromwell had the Dunster fortifications destroyed. The house was left standing, and is now incorporated in the nineteenth-century replica of the mediaeval castle. The great stone stables outside the gate, sometimes called Cromwellian, seem to have been built two or three decades earlier and they would have housed the war-horses of each side in turn. Fortunately they were not demolished; any cavalry officer would be bound to admire their spacious strength, and want them kept.

Minehead rang its church bells to celebrate Parliamentarian victories at Bristol and Colchester – and at the surrender of

Dunster Castle. The last occasion must have caused some bitter local resentment, since Luccombe and Selworthy, only a few miles away, were Royalist. Blake's dragoons were stationed there for a time, commanding the coastal road and foraging locally. Mr Steynings of Holnicote found their demands excessive; 'at least forty will not only have hay but oats too for their horses', and he feared for his own winter supplies.

Most of the seaports had Parliamentary sympathies; their livelihood was endangered when all ships were requisitioned for the King's service. For a few years this entirely stopped the important trade of the Western Venturers with the Newfoundland Cod Fisheries. The traders brought home dried salted cod (much of it reshipped to Catholic countries to be eaten on fast days!). Their worst risk at sea had long been from the Barbary pirates, waiting as they drew homeward to the English coast, raiding the convoys and selling into slavery any sailors they could seize. When Admiral Blake of Bridgwater had an English fleet in the Mediterranean in 1655 he was mindful of this, and sailed to Algeria and destroyed the pirates' ships.

In 1646 Cromwell's New Model Army came west, and, under Fairfax, defeated the Cavaliers so thoroughly at Torrington that the capture of Exeter and Barnstaple was easy, and virtually ended the war in Devon and Cornwall. A discovery made a century ago at Thornham farm, East Worlington, some way south of the moor, may be a sad legacy of that defeat. The farmer and his men, repairing a hedge-bank, came upon three cloamen jars – earthenware crocks – filled with hundreds of small silver coins, Tudor and Stuart but none later than 1645. In 1646 the then owner of the farm, a well-to-do Cobley, had gone away to join Hopton's Royalist force and he was killed in the battle. It was related that as he lay dying he tried to give a comrade a message for his family but the only intelligible words were 'in the orchard'.

The bank in which the jars were found was in fact the old orchard boundary. It seems likely that Cobley had hidden the money from possible marauders before he left for Torrington, and kept the place a secret even from his family. Ignorance might be safer for them. Neighbours might pry – East Worlington was Roundhead, West Worlington Cavalier. The hoard, now in the British Museum, was the biggest collection of coins so far found in the South West,[4] but in that troubled decade it is unlikely to have been the only one buried. Perhaps others were safely recovered by owners who came back or by relations who did know the place of concealment.

The armies seem usually to have followed the ancient ridgeways rather than labour up and down the rough hill tracks. And though there were farms and villages in the purlieus, the central Forest was still an uninhabited and treeless waste, inhospitable to soldiers living off the land. The moor may have escaped most of the fighting and foraging – though cannon-balls found in the parish of Challacombe are thought to have been fired by Prince Maurice's troops – but the religious changes, Puritan now, penetrated every moorland parish, as the Protestant reformation had permeated it a century earlier, and some of the damage to churches may have been done by wrathful Cromwellian soldiers rather than by King Henry's or King Edward's sober-sided commissioners. It is not clear, for instance, when the large and lovely church of Selworthy, overlooking the Minehead–Porlock road, lost its rood-screen and its stained-glass windows. It might have been while the dragoons were there – but would Blake have allowed the vandalism? (Throughout his long siege of Dunster Castle the beautiful fifteenth-century screen in St George's church was unhurt.) At some time – then, or earlier, or perhaps even as late as the Commonwealth – the fourteenth-century preaching cross in Selworthy churchyard was broken, leaving only a shaft on a plinth. The same happened to others, as old or older, outside smaller churches – Twitchen, Hawkridge and Exton and many more – where the weather-worn shafts still stand, usually near the south porch.

In the churches the records and memorials tell the Royalist side of the story; but most of the injury was to objects, not to people. Compared with the Thirty Years' War which was ravaging the continent, the Great Rebellion, as later Royalists called it, was short and temperate. Many country rectors were dispossessed, some of them were treated roughly, and a few were imprisoned as 'delinquents', but they were not killed. And the preacher appointed by Parliament to replace a dismissed rector was obliged to give one-fifth of his stipend to keep the evicted man's family from starving.

At Rose Ash, south of the moor, Parson Trosse had provided a horse for the King's men, and when the Roundheads arrived that generosity cost him dear. They plundered his rectory, took him two miles from home and there stripped him and sent him back to manage as best he could, with his wife and five or six children, in his kitchen. The living, of course, went to Puritans until the Restoration. At Molland a dignified memorial on the chancel wall tells of Daniel Berry, 'some time minister of this church and of that of the parish of Knowstone, wherein he was born. Who for his zeal in the support of the Church of England and loyalty to that martyred king, King Charles I, was first sequestered by the then rebels and ever after persecuted until he died' – seven years before the Restoration, in his forty-fifth year, but 'persecuted' may have meant only 'harassed'. His second son John became an admiral, was knighted by Charles II 'for his long and many good services at sea', and 'honouring the memory of all orthodox and loyal men of the late times and out of a pious regard to his father's sufferings, erected this monument'.

More is known about Dr Henry Byam, rector of Luccombe and Selworthy. Born eight years before the defeat of the Armada, he was a distinguished scholar at Oxford when the old Queen died, and on taking orders was, according to an Oxford antiquary, 'looked upon as the most acute and eminent preacher of his age'. Perhaps this claim was a little biassed – there were some magnificent Anglican preachers at that time – but certainly he was a respected divine, a prebendary of Exeter cathedral and active in the diocesan affairs of Wells. At Luccombe he succeeded his father, at Selworthy his father-in-law, and through the rector's manorial rights he controlled a sizeable estate, including Cloutsham and Sweetworthy.

He was in his vigorous sixties at the outbreak of the Civil War, and though he and his parishioners had signed the 1641 Protestation, hoping for a moderate solution, he at once raised a troop of horse for the King, and at least five of his sons took up arms. (Two of them 'died honourably in the service of their Prince', said the colleague who preached at his funeral.) For this he was arrested, at Luccombe, by Blake, as yet only a captain of dragoons. His wife tried to cross the channel to Wales, taking their young daughter and a maid-servant, but a fierce storm blew up, and all three were drowned, 'swallowed up quick by the merciless waves', as survivors testified. Byam escaped from captivity and joined Charles I at Oxford; he was awarded a Doctorate of Divinity at the King's wish, and then accompanied the Prince of Wales to Scilly and to Jersey, and served as chaplain to the royal garrison until it surrendered – two years after the execution of the King. As a 'delinquent' he was permitted to compound for his sequestrated lands at the legal rate, and could live there privately until the Restoration. Then, at the age of eighty, he was reinstated as rector of both parishes. He lived for another nine years, and was buried inside Luccombe church, where a memorial tablet describes him as Chaplain to King Charles II. So much ungrudging loyalty perhaps deserved a more generous reward.

The eleven years of the Commonwealth had been a cheerless time, because the Puritans – or the Presbyterians, who predominated – mistrusted all worldly pleasures. The theatres were closed on the grounds that they encouraged impiety and loose living. Actors and Puritans had been at odds for a long time; Shakespeare's bibulous Sir Toby, in *Twelfth Night*, carousing with his cronies in his niece's house, mocked her Puritanical steward Malvolio (or 'Ill-will'), 'Dost thou think because thou art virtuous there shall be no more cakes and ale?' By 1650 this was exactly what Parliament thought, and tried to enforce. Up and down the country, parish revels, church ales and village sports of almost every kind were forbidden, as hotbeds of drunkenness and fighting. Even bell-ringing was a levity; Bunyan in youth felt bound to give it up, but was still drawn to watch his friends ringing, until it occurred to him that God might, as a judgement, cause a bell to fall upon his head. It was a time of strict Sabbath-observance and immensely long sermons, of belief in predestination, fear of Jehovah and of hell-fire. Bunyan's 'Grace Abounding to the chief of Sinners', a kind of spiritual autobiography, shows the terrors this might hold for a hardly literate young man of powerful imagination. He was fourteen when the Civil War began, and at seventeen he enlisted in the New Model Army; but as a boy of nine, he says, he was so possessed by the sense of sin that he saw no hope of getting to heaven, and often wished either that there were no hell, or that he had been a devil, 'supposing they were only tormentors', so that if he needs must go thither, he might rather be a tormentor than be tormented himself.

Cromwell died, and was buried in Westminster Abbey. His son Richard, who succeeded him, was a nonentity, and before long, army and Parliament were at loggerheads with each other and divided among themselves. Finally (in 1660) part of the army, under Cromwell's generals Monk and Fairfax and Lambert, brought back the exiled heir to the throne, by invitation, amid widespread rejoicing. By and large, the country had had enough – enough not only of Puritan gloom but even more, perhaps, of the political quarrels and the fighting. Only five years earlier a Royalist rising in the South West had failed miserably, for lack of support, while the future King Charles II waited on the French coast for news of success. The Cavaliers had raised his standard at Salisbury and moved westward, but few recruits came in, and many, discouraged, went home. A dwindled force of less than two hundred tired and hungry men settled like locusts in South Molton at about seven o'clock on a March evening, hoping for a good night's rest in comfortable billets. But a Parliamentary soldier, Captain Crook, who with his troop of sixty had been seeking them for days, 'beat up their quarters about ten of the clock'. He said they disputed it very much with him in the houses for more than two hours, 'firing very hot out of the windows'. His men 'broke open many houses', took some fifty prisoners, nearly a hundred and forty horses and a supply of arms. Colonel Penruddock, who with his father and brother had fought for Charles I, was captured, and so were the leaders of the other troops which, like his, were to have grown into regiments. Sir Joseph Wagstaffe, a genial but unprincipled soldier of fortune from the exile's court, whom they had asked for as military commander of the rising, escaped. Crook tried in vain to trace him; the tradition is that he leapt his horse over the north wall of the churchyard, thereafter called 'Wagstaffe's Wall', beside 'Wagstaffe's Gate'. A few months later he was back in Holland; a lot of people must have helped him away. Penruddock and another leader were beheaded – a quick and in those days honourable death. Some were hanged, others sent to the plantations. Sympathizers in Exeter gave them good food in prison, and provided decent burial for those who were executed.

As soon as the fighting in South Molton was over, Captain Unton Crook sat down, well after midnight, to write triumphantly, almost breathlessly, to the Lord Protector, describing the affair and concluding, 'My lord, they are all broken and routed, and I desire the Lord may have the glorie'. (Or in an older style, 'Non nobis, Domine'.) He begs Cromwell to 'pardon this unpolisht account', saying he can indeed hardly write, 'being so weary with extreme duty', but hopes to send more detail later. Next day, writing from Exeter, he says that he has handed over the prisoners to the High Sheriff, that 'the Mayor of South Molton being with me in the Streets was shot in the body, but like to do well', and that 'the Country' is catching stragglers every hour. Meanwhile, the householders of South Molton, involuntary participants, had to set their damaged houses to rights.

There had been too much disorder and strife, for too long. The restoration of the monarchy seemed to promise more toleration and a broader freedom than had lately obtained, and a settled constitutional government by King and Parliament together. But the deep divisions remained, and many sincere Puritans despaired, their cause seeming utterly lost. Milton's Samson in the power of the Philistines was a reflection of their mood. Many emigrated, to join an earlier generation on the eastern seaboard of America; from Barnstaple and Bideford some of them sailed to the Newfoundland fisheries. Religious persecution did not end; the Quakers suffered badly, and only late in Charles II's reign were they allowed to emigrate. Then, on the initiative of William Penn, they went further in from the coast, cleared the virgin woodlands; and called their colony Pennsylvania. Not far from their Quakertown, the place-names Bethlehem and Nazareth show what kind of men and women they were.

The new court was at the opposite pole. 'Joy ruled the day, and Love the night', said Dryden, adding that the lovers were all untrue. At the centre was the 'Merry Monarch', easy, pleasure-loving, idle, delighting to saunter in the park with his spaniels and his witty courtiers. This was the impression he made and sedulously maintained. Only gradually did the darker side of his character appear – the cynic, devious and utterly unscrupulous. Lord Rochester, no saint himself, put about the wickedly memorable epitaph:

> Here lies our sovereign lord the king,
>   Whose word no man relies on,
> Who never said a foolish thing,
>   Nor ever did a wise one.

King Charles's treacherous intrigues with Louis XIV and his personal inclination to the Roman faith were strictly secret, but as time went on suspicions spread. His Catholic mistress Mlle de Kerouaille was cordially disliked, on rumour or sound instinct; in fact King Louis had sent her over as a well-nigh irresistible agent. But Nell Gwynn of Drury Lane was no mean rival, and far more popular; when she was mobbed in her fine carriage, in Oxford, she understood the mistake, put her head out of the window and said, 'Pray, good people, be civil; I am the *Protestant* whore!'

The political settlement had been unvindictive, by the standards of the time. The King had promised a general pardon, though some of the regicides and a few other leaders were executed. At Parliament's instigation, not the King's, Cromwell's body had been taken out of its grave in Westminster Abbey and hung on the gallows at Tyburn. Blake's body, too, was removed from the Abbey and thrown, with others, into a pit on the north side. Charles himself went warily, determined, he said, not to set out on his travels again. He proved better at pardoning his enemies than at rewarding his friends.

This would soon be noticed in the country, not least on Exmoor, while the political chicanery was not yet known. Loyalists who had lived in England throughout the years of the King's exile did not forget so easily. The clergy were welcomed home to their rectories; Luccombe and Selworthy rejoiced at Dr Byam's return. A local regicide, John Venn, had died soon after signing the death-warrant of Charles I, but his memory was detested; the font in which he had been baptized, in the church of Lydeard St Lawrence, was turned upside down, and a new bowl hollowed out in the former stem, so that no child should ever be contaminated at christening. It is still inverted and still in use.

An older political gesture was revived, in an order that the King's arms be displayed on a large painted board in every church, at the expense of the parish. The practice had begun at the Reformation, to emphasize that the King, not the Pope, was head of the Church of England. Henry VIII's arms survive near Exeter, and those of Edward VI at Westerham in Kent. Under Catholic Queen Mary the boards were removed, but with the accession of Queen Elizabeth I the statement had to be made again; at Honeychurch, near Sampford Courtenay where the Prayer Book Commotion had begun in her half-brother's time, the Queen's arms were painted as a huge fresco opposite the one door of the little church. Later, this was plastered over, and has only recently been, in part, uncovered. Cromwell's men must have destroyed any Stuart insignia they found, but they missed a fine large James I at Winsford.

The renewal of the edict at the Restoration was secular – the monarchy asserting itself not against the Pope but against Puritan republicans, Commonwealth men. (At Luccombe the display of the King's arms cost the parish £4.8s.0d. in 1661; Dr Byam would certainly have it done in style.) But after 1715 the Stuart arms were painted over or taken down, by order, and most of the boards remaining on Exmoor now are Hanoverian, set up to discourage any interest in the papist Stuart heirs. A few survived. In remote Martinhoe the arms of Charles II were still to be seen in 1853, and probably until church alterations in the following decade. At East Worlington, south of the moor, home of the royalist Cobley who died at the Battle of Torrington, the board was repainted with the arms of George I, but the Stuart badge, a red and white rose, small and inconspicuous, was left undisturbed in a lower corner. Dunster has an enormous painted board of the arms of Charles II, dated 1660, on the wall of the nave. It can hardly have been flaunted there in Hanoverian times, and Page, describing the church in 1890, does not mention it; but whether old or new it is a reminder that the Castle was held by Royalists and that Charles, as Prince of Wales, had been a guest there for a few nights during the Civil War. (As time went on, these boards became simply a token of loyalty, without political force. Many, in towns, were cleared away in the nineteenth century, when High and Low Church reformers agreed on the removal of secular objects. Exmoor parishes did not change their ways so readily – Countisbury has the arms of William IV, Hawkridge those of Queen Victoria, and Trentishoe those of George V, all still to be seen.)

The King was Defender of the Faith, but religious toleration was restricted by Parliament. On Exmoor the Independents gathered to worship secretly in wooded combes, and Jesuits were hidden by the recusants, as before. Charles, always trying to win religious freedom for the Catholics, offered a general indulgence for them and for all Nonconformists, but by then his Protestant parliament mistrusted him too much. James II, openly Papist, and, like his brother before him, surreptitiously taking a subsidy from France, made a similar offer, from the same motive. Bunyan was one of the Dissenters who recognized the bait. He saw James trying to buy their support for his plan to undermine the Church of England, and was reminded, he said, of the promise of Polyphemus to Odysseus, 'that he would eat his men first, and do him the favour of being eaten last'. When the Protestant Queen Mary and Republican William of Orange came to the English throne, liberty of conscience was extended to almost all. It was still considered too dangerous to appoint Catholics to high office in church or state, while successive Stuart claimants to the throne were being harboured in France, and the risings of 1715 and 1745 justified this caution. King William urged in vain that the Puritan dissenters would be no political risk; they too were excluded from power. But religious oppression was virtually over. Voltaire remarked later that an Englishman, being a free subject, could go to heaven by whatever road he liked.

All this time, Exmoor was suffering from a very different, wholly secular, result of the Civil War – Parliament's sale of the Royal Forest in 1652 to the quarrelsome 'Sir Positive', James Boevey. When ownership reverted to the Crown, Boevey ingeniously acquired the tenancy, as Warden, and before long he tried to claim all the surrounding commons too. This led to his great defeat by exasperated neighbours maintaining their ancient rights.

As early as 1630, long before Boevey's day, there had been talk of 'improving' all the 'unnecessary Forests and Waste Lands' in Somerset, Devon and Cornwall. A memorandum by Crown officers recommended this; provided that some great person were authorized by his Majesty to undergo the weight of it, they said, 'the business would proceed happily; but without such assistant, those works are not to be dealt in.' They envisaged sixty-year leases, at 4d. an acre, for improving the Forest and making it useful for the country and profitable to the King. (Charles I, trying to rule without Parliament, was very short of money.) Since there were already leases and sub-leases in force (the Pollard family of King's Nympton held the Wardenship) this came to nothing. But the memorandum remained, and when Sir Hugh Pollard's estates were sequestrated, and Parliament had annexed those of the Crown, there was no such barrier. Perhaps some knowledge of this proposal influenced Boevey towards purchase; in one of the legal documents he guarded the security of hypothetical tenant-farmers, though in fact only the home-farm at Simonsbath was enclosed in his time.

He may also have been attracted by the chance of claiming tithe on agisted stock. This came of an innovation in 1633. Exmoor was extra-parochial, and had always been tithe-free – a great advantage to the farmers; but Charles, in search of funds, 'granted' the hitherto non-existent tithe rights to a stranger. Many farmers ceased to put sheep on the Forest, the Warden reimbursed himself by increasing the cost to the others, the matter was repeatedly disputed in the courts, and was only finally settled after the war when Boevey had become owner. The judgement was in his favour.

When Mr Jeremie Baines, Parliament's envoy, came to survey and value the Forest in 1651, he spent eight or ten days going

81

round it; the Deputy Forester, Nicholas Rawlinson of Exford, said long afterwards that he had been with him for two of them. It seems likely that this was in the short days of late autumn or winter; Baines was working in unfamiliar and very rough country, and Rawlinson, who held office from the Royalist Sir Hugh Pollard, may not have been particularly helpful. The record contains one bad topographical muddle (at Kinsford Cross) and some bewildering versions of local names. For one of these, a new explanation seems persuasive. Baines went southward down Spraccombe Water 'along by the ground called the Orchard and Reddbrookes house unto the river Exe'. Who was Reddbrooke? There is no local trace. But there are *Edbrookes* on record. John Edbrooke of Winsford was one of the husbandmen who, a century earlier, raided the Halscombes and impounded the stolen cattle at Hawkridge. In 1606 it was Richard Edbrooke of Exford who hurt a little boy's finger on a meare-stone to make him remember it. And soon after the survey and sale Boevey was quarrelling with Robert Edbrook of Exford, a leading farmer who paid the highest rates in the parish (12s.6d. a year) and who, with others, was claiming rights of common on the Forest. Did Baines make a note of R. Edbrook and then misread it as one word? Tumbledown walls remain, on the left bank of the stream, immediately outside the Forest boundary, at the edge of Westermill farm, and if Edbrook lived there he would have had borderer's rights. In the 1815 perambulation it is 'the site of a house called Orchard House otherwise Redbrookes house'. Was the written mistake revived, by reference to Baines, when Orchard had long been the spoken name?

In spite of some inaccuracy, the survey is full of valuable information about the customs and laws of the Forest at that time, the rights and duties of Free Suitors and Suitors at Large, the Swainmote courts, and much else. The general assessment is clear and uncompromising:

> 'Memorandum – that the said Chase is a mountainous and cold ground much beclouded with thick fogs and mists, and is used for agisting and depasturing of cattle, horses and sheep, and is a very sound sheep pasture, but a very great part thereof is overgrown with heath, and yielding but a poor kind of turf of little value there, and a considerable part thereof lying upon the sides of the combes lies near the rock and is capable only of being a sheep pasture, and the residue thereof being only some of the balls or hills, if they were enclosed might be capable of improvement being a good soil, all which we have considered in our valuation of the same.'

Remote, threaded only by rough tracks, the moor was lonely

at any time, and in winter was left entirely to the deer and wild ponies. The previous Deputy Forester, Humphrey Venner of Chittlehampton, had told a court enquiry in 1635, 'No person inhabits within the said forest'. There was still no house of any kind at the time of the survey, but in the 1620s Sir Lewis Pollard of King's Nympton, the Warden or Chief Forester, had obtained permission to build a lodge with an enclosure. It may well have been he who selected the perfect site at Simonsbath, right in the middle of the Forest, where the old Dunster–Barnstaple road crossed the Barle by ford and wooden bridge. At Yard Down, that road slanted across the old one from Lynton to South Molton, with King's Nympton not far beyond. A track from the north coast joined the mediaeval road at Simonsbath ford, and probably a path already ran westward along the left bank, to Challacombe. The site was sheltered from the north, bounded east and west by streams, and looked southward down the loveliest reach of the always lovely Barle, where trout and occasionally one or two salmon swam, and deer would come down to drink. Sir Lewis, a keen sportsman, could not have chosen a better place for a hunting lodge. If the plan was in fact his, the Dutchman from London saw some of its merits, and lost no time in adopting it. The date 1654, carved on a beam in the house he built, shows his promptitude. Shortly afterwards he brought his wife and household, and settled in. From here he managed the estate, and conducted his quarrels. Much of his house remains, with later additions, and the big new Forest pound he made for strays can still be seen beside the line of the old road down to the ford – by which John Knight's 'Pound Cottages' stood, until they were pulled down recently and their name transferred to others, across the road.

Perhaps, too, in the years when he was owner not tenant, Boevey had a warrener's cottage built where the present Warren farmhouse stands. Pillow-mounds – long man-made banks in which wild rabbits could burrow easily – lie near the house, and are thought to date from the sixteenth or seventeenth century. The Rev. T. H. Cooper of Lynton, in his guide-book published in 1853, mentioned a ruined site which he had been told was still visible on 'the warren'. His informant may have seen and spoken of it a few years earlier, before the Knights' farmhouse and buildings were made – when the old stones would have been reused. On the 1819 Inclosure Map 'the warren' is shown north of the Exe, and Honeymead neighbouring it, south of the river but *north* of the Exford–Simonsbath road. This was before the 'reclamation', of course. It may be that Boevey depended on that area for honey as well as rabbit-meat; his warrener and bee-master might have been the same man.

Since Boevey's quarrels were concerned with grazing-rights,

tithes, and finally the ownership of the commons, they reached beyond the Forest into all the surrounding parishes, and the oral depositions, all on record in MacDermot's book, give a convincing picture of the unpretentious 'husbandmen' of the time. The dispute about the commons was deadly serious for all who were entitled to graze stock there or claim tithes, and their solid opposition defeated him at last.

After that Boevey's rule was less troublesome, though it lasted nearly to the end of the century. It covered the period in which Blackmore, writing two hundred years later, set his romance of *Lorna Doone*, and the testimony recorded in the boundary dispute shows the wide – and perfectly legitimate – difference between fiction and fact. A hundred local witnesses would not all have been silent about the Doones if such marauders as Blackmore describes had been living in Badgworthy, only just outside the Forest, nor is it imaginable that Boevey would have tolerated them as neighbours. But these depositions were not known when *Lorna Doone* was published in 1869; MacDermot's immense work on the documents in the Public Record Office in London was done after Blackmore's death. Rawle, a North Devon antiquary, and the scholarly West Somerset historian Chadwyck Healey, writing at the turn of the century when unsophisticated readers of the tale were beginning to mistake it for history, both demurred. In much reading of seventeenth-century records they had found nothing at all to substantiate it. Chadwyck Healey speaks, however, of the Doone legends current before Blackmore used them. Some had been told to the Rev. W. H. Thornton, curate of Countisbury; in 1848 the farmer of Yenworthy had shown him the famous 'long gun' and told him 'with great satisfaction' that with it an ancestor of his had shot a Doone who was prowling about his farmyard by night. In 1853 T. H. Cooper told this and other Doone stories, and a number of Faggus tales. He gave a neat and succinct version of the waylaying of Faggus in Exford, when the highwayman arrived in disguise and outwitted the armed men awaiting him.

There seems to have been, at some time, a cluster of thieves who stole sheep and plundered hen-runs and perhaps settled in the longhouses where centuries earlier the 'Hermits of Badgworthy' had lived. Around the reports of their misdeeds, tales for the winter fireside accumulated – perhaps some of them had been told ever since the Danish raids. Blackmore had heard them in his boyhood – blood-curdling tales retold after lights-out in the dormitories of Blundell's school – and he was convinced that some of the barbarities had been committed. He wrote in his first preface to the book that any son of Exmoor reading it would remember 'the nurse-tales of his childhood' about the 'savage deeds of the outlaw Doones in the depth of Badgworthy Forest, the beauty of the hapless maid brought up in the midst of them, the plain John Ridd's Herculean power, and the exploits of Tom Faggus'. He describes himself as 'shaping this old tale', and says he 'neither dares, nor desires, to claim for it the dignity...of an historic novel'. It has the ideal ingredients of a 'nurse-tale' and it follows the old soothing recipe for popular success – 'Boy meets girl, boy loses girl, boy gets girl'. Moreover it is set in remote and beautiful country which the author had known and loved all his life. No wonder it has given pleasure to innumerable readers.

To swell this simple tale into a full-length Victorian novel for family reading, much more was needed, and so Blackmore drew from national history, local personalities, moorland landscape and the Exmoor farming of his own time. He selected and enlarged, added and rearranged, for the sake of his story. For variety, his young moorland farmer was twice despatched to London; on the first visit he was interviewed by Judge Jeffreys and on the second he managed to be in the ante-chamber of the royal chapel in Whitehall Palace when King James II went in state to mass. To keep the reader's interest while hero and heroine were separated ('boy loses girl') Blackmore manoeuvred John Ridd to the battlefield of Sedgemoor, as a neutral, arriving only when Monmouth's rebels were in flight, and Colonel Kirke's 'Lambs' were slaughtering survivors.

He carried the story to the fringes of recorded history whenever he could – the capture of Major Wade at Farley farm is authentic, though irrelevant. Tom Faggus was half fact, half fiction – a blacksmith in North Molton until he took to highway robbery. In real life he was finally caught, and hanged at Taunton, but that could not be allowed to happen to the hero's brother-in-law in a romance. Instead he reforms and settles down to farming, and the happy ending is not clouded. References to well-known local families – Bampfylde and de Wichehalse – help the illusion. Minor names are indigenous – Muxworthy or Slocombe – and a grotesque head carved on the tombstone of a Thomas Fry, just outside the porch of Countisbury church, might serve very well as a portrait of the lumpish John Fry in the book.

The landscape was treated equally freely, always to suit the tale. Persuasively he brings his characters up from Dulverton by a recognizable way. They take what is still 'the old coach road' as far as Heathpoult Cross; there the fine carriage with Lorna in it turns right, along the Brendons, for Watchet, and the young hero and John Fry keep on over the winter route of the Harepath through Cutcombe parish to Blagdon Cross and Dunkery Gate. Once on the open moor, in darkness and mist, they are in the land of the romance, and thenceforward only Oare church is immovable. Hills become mountains, combes are gorges; a fine waterfall in one combe is moved to another as the impressive 'waterslide'. The

Badgworthy ruins are magnified and transformed. Simonsbath House is omitted – a new mansion in the wild would have been a hindrance. Needing an abandoned farmhouse on the warren, inside the Forest – an impossibility at that time, unless it was prehistoric – he may have picked up Cooper's reference to a ruin, and made a farmstead of what may have existed as a warrener's lodge. The moor was still remote in Blackmore's day, and he had plenty of elbow-room.

Four years after the publication of *Lorna Doone*, in a new preface for the sixth edition, he said how surprised he was by the success of 'this simple tale' and how gratified to have pleased 'those who are at home with this scenery, people, life and language, wherein a native cannot always satisfy the natives'. Again and again in the novel comes the affectionate observation of detail which to many lovers of Exmoor is its chief delight. It may be John Fry's 'Sunday hat with a top to it',[5] or 'the little stubby trees that stand here and there like bushes with a wooden leg', their branches drooping with wet mist; or light frost, 'just enough to make the blackbirds look big in the morning', or reapers with their sickles, moving across the cornfield 'like half a wedge of wildfowl', or sheep alive in a snowdrift, where their breath and the warmth of their bodies have scooped out 'a coved room'. Thomas Hardy, fifteen years his junior, wrote to him in 1875, the year after the appearance of *Far from the Madding Crowd*, to say that he had just read *Lorna Doone*, and found in it 'exquisite ways of describing things' which were entirely after his own heart. 'It seems almost absurd,' he continued, 'that I had not read it before, considering the kind of work I attempted in *Far from the Madding Crowd*,...Little phases of nature which I thought nobody had noticed but myself were continually turning up in your book – for instance, the marking of a heap of sand into little pits by the droppings from trees ... A kindred sentiment between us in so many things is, I suppose, partly because we both spring from the West of England.'[6]

Monmouth's rebellion, ill-prepared and ill-fated, was brief – less than a month elapsed between his landing at Lyme in June 1685 and his crushing defeat in a short night-battle on Sedgemoor in July, and ten days after that he was beheaded. Old Parliamentarian and Puritan loyalties made the cloth-town of Taunton and the port of Bridgwater prefer Charles II's bastard son, the Protestant Duke of Monmouth, to his Catholic brother who was now lawfully King James II. In Taunton, the Duke's rallying-point for the west, there were June flowers in every doorway to greet his arrival. In a charming little ceremony Miss Mary Blake, the headmistress of a girls' school, with her assistant, Susannah Musgrave, led her twenty-seven 'Maids of Taunton' to welcome him. She offered him a sword and a Bible, and each girl brought him a banner she had embroidered for his cause. He responded with characteristic grace – Dryden had written that

> Whate'er he did was done with so much ease,
> In him alone, 'twas natural to please.

More and more recruits came in. But his illegitimacy made many of the country gentry hold back, and in addition this favourite son of a very indulgent father had long shown himself to be politically unstable, or worse. King James had no son; both his daughters by his first marriage were Protestant, and Mary, the elder, was wife to William of Orange. To many it seemed better to wait, if possible, for the lawful succession. So the forces of insurrection were not as strong as Monmouth had hoped. The volunteers who marched behind his standard, 'Fear Nothing but God', were sturdy and convinced Protestants, ready to die for their beliefs, but they had no chance against the King's professional army. They did not get beyond Somerset, and the marching and fighting were well east of Exmoor and the Quantocks. The recruits from Minehead, Porlock and Dunster may have been the sons of men who had fought under Fairfax or Blake. They had a good cause and deserved a better leader.

The savage sequel is notorious: Colonel Kirke and his soldiers had no mercy. The defeated men were either slain without ceremony or herded to prison until the assizes – the Bloody Assizes, at which Lord Chief Justice Jeffreys, willing instrument of the King's vengefulness, condemned most of them to death or deportation. The deported were sold as slaves to planters in the West Indies. The death sentence was usually for treason – the prisoner to be hanged, drawn and quartered in his own village or small country town. The heads and quarters, boiled in salt and tarred, were displayed separately on poles in the streets and highways, and left there as a warning. Very soon the countryside was an appalling sight. A distinguished observer, Col. Sir Charles Lyttleton, a life-long royalist, wrote from Somerset to Lord Hatton in October, 'I cannot but believe we shall hear more of this when parliament meets … the country looks, as one passes, already like a shambles', and with the assizes still raging he expected far more of these brutal executions. Stogumber had three of them, Stogursey two. Some were hanged in iron chains on the gibbets. Nobody could, or dared, take the bodies away for burial unless this had been granted as a most exceptional favour – at a very high price. Three Dunster men were strung up on a tree beside the road to Timberscombe. Six rebels were hanged at Minehead, three at Dulverton, two at Porlock. A close watch for fugitives was kept at South Molton, and five were captured there and sent to Exeter gaol; a Major Wildboar was so enraged by this that he threatened to shoot the Mayor for causing one of the arrests.

Those who managed to slip home safely across Exmoor kept very quiet; they hid their swords about the farm or under floor-boards, or flung them away in remote parts of the moor, where they would tell no tales. Harbouring a fugitive rebel was accounted treason, and for a woman that meant being burnt at the stake. (Jeffreys condemned one old lady in her eighties to this fate; in response to urgent appeals from her friends, the King relented so far as to change the sentence to beheading.) Yet in spite of the fearful risk a great many people must have sheltered the hunted men, or helped them away. After the September assizes in Exeter, well over 300 Devon rebels were still at large. So, in Somerset, was the Taunton schoolmistress, Susannah Musgrave. Twelve of the Maids of Taunton were taken away and held to ransom, and their headmistress died in Dorchester gaol, but Susannah escaped to Exmoor and must have found friends. The vicar and parish constable of Dulverton tried to capture her, many months later, but had no success.

In the north-west of the moor, an attempt at concealment is known because it failed – when Wade was caught at Farley farm through the efforts of the Rector of Brendon. 'Major' Nathaniel Wade, a civilian who had been in Holland with Monmouth and was commissioned by him during the crossing to Lyme, had proved to be one of his best officers. When the short battle of Sedgemoor was unmistakably lost, and the Duke and Lord Grey had ridden away, hoping to escape, Wade, finding his own infantrymen 'not inclinable to stand', organized them into 'a kind of disorderly retreat', and after suffering another attack from pursuers, marched with about 150 survivors back to Bridgwater (where he met 'two or three full troops of horse that had run away out of the field without striking stroke'). With his own horses and a party of about twenty mounted men, he rode westward to meet others who had been sent to Minehead for cannon – now of course, too late. His own account of the campaign continues, 'With part of them, amounting in all to near 50, we went to Ilfracombe and seized on a vessel which we victualled and put to sea but were forced ashore by two frigates cruising on the coast, after which we dispersed and fled into the woods. I for my part was alone from that time to the time I was taken coming out of the house of one John Birch in the parish of Brendon in the county of Devon.'

This brevity about his flight and capture was deliberate. Wade composed his narrative when, a badly wounded prisoner, he had been moved from the Tower of London to Windsor Castle, and had been promised his life if he wrote a full confession with plenty of names in it. But he contrived to win his pardon without endangering anyone. He had been allowed to send his linen out of the Tower for laundering and he hid a note in the bundle imploring one of his friends to give him the names of those rebels known to have been killed in battle, or executed, or to have escaped abroad. When his shirts came back crisply ironed, the information was hidden in their pleats.[7] So the narrative gave plenty of names, indeed, but did no harm. Farmer John Birch had already hanged himself, to avoid capture and a shameful death.

It is not known where the requisitioned ship had run ashore. The defeated rebels had been sailing up-channel, probably hoping to slip across to Wales. Woody Bay, Lee Bay or Lynmouth – a very small fishing-hamlet then – might fit the scraps of evidence. One of the fifty-odd men was Captain Hewling, who had been among those sent to Minehead for cannon, and had missed the battle. He and his brother, it is reported,[8] and perhaps others, having got ashore at the risk of their lives, over dangerous rocks, saw the country filled with soldiers, 'and being unwilling to fall into the hands of the rabble, and no way of defence or escape remaining to them, surrendered themselves prisoners to a gentleman whose house was near the place they landed' (perhaps the J. P., John de Wichehalse, at Lee?) 'and were from thence sent to Exeter gaol, on July 12th.' Captain Hewling was executed with eighteen others at Taunton at the end of September. 'He was but 22 years of age, a Londoner, and as some say a relation of Cromwell.' A local story set down much later is that another of the fifty was caught and killed in Bonhill Wood, just above Lee Bay, and his quarters impaled on a gate across the road. A rapier was found nearby, and a sword down a well at Cheriton.

Wade does not mention his first rescuer, a farmer's wife, Grace How[e] of the small farm at Bridgeball, but he remembered his debt to her for the rest of his life, and left her an annuity when he died. She had found him hiding among the rocks at 'Illford Bridges' (Hillsford Bridge, half a mile downstream from the Howes' farm). He explained his danger, and she took food to him there for a day or two, until she and her husband Philip could arrange something better. Bridgeball, on the way up to the church of St Brendon, which was at that time the parish church, was too accessible to be safe, but they confided in John Birch at Farley, further out towards the moor. She led Wade up there, and Birch sheltered him and two others. The neighbours were sympathetic and discreet, but the Rector, the Rev. Richard Powell, began to think his parishioners were keeping some secret from him, and he made a few enquiries. He was told that the nearest inn was reserving the best beer for somebody who came down for it every day. According to a thin but strong thread of local memory South Cheriton farmhouse, near the church, was then the rectory; from there, anybody looking east across the Lyn valley would have a very good view of Farley farm; with a telescope, he could see most of the comings and goings. Before long, Powell's suspicions made him ride over with a friend – both of them armed – to John de Wichehalse. The Justice brought along a servant, Babb, as fourth man. They searched three houses at Bridgeball in vain, and went on to Farley where they surrounded the farmhouse, watching both doors. The Rector knocked at the front; after a short delay, Grace Howe opened to him, and all three fugitives bolted out by the other door. Wade – disguised in Farmer Howe's clothes – was shot by Babb, and fell, very seriously wounded. The other two got clean away and he said nothing about them in his narrative.[9]

The Rector's activity had resulted not only in the capture of Wade – for which he claimed £100 reward – but also in the suicide of one of his parishioners. The people of Brendon must have made their feelings plain; the parson left the parish in the following year. As at Dulverton, the Protestant clergyman supported a Catholic King in his hideous cruelty. Was it purblind self-interest? Did both of them retain some bitterness from the Puritan sequestrations? Or were they simply two very insensitive men? Certainly their behaviour – especially Powell's – must have left an almost indelible memory among country people, far into subsequent reigns.

The rebellion so vindictively suppressed was a tragic waste of lives. Within three years of it the unforgiving King had antagonized nearly all his subjects and was obstinately defying Parliament and the Church and the preceding 150 years of English history. In 1688 his second wife, the pious Mary of Modena, whom he had married to please Louis XIV, bore him a son, who would inevitably be brought up as a Catholic. This was decisive. Whig and Tory leaders together, confident of national support, invited William of Orange to come over with a big enough army to ensure success. He landed in Torbay and was welcomed like a liberator as he advanced to Bristol, through towns and villages so lately tormented. (When his advance party, riding ahead with the news, reached Tiverton, they found tarred limbs of Monmouth's men still displayed on posts; they took them down and buried them in the churchyard.) All over the kingdom risings in his support succeeded without bloodshed, and King James fled to France. Parliament, offering the crown to William and Mary, bound them to maintain the Protestant religion and the laws and liberties of the realm, in a Declaration of Rights which was like a second Magna Carta. They promised, and kept their word.

The church bells rang for another coronation, and every parish bought ale for the ringers.

CHAPTER SIX

The poor man at his gate

Early in the eighteenth century Daniel Defoe, who as a young man had fought in Monmouth's army at Sedgemoor, was near Exmoor again, and wrote about it in his *Tour through the whole island of Great Britain*. Observant Londoner that he was, he enjoyed the bustle of prosperity in the cloth towns surrounding the moor, and in the harbours of Ilfracombe and Minehead, but untilled land did not appeal to the author of *Robinson Crusoe*. He quoted an Elizabethan judgement: 'Camden calls it a filthy barren ground, and indeed so it is.' On his way north from Taunton to look at the coast he crossed a corner of Exmoor – probably by the Brendons ridgeway and Hillhead Cross to Porlock – and wrote, 'It gives, indeed, a melancholy view, being a vast tract of barren and desolate lands; yet on the coast there are some very good sea-ports.'

In fact it was a vast sheep-walk, with villages hidden in the combes. It provided much of the wool for the thriving cloth-mills, though not all: both wool and yarn were being imported from Ireland to Barnstaple and Minehead. Dunster Yarn-Market, built about 1590 and repaired in 1647 after the long siege of the Castle, kept Irish yarn dry for the weaving of 'Dunsters'. In Tiverton Defoe was informed that all the people were fully employed, except a few scrimshankers. In Taunton, where 1100 looms were kept busy, an important clothier told him there was not a child in the town or neighbouring villages but could earn its own bread by the time it was five years old, unless it was neglected by its parents, and untaught. He records this with approval. Women and children were the spinners, men the weavers. Merchants sent packs of wool out weekly to the villages and hamlets, where it was combed and spun, and returned when the packhorses came again. The dyed yarn was woven in long rooms or workshops in the country towns, where fullers then cleaned and thickened the loose-woven fabric in the tucking-mills;[1] Dunster and Dulverton had had these since the thirteenth century, North and South Molton since the fourteenth. Finally, the compacted cloth was stretched and dried on tenter-racks in the fields – there is still a 'rack-close' in Selworthy – and the best of it was brushed by teasles to raise a good nap. (These were a difficult crop to grow, but some stragglers survived until recently in a Selworthy hedgerow, not far from the rack-close.) Then it was sent away in bales, each stamped with the stapler's mark.[2] (One such mark is moulded on a house-wall in North Molton square; it seems to form the initials of Thomas Parker, chief clothier there in Tudor times.) It was carried by pannier-ponies to the bigger market towns, or to the ports and thence to willing buyers overseas. The looms have gone, and the mills were adapted for other work, but Tucker, Webber and Comer are still common surnames around the moor.

Up on the Forest thousands of sheep were agisted – especially in early summer, to save the farmer's own grass for hay. After Boevey's death, the Wardens did not live at Simonsbath: most had their own estates to manage, outside the boundary, and held the lease of the Forest from the Crown for varying lengths of time. Simonsbath house and farm were sub-let. Given the remoteness, and the long winters at more than 1000 feet above sea-level, the tenancy can hardly have been attractive to farmers who could afford anything else. A tenant called Dennicombe, who held it at a low rent from 1704 to 1719, neglected the repairs; 'the premises,' said the Warden, Robert Siderfin of Carhampton, 'fell into very great decay and became ruinous', and when at last he was evicted one of the charges against him was that he or his family had broken and burnt gates, floors and 'timbers of the house'. The few trees planted to shelter Boevey's house would provide very little firewood, and there were no others for miles except a few stunted thorns. A man desperately failing, and very badly in debt to his landlord, was pulling the place to pieces to keep his family warm. In any bad winter Simonsbath is still cut off by deep snow.

The house was repaired and let again – usually to the deputy forester who managed the estate. In 1767 further expensive repairs were undertaken – with timber cut specially at Hacche Farm, South Molton, and hauled from there over the high ridge. In 1789 it was licensed as an inn – convenient for travellers from Dunster or Barnstaple and for graziers visiting the estate office on business. Thenceforward, the deputies appointed by the Wardens – Aclands now, in long succession – must have lived outside the estate. They were still concerned with letting the grazing, paying the tellers, checking the boundaries, and, within them, keeping the roads passable; the eighteenth-century account books record small sums paid for repairing highways, cutting out bogs, and on one occasion 'putting up a stone in Kinsford Road' (Leland's route). More urgently, the Forest pounds would have to be kept stock-proof. The 'Little Pound' at Withypool was still in use, and in 1736 its wall and gate had to be repaired; at Simonsbath in the same year Boevey's pound needed a new gate-post and the Forester had also to buy timber to mend the gate itself; a carpenter was paid 1/4d. to do the work, which took him a full day. Then, as a separate item, 8/2d. was spent on 'repairing the pound wall at Simonsbath after a great flood' and a further 3/- for 'drawing and carrying of stones'. The drifts and preys continued – the poundherd had special pay for 'warning the Suit' and attending the drifts. Free Suitors and Suitors at Large still had their privileges and duties, including the perambulation of the Forest every seven years, and the two Forest courts were still held regularly at Lanacre and Hawkridge, at the Warden's expense. Besides the steward of the courts, the poundherd, who might be an important witness, was paid to be present at both.

Looking back, it seems an anonymous time on the moor. Carpenter and poundherd did their work, and would take pride in doing it well, as would miller and smith and farrier in the villages, and hill-farmers incessantly pitting their wits and their muscles against a difficult and unpredictable climate. Few traces of all this remain. Families in the big manor-houses down in the foothills wrote and kept letters and even diaries, preserved the estate account-books, and when they died were buried in vaults or inside the church under handsome and informative monuments. Their houses, altered or enlarged by successive owners, reflect changing customs and interests, and follow, perhaps tardily, the changes of architectural fashion. But up on Exmoor the farmhouses, inns, church-houses or surviving cottages were built according to almost ageless tradition. Farm buildings might enclose a sheltered garth, Saxon-fashion, and new farms in the nineteenth century, like Wintershead and Horsen high on the moor, still used this practical design. Even the prehistoric 'longhouse' pattern, home and byre under the one roof, went on suiting the poorer farmers for a very long time.

Lanes wore steadily deeper between their hedge-banks; they filled with snow in winter, or became torrents after heavy rain. Clammers had to be kept firm, or hoppers – stepping-stones across a ford – replaced. House and shippon (called cowshed up-country) needed new thatch every few years. Here and there, reminders of what must have gone on everywhere can still be seen, but very seldom was any record kept. Careful memory, uncluttered by printed news, met every felt need in farmhouse or cottage; 'My grandad used to tell how his grandad ...' might be said to the speaker's grandchild and span seven generations – 200 years or more. The main facts of private and public life were set down tersely in parish registers or account-books, and the latter might embalm some practical little custom like the payment of the dog-whipper. (Farmers would ride to church with their dogs at heel – the dogs would want to follow their masters into that building as into any other, not wait outside by the pony-rail; so a dog-whipper was paid to keep them in order during services; his fee was 2/- a year in 1660 at Luccombe, but 8/- in 1665; in 1678 Jasper Kebby was paid only 3/- at Countisbury – a smaller church.) The parish also paid for the killing of animals considered vermin. In 1678 Countisbury paid a fox-catcher 15/- for the year, and 2/- to somebody who killed two 'grays' or badgers. In 1749 Luccombe enlisted Thomas Smith of Countisbury to kill their foxes too – at 10/- a year. They also thought it worth paying 2d. a head for hedgehogs – sixty-five of them in 1692; what harm were they thought to do?

Few voices speak from the moorland parishes. Reading and writing were not yet everybody's skills, and if people could win a precarious livelihood, family affection and the respect of neighbours, why should they bother about the opinion of strangers in time to come? Those who were defeated had to 'go on the parish' for relief, and in the end had a pauper's funeral – decently conducted, and the passing-bell was tolled, but parish money did not pay for memorials. The dead man or woman would be shrouded (in wool, for the sake of the cloth trade) and carried on a bier to a simple grave; coffins were not provided for the poor until well into the eighteenth century, according to the parish accounts of Luccombe, in which these funeral expenses were meticulously listed. Relief to needy vagrants is recorded there too; they were often maimed soldiers and sailors trudging between Minehead and Porlock. Countisbury, too, often paid small sums for relief to passing seamen and soldiers, some of whom had their wives and children with them. In 1678 the comparatively large sum of 1/- was spent on a petition for Hannah Harris to redeem her husband from captivity in Turkey.

North Molton, a four-shop village now, was a small industrial town for five or six centuries. Its records, analysed in an excellent unpublished work by Norman Annett, schoolmaster of the parish in the middle of the present century, illustrate the continual changes of fortune in the eighteenth.[3] The cloth-trade swung between decline and prosperity as the wars closed or peace reopened the continental ports. When export to western Europe was barred, the south-western industry was saved from collapse by large sales to the East India Company, which used the cloth to pay the Chinese for their tea. Meanwhile, competition from East Anglia and Yorkshire was increasing. These vicissitudes would be felt by the sheep-farmers as well as by the clothiers and their teams. Difficulties worsened when the copper and iron mines, briefly exploited in earlier centuries and more thoroughly developed in the eighteenth, stopped production in 1770. They were not seriously reopened for another fifty years. The wool hamlet of Heasley Mill, being even nearer to the mines, shared the history of the town, and at some periods both were far more populous than they are today, and crammed with tiny cottages now long demolished and almost forgotten. Two hundred people lived at Heasley Mill, and in the whole parish the population rose from 1500 to over 2000 in the mining boom of the nineteenth century. (It is now 1000 or so.) Wage-earning labourers and their families came and went. Weavers or combers left to seek their own kind of work in South Molton or Tiverton. Miners arrived from Cornwall, South Wales, Durham and even Germany; when the mines closed again a few settled locally, but most went home.

The industrial life – much of it indoors or underground – the high proportion of newcomers, the urban troubles of overcrowding, insanitary conditions, inadequate food, and the frequent bad epidemics (including smallpox and cholera), combined to differentiate the borough of North Molton from Exmoor itself, but the parish – distinct from the borough as late as the sixteenth century, separately taxed and richer – remained a sheep-farming community, with some ploughland on the lower slopes and rights of agistment up on the Forest, like any other parish bordering the moor. Unlike the rest, it had to feed the fluctuating population of two industries. This was fine for everybody in good times, but very bad when a harsh winter was followed by a wet summer, so that hay and corn harvests failed, and food prices climbed out of the reach of the poor. Sometimes the number of pauper burials rose to half the total for the year, and even more.

Records show the parish looking after its poor conscientiously, some of them in its workhouse, which could house only thirty to thirty-five people, and some in their own homes, by relief in cash or kind, or both. In 1767 extra money was given to the poor in the bad weather, and some more in 1784, 'given away in the great snow when the Poor was starving'. Clothing and shoes and stockings were issued to whole families – gown, coat, breeches, a woollen apron for the wife and enough canvas to make (very coarse) underwear for herself and three of her children. The parish detailed the doctor to visit sick or injured people who could not afford fees; in 1785 it 'Pd. the Physician for attendance to North Molton when the poor was very bad £1.11.6.'

To make all this possible, by a poor-rate which gravely impoverished some of the contributors themselves, the parish had to insist on the law of the time that regular relief was the business of the pauper's birthplace – except in some special circumstances which counted as 'settlement'. So it would pay a Cornishman's fare home, but might have to provide for former parishioners who had gone away to work and were being sent back destitute.

Out on the farms, the struggle with the climate went on, year by year. John Thorne of North Radworthy kept a farm notebook[4] from 1790 to 1827, which covers the years of near-famine at the turn of the century. The farm lies in the highest part of North Molton parish, not far outside the Forest boundary, and the weather he records must have prevailed all over the moor. At Christmas in 1798 a very harsh frost spoiled all the turnips and some of the potatoes, and damaged the wheat. In February 1799 a great snow, falling for two days and two nights, buried the sheep and many lambs were lost – thirty on one farm. Hard frost and cold, with almost incessant east and north-east winds, continued until mid-May. June was very dry, but a wet July and August spoiled the hay. A week of fine weather saved much of the wheat in the corn country, but another six weeks of rain in September and October ruined all the corn crops in the hills. The winter (1799–1800) was mild, but after the failed harvests food and clothing were selling at double price ... 'So 'tis the hardest times for the poor ever known in our time' wrote Farmer Thorne. By May and June scarcity had driven prices far above what had seemed dreadful a year earlier; in June a three-month drought began, and cottage gardens lost their potatoes, vegetables and fruit.

A better harvest eased matters, but not for long. All grain, potatoes and meat were soon in short supply again, and ruinously dear. By the following spring, 1801, with wheat at 21/- the bushel, barley 14/-, and potatoes 11/- the bag, against only 1/6 in 1796, famine was so near that the people 'rose in a mob' and made the farmers promise to sell their produce for much lower, stipulated, prices, and only in their own parishes, carrying none out. For three weeks nothing went to South Molton market; then wheat was taken in from other parishes and sold at a guinea a bushel again – far beyond cottagers' means. The vestry bought 'ship corn' from Barnstaple and further wheat and barley from Exeter, and to eke this out, rice and potatoes, herrings and butter, to be shared among the neediest at cheap rates. Nearly £1700 was paid out to the poor this year.[5] Mercifully the next harvest, in a fine summer, was exceptionally good and the end of the first Napoleonic war helped to bring prices down.

The winter of 1814, though, was one of those which are remembered and talked of for a very long time, and John Thorne rightly considered it worth full description:

1814 The Terriblest Winter this year ever since that one in 1776 that is 38 years ago. Began the 6 Day of January Snow and 3 or 4 Snows else then a days Rain and Froze to the Ground, Bushes, Trees, Hedges, Broke them all Down with the Weight, which was 2 and 3 inches thick in some Places of Ice. then before it broke away, it snowed 2 Nights, and most 2 Days with a

Tempest of Wind that blowed the Snow in the biggest Drifts ever known. the Ice lay on the ground for more than a week, many Sheep under Snow, 29 Shortecombe under and 9 of them Dead, forced to take in every Sheep from Shortecombe in the in Ground and Give them Hay. There was not a Sheep on the Darlicks, Shortecombe Easter and Wester Butterys, all forced to take them in and give them Hay by Reason of the Ice, that they could not taste a bit of grass Twig Furze nor any thing, for the Furze and Wood and Hedges was all Bowed down with the Ice and then covered with the Over whelming Snow. forced to give Hay to the Exmore Colts and other Colts, Go to mill on foot, no Horse could go the Drifts were so high, forced to go over the Fields, the Roads mostly full, it were 8 snows, it hold most 5 weeks then Thawed.

Those trapped by poverty and unemployment had small chance of escape. During war time some joined the army – as early as the 1740s Fielding noted, in *Joseph Andrews*, that the bigger wool-towns such as Frome were good for recruitment – but peace might send them home, maimed, to vagrancy, and in the end parish relief. Some emigrated – though fewer in this century than the next. Illiteracy was a further handicap.

Schooling was very scanty, and many of the poor had no chance of learning to read. A young farmer like John Thorne was luckier; he was probably taught the three Rs in North or South Molton, but perhaps the chronicler's instinct in him would have impelled him to learn somehow, whatever his circumstances. He obviously enjoyed writing – in verse as well as prose – and did it so vividly that his notebook was treasured, not thrown away. It includes a long account, in lively doggerel, of Sunday church-going. He dated it 1811, though part of it must have been written seven or eight years earlier, before Trafalgar, and he called it *The Country Church-Yard or the Impropriety of Worldly Conversation on the Consecrated Ground*. There is very little about the impropriety and much relish of the worldly conversation – the farmers exchanging the week's news and the women their gossip. The parson arrives, and they hurry into church.

> Out comes the Book, Confession's made
> We all like sheep have err'd and strayed,
> And some you'll hear in whispers low
> Will read the Absolution too.

They settle down for the sermon; the parson *reads* it and *nearly* sends them to sleep. The end comes, they snatch down their hats from the pegs, and home they go like schoolboys set free. The wooden pegs can still be seen in one or two Exmoor churches – or could, until recently; the good-humoured chaff is timeless and might be heard today on those of the hill-farms which are still in proper Exmoor hands.

At Ilfracombe in 1729 the only school-master was so busy as deputy-controller of the harbour and skipper of his own little boat that he had not taught his school for ten or twelve years. Combe Martin boys were better off; navigation was in their curriculum. Knowstone, where long tracks meet on the Chulmleigh–Dulverton ridgeway, had had a village school even in the reign of Queen Elizabeth I, but that was exceptional. (Had the Wadham family, lords of the manor since before Domesday, any part in this? The younger branch was still in Knowstone, though the elder had migrated long since to Somerset; from Ilminster, early in the seventeenth century, Nicholas Wadham, who died childless, founded the Oxford college named after him; it was built by the architect who had renovated Dunster Castle, and among its early undergraduates was Robert Blake of Bridgwater, who afterwards laid siege to the Castle on Parliament's behalf.)

Before the Reformation, even such a small abbey as Barlynch, near Dulverton, had had its little school, planned for novices but admitting a few outsiders. Part of a pupil's Latin notebook used there has recently been found – a tiny window letting in a dancing ray of light.[6] The teacher, Master David Juyne, dictated some of the notes and exercises, and the boys contributed a few of their own. 'Ego sum bonus puer' recurs. One day this 'good boy' wrote that he had come to school by a roundabout way – explaining his lateness on a sunny May morning perhaps? Another sentence, containing a new word to be learnt, complained that the chamberlain bustling about the dormitory at dawn made further sleep impossible. Whether boarders or day-boys, they began lessons at six in the morning, and were taught Latin and morals and table-manners.

After the dissolution of the monasteries, a few benevolent individuals – a Blundell here, a Wadham there – founded grammar schools or colleges. In the eighteenth century the Church of England began to provide 'charity schools' in poor areas. But a child's chances might still depend on geographical accident as much as on his father's purse and inclination. There were those five-year olds earning their own bread under the clothiers of Taunton, in 1700 or so. In 1818 schooling in country parishes was still so haphazard that a 'Select Committee on Education of the Poor' was appointed to investigate. The returns from Somerset villages on the Exmoor coast make sad reading. Culbone had 44 parishioners and nobody taught their children. Porlock's population was 633 and it had only a small day school, supported by voluntary subscription and attended by 23 pupils. Oare had nothing at all. Luccombe, with 417 souls, had only a Sunday school. In Stoke Pero 'a few children' were taught to read by an old woman whom the parish paid. Clergy making the returns reported, one after another, that the poor were anxious to have their children properly educated. This was in the years of unemployment after the Napoleonic wars.

For a long time the children of South Molton were exceptionally fortunate, thanks to the town's benefactor, Hugh Squier, whose portrait bust on the Guildhall facade looks over the old market-place – now the Square. Back in the 1680s he had founded a Free School of a new kind. He was what that century called, with warm approval, a 'worthy'. He was born in the parish, of well-to-do yeoman stock, in 1625, and being a younger son went away to London to work. He prospered there as a merchant, and settled in Westminster, but he leased the manor of South Molton from his brother and came to it often. When he was nearly seventy, and an attempt was being made to distort his charitable work, he wrote in a letter, 'I love the place of my nativity, and the very ground of the place, and the people that go upon the ground, and the chief good I can do them is to help them that they may not mis-spend their precious time.' His four children had all died young, and thereafter, with his wife in full accord, he devoted a great deal of thought and money to the needs of the people of his native place.

He decided to build a school. 'While others build almshouses to relieve the poor, I do design to prevent them from ever being poor, and instead of living in others' almshouses that some of these may in time build almshouses for others to live in.' He thought there was far more emphasis on Latin than was sensible for country children, and it had 'afforded [him] matter of compassion these many years, to see the godly good old wife (in the midst of all her other pressing affairs) take pains to pack her boys away to school (because she thinks 'tis for their good)' when they would be taught nothing more useful than the very rudiments of Latin, although the parents would not be able to keep them at school for more than two years. After that, he said, they would either forget all they had learnt, or else brag of having been two years at the grammar school and air their scraps of false Latin, which no more suited them than a saddle on a sow. Either the boy should go on and learn his Latin thoroughly, if he meant to be a parson, a lawyer, an apothecary or a gentleman, 'or else 'tis madness to begin'.

So this school was to give free instruction to twenty boys of the parish. (Later, before the founder wrote his will in 1709, the number was thirty.) It was not to be *only* for teaching Latin or grammatical rules, nor was it to be 'a horn book school to teach little children to read' (pupils were not to be admitted until they were literate). Its chief purpose was to teach good handwriting and arithmetic ('so necessary both by sea and land'). Provided there were twenty Free Scholars in attendance, the schoolmaster might admit any others who came to learn, at a fee to be agreed with the parents, and a Latin master was to be provided for these fee-payers (Coleridge's father, the clergyman son of a South Molton wool-merchant, held that post for a time). But the education of the Free Scholars was always to come first. This was never to become 'a common Latin school'.

Soon after Squier's death another school was founded, in the churchyard, a Blue Coat charity school where poor boys were taught to read, and grounded in the tenets of the Church of England. A second branch was added, 'for teaching poor girls to read, [to] say their catechism, to sew, and to knit'. There is no mention of writing or arithmetic, for either sex. The Free School near the bottom of East Street was far in advance of its time and it lasted until the national education reforms of the 1870s. Later – in 1893 – John Cock, in his history of the town, wrote proudly that there were many still living, occupying positions in honourable professions, and others retired from business, who owed their success in life to having been elected to Hugh Squier's Free School at South Molton.

There were many people, however, up and down the country, and not least in the South West, for whom the tenets of the Church of England had no appeal. Some of those who had fought under Cromwell for political and religious freedom had despaired at the Restoration and sailed away to the American colonies, but others had stayed quietly at home, bringing up their children on the Bible and *Pilgrim's Progress*, as did the Taunton merchants whose daughters attended Mary Blake's school and greeted Monmouth as the Protestant deliverer. Sedgemoor and the Bloody Assizes thinned their ranks.

Under William and Mary it had become lawful for Dissenters to hold religious meetings, and the secret gatherings in the woods had come to an end. Defoe, soon after 1700, found Nonconformist communities flourishing in the towns round the moor. He saw a fine new meeting-house in Bideford, and another in Bridgwater which had a special seat for the mayor if he should happen to be of their persuasion. In Taunton there were two big parish churches and two or three meeting-houses. By that time, since Dissenters as well as Catholics were debarred from the universities, the former had begun to establish their own academies (he records one in Taunton and one in Bridgwater) 'to breed up their preaching youth'. He himself had been educated at one such, near London, but took to politics and journalism instead of the ministry. Generally, though, the professions and public service being closed to them, the abler Nonconformists throve in trade, in the towns.

The Catholics – more often living on country estates – were

RIGHT: 11. Combwich causeway (*R. Beck, 1987*)

12. Stone Down (*R. Beck, 1984*)

13. Tarr Steps and the Barle in spate (*Exmoor National Park*)

14. Admiral Blake
*(Anonymous seventeenth-century miniature,
believed to be the only authentic portrait)*

JAMES D. DE MONMOUTH

15. James, Duke of Monmouth
(after W. Wissing, c. 1683)

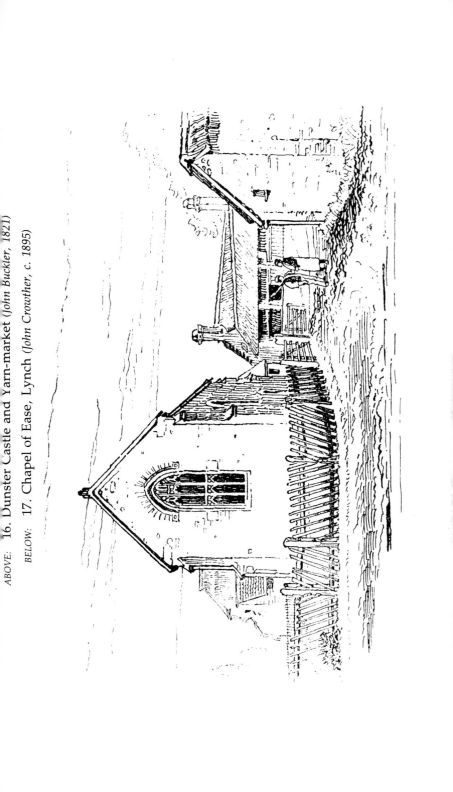

ABOVE: 16. Dunster Castle and Yarn-market *(John Buckler, 1821)*

BELOW: 17. Chapel of Ease, Lynch *(John Crowther, c. 1895)*

18. Molland church: eighteenth-century chancel *(R.C.H.M.E.)*

a political risk; the Old Pretender in 1715, and Bonny Prince Charlie in 1745, looked to them for support. In 1715 the Duke of Ormond crossed from France to the Devon coast on behalf of the Pretender and called for a rising, but he had no success. The leader of the English Jacobites was Sir William Wyndham of Orchard, near Williton, whose predecessor had held Dunster for the King during the Civil War and afterwards helped the future Charles II, 'the Black Boy', to escape southward after the battle of Worcester. Now, at the threat of invasion by the prince who hoped to be James III, Sir William had been taken into custody in the Tower, and without him nobody in the west would stir. He was released when the rising in Scotland had completely failed.

The Dissenters were no such danger. Their foreign friends were the Protestant Dutch, Germans and Swiss. But during their years of power the narrowest fanatics had predominated. These had exasperated Cromwell by their arrogance, and were remembered with distaste. So the first free Protestant parliament, which welcomed William and Mary, would not give them the entry to universities and state service which it was denying to the Jacobites, and Dutch King William's good counsel was overruled.

Consequently division deepened, when reconciliation was badly needed. It was a deprivation for society, as well as for individuals. Many of the Dissenters were poor men, self-taught like Bunyan, or self-opinionated (as he never was), and the new exclusion from educational opportunity might be both narrowing and embittering. (If they had been born into this later time, Robert Blake could not have gone to Oxford nor John Milton to Cambridge.) It reinforced social differences. Defoe's pleasure at finding, in Bideford, an exception to this generalization is revealing:

> The person who officiates at the meeting-house in this town, I happened to have some conversation with, and found him to be not only a learned man, and master of good reading, but a most acceptable gentlemanly person, and one who, contrary to our received opinion of those people, had not only good learning, and good sense, but abundance of good manners, and good humour; nothing sour, cynical, or morose in him, and, in a word, a very valuable man. And as such a character always recommends a man to men of sense and good breeding, so I found this gentleman was very well received in the place, even by those whom he differed from in matters of religion, and those differences did not, as is usual, make any breach in their conversing with him ... I wish I could say the like of all the rest of his brethren.

After so many decades of political and religious passion, England sank into torpor in the early part of the eighteenth century. The government was cynical – 'Every man has his price' was a prime minister's maxim. The universities were slothful, the Church stagnant. 'Enthusiastic' became a disparaging word. Common sense was admired, though it might be only dreary self-interest. The brilliant Catholic poet Alexander Pope, impatient of rubbish, flashed his malicious rapier: he predicted the eclipse of all moral and intellectual endeavour, all art and wit and learning, at the pompous approach of the great goddess Dullness, daughter of Chaos and primaeval Night.

Worldliness was uppermost, and the clergy were politically divided. Bishops appointed by the Whig government to support the House of Hanover were more interested in place-seeking at Westminster than in diocesan duties, while many country parsons owed their benefices to Tory squires who still toasted the King over the water. It was a time of absentee rectors, plural benefices far apart, cautious trimming – mocked in the song about the Vicar of Bray – and sheer laziness.[7] The miry roads of Exmoor must have provided many an excuse; even Eggesford and Mariansleigh in the southern foothills had no services in winter, because their non-resident parson pronounced them inaccessible.

In remote farmsteads on the moor a few little Chapels of Ease had survived since the late fourteenth century. That, too, had been a time of self-indulgent clergy and neglected laity, when Wyclif's long struggle for reform was the beginning of English protestantism. Some lords of manors a long way from the parish church had obtained the bishop's licence to have daughter-chapels consecrated in or very near to their own homes. Most of these fell into disuse during the Puritan ascendancy, and were used as outhouses or barns until they tumbled down for lack of repair. In 1705 a rector of Selworthy recorded that only one of the four in that parish was in good order and still used for worship. (Two of them, Lynch and Tivington, have since been restored.) In 1744 a diocesan enquiry about chapels and ruins of chapels drew from the incumbent of the very large hill-parish of North Molton, where three had once been licensed, the brief reply 'No chapels'. Apparently he did not bother himself to ride out to South Radworthy and Bentwitchen, where he would have found two derelict ecclesiastical buildings. Both of these were converted into cottages during the eighteenth century; South Radworthy's then declined into a cowshed and eventually fell down, Bentwitchen's is said to have become one of three cottages, and to have been used for Methodist meetings in the 1830s. Two of the three have been modernized past recognition, but to the west of them an air-photograph taken about twenty years ago showed the floor and wall-footings of a rather larger ruin, now buried under the grass. The Bentwitchen farmer, Jeremy Thorne (of the Thorne family long at North Radworthy), believes this to have been the Chapel of Ease. The third such was at Holywell, so far from any habitation that it may have evolved from pre-Christian well-worship, perpetuated by the Church in the Holywell Revel. (See Chapter 10.)

The village churches did not fall down, or become cowsheds; they were merely altered as the centuries went on – repaired, enlarged or almost rebuilt. Sometimes the congregation had increased, and private benefactors paid for the work to be done. Often the architecture tells more or less when a chancel was lengthened or an aisle added; sometimes parish records date it exactly, and show that new styles spread slowly. The churches of towns and ports round the moor – North and South Molton, Dunster, Minehead – acquired their Perpendicular character towards the end of the fifteenth century, when the wool industry was thriving, and newer generations of masons had replaced the victims of the Black Death. They were later than some of the great lofty churches of Norfolk and Suffolk which have stood in open country ever since that plague. The beautiful south aisle of Selworthy was added later still, when the Reformation had begun, and Thomas Cromwell was promulgating changes of doctrine which would eventually clear away side-chapels and rood-screens, remove all images and all decoration, and replace the chancel altar by a communion-table in the nave.

The remoter parishes were too small to afford the glories of the Perpendicular and some of their tiny churches retain an older and touching simplicity. Culbone keeps its Saxon window, Hawkridge its Norman door and font. Norman fonts often survived mediaeval alterations to the church – as at Winsford, at West Anstey, and a number of others. They were carefully kept because they represented the church's authority to baptize; when St Brendan's was transferred from Cheriton to its present site in Brendon in the eighteenth century, the Norman font was taken over. Indeed, nearly all the stonework was moved; it is locally reported that the hamlet of Cheriton had been emptied by plague.[8] The labour must have been immense – everything to be dragged three miles downhill and up, on some kind of sledge, in dry weather when Farley Water was low; but good material was not to be wasted, nor old associations forgotten.

Church interiors have changed continually, with the swings of doctrine and fashion, but two Exmoor churches, Molland and Parracombe, have remained almost as they were in the eighteenth century. They reflect the war-weary compromise (altars were restored, rood-screens were not), the lazy tenor of Church of England worship at the time, and indirectly, the changed relationship between Church and state. The days when fugitives ran to the church for safety were long past – though the heavy door of Molland church still has its sanctuary ring. Now the squire, more powerful than the parson, governed the parish as Justice of the Peace and chief employer; he owned the parish stocks, and when they were not being used to punish offenders in the middle of the village, they were kept in the churchyard or in the tower. They can still be seen in an unused pew at Molland – a set made to grasp three pairs of ankles, very close together.

Except for its Norman font, Molland church was completely refurnished in Queen Anne's reign, and escaped later alteration. The houses of the time were elegant, practical and comfortable, so the House of God was similarly domesticated. There was no mystery or secrecy; all was light and clear; plain glass replaced the richly coloured story-telling of the mediaeval windows. Wall frescoes which had illustrated other stories for simple congregations were everywhere plastered over – a part of one lately uncovered at Timberscombe shows King David playing his harp. The old division between chancel and nave – the screen half-concealing the movements of the clergy, and the rood-beam above it holding aloft the figures of the Crucifixion – had gone too. The Molland beam had been taken to the stable of Copp Hall, where it was identified in our own century.[9] The narrow, richly carved panels of the old screen had been removed, but kept, and some of them now form a handsome reredos. The Queen Anne craftsmen made a new and simpler screen, rustically graceful, with an empty oval like a cheval glass forming the upper half of the door. It invites decent respect for the chancel, but hides nothing.

Instead of the rood loft a painted tympanum displays the ten commandments, because emphasis had shifted to the Old Testament and Mosaic law. Literacy was implied, though probably few of the country parishioners could read. In the centre, and rather higher, between two panels of commandments, is the coat of arms of George III, and in the highest place of all was painted in good clear letters the name of the reigning churchwarden, L. Mogridge.

The pulpit, rather than the altar, dominates the church. It is a sturdy three-decker, with reader's lectern and clerk's seat below the parson's eminence; there is a fine sounding-board above it to carry his voice outward, and on top of that the wooden figure of an angel blowing a trumpet. The preacher's flock was neatly packed in box-pews – two large square ones in front, for the squire's household and his own, and rows of plain oak oblongs for the rest. The musicians sat behind, near the tower, and to their right was built, then or later, at the back of the last pew, a raised floor with two little benches designed for the short legs of the Sunday school children, who could thus see and be seen. Their elders were comfortably shut into their boxes; once the door was closed the high panels must have kept most of the draught out and some warmth in. Sermons were not as immoderately long as

104

in Commonwealth days. (Almost the first thing Luccombe parish bought after the Restoration was an hour-glass, like the one at Selworthy, to be set up beside the pulpit where parson and people could all see the sands running out.) Even so, a dull voice and the seclusion of the pew might bring on drowsiness.

The clerk, who had charge of the music and led the singing, felt responsible for the good behaviour of the congregation. In the following century one man – George Ayre – was clerk of Molland for fifty-one years. He used to move down from the three-decker and sit on a hinged seat near the porch during the sermon, and if anybody snored he went forward quietly with his staff of office; at one end it had a wooden knob, for rousing male sleepers by a rap on the head, and at the other a bunch of feathers which he would brush over a woman's face until she woke.

Sometimes it was the squire who looked after decorum. Early in the century Addison described his fictitious Sir Roger de Coverley as generous to the church and on good terms with the parson, while in the next village the reverse obtained. Being landlord to the whole parish he kept his tenants in order, and would suffer nobody to sleep during service except himself. If he had 'been surprised into a short nap at sermon' he would stand up when he woke and look about him, and if he saw anybody else nodding, would send his servant to wake them. Nearly two hundred years later, the Sir Thomas Acland of the day, the well-loved 'Old Sir Tummus' who occupied the Squire's Pew above the porch at Selworthy, could look down over the congregation and after the service would quietly reprove any tenant who had misbehaved. (An affectionate myth alleged that he took his fishing-rod to church with him and cast a line – but no hook – over any sleeper within range.)

The characters of the squire and the parson, and the relationship between them, were very important, for better or worse. In Exmoor's forty parishes, in the long duration of the squirearchy, there must have been great variety. Remoteness would breed eccentricity. Glimpses here and there in family archives or letters whet the reader's appetite, but they are brief. Nobody local, it seems, was looking round and trying to tell the whole tale. But in the 1740s there was a great comic novelist observing country matters not so very far away – the author of *Joseph Andrews* and *Tom Jones*. Fielding grew up in the South West, was educated at Eton and went to London, where he became first a playwright, then successively a barrister on the Western Circuit, a J.P. for Westminster, and Bow Street magistrate. He knew his world rather as Chaucer did, and he insists that his people and incidents are drawn from life. Of course he selects and heightens for dramatic effect, but he is a witness to be trusted.

The neighbouring landowners in *Tom Jones*, Squire Western and

Mr Alworthy, are on friendly terms, but opposite in nature. Alworthy is as his name suggests, and universally respected. The Squire is uncouth, tempestuous, harsh even to the daughter Sophia whom he loves only slightly less than his horses and dogs. He hunts foxes, preserves pheasants, speaks broad dialect, shouts and swears, pronounces the government 'a parcel of roundheads and Hanover rats', and regularly goes to bed drunk. He invites Parson Supple to meals, and is glad of his company on an expedition to London, but threatens to cast him off for ever when he ventures to advise a little gentleness towards Sophia. In *Joseph Andrews* the learned, simple-hearted, underpaid and Quixotic curate Parson Adams is admitted only to the kitchen of the squire, Sir Thomas Booby, who regards him as a mere servant of that thorn in his flesh, the rector.

Fielding does not romanticize either rich or poor. Tom travels through Somerset, Gloucestershire and Worcestershire; the country is rough and wild, and so are many of the people he meets on the ill-defined roads or in the alehouses and inns. Cupidity and cunning do well in the hostelries. Robbery by horsemen on the highways, or by footpads in the lanes, is a recognized risk of travel. How far this would have applied on Exmoor can only be guessed. There would be fewer travellers and fewer inns; but the roads were certainly atrocious, and a highwayman's horseshoe – an oval, to baffle pursuers – found near Ash Mill, which was on the old packhorse route from Tiverton to South Molton, is good accidental evidence.[10] Tom Faggus, the blacksmith turned highway robber, was fresh in memory. People in lonely farmhouses and cottages tucked away in combes below the ridgeways would be careful not to attract any attention at night – and in any case, candles and rushlights were not to be squandered. A stranger who had missed his way at dusk might wander until morning, unless he was willing to sleep in the heather.

Dissatisfaction with the torpor of the Church moved a little group of Oxford students, in the 1730s, to meet regularly for prayer and devout study. Others laughed at them, and by analogy with an old school of medicine nicknamed them Methodists. They were led by three young men who were soon afterwards ordained as Anglican clergy – John and Charles Wesley and George Whitefield. The Wesleys were sons of a country rector, who though he had nineteen children managed to give these two and their elder brother Samuel 'the finest education to be had in all England' – at Charterhouse and then Christ Church College, Oxford. They were High Churchmen at their ordination, and remained within the Church of England all their lives. Whitefield was working his passage as a servitor (an exhibitioner with some menial duties) and was probably the most eloquent and impassioned of the three. He became a Calvinist a few years later, and initiated, both in America and England, a Calvinistic version of Methodism which was repudiated by the Wesleys; they wished only to found a reforming society within the Church. Their aim was not unlike Wyclif's 400 years earlier, a recall to purer Christianity from the prevailing apathy and clerical sloth. Charles Wesley's hymns show the return from Old Testament values to New; they dwell on forgiveness, and 'Love divine, all loves excelling'. They are as limpid as George Herbert's poems and reflect similar humility and sweet nature. He was very far from Calvinism.

All three men set out on long missionary tours. At first they preached from the pulpits, and when, later, these were closed to them, they spoke in fields or market-places, from inn-steps or upping-stocks.[11] They went to the collieries and to William Blake's 'dark Satanic mills' in the northern towns, where conditions were appalling and the human scene was one of poverty, ignorance, drink, crime and hopelessness. Their work met a great need, and flourished. John Wesley addressed a crowd of 14 000 on Blackheath. Whitefield, speaking to 20 000 Bristol colliers at an outdoor gathering, saw their tears 'making white channels down their blackened cheeks'. More and more preachers were enrolled – first clergy, then laymen too – and styles varied. Sometimes, men and women at the enormous meetings became hysterical and fell down in faints or convulsive fits. Relations and neighbours, thinking the converts were being driven out of their right minds by the new preaching, tried to break up the meetings; the mob might drive an ox or a baited bull through the crowd or towards the improvised pulpit. Some of the gentry and clergy deplored the revival as 'enthusiastic' and unsettling, and took an active part in opposing it. Hostility built up.

The new influence reached Exmoor early, from the Wesleys. Their eldest brother, Samuel, had become headmaster of Blundell's and they stayed with him in Tiverton on their journeys to Cornwall, where they soon had a large following among the tinners. Sometimes they crossed the moor, and lengthened their journey to visit the miners and weavers of North Molton.

They kept diaries, which contain matter-of-fact but illuminating comments. Both preached at North Molton, John at least three times. There was already a congregation there in 1745, and he recorded that it was seriously harassed. 'A neighbouring gentleman has threatened them much unless they will leave this way, has turned many out of their work or farms, and headed the mob in person.' A Cornish convert, William Roberts, moved to Tiverton and travelled regularly to North Molton on the newly formed North Devon circuit. When John Wesley returned, twelve years later, things had improved; 'there have been great tumults here since I saw them before, but God has now rebuked the storm.

When the gentry would no longer head or pay the mob, the poor rabble were as quiet as lambs.'

Charles Wesley had an uncomfortable ride from Tiverton to Barnstaple, by way of North Molton, in wet September weather in 1758, when he was fifty-one. He sheltered at an alehouse soon after leaving Tiverton, then went on his way, 'and a vile one it was'. It must have been the route of the later turnpike, the main road from London, passing Ash Mill, but it would be no more than a very muddy packhouse track at that time. (A renegade Anglican clergyman tried to use it on his way to plague William Roberts and the North Molton congregation but strayed into a bog, sank in waist-deep and died in its grip; when they found him, he was covered in snow.) Wesley put up at North Molton for the night; the food – the best his 'friendly old host' could offer – was tougher than he could bite, but 'clean warm beds made us amends'. He preached in the evening, 'with more comfort and life than I have done since I left Bristol', and again to a full room at five o'clock next morning. He left in heavy rain for Barnstaple, via Filleigh, where he sheltered again in the park-keeper's lodge.

On another occasion John Wesley rode from Cornwall to Minehead, where he preached 'near the seashore' to almost all the inhabitants, including, he said, most of the gentlemen of the town, who 'behaved with serious decency'. Next morning he crossed to Wales. He must have ridden over the moor, most probably by Leland's road through Barnstaple, Brayford and Exford. He seems to have been unmolested on these journeys, but in North Tawton, between Exmoor and Dartmoor, where in 1765 he tried to preach from the steps of the inn, the rector and several other gentlemen called out the huntsman and hounds against him. He was in his sixties. The barbarous squire in *Joseph Andrews* who set his pack on Parson Adams was not greatly exaggerated, it seems; but Wesley was able to record that 'the dogs were wiser than the men, for they could not bring them to make any noise at all'.

The movement strengthened; its temper suited many on Exmoor whose forebears had fought under Cromwell's generals, had sheltered fugitives after Sedgemoor, and been steady Dissenters ever since. They were reinforced by the Cornish miners – some in the eighteenth century, and far more in the nineteenth, when iron and copper were being mined not only near North Molton but also near Simonsbath and in the Brendon Hills, and when some of the new Nonconformist chapels were built with the Cornishmen's help. The opposition of the squires and clergy (not all but many) and the belligerence of some of the Methodists (not the Wesleys) at length made the rift inevitable. On Exmoor as elsewhere church or chapel became a deep division, religious, temperamental, often social, often lurking in party politics. Civilly concealed, it is still potent in the villages of the moor.

CHAPTER SEVEN

The coast and the wars, 1700–1815

North of the coastal ridgeway lies a different Exmoor, in partnership with the sea. It has always been so. The ridge is a natural boundary: southward the moorland stretches to the horizon, fold upon fold of hills and combes, but on its north flank the characteristic gentle slopes either end abruptly in a sheer drop to rocks and waves far below, or fall away only a little less sharply in woodland right down to the water's edge. Here and there rivers from the moor leap down to the sea in cataracts, or run down through combes or cleeves to tiny beaches or little habitable bays. When roads were only steep tracks, slippery with mud or loose stones, the hill farmers would need good reason to make the precarious descent and the long climb back, and the hamlets at the foot depended for centuries on the fishing and on what could be brought in by sea.

So the people of these northern parishes looked outward. They had always been seafarers; in Saxon times their little ships were trading up and down the coast, and in still smaller boats, like coracles, yet earlier inhabitants must have been fishing to feed themselves. In the second half of the eighteenth century William Chapple, an observer with long experience of mid-Devon agriculture, was distressed by the hardship and gloom among labourers when estates were enlarged, and arable became pasture, which needed fewer hands.[1] He remarked that the poor in maritime parts of Devon were more fortunate, because they had unlimited supplies of salt-water fish of many kinds, 'fresh and good at a cheap rate, whilst the better sort of people in the inland counties are glad to have them at almost any price, stale as they must be before brought thither'.

The herrings were never allowed to go stale. Big shoals used to come up the Bristol Channel, and in 'Red Herring Houses' built on the quaysides at Lynmouth, Porlock Weir and Minehead, the fish were cured, for storage or sale, except in the rare years when the shoals failed to appear. The salmon caught in the fish-weirs, or the oysters dredged off the Foreland, might be sold locally; sometimes, one hopes, they provided a tasty treat at home for the fisherman and his family. But the herring, not the salmon, was accounted – by Westcote, in 1630 or so – 'the king of fishes'.

Alongside the fishing was the coastal trade, up to Bristol, down to Cornwall, or across to South Wales. The ketches took away dried fish, oak-bark for the tanneries, butter and eggs, and occasionally a few cattle or sheep, and brought back coal, salt, wine and 'victuals' unspecified. The merchants of Minehead addressed a petition to Queen Elizabeth I, saying that their pier was in such bad repair that they risked losing the 'ancient and daily passage' to and from the Glamorgan ports, which had kept the Somerset fairs and markets stocked. Irish wool-yarn supplemented huge local supplies, and linen was brought from Dublin and Waterford. So were ox and cow hides; Exmoor manors, farms and villages must have needed much more leather than they could produce; sheepskin would not be strong enough for harness or boots, nor even, perhaps, for the fireside bellows. There was a coastal ferry for passengers between Porlock and Minehead in the eighteenth century, and a traveller could always hire a boatman to take him over to Wales if weather and tides allowed. And schooners and brigs had long been trading from the Bristol Channel to Iberian and Mediterranean ports and to the North American colonies.

Living so differently, hillmen and shore-dwellers grew apart – except round Porlock, with which a good harbour, gentle climate and sheltered fertile fields, had the best of both worlds. Further west the difference became social; the families did not intermarry. This may have been partly practical, on both sides; it would be best to have a helpmate bred to the life she would have to share. But there was more to it than that. The owner of even the smallest boat was his own master. Independence gave him a sense of superiority, and he would choose his wife from another port, rather than from inland. That might also mean that his sons and daughters would inherit boats or cottages in two little harbours, not one. Then in the eighteenth century bigger vessels were being built for the foreign trade, with several well-to-do local tradesmen or gentry taking shares in the enterprise and its financial risks, and they would sign on seamen they knew, to contend with the dangers of wind and weather, pirates and privateers.

The sailing hazards for ships on the Biscay run were formidable. South of Harty Point high stony cliffs faced the Atlantic, and when the prevailing westerly winds strengthened to gales, ships were driven towards the rames, wicked parallel ridges of jagged rock, half-submerged, reaching out lethally from the cliff-foot into the great ocean waves. Wrecks of iron steam-ships are strewn along the coast; the timber-built sailing-ships of older days needed consummate seamanship to get them past, and some must have been smashed to shreds. Deliberate wrecking, by showing false lights on the cliffs, was customary between Hartland and Bude. The wreckers ensured that no sailor survived to tell the tale; besides, if any living person reached the shore, the ship was not legally a wreck – not lawful plunder. At Morwenstow the vigorous rector, Robert Stephen Hawker, insisted on being summoned whenever a ship ran aground, because, he said, the parson must have his tithe; in fact, of course, his presence made murder more difficult. But there is no record of that savage crime anywhere on the Exmoor coast. Wrecks there were, but the shore folk, being sailors, would be reluctant to add to the perils of the sea. On the contrary, they built up a rescue service which in the nineteenth century became very impressive indeed. Vessels bound for Bristol might have put into Ilfracombe for shelter; so might, now and then, a foreign trader caught in sou'westerlies near the Scillies, and blown far off course. In such weather outward-bound ships would not attempt to leave port.

There were other dangers from pirates and privateers. The pirates, maritime counterparts of the highway robbers, found Lundy a convenient base. During the recurrent eighteenth-century wars, mostly against France or Bourbon-ruled Spain or both, privateers were legitimized pirates. Their owners or captains were allowed to sail armed on private business, and at the same time were commissioned by government to attack the merchant ships of hostile nations. It was a game both sides could play, and did. The French grand fleet was virtually immobilized – defeated so thoroughly at La Hogue that Louis XIV neglected it thereafter and poured money into the land conflict with Marlborough. So the French seamen took to privateering instead. Any merchant ship risked being boarded, captured and sailed into an enemy harbour by a prize crew; but on the way she might be recaptured, and change hands two or even three times during what began as an innocent trading voyage. The western approaches to the English Channel and the Severn Sea provided very good hunting. British sailors brought their prizes into Ilfracombe or up to Bristol, and any neutral vessel driven up past Hartland by the gales was liable to be seized between Exmoor and South Wales – an interesting spectacle from either coast.

Britannia ruled the waves, but her ships could not enter enemy ports. Consequently the wool trade of the south-western counties suffered in every war. Weavers and combers and tuckers from the cloth towns, labourers from the surrounding country, losing any prospect of work, reluctantly enlisted in the King's service. Recruitment was locally conducted: each parish had to supply a fixed number of men, and a prosperous conscript might pay a nearly destitute neighbour to take his place. The money would help the poor man's family for a time. Inland recruits became soldiers rather than sailors – they preferred solid ground under their feet, however far from home.

They might be sent to fight their own compatriots in the American colonies. The settlers now rebelling against an English tax and a stubborn Hanoverian King were descendants of voluntary or unwilling emigrants. Puritans who had left Stuart England for religious freedom had by now been carving out a life on the eastern seaboard of America for several generations, and like Hampden before them, wanted a say in how their money was spent. Further south were men whose grandfathers had been sent out into slavery in the plantations for following Protestant Monmouth. They would not have been forgotten at home, and there must have been second cousins from this side with little heart for the campaigns. Conversely, there were colonists who were magnanimous to the defeated – as was the English-born General Gates, after Saratoga, to his wounded prisoner, that 'most confounded Tory' Major John Acland, and his intrepid and charming wife Lady Harriet.[2]

Meanwhile, the British East India Company was at work in Madras and Calcutta, unconsciously founding a second British empire. In America and India, within a single quarter of the eighteenth century, the balance of the world's future altered; and the shadows of both changes reached one lonely old farmhouse near the Exmoor coast. In Countisbury church a slab of dark grey slate commemorates four brothers, of whom three, being too many for a small farm to support, went overseas to seek their fortune. They were the sons of 'Mr John Fry of Wilsham in this parish', who died in 1762, and his wife Mary who outlived him by only a few weeks. The three died abroad, all in their twenties or thirties – Walter in Bengal 'in ye East Indies' in 1783, William in Georgia in 1789, and Richard in Jamaica in 1796. John, the eldest, stayed at home and farmed Wilsham, and at length raised this handsome memorial. Space was left at the foot of it, and there, in slightly different lettering, is the record of his own death, in 1829, at the age of eighty-one.

Not one of the three who went so far away is likely to have been in any battle. Walter must have joined the East India Company some twenty years after Clive had conquered Bengal (and how should John, at home in Countisbury, distinguish between East India and the East Indies?). William's death in Georgia was eight years after America had won independence. Richard, in the British island of Jamaica, lived longest. Perhaps disease, perhaps unhealthy conditions, killed each of the brothers in turn – far apart from each other in hot climates, and very far from the airy hilltops and misty combes they knew in boyhood, besides the cool clear waters of the Lyn.

Countisbury parish lies athwart the ancient ridge-road which dips to the sea at either end – Lynmouth and Porlock – and marks off the cliff country from the moor. North of the road, the church stands up to all weathers, on the slope of the Foreland. South of it, almost opposite the church, a row of cottages – probably Tudor – became an inn early in the nineteenth century, and was called, in parish records and on the 1841 Tithe Map, 'The Blue Ball'. It was a good name to hearten Jack ashore; in the great days of sail, a single blue ball hoisted by the coastguard meant, 'Now safe for small craft to berth in harbour'. The signal dropped out of use early in the present century. The inn-name kept the link with the sea until, in the mid-1980s, a rich stranger enlarged the building and called it 'The Blue Boar', then sold it to another who entitled it 'The Exmoor Sandpiper'. Exmoor people hope that a future owner will restore the proper local name.

The welcoming sign may or may not have encouraged some of the smugglers who used this wild coast during and after the French wars. It is on record that in 1832 the Customs Riding Officer seized near Countisbury sixty-eight tubs of spirits and three horses which should have carried them away. (The cargo was believed to have been landed from a gentleman's yacht.) Perhaps the ridge-road, however rough, was more convenient for the Lynton-based officer than was healthy for the law-breakers; but an inn had stables and fodder, as well as cellars where illicit barrels might be concealed for a day or two among the rest. And the distributors of contraband had many friends. Unlike highwaymen, they were no threat to people who left them alone, and the country partners in the team worked more by their wits than by fighting, though the captains and crews of the ships which brought the contraband up from Brittany and the Channel Islands, sailing dangerously near the coast to escape notice, might be violent men who had few scruples. Sometimes armed sloops landed their dutiable cargo on Lundy, where it would remain until, on a favourable tide, local boatmen could row across to one of the little Exmoor bays, deliver it to collaborators waiting on the beach, and slip away while these carried it to a safe hiding-place – as near as possible, for speed. Next night, or very soon afterwards, others would come from landward, sometimes with pack-ponies as though in the normal way of trade, and take it much further inland, to willing buyers.

Few people thought it any crime to cheat the Customs. The national purse suffered, and so did honest tradesmen who paid duty and had to charge more. That did not worry parson, squire, or farmer, and there was no lack of hiding-places. Churches were conveniently lonely at night. Old Cleeve chapel is said to have burnt down with kegs of spirits blazing under the old pews. Trentishoe church, believed to have been a favourite with smugglers, was ideal for their purpose. The belfry would hold plenty of small barrels. The southern approach, by narrow lanes winding up and down wooded hills, would be difficult for strangers and easy for secret distributors; from the sea a very steep climb led up from Bosley Gut, and rather easier ways from the Heddon valley. A hint of corroboration appeared a few years ago, when a little white flower, Cardamine Trifolia, was found growing in the highest and furthest corner of the churchyard. It is not indigenous; botanists wonder whether the seed came from France on muddy contraband. The men who carried the little barrels up from the beach might have dumped them over the wall for Trentishoe confederates to stow away in the tower. 'Brandy for the parson, baccy for the clerk' would keep all safe and secret.

The rocky cove at Heddon's Mouth was used for a long time. Even a sloop, the *Hope*, came close inshore one moonlit night at the turn of the century and landed ninety-six barrels of spirits, but then, sailing westward under the shadow of the cliffs, struck a rock and sank. As late as 1827 a huge haul, brought up from the cleeve, was discovered on a Trentishoe farm. Somebody had laid information against the farmer, John Hoyle or Hoyles, and the officers found newly dug holes in the floor of his barn and seized 262 tubs of spirits as well as wine, cordials, and even a case of preserved fruits. They thought they had captured Hoyle, but they were defeated by a well-tried local ruse. Like many other farmhouses and cottages, this one was built right into the side of a hill – a few such can still be seen. There appeared to be only one entrance, so the preventive men watching it did not mind letting their prisoner out of sight, indoors. They knew nothing of the attic window opening on to the hill behind. Hoyle was soon far away, and they did not find him again. The booty was all secured, but the farmer was a near relative of Cook, whom the revenue men accounted 'the most notorious smuggler in this part of the country'. Friends and neighbours supported the vanished man so effectively that nobody was ever tried for harbouring the contraband. The informer must have had an uncomfortable time.

Moonlighting was skilled and adventurous work on the steep western cliffs, and must have had an appeal besides profit for lively young men. Down near Porlock, and east of Minehead, where the harbours were easier and the farmers and tradesmen more prosperous, the character of the enterprise was different, and not at all romantic. The landing and distribution were well organized, and a recognized part of local life. Pack-horse trains or carts coming up with lawful cargo from the weir could easily carry a little extra, or call in at a big farm and pick up a further load. Chadwyck Healey describes an elaborate hiding-place at Higher Doverhay which must have been used over a long period of time. It was contrived between the old wall of the dairy and a false one

114

built outside it. The way in was through a creep-hole in the dairy, small enough to be concealed by a milk-pan standing in front of it. When the cavity was discovered during building alterations late in the nineteenth century, the stands for kegs of brandy or rum were still in position. Another capacious hide was a room 9 or 10 feet square, deep underneath a small field near Bossington. The secret was kept until by chance, in about 1850, a hunted hare disappeared into a hole, and the huntsman enlarged it and sent a man down after her. During the construction of such places a good many local people must have used their eyes and held their peace.[3]

In 1682, towards the end of Charles II's reign, the Surveyor-General of Customs, William Culliforde, came to enquire into the loss of revenue from these busy little ports, and the alleged corruption of some of His Majesty's officers. He found a great deal amiss, though in Porlock things seemed – at that time – to be orderly. The Customs officer there was 'an active young fellow' well deserving permanent appointment and twice the payment he was receiving, 'it being a place of trade and where great quantities of herrings are taken and cured, which begets a great concourse of people and small craft, that may be of dangerous consequence to the Customs unless well guarded'.

At Watchet the depositions made to the Surveyor describe blatant running of contraband direct from ships in the harbour, and a corrupt officer, Mr Dashwood, allowing it. The rule was that nothing except coal should be landed at Watchet unless it had been cleared at Minehead. One ship which had openly evaded this was the *Industry*; another, arriving a month later, was the *Adventure*, loaded with wine, brandy, linen cloth and salt. 'The salt entred and paid duty at Mynehead, but the wine, brandy and cloth all run and was a very considerable parcell for there was not lesse than 30 men at worke between two and three hours delivering the same and all that while Mr Dashwood was drinking sack with the Master at the Shipp tavern and was privy and consenting to the same.' Mr Culliforde suspended Dashwood, whose long connivance had made the town a free port and remarkably rich. He appointed a temporary replacement and recommended him for permanent appointment 'for as much as the said Mr Perry fore making the discovery and doeing the king service, has begotten himselfe a generall hatred throughout the Town of Watchet (which belongs to Sir William Windham who patronises them in all their actings) – and for that the said Perry is a person well qualified for the said service...' The sequel is not known.

Minehead was as bad or worse. A shoemaker who lived on the quay gave information on oath: 'About a year and a halfe since came into this harbour a vessell belonging to Bristol and stayed here not above two days, on which said Vessell, James Hellier was Tydsman' (inspecting officer) 'and afterwards went to Bristoll upon the said Vessell during which Vessell's stay in this harbour, in the night time this Informant saw run out of the same about forty packets of cloth which was brought from on board the said Vessell by Thomas Jones, Roger Tapscall, Wm Geen and others and was by them carryd to the Backwall of Mr Thos Wilson's house, mercht, living on the key in Minehead and there by cords drawn up the walls into the court yard. When this informant went to lye down on his Bed being about 3 o'clock in the morning he left the said persons at work who continued so to do till it was almost day.' (The information was laid in June; 'about a year and a half', if accurate, makes it a midwinter run, with daybreak very late.)

Another informant, a mason, had seen casks of wine and brandy being carried at night, later that year, from a ship called the *Merchants Adventure*, and a further consignment from the *Swallow*, to the same Thomas Wilson's house on the quay, and he said James Hellier was privy to the landing. Much more was landed at the same time, 'and within some few nights after Mr Hooker's waggon of Taunton came severall times and fetched away the said wine and brandy in the night time, at one of which times James Hellier and Henry Clement, the Tydsmen, were present at the loading of the said waggon'. Hellier was suspended by Culliforde; the mason was severely beaten by the master of the *Swallow*.

It was all too profitable, and too deep-rooted, to be eradicated by a few dismissals. It grew steadily throughout the eighteenth century and reached a peak during the Napoleonic Wars. In 1804 the Collector of Customs for Barnstaple reported that smuggling had increased to an alarming extent, and was so systematic that the inhabitants of Devon and Cornwall were regularly supplied with smuggled spirits at well below market price. The loss of revenue must have been very great. But so was the national danger, and the consequent impressment of men for the fleet. In that anxious time the Barnstaple officers also reported, 'We are told a large quantity of goods are landed near Hartland where the Coast Waiter is 80 years old and the Riding Officer at Clovelly is over 70 – has not been on horseback for 20 years'. Shorthanded and underpaid, the preventive men had an almost hopeless task.

In the spring of 1798, a young stranger, William Hazlitt, happened to describe the country in which they had to work. He walked, with Coleridge, from Nether Stowey to Lynton; he observed with a painter's eye, and recalled the journey long afterwards. 'We walked for miles and miles on dark brown heaths overlooking the Channel, with the Welsh hills beyond, and at times descended into little sheltered valleys close by the sea-side, with a smuggler's face scowling by us, and then had to ascend conical hills with a path winding up through a coppice to a barren top, like a monk's shaven crown.' It was nearly midnight when they reached Lynton, and knocked up somebody to give them lodging. They were tired and hungry, and their hostess, roused from bed, cooked them 'some excellent rashers of fried bacon and eggs'. They stayed three days, and loitered happily on Lynmouth beach all one morning. There, 'A fisherman gave Coleridge an account of a boy that had been drowned the day before, and that they had tried to save him at the risk of their own lives. He said he did not know how it was that they ventured, "but, Sir, we have a *nature* towards one another".' On the third morning they set out for home, 'and Coleridge remarked the silent cottage-smoke curling up the valleys where, a few evenings before, we had seen the lights gleaming through the dark'.

The scowling smugglers were regulars, but there were casuals too. Hazlitt's fishermen and cottagers were not the people to let a windfall lie. A few years later a big lugger loaded with contraband was being chased along the coast by an Excise cutter, kept too close inshore so as to evade her, and ran aground near Lynmouth pier. More than 600 casks of spirit were landed and stowed for the night in open fields. Within two days every barrel had been carried inland, without any customs officer knowing anything about it.

Changes were made to improve the preventive services, especially after the end of the war. Three lines of defence were established – Revenue cutters out at sea, the Preventive Water Guard in galleys and gigs closer in, and ashore the Riding Officers, each one expected to patrol a long strip of coast and 10 miles inside it. Yet even after the 1815 reorganization there was a gap from Combe Martin to Lee, between the beats of the Braunton and Lynmouth riders; the Collector of Customs for Ilfracombe suggested mildly that it might be useful to recruit another man for this stretch – which included Trentishoe, Heddon's Mouth and Woody Bay! It was risky work along there. A tale told locally of Smuggler's Leap, just above Lee Bay, is that a Riding Officer, chasing a smuggler at full gallop, caught up with him there and grabbed his bridle, whereat both horses reared, and plunged over the cliff.

Further east, well clear of the high road (such as it was) and at the foot of steep cliffs, right at the corner of Countisbury parish and close to the Devon–Somerset boundary, the Coscombe beach (Glenthorne now) was a natural invitation which smugglers did not fail to accept. The Rev. W. H. Thornton, active young curate of Countisbury in the early 1850s, and a private pupil at Selworthy before that, inevitably knew a little of what was going on – a neighbouring parson's horses 'borrowed' at night, for instance, and a keg of brandy found in the manger and appreciated. Long afterwards a very old smuggler, dying in bed, told him 'how he used to have a donkey with a triangle on its back, so rigged up as to show three lanthorns, and how chilled he would become as he lay out winter's night after winter's night, watching on the Foreland or along Brandy Path, as we called it, for the three triangled lights of the schooner which he knew was coming in to land her cargo where Glenthorne now stands, and where was the smugglers' cave. "Lord bless you, sir", and the dying man of nearly ninety chuckled, "we never used no water, we just put the brandy into a kettle and heated it, and drinked it out of half-pint stoups, us did, and it never did us no harm whatsomdever, it was of that quality it were." ' From the hiding-place at the boundary, agile men would take the contraband east or west, into whichever county offered, just then, the safer welcome.[4]

By mid-century, look-out posts had been built to command a view of likely landing-places – there is still one near Glenthorne – and the three services had been combined into one, 'the Coastguard', charged with the prevention of smuggling. But the 'fair trade' was a long time dying, and perhaps its end was partly due to something quite different: as the nineteenth century wore on, the coast became much less lonely.

Coleridge and the Wordsworths, and then Hazlitt, were among the first outsiders to come to Exmoor purely for its own sake. Taste had begun to alter profoundly, and the wildness of mountains and cliffs, crags and cataracts was coming to have more appeal than smooth, long-tamed country. Then from 1793 until 1815 the war with Republican and subsequently Napoleonic France kept most English people from visiting the 'romantick' Alps or Rhine, so they looked for impressive scenery near home. Wordsworth's poetry, imbued with a new nature-mysticism, directed attention to the lakes and mountains of the north-west; Turner and Girtin travelled to paint wild Wales; and soon Sir Walter Scott's verse and novels, romantic in every sense, were to win him wide popularity as 'The Wizard of the North'.

The conventional idea of Exmoor as a barren waste began to be modified. In 1791 Collinson, a Somerset local historian, had little to say in praise of the moor, but much for the dramatic coast. He describes Culbone: 'This spot is as truely romantick as any perhaps which the kingdom can exhibit. The magnitude, height and grandeur of the hills, rocks, and woods, at the back and on each side of the cove; the solemnity of the surrounding scene; the sound of the rivulet roaring down its craggy channel ... During the three winter months the sun is never seen here; being entirely hid by the height of the surrounding hills.'

Six years later, William and Dorothy Wordsworth were living for a time at Alfoxden, in the north Quantock parish of Holford, and Coleridge was nearby in Nether Stowey. They were young and hardly known, but full of ideas and energy. They had heard of the Valley of Rocks, and Coleridge, who read everything, must certainly have read Collinson. So the three of them set off late one afternoon in mid-November to walk to Lynton, by the coastal path through Culbone Wood in its winter shadow. Dorothy recorded in her journal that the evening was dark and cloudy; they walked the first eight miles to Watchet and there put up for the night. During those miles, she said, Wordsworth and Coleridge were planning a ballad. What emerged was *The Ancient Mariner*. They worked out its powerful scheme together and at Watchet in the evening sat down to write it jointly.[5] Before they had done much, Wordsworth realized that his help would be a hindrance, and sensibly took no further part. Coleridge, his imagination thoroughly kindled, must have had the embryo of the poem in his mind all next day as they followed the cliff path from Porlock to Lynton, with the sea and ships far below on their right. He worked on it at Nether Stowey during the winter, and at the end of March walked over to Alfoxden with the manuscript of the long poem finished – and incomparable.

The poets told their friends about the coast; Southey stayed at Alfoxden and visited Porlock, Lynmouth and Lynton. Half a generation later, still during the war, Shelley brought his young bride to Lynmouth for a few summer months. They were enthusiastic, but came and went like the swallows. The Wordsworths remained in the Quantocks for a time. Coleridge spent a few months at one of the farmhouses above Culbone, where he dreamt his exotic poem *Kubla Khan*. They wrote little about Exmoor, except in letters and diaries, and their delight in this wild landscape brought no immediate flood of tourists. Inland, the moor was still difficult for strangers to reach; for some time yet it was to be accessible only to travellers on horseback or on foot.

Another new fashion was the seaside holiday, and this brought summer visitors to the north coast faster than romanticism did. For about half a century doctors had been promulgating a new faith in salt-water cures. Scarborough and Margate had become bathing-resorts. At Weymouth King George III was trundled a little way out to sea in a bathing-machine, for his health, and as the attendants plunged him into the water the town band, on an accompanying cart, struck up 'God save the King'. The hamlet of Brighthelmstone, developed for Dr Russell's cures, grew rapidly into the Prince Regent's fashionable and sophisticated Brighton. Before long, the seaside was visited quite as much for pleasure as for health. The custom spread along the warmer south coast, from Lyme Regis on to Sidmouth, Teignmouth, Shaldon... By 1825 even Ilfracombe had a 'Ladies' bathing beach' and those who shirked immersion still felt better for the sea-air. Wherever there was a sandy cove, or a way down to the sea, as at Lynmouth, fishermen's and farmers' wives added to their scanty income by taking in family parties. Smugglers must have lost their help during the holiday season – it would be unsafe. And young holiday-makers scrambling about the rocks and cliff paths might find traces of moonlighting which the coastguard had not noticed.

Meanwhile the war with France continued, with two brief interludes, for twenty-two years, and sometimes the danger to this country was very grave indeed. The French Revolution had aroused Whig enthusiasm and Tory distaste, and Pitt had kept England on terms with the new Paris government for a time; but the excesses of the later and more violent revolutionary leaders, and their offer to support any rising against any monarchy, swung English opinion against them, and when France declared war on Britain in 1793, enmity quickly prevailed. It was not lessened by the boast of the French Minister of Marine that he would land in England with 50 000 Red Caps of Liberty to overthrow the government. Fears of plots and conspiracies grew to panic strength, and though they were almost without foundation, any political opposition was repressed, Habeas Corpus was suspended, and the advocacy of any reform at all was accounted seditious, and might land the speaker in gaol. In 1797 things looked very bad indeed. England's continental allies had withdrawn from the coalition, and in the spring there was serious mutiny in the home fleets at Spithead and the Nore. The war even came near Exmoor one February afternoon when three French ships – two frigates and a lugger – passed Lundy, with troops on board. They had orders to sail as far towards Bristol as they could, causing as much damage as possible. A channel pilot reported that they were off Ilfracombe; the alarm was raised about midnight, the North Devon Regiment of Volunteers was ordered out, but by daybreak there was no sign of the ships. Some warning must have reached them. They had turned across the Channel to Pembrokeshire, where their 1400 soldiers disembarked, and then surrendered peaceably to the Cardigan militia.

During that anxious year the two young poets, both strangers, arrived at Nether Stowey in the Quantocks and walked by day and night in the hills overlooking the sea.

A government agent was sent to shadow them. Wordsworth on his first visit to France in 1791, while he was still at Cambridge, had been enraptured by the Revolution, and wrote of it later as a blissful dawn. Coleridge and Southey, as undergraduates, had planned to form a communistic colony, a 'pantisocracy', in Pennsylvania, but the idea came to nothing. More recently, as a Unitarian minister, Coleridge had preached about war and peace, Church and state, worldliness and Christianity, and had inveighed against the practice of 'crimping' – the impressment of country lads for the army.[6] A 'Republican', John Threlwall, came visiting, and he and Coleridge walked in the hills, calling each other Citizen Samuel and Citizen John. Wordsworth and Coleridge discussed philosophy, and the spy, who happened to have a long nose, complained that they were always talking about him as Spinoza. Coleridge, being a Devon man, was comprehensible, but Wordsworth spoke – said Hazlitt – with 'a deep guttural intonation, and a strong tincture of the northern burr, like the crust on wine'. The villagers watched and pondered, and concluded that Coleridge had little harm in him, 'for he was a crack-brained, talking fellow; but that Wordsworth, they said, is either a smuggler or a traitor, and means mischief. He never speaks to any one, haunts lonely places, walks by moonlight, and is always *booing* about by himself.'[7]

There was little harm in either of them, really. In 1798 the continental kaleidoscope shifted a little, and Wordsworth and Coleridge both left for Germany, a home of Romanticism and philosophy at that time. By then they had published their little volume of *Lyrical Ballads*. It was a great landmark of change in poetry, but they were not the men for active revolution.

The fortunes of war swung back and forth. The naval mutiny was contained, the sailors' grievances partly redressed, and very soon the ships were at sea again, first defeating the Dutch and then, at the Nile, under the brilliant young naval officer, Nelson, ruining the fleet – and the ambitious plans – of the brilliant young Corsican general who was soon to be First Consul of France. Four years later peace was signed, but it was little more than an armistice. Buonaparte used it to strengthen the French navy (while we made economies in ours). In 1803 war was renewed, England stood alone, and again the future looked very dark. Napoleon had 100 000 soldiers encamped at Boulogne for nearly three years, waiting to invade, but his ships could never get past our navy to bring his army across the Channel.

Here, everything possible had to be done to reinforce the fleet, the mainstay of defence. Merchant ships and their crews were requisitioned in very large numbers. The levy fell hard on the Western Venturers, and combined with enemy attacks at sea, it virtually ended their Newfoundland trade. There were Exmoor sailors with Nelson and Collingwood, and Exmoor soldiers with Wellington at Waterloo, but they have no memorial. Some died and were buried at sea or on foreign battlefields. Some came home maimed and depended on parish relief. Some returned safe and sound, with their tales to tell. Parson Thornton said that as a young man he had known 'many of the tough fellows who, often unable to read or write, fought under these great commanders – men who, against great odds, had held Hougomont for twelve hours', or had made one enemy battleship a bridge to get at another.

There was no doubt about the risk of invasion: on a sunny day the glint of the French bayonets could be seen from Dover, as the soldiers marched and drilled, and enterprising boat-owners on the south coast went part-way across the channel to have a closer look. King George himself insisted on sailing further out from Weymouth than his retinue thought wise. Napoleon's transport barges were ready to be towed across, but – like Hitler's in 1940 – they were never used. Thomas Hardy, who had been fascinated in boyhood by the reminiscences of old Dorset villagers, gives the whole flavour of the time in *The Trumpet Major* – dragoons encamped on the downs behind Weymouth, farm-hands being instructed before Sunday service in the use of rifles, even if they only had pikes, press-gangs taking young men for the navy, old men tending the fire-beacons, and a false alarm which sent half-trained volunteers cantering to defend the beaches, while the womenfolk went inland in gigs or carts.

Exmoor was not immune. Napoleon might attempt a surprise landing from the Bristol Channel, so the whole south-western peninsula was preparing to fend him off; the sea was watched, the beacons were manned, the militia was strengthened. A most remarkable young cavalry officer, Sir Robert Wilson, was appointed as inspecting officer for Somerset and Devon. He was then twenty-six years old; nine years earlier he had distinguished himself in Flanders by helping to prevent the capture of the Austrian Emperor, who in gratitude gave him a medal specially struck and made him a Baron of the Holy Roman Empire – hence his English knighthood. Then he fought at the Nile, corresponded with Nelson, and wrote a brief history of the campaign. By temperament he was a freelance and a firebrand; he was said to be 'never out of action if within possible reach'. In 1803 there was none available, but safeguarding the threatened shores was a useful alternative. One little group of his men was billeted in North Molton; his personality made such an impression that the cottages they occupied were later named after him. (The officers' quarters still stand, and so does the shed in which their horses may have been stabled; the very humble lodgings of the private soldiers have since been replaced by garages, and their name – Wilson's – transferred to the stronger cottages, formerly Prospect Place.) The soldiers had only a few miles to ride, up rough tracks, to the ridge from which, in good weather, the whole westerly sweep of Barnstaple Bay is clear, right down to Hartland Point and over to Lundy. There must have been other platoons, now forgotten, at vantage points along the northern coast. Hints may survive in parish registers; at North Molton several men with up-country surnames, described as 'sojourners', married local girls at that time.

Meanwhile, contingency plans were made, and directions sent to every parish for evacuation and a scorched-earth policy if the French should land. Few copies of these survive, but there is a set, photographed and framed, in Molland church. The general instructions were printed; this set came from Exeter, but they must have been nationally devised, and sent to county towns for completion. Spaces were left on each form for the insertion of names and local particulars, which can only have been gathered by enquiry on the spot. (Hardy mentions a 'government man' visiting 'Overcombe' in Dorset for that purpose.)

The Molland papers are four, called 'Schedules for the removal of the Stock etc. etc.' and dated 1803. The instructions for stock-owners are addressed to Mr James Quartly. On receiving orders, he is to direct four named drivers to proceed with their animals to Molland Town (the high ground beside the church, above Town Meadow). They are to take provisions for a few days, and put themselves under the command of Mr Henry Quartly. The handwritten note which follows gives the number of people who have livestock to remove if the French approach, and the superintendents are to see that they are fully informed of the relevant plans, and the line of march as soon as that is decided. (The Quartlys of Great Champson and West Molland, breeders of the famous Red Devon cattle, were the obvious people to take charge of this.)

Next is a schedule addressed to 'the Conductors and Overseers of Stock'. These were Messrs Henry Quartly, Richard Frost, John Cockram of West Lee, and James Loosemore. The printed instructions are: 'On receiving Orders, you are to proceed to ... (Molland Town) there to take on you the Charge of conducting the Stock under your Care, to such Place, and by such Route, as shall be pointed out to you by the Superintendent of your Parish, and you are to take with you, Provisions for yourself for a few Days, and a Blanket: as your Route, in all probability, will be either towards the open Grounds about Somerton, in Somersetshire, in one case, or towards Dartmoor, in the other; you will proceed by the Roads that are pointed out to you below, taking care, in all Cases, to avoid the public Roads, which are to be left open for the Troops, Ammunition-Waggons, etc, and for this Purpose you will take proper Tools for breaking down Hedges, etc.' Then follow, handwritten, the alternative routes. If the landing is on the south coast, they must go from Molland Town over Molland common to Dulverton, then cross the Wiveliscombe roads and pass Gore Inn on their way to Langport and Somerton. In the event of a northern landing the line of retreat is to Dartmoor, and their way is from Molland Town to Bishop's Nympton, on to Mariansleigh and Meshaw, and thence to East Worlington, Lapford, Zeal Monachorum, Sprayton,

Chagford, and 'From Chagford to Dartmoor', where the animals could be turned loose.

Mr James Quartly was not to go with his four drivers; he and Mr John Palfreman and Mr George Frost were appointed to take charge of the 'Dead Stock'. Their brief was 'You are to remain in your Parish and to act as you shall receive Orders from the General Officer, or Deputy Lieutenants of your Division. If the Enemy should approach very near you before you can receive Orders so to do, you are to destroy the Hay and Corn, and the Cattle of all Description, particularly the Horses not retained for public Service, and render useless all the unemployed Carts and Waggons, before you remove yourselves; but this step is not to be taken, unless in the last Extremity; and you are to assure all those, whose Property is thus destroyed, that they will be repaid for their Losses, provided it shall appear that they have complied with the proposed Regulations of Government, and lent their best Aid to promote the Public Service.'

Two schedules are humanitarian. Instructions go 'to the owners of waggons and carts appointed for the removal of the sick and infirm', and 'to the conductors and overseers of the said waggons'. All are to repair to Molland Town on receiving orders so to do. The first document names four owners, John Cockram and three others. Each is recommended to send provisions for his horses and driver for two days, and a spare set of shoes and nails for each of his horses, 'together with Pickaxes, and such other Tools as are fit for the Use of the Pioneers, which will be required for the purpose of making Breaches through Hedges, in case it should be found necessary'.

The next schedule tells the two conductors – John Cockram and another – the alternative lines of march, and enjoins them, too, to leave all public roads clear for the army, and be sure they have proper tools for breaching hedges. (This could hardly be said too often; a diversion of all the carts and sheep and cattle of even one moorland parish into a deep and narrow 'highway' might have been a crucial hindrance to troops.) The printed order ends: 'You are to be very careful of all those placed under your Charge, and provide for them in the best Manner you shall be able.'

The instructions to the owners raised difficulties. The general order had ended, 'The List of Persons to be conveyed in your Waggon is subjoined', and the heading 'A List of Names' was printed above a space ruled into three blank columns. But what follows instead is a long handwritten note with two postscripts.

'N.B. There is in this parish 41 Old and Infirm people Incapable of removing themselves and 105 Children under ten years of Age. And there being but 7 Draft Horses and 80 pack Horses in the parish. It is to be suppos'd that those Horses must be retained for the removal of the Infirm folks and Children and to be placed

124

in the Waggons and those Carts and on Horseback in pursuance of the directions to be given by Messrs Francis Quartly and John Mogridge the appointed Superintendents.' Given the awkward numbers, a little incoherence is not surprising. The postscripts are helpful, none the less: 'N.B. Mr John Palfreman has one light Waggon that he must retain for the removal of his own numerous family. And one cart with convenient horses Mr Palfreman retains for the publick services.' And finally, 'N.B. George Andrew will drive his own Cart.' George Andrew was one of the owners named; John Palfreman was not, so his would be a fifth available cart. He himself had been detailed to stay and destroy the 'dead stock'.

The need never arose, but for two full years the invasion was expected, and every village had plans like these. John Thorne of North Radworthy listed the danger cheerfully among the topics of churchyard talk on Sunday mornings:

> What Battles have been fought at sea
> And who has gained the Victory
> What ships are took'd or cast away
> And when to Depford or to Dover
> Buonaparte is coming over
> And when he comes how we shall fare...

'When' he says, not 'if'.

Nelson, chasing the French fleet across the Atlantic and back, was so much too much for its admiral, Villeneuve, that Napoleon gave up hope of ever getting the ships to Boulogne, and marched his soldiers away to Austerlitz in Moravia, where he overwhelmed the Austrian army. Just after he left the Channel coast Villeneuve's fleet came out of Cadiz harbour and was shattered at Trafalgar. Though Nelson died in the action, his work was done. The risk of invasion was over.

At home, this was immediately recognized, and the whole country celebrated its relief, though it mourned its hero. South Molton declared a week's holiday, and among the events was an ox-roast in a field at North Molton. Almost the entire population of South Molton set out for this, on foot or on horseback, calling at twenty-three ale-houses on the way. (The distance, by the 'old road' is less than 3 miles, all farmland now.) When they arrived at the appointed field the gateway proved too narrow for the Mayor's coach, and a team of horses had to be fetched to drag up one gatepost with chains – an old longstone, perhaps? There must have been similar rejoicing in every moorland and coastal village and town, and spontaneous parties to welcome sailors home. Maybe some medals or souvenirs are still treasured by descendants – Trafalgar mugs or plates perhaps, rare now but very popular at the time, or a table inlaid with darker wood at one corner in sad commemoration. There seem to be no records or memorials on Exmoor, but it is pleasant to wonder whether the five guns which serve now as bollards on Lynmouth quay were trophies from a French ship, taken as prize by a crew containing officers or men from this tiny fishing-port.[8]

The war turned away from the coasts. The five-year struggle in the Iberian peninsula began in 1808. (Sir Robert Wilson of the 20th Light Dragoons, by now a brigadier-general, was there, true to form, commanding a 'Lusitanian Legion' of Portuguese soldiers whom he had recruited and trained himself.) At home, hardships and shortages continued. The price of Exmoor ponies rose, from £120.5s.0d. for twenty-seven in 1805 to £201 for twenty-eight in 1809; were they too, sent to work with Wellington's army in mountainous Spain?

Then Napoleon made his fatal mistake – the invasion of Russia. (Wilson heard of this at the British Embassy in Constantinople, and set out at top speed for St Petersburg, with only a pair of saddle-bags as luggage. He paused for a few days with the Russian army, which was defending Smolensk against the advancing French, and then hurried on to Petersburg to see the Czar and the British Ambassador and get himself appointed as an attaché in the field. He missed Borodino and the burning of Moscow, but rejoined Kutuzow's army for the long pursuit of the French in their terrible winter retreat. 'The English General' insisted on riding all the way, like his Cossack friends, and spent much of every night writing despatches and letters and keeping a journal of what he had seen and heard, thought and done, each day.)[9] Buonaparte abandoned the remnant of his army at the half-frozen Beresina, hurried to France and raised new regiments, but was defeated by Austrians and Germans at Leipzig; in 1814, encircled in France itself, he was unable to enter Paris, and abdicated.

That seemed to be the end of the war which had begun twenty-one years earlier. The young generation had no memory of peace, but had been brought up to execrate Boney, who was now an exile in Elba. The whole nation rejoiced – as in 1918, and as in 1945.

South Molton was adept at such festivities. It had held others – for the victories of the Nile and Trafalgar – and there would be another in a year's time, when Napoleon had slipped out of Elba, rallied the French army to his leadership once more, and been narrowly but finally defeated at Waterloo. In 1814 the little town kept holiday for a week and the rejoicings were recorded in vivid detail.

They began at three o'clock in the morning on Monday, 13th June, with church bells ringing and two bugles sounding. The inhabitants were soon busy 'dressing all doors and windows with laurels and flowers and evergreen, so that the streets had

126

the appearance of a shrubbery'. There were tables in 'Market Street' (the Square) for 1700 people, the places all numbered and allocated, and the company dined on roast beef and plum pudding, 'as quiet as ten would in a parlour, and all had as much beer as they would drink'. The waiters were the gentlemen and chief tradesmen of the town; on a high scaffold in the centre a band played merrily all dinner-time, and mirth and harmony continued – the numbers growing to more than two thousand – for the rest of the day.

On Tuesday a procession of all the trades in their uniforms was perhaps a rehearsal for greater things on Thursday; there were 'music, singing and dancing – rich and poor together – on the pavement, also tea thereon for all the weavers', and at midnight a firework display. Wednesday was Fair day, so 'very little worth record took place' but everyone was in happy holiday mood.

Thursday was the real gala day. Early in the morning the two bugle-horns were blown, to remind every trade to be ready by ten o'clock for the procession. The school-children headed this, followed by the constables and mace-bearers, the Corporation 'in their scarlet dress' and a great number of other gentlemen and ladies. Next came the first contingent of craftsmen, the Gardeners, each with a belt of flowers, an orange growing in a pot, and a cucumber fastened to the right arm with blue ribbons. A plough ('drawn by two well-trained oxen') preceded the Seedsmen, Reapers and Mowers in their Holland shirts, 'with their hook and scythe neatly beautified'. Then Farmers and Labourers, their emblem a white rod, corn and laurels tied to it with ribbons, 'and so on with the whole art of agriculture'. Suddenly wider vistas opened – 'a Cossack soldier on a grey horse in all the Cossack uniform', and silk flags with gold-lettered texts, *King and Queen* and *Friendship and Unity*. A large bevy of women weavers was evidence of change wrought by the long war; 250 of them took part, 'with their shuttles, some gilded, some painted blue, but all fastened on the top of white rods with garlands and ribbons'. After them came the Bishop and his chaplain, their carriage drawn by four greys, 'then the Shepherd and Shepherdess, Lamb and Dog, the Shearers, Jason with the Fleece on the top of a pole in the midst of a beautiful garland'. There were Combers, Shopkeepers and 'Tailors accompanied by a great number of Needle Women dressed in white, each having by her side a blue silk work bag, their scissors hung round their necks with blue ribbons'. Again interest swung further away – 'Four couple of sailors, four carrying a ship and four with flags'. Behind them came members of all the other trades which sustained the community – butchers, maltsters, masons, cabinet-makers and carpenters, rope, bag and twine-makers, 'all the rod and basket-workers', thatchers and waggoners; and 'every man had a belt made out of their profession, and every one carried an implement of their employ'.

About 1500 people took part; they had thirty-two flags in all, 'most handsome and painted for the different professions'. Travellers thought it a grand sight, and said so. By evening there was an immense crowd from neighbouring parishes; 'the day closed with near 500 couple of rich and poor all in harmony together, dancing on the pavement'.

They had great stamina. On Friday there was a public dinner and tea in the streets for labourers – partly at their employers' expense – and in the evening the Corporation gave a supper and ball at the Town Hall for 200 people. The ball lasted until seven in the morning and concluded the week-long celebration.

It showed the good side of a system which, like most others, left much to be desired. In this small community, town and country interwoven, everybody's place was clear, and was maintained with modest pride; the needlewomen with their scissors were honoured with the rest. Soon the wool industry would decline and the social pattern would crack, but still hold for a time. Change was coming to Exmoor, comparable with the great Tudor rearrangement, but in this midsummer week of well-planned rejoicing one can still catch a glimpse of the England of the mediaeval guilds, of Chaucer's weaver and dyer in their solemn livery, of his random company making their pilgrimage a holiday, rich and poor together, and the host of a Southwark inn organizing their mutual entertainment and keeping the 'harmony' when it came under strain.

PART III

YESTERDAY ON THE MOOR

CHAPTER EIGHT

Continuity and change

New ideas about farming had been developing in other parts of England in the eighteenth century and began to spread to Exmoor during the long gruelling Napoleonic Wars. For fifty years or more, owners of great estates had been experimenting to improve their stock and increase their yield; the total acreage of farm land had been very much enlarged by the drainage of fens and marshes, which had begun in the seventeenth century under Dutch guidance. 'Agricultural improvement' became a fashionable interest as well as a profitable investment, and attracted men of enterprise, ability and wealth like 'Turnip' Townshend and Thomas Coke of Holkham.

The market was expanding fast, for a rapidly growing populace. Hungry workers in the overcrowded industrial towns had nowhere to grow their own food, and the frequent wars had checked supplies from overseas. A few months after the outbreak in 1793 of the long struggle with France, Parliament recommended to the King ('Farmer George') that a 'Board of Agriculture and Internal Improvement' be formed, and promised that 'His Faithful Commons would cheerfully defray any expense up to £3000'. This was inaugurated at once, under the chairmanship of the eminent investigator and agricultural writer Arthur Young. Its first move was to invite authoritative surveys, county by county, of current farming practice, with suggestions for improvement. Exmoor and its fringes in west Somerset and north Devon were considered in both the county reviews – Billingsley's of Somerset in 1794, and Vancouver's of Devon in 1808. Consequently, we have vivid accounts of how it all looked and what work was being done and how, just before the face of the moor was altered by enclosures, draining, cultivation, the new machinery and the intermittent mining.

These experienced countrymen described carefully, for the strangers on the Board in London, the particular difficulties of climate and contour in the hill country, and the measures taken locally to overcome them. Looking through their eyes we see teams of beautiful Red Devon oxen ploughing the lower slopes, packhorses carrying dungpots up to the higher fields, pannier-fashion, while the native sheep – sturdy little Exmoor Horns – grazed indefatigably out on the moor. There are minute accounts of the hedgers' work – making the earth and stone banks, planting beeches or other hardwoods along the flat tops, and then sowing fir, elder, blackthorn and brambles on the windward side, above the reach of browsing cattle, to protect the growth of the slower trees; Billingsley noted that beeches were the most resistant to salty winds. Vancouver explained exactly how the farmers' wives clotted their cream, how the apprentice system worked – well for boys, badly for girls, who were too often put to outdoor work instead of being trained by the housewife – and how the wrestling bouts, the young men's favourite sport, were arranged.

At Great Champson and West Molland the Quartlys, tenants there during the greater part of the eighteenth and nineteenth centuries, were breeding the Red Devons to a very high standard. Coke of Norfolk stocked Holkham with them and spread their fame. Arthur Young visited Champson and thought very well of them; Billingsley said they were universally considered the best draught-oxen in the kingdom.

Vancouver describes their working life. After a year's gentle initiation while they were two years old, they were put to all the 'ordinary labours of the yoke' for about eight hours a day, from the age of three to five or six; farmers reckoned that from three to five their value for labour increased by a shilling a head every week. In summer 'these patient animals' were sent to forage for themselves in the coarse pastures; in winter their range was much the same, but with access to the straw-yard for fodder and lodging. There they would spend the night if the yard was not too wet and uncomfortable, but if it was, they would leave it and look for somewhere better.

At Swincombe farm, Challacombe, on the western border of the Forest, family memories go back a long way. Jack Huxtable, who retired from farming it in the 1980s, and his brother George, recount what their father heard from an old countryman, Richard Jones, who had ploughed in Challacombe with draught-oxen when he was young.[1] Early in the morning, he said, three pairs of the Red Devon steers would be herded quietly into a paddock near the road, yoked, and led to the field. Then one man with a long goad piloted them on a straight course, encouraging them by name all the way, while another steadied the plough. Names the old man recalled were Fortune, Beauty, Honey, Speedwell, Good Luck, Pretty Boy and Flower.

A similar memory handed down for three generations at Knighton farm, Withypool, was that the ploughman had a kind of *chant*, in which all the names were used. Harry Reed, the farmer telling me of this in 1950, could only call two lines to mind:

> Good Luck come and Merry,
> Pretty, Spark and Cherry.

He explained that the use of the names was essential. The owners chose names that would 'run well together', and if a bullock died, the newcomer must have the same name, or one that would slip equally easily into the verse. 'Whether it kep'm in a good temper, or whether they walked to the rhythm, I don't know. I don't know how they got the oxen to know their names, but all the names had to be in – and that chanting was the essentional thing. (Harry often lengthened a long word, to give it still more force.)

In *A Shepherd's Life*, in 1910, W. H. Hudson quoted from an old travel book, published in 1808, a long account of Cornish ploughmen talking to their teams in a simple but melodious chant.[2] Hudson could not discover any living memory of this, though he asked very old men who had worked on the land all their lives, but in the same year as the record from Cornwall, Vancouver in Devon described the same thing with brief precision, though neither gave any of the words. He said that the ploughboy, who would be walking beside the leading pair, cheered the team on 'with a song he continually chants in low notes, suddenly broken and rising a whole octave. The ceasing of the song is said to occasion the stopping of the team.'

Harry Reed's grandfather, as a boy, learnt to coax the team along like this, somewhere about the middle of the nineteenth century. Perhaps ox-ploughing, like other customs, continued longer on Exmoor than elsewhere, and as the old ways died out, details like this were preserved in talk at the fireside on winter evenings. Neighbours lived a long, muddy journey away, and there was of course no entertainment coming over the air. Well told, the anecdotes about known characters or their forebears, set in familiar surroundings, were better than fiction, and not so strange. They may not be remembered much longer now.

The Red Devons made very good meat, when their few years at the yoke were over. (Until half-way through the present century they were the normal cattle on the moor, kept for beef and for their rich creamy milk.) Billingsley says their value in the London meat markets drew graziers from the Midlands to buy them for fattening; Vancouver speaks of buyers from the Somerset lowlands feeding them up to sell to butchers in Bath, Bristol or London. A few decades later the farm-hands who knew the animals might drive them to the great cattle-fairs. Richard Jones described how he had helped to take a drove of 300 from several Challacombe farms to Blackwater Fair, 9 miles west of London, where they were all sold. For field work they would have been shod lightly – on both sides of the cloven hoof in front, because the shoulders were taking the weight, but the hind feet outside only, or not at all. For long journeys all four feet might have half-shoes on the outer side only, allowing for the splay. On the three weeks' walk by primitive roads from Challacombe to Blackwater the 300, divided into three equal groups for easier handling, were attended by a farrier, with his tools slung over a pack-horse's back, and at the evening halt he shod or reshod any beast which might otherwise go lame. After the fair, it took the Challacombe drover just a week to walk home. Recalling it all, long afterwards, he said they had passed close to 'one of the seven wonders' (Stonehenge, lonely and impressive beside the ancient track). And he regretted that when he was so near London he had not 'been in to see it'. (Exmoor people until two or three generations ago said that if you had once been to London you wouldn't die a fool.)

There were very few carts yet – the moorland 'highways' were too steep and rough. Pack-horses were the carriers: Molland, with its seven draught-horses and eighty pack-horses, was probably typical. These invaluable animals were a special breed, bigger than the native Exmoor ponies, but developed to their best in these hills, and sought after by discerning buyers from up-country. Fourteen or fifteen hands high, they were sure-footed, had powerful shoulders, and were willing as well as strong enough to travel eight or nine hours a day carrying a load of 240 lb (a 'seam' of corn or dung, or a 'pack' of wool). Ten or a dozen horses in a string followed the best one, always placed as leader. They would carry anything which would go into the panniers on either side of the saddle, and they were used about the farm as well as on long journeys.

If the load was unwieldy, tall wooden 'crooks' were fixed to the saddle instead of panniers, and at harvest-time the sheaves were wedged one upon another between these. When the corn had been delivered in the barn or at the stack, the horse was ridden back to the field for its next load, and the whole harvest was safe under cover in a shorter time – according to a contemporary observer[3] – than could be managed by waggons or in any other way.

The wild ponies, the sturdy native Exmoors, were tamed at need for rough riding. The Forester had a yearly sale of them at Simonsbath, and local farmers then and long afterwards relied on the ponies' sure knowledge of the moor and on the untiring strength which would carry them through a long day's work, shepherding or cattle-droving or travelling to a distant market and back, and perhaps a little poaching after dark. (To quote, anonymously, a farmer's praise: 'So soon's pony felt the fish on 'is shoulders 'e was away, and no river-bailiff couldn't have caught us'.)

They are almost the last pure survivors, anywhere, of the primitive horse. It may be that about 100 000 years ago their ancestors came by land from Canada to the north of Scotland and wandered down the hill-ridges of England and Wales and into the far south-west.[4] Much later, human invaders brought bigger horses from the continent, and nearly everywhere these, by deliberate or chance crossing, changed the identity of the ponies. On the Forest the strain was still pure when John Knight bought the land, and a few herds were saved – by the Aclands, who ran them on Winsford Hill, and by the Miltons of Withypool – and were carefully kept from adulteration. Both Knights, father and son, tried to 'improve' the ponies by crossing them with hunters, and even with Dongola Arabs, but the hybrids at once lost the characteristics which had kept them independent in the wild for so long. Recently, some new herds have been formed, by careful selection, but there are new risks, man-made – more fencing, heavier grazing of the moor by sheep and cattle, and very little demand from farmers – and the survival of the true wild ponies depends on the devotion of a few owners.

The pure Exmoor – small, brown, with distinctive mealy muzzle – is perfectly adapted to endure the harshest weather. Its deep-set eyes are well guarded from stinging winds and driving rain; in winter it has two coats, one of fine hair, warm, next to the skin, under a great thick, shaggy, greasy overcoat which keeps the cold out and the body-heat in. Snow lies on this coat without melting, and can be shaken off from time to time; the tail is similarly protected by a 'snow-chute' of short hairs, fan-like at the top. Most important of all, the ponies can always find food, even when the hills are deep in snow. The loss of this ability in the mongrels meant they had to be given hay; to the working farmer that made the thoroughbred far more valuable.

Billingsley thoroughly approved. Writing at the beginning of the wars with revolutionary France he estimated that horses which were stabled in winter needed, for fodder, as much land as under normal cultivation would feed five men; so, he said, 'every man who keeps an unnecessary horse is an enemy to his country by retarding the increase of his own species'. But he was enthusiastic about the Exmoors bred on the Forest: 'The small horses (in the whole upwards of 400) are not taken into better keeping, nor to more sheltered grounds, during the severest winter. When

133

the snow covers the forest to the depth of many feet, these hardy animals are seen in droves, traversing the little vallies and sheltered parts, gathering their scanty fare from the banks of the rivulets and warm springs, but the sheep are almost all driven off for the winter, in the months of November, December and January, according as the season is more or less severe.'

The winters of really deep snow, testing the hardihood of man and beast, did not come every year. Wet summers might be a worse worry, ruining the hay and corn and threatening famine, as John Thorne of North Radworthy had recounted in his diary in 1799. In the years after Waterloo he wrote of dreadful weather again: '1816. From Midsummer to Lady Day 1817 the Wettest Time ever known in our age. The Hay Badly made. The Corn badly saved, no wheat in the Hill Countries would make dry bread.' Six years later it was worse still. '1823. Very wet summer ... July and August very wet. Worst Hay made ever known. September a fortnight very wet weather for the late hay and In country Harvest. Snow and High Wind blowed down 100 trees at Castle Hill and Hundred in North Molton. There were sheep under snow on Exmoor in this Storm it was on the 30th Day of September. Us had a very wet corn Harvest this year.' Then in 1825 and 1826 the trouble was drought – worse in the second year, when all the springs were feeble and North Radworthy well was so low that they 'could get no good Water, even in the Morning'.

Difficult country, a difficult climate and a hard life – and worst for those who had no money to cushion them against misfortune. We hear of them, but not yet from them – so few were literate. Exmoor had no ploughboy poet, no Robert Burns or John Clare. But far away, *The Rights of Man* had been written, the French Revolution had led on to the Reign of Terror, and Billingsley and Vancouver, themselves kindly and well-educated men doing good work, were wary about literacy for peasants. Both urged, with obvious sincerity, that they wanted to see cottagers industrious and contented, but both said that the poor had lost their proper pride through having to take parish relief during the bad years.

Billingsley deplored 'a growing dissoluteness in the manners of the poor, which ever accompanies national improvement'. He said that higher wages, due to scarcity of labour, instead of disposing the workman to keep his family in greater comfort or to save for a time of need, had encouraged him to work a shorter week. More sympathetically, he recommended the establishment of Friendly Societies, which would help the labourer at the most difficult time, when he had five or six small children, could barely feed them, and had to borrow if he fell ill. If this kept happening before he could clear his debts, his spirit was broken. Friendly Societies would involve the bachelor in helping the married, and this might have the further advantages of checking 'the celibacy too evident among the lower orders of mankind', and adding to the comfort of wedlock and to the population of the realm, alarmingly depleted by the wars.

Vancouver, after making his practical recommendations on draining and moorland reclamation, broke out eloquently against the idea of *educating* the poor: he was shocked to learn that even the King and Queen had been encouraging this. Reading and writing, and consequent communication by letters and pamphlets, bred discontent and emigration, he said; and 'the number of pen and ink gentry on board our ships of war' had created and maintained the mutiny of 1797. 'In short, the peasant's mind should never be inspired with a desire to amend his circumstances by the quitting of his caste; but every means the most benevolent and feeling heart can devise, should be employed to make that situation as comfortable and as happy to him as possible.' The best means would be to foster a pride in doing *any* job well, even stone-breaking for limekilns or highway repair.

Spoken of collectively like this, 'the poor' seem faceless; but centuries of Christian teaching had hallowed the term, and in the villages the poor were not segregated. The parish councillors, the parish clerk, the farmers paying the parish rate on which the unfortunate depended, knew them as needy neighbours, hard-working or feckless, awkward or agreeable, honest or light-fingered. Eighteenth- and nineteenth-century wills show the sense of local obligation. Farmers had solid property to leave, but not much ready money; they provided for their families with land or possessions, perhaps supplemented by an annuity, or one or two golden guineas to be paid within six months. So a bequest of money to the poor of Withypool in 1732 is noteworthy. £5 was to be shared among them, 30/- the day after the testator's funeral, the rest in equal parts quarterly for a year, and in addition £5 was to be invested in stock for ever, the interest to be divided among them year by year.

That was James Hill, yeoman farmer of Newland, Withypool. His family held this small farm on the sunny side of the Barle valley from 1657 until 1920, and probate copies of all the owners' wills, and most of the deeds as they leased, bought or sold neighbouring lands and tenements, have survived together.[5] Father was succeeded by son, John and James, John and James, until in 1810 the second James, who had no children, left it to a nephew, another John Hill, not yet of age. He, in 1862, bequeathed Newland and Hillway to his two sons, John and James, both minors. Only the elder lived to inherit, and before long he left the moor, mortgaged and let Newland, and ultimately, in 1920, as an old man, sold all his remaining Withypool property.

He was of the sixth generation, but was the seventh owner (his great-grandmother, Mistress Joan, had ruled for nine years after her husband's death) and nearly all of them bequeathed money to the poor of Withypool. The matriarch Joan, in 1777, decreed that every person on parish relief and over the age of twenty-one was to be given one shilling, 'to be paid unto such of them as will apply for the same the Sunday after my interment'. Her son, the second James, was more imaginative. In 1810 he thought about the need, in those war years, of the poor labourers who, though parishioners, were *not* drawing monthly relief. (Either they were not quite poor enough to qualify, or they had kept the pride in independence which Billingsley thought was lost.) £5 was to be divided equally among them and paid within six months of his death. Also he wished *all* the poor of Withypool to be invited to his dwelling-house at Newland farm the day after his funeral, 'then and there to have plenty of Meat and Drink to the discretion of my Executor'. (There is no punctuation, but perhaps a comma after 'meat' was implied?)

However difficult the times, the long chain of wills shows an enviable confidence in stability. The farmer would leave land to his lawful heirs 'for ever', and it was to be properly farmed, fences maintained, farm gear and household goods treated with respect, and all passed on in good condition. And as far as possible the whole family must be left secure. The documents illuminate the life that went on in the same place, and in much the same way, for rather more than 200 years.

It began in 1657 with the John Hill who was Boevey's Deputy Warden. In 1653, when Parliament had confiscated all royal estates, the Londoner of Dutch Huguenot origin who bought Exmoor depended, of course, on local men for knowledge of the Forest. At first he retained the last Royalist Warden's deputy, Nicholas Rawlinson of Exford (the guide who had given only scanty help to Parliament's surveyor, Jeremy Baines) but after a year they parted, and Boevey appointed the young farmer John Hill instead. Three years later Hill took a ninety-nine year lease of Newland, by agreement with John Menefie of Halberton, owner since 1629. (The last *occupant* had been 'Dorothy Hill, widow, deceased'.) In the conveyance John Hill is described as 'of Simonsbath'. Perhaps he was encamped in some corner of Simonsbath House while it was being built: there was no other.

He held office as Boevey's deputy for twenty years, and left shortly before the great dispute about the ownership of the commons. He was called as witness by both sides, and his testimony was suitably discreet. Other depositions show him as a respected agent, proclaiming the annual agistment rates ('crying the moor'), conducting the perambulations, punishing farmers who stole cattle or sheep off the moor by confiscating theirs. (The clerk of the court, impressed, described him as 'gentleman'.) As a Free Suitor – Newland carried three 'suits' – he was entitled to free grazing on the Forest for 420 sheep, fifteen mares and foals, and as many bullocks as he could keep on the farm in winter. Whether he used his full entitlement is not sure: the inventory made for probate in 1693 gives 'sheep of all sorts £20' and 'horses and foals £10' but no cattle. His total estate was valued at £110.1s.8d. That would have to be very much multiplied to give its modern equivalent; there are readier indications of homely prosperity in other items:

In brass crooks and other brass[6]	...	£6. 5. 0.
In pewter	...	£2.10. 0.
In linen	...	£2. 0. 0.
In plate and rings	...	£5. 0. 0.

He had made his will eleven years earlier, when he was fifty-four; it is simple, devout and unpretentious. 'I John Hill of Withypoole in the county of Somerset yeoman being sick and weak of body but sound of mind and memory thanks be to Almighty God ... do now make and ordain this my Last Will and Testament in manner and form following. First my soul I humbly recommend unto Almighty God my great Creator hoping in and through the only merits and mediation of the Lord Jesus Christ my Redeemer and Saviour to obtain the pardon of all my Sins and Eternal life when these my days shall have an end. And my body I commit to the Earth therin to be decently interred by Christian Buriall.' Then comes the disposal of his worldly belongings, chiefly the real estate. He provided well for his 'dearly beloved wife Mary', leaving her four properties – in South Molton, Bishop's Nympton, Chulmleigh and one, Greenwood (now Newland Wood), in Withypool. She would draw rent from these, besides an annuity of £20 to be paid quarterly from the Newland estate. She was also to have, for life, 'the full and free use and possession of the two little rooms or chambers lying over the Buttery of my dwelling-house of Newland', half the household goods, and all plate, rings and jewels except one silver watch, which he bequeathed, with everything else, to his son James.

This James held the farm for forty-seven years. His wife must have died before he made his will, in 1732, eight years before his own death. Apart from the £10 already mentioned, to the poor of Withypool, all his estate went to one son, one daughter, the son's daughter Dorothy (£20 to be invested for her until she was twenty-one) and the other grandchildren (a guinea each). His son John was heir to all his lands and tenements in the parishes of Withypool and Hawkridge, but his married daughter, Mary Adams, was to have the remainder of a lease in Little Torrington (these scattered properties must have been bought in good times as safe investments), besides two golden guineas, and half his sheep – the other half going to John. He also left her 'the feather bed on which I usually lay, the Bolster and drawer,[7] two short pillows, one flowered Greenish coverlid, two of my best brass milk pans, one Oak Box marked with the letter E with all those things lockt up in the same, One Oak eight-cornered table board that usually stands in my bed Chamber, and my Exmore Gray Mare with all her increase that is or shall be.'[8]

When John made his will in 1773, he distributed his land and money among a much larger family, headed by his dominant wife. He did not bequeath the farm directly to his elder son, as was customary, but to his 'dear and loving wife Joan' in trust for James and his sons and grandsons. Two trustees were appointed. The will confirmed all that he had previously settled on his wife *or intended*, and she was sole executrix. He had already given dowries to their three married daughters, and now he provided an income for the unmarried one, another Joan, who presumably lived at home. She was to have £50 paid in five yearly parts from a property called Hawse, where she was empowered to distrain if necessary, and also Lanacre until his rights there expired. (They remained in the family until 1843.)

Four years later he died. Almost at once his widow set about making her own will. Very little of the land was hers to bestow, but she had furniture, kitchen-ware, silver and pewter, and plenty of clothes, and she distributed all this in four pages of exact description, signed with her mark and duly witnessed.[9]

James the heir was to have 'the large silver two-handled cup with West Anstey engraved thereon' and three pieces of heavy furniture (the bedstead in the buttery chamber, 'the Beaufet in the Parlour', and the large settle in the kitchen). To his brother John she gave her clock and case, plated tankard, small silver two-handled cup engraved with three letters and the figures 1736, and her tack and weights. So much for sons; then on to the livelier task of sharing personal treasures among four daughters and fourteen grand-daughters. Some of the clothes were already old, and she lived for another nine years, but perishable and durable were fairly balanced in most of the bequests.

The married daughters came first. 'Unto my daughter Dorothy Adams' (who as Dorothy Hill had had £20 invested for her under the will of her grandfather James) 'one silver Salt and silver salt Spoon my plain blue gauze Handkerchief and my white stampt Laun Apron'. To Mary Rock 'my Bed in my Parlour Chamber the under part of my Chest of Drawers my large Oak Table Board my large silver shugar Castor my black silk Gown one of my double-laced Mobs my best laced Handkerchief one of my small flowered Glasses and one of my Mourning Gold Rings'. (The upper part of the chest of drawers went to her grand-daughter Dorothy Hill, who married Richard Rawl of Challacombe.) 'Unto my Daughter Elizabeth Zeale my silver pepper Castor my black Barcelona Handkerchief my old black Quilted Coat my best Stays my red Gown and black silk Hat.'

In addition, Mary and Elizabeth were to have small annuities, to be paid to them 'apart from their present or any after taken Husband or Husbands'. The same precaution applied to 'the dwelling-house in Withypool in which Dorothy Adams now lives'. It was to remain Dorothy's for life, in trust for her unmarried sister Joan – no present or future husband having any right therein.

The bequest to Joan is the most important. First comes an engraved silver cup, then a silk gown trimmed with gold lace, then 'my black laced silk Handkerchief my double laced black silk Handkerchief my best doubled laced Mobb my Hackney Mare my best Bed performed' (meaning complete, with mattress and probably curtains) 'my best Bed Quilt my best Holland sheets my largest and least Copper Boilers my round Mahogany Table Board my large Oaken Table Board my largest Salter except one ... my largest Trendle three of my largest Pewter Dishes four of my best Chairs ... two Half Hogsheads two new Quarter Barrels silver Tea Tongs Silver Salt and salt Spoon'.

It was thoughtful provision for the daughter who had stayed at home and might soon have to live alone. And she was to have the best. In the only gold-laced silk gown, and with two rows of lace round her mob cap and black silk handkerchief she should cut a dignified figure at her round mahogany table – and probably few Exmoor farmhouses could rival that, because the handsome red wood from the West Indies had not long been used in England. Her bedroom, parlour and kitchen would be well-equipped; the second largest salter may have been the most convenient size for her, and the largest trendle would help her through the winter.

Joan was also residuary legatee and as sole executrix had to distribute the legacies to fourteen grand-daughters. (James and John may have been glad to escape that task.) There were three more handkerchiefs and two more aprons, and narrow-laced mob caps. There were two pairs of white gloves, a 'white flowered Coat', a 'cloudy silk Gown' and a white silk hat. A flowered petticoat and an old blue quilted one went to Mary's third and fourth daughters. The first two did better; 'unto my grandaughter Dorothy Rock my blue corner Cupboard in the Parlour one Pewter Dish and half a Dozen Clome Saucers' (which would be sauce-boats) and 'to her sister Mary Rock my white Corner Cupboard a little Trendle my black beaver Hat and one Pewter Dish'. Another grand-daughter was to have the clothes-press and 'my green Cloak with Lace', and yet another 'my white Cloak with Lace'. Arrayed for a wedding or a christening, Easter or Harvest

Home or a shearing feast, Mistress Hill of Newland must have been a fine sight to see.

One hopes she had a good funeral; she had provided for hatbands and gloves to be given to the pall-bearers, her sons-in-law, and mourning gloves to all her grandchildren. It was a pity that the paupers had to *apply* for their shilling a head.

In 1786 her will was proved, and the second James inherited at last. He was gentler than his mother, and more thoughtful – his was the funeral feast for the poor of Withypool, and the legacy for indigent labourers not drawing parish relief. There were shadows in his life. He had no son or daughter. In 1809 his brother, John, the next heir, was seriously ill, and made a will in favour of his one son, another John, not yet of age, asking James to be executor in trust. He must have died soon afterwards; probate was granted in January 1810.

Later that year James made his own will, 'being weak in body but of sound and perfect mind and memory (thank God for it)'. Like his forebears, he bequeathed his soul to God and his body to the dust to be decently buried, and then disposed of his worldly goods. His nephew inherited the farms; there were legacies of money to all his brother's and sisters' children who were living, and to the children of the eldest Dorothy Rawl, who had died. The new tenant of Lanacre was to have 'all my wearing Apparel except my New Buff Breeches',[10] and Sarah Comer of Hillway £5, to be paid at once so that she could buy a suit of mourning for his funeral.

But his first and chief concern was for his wife. The young nephew might not be considerate enough, and the trustee, a solicitor, was 10 miles away in South Molton, so all was carefully set down. 'First I give and bequeath to my wife six and twenty pounds a year of lawful Money of Great Britain to be paid to her every year during her life in lieu of a third of my Lands. Also I give my wife the use of my Parlour and Parlour Chamber with all the furniture in them and the two Rooms the West side of the Passage the Chambers over them and one Bed performed that I commonly Sleep in and convenient Outhouses to keep her fuel in during her life and at her Death and decease it shall descend and come to my Executor but she shall not wilfully do any damage to the Rooms nor diminish any of the furniture nor suffer it to be done. Also I give my Wife Two hundred faggots of wood every Year of her life and the Carriage of all her other fuel to be brought to her when she hath occasion. Also I give my Wife one of my Milk Cows which shall be kept with other Cows in every respect she paying four pounds a year of lawful Money of Great Britain for the keeping on my Estate to my Executor during her life.'

John the nephew was enjoined to occupy the estate himself all his life, and not to sell any dead or living stock except in the normal way of business. He lived a long time – inherited in 1812 and died in 1862 – but at some date he moved away to Old Cleeve, east of Minehead. From there, in 1843, he signed away Lanacre, and the chief rents of Wayhouse, Foxtwitchen, Weatherslade, other Withypool properties including the 'encroachments adjoining Brightworthy', and his manorial rights.

His own will, dated from Old Cleeve a few months before he died, is very long and legalistic – worded by the solicitors at his bedside? Both his sons, John and James, were minors, and he divided the real estate between them, John to have Newland, James to have Hillway and several small 'parcels' including the enclosure on Hawkridge Common now called Four Fields (formerly Tudball's Splats). He wished his wife – unless she remarried – to live with their sons until both were of age, keeping house for them and sharing the use of furniture, books, plate, china and glass, and utensils for the kitchen, dairy and brewhouse. She was also to have an immediate payment of £20, and annuities amounting to £30 a year.

This is the first we hear of books (though the family Bible must always have passed to the heir). They were Dr Clarke's Commentary on the Old Testament, and Butterworth's Concordance, left to the elder son, and the companion Commentary on the New Testament, left, with two volumes of Wood's Dictionary, to James. The dying man was a staunch Wesleyan – as a young owner he had given land on which Withypool's first Methodist Chapel was built[11] – and this coloured his will.

He began by dividing his household goods between the two sons. The list of furniture reflects increased prosperity and ponderous Victorian taste. It includes mahogany and oak tables, two carved oak armchairs, and six mahogany chairs, hair-seated. There were 'sofa and chairs to match' besides a brass pole and scarlet curtains, a pianoforte, a large furnace, a weather-glass, an oak washstand, a pier looking-glass, best and second-best feather-bed and bedstead, and more brass and silver than of old. Even a mahogany bread and cheese tray has separate mention. But after all this the mood changes.

A clause of a new kind empowers the trustees to spend up to £200 per person, for any presumptive heir to any part, 'if they or he shall think fit', for placing him 'in or to any trade profession or employment or otherwise for his or her benefit or advancement in the world'. Then comes an exhortation to the two young sons: 'I earnestly request and enjoin my children ... to receive and entertain the Wesleyan Methodist Preachers and to attend their Ministry at Withypoole at all seasonable opportunities and to assist in supporting the Wesleyan Sunday School at Withypoole it being my fervent desire that my Children may be religiously educated and that they may thereby acquire vital Godliness and to the utmost of their power promote and encourage the same in their houses and families and amongst their neighbours. And it is my strong recommendation and desire that my sons should reside at Withypoole and farm the properties which I have given to them by this my Will for the period of Seven years at least after my decease.' He wished to be buried in Withypool churchyard, and he left £5 to buy bread for the poor of the parish as need arose.

His plans went awry. The younger son died in his minority, so the fourth John, at eighteen, inherited both farms – and indeed both volumes of Dr Clarke's Commentary. Like his father before him he disregarded the testator's wish that he should live on the property and farm it; within five years he was at Watchet, and from there mortgaged Newland for £2000. His mother drew her annuity until her death in 1892, and he found tenants for the farm. In 1920 he sold it for £3170 to Stanley and Frederick Bawden, Exmoor brothers who had been farming near Stonehenge, fattening western sheep for the big up-country markets. He paid off the mortgage and made a statutory declaration that he had owned the property for more than fifty years and that nobody else had any claim on it. So the family's long tenure came to an end.

There may have been both practical and temperamental reasons for the dwindling enthusiasm of the last two John Hills for moorland farming. When the elder inherited, in 1812, farmers were getting good prices, but these dropped in 1815, at the end of the long war. In 1814, 1816 and 1823 Exmoor harvests were ruined by rain, and in 1825 and 1826 by drought; it was a discouraging start for a young man. In 1819 the long deliberations about the future of the Royal Forest ended with inclosure and sale, and allotments were given to neighbouring landowners in lieu of their grazing rights. By then the Hills, as Free Suitors of Newland, East Hole (Hallfield) and Higher Lanacre, had six suits. Their compensation was considerable – 171 acres. But the insatiable buyer of the Crown Allotment was offering high prices for all fragments of the old Forest, and in 1828 John Hill sold him the greater part of his allocation. After the further sales in 1843 much less land remained for the next John, and he preferred a different life, as a seed-merchant in a small town.

Legal enclosure of common lands, characteristic of eighteenth-century farming elsewhere, hardly reached Exmoor until the middle of the nineteenth, except on the Brendons, where Cutcombe and Exton commons were enclosed in 1797, and King's Brompton, Upton and Skilgate in 1804. Neighbouring landowners reclaimed the ground and improved the yield just when the national need for more food was becoming acute. At Brendon Hill farm, for instance, John Roals, Lord Porchester's first tenant, understood the land and the climate so well that he could tackle the job 'right-handed'. His success was recognized and admired, and an article he wrote about his conversion of 'a Moory Hill-Side into Catch-Meadow' won a prize, and was later published in the journal of the Royal Agricultural Society. Further north and west in the old 'purlieus' there was little change yet, but towards 1814 the imminent expiry of the Acland lease of the Forest compelled a decision about the whole future of the King's rough Exmoor estate – and the King, though old and declared mad, was still 'Farmer George', patron of improvement some twenty years earlier.

When Billingsley was asked to make a survey for the new 'Board of Agriculture and Internal Improvement' and make practical suggestions, at the end of the eighteenth century, his advice about Exmoor was not unlike that given to Charles I in 1630, but it was far more detailed. He was well known for his own reclamation work on Mendip, and on Sedgemoor where he was helped by an outstanding landowner and surveyor, Richard Locke of Brent; and to assess the farming potential of Exmoor he probably relied chiefly on Locke, who could draw on personal knowledge.[12] The report is full of sound observation. This part of it begins by saying that in an agricultural survey of Somerset 'it will naturally be expected that particular notice should be taken of the forest of Exmoor; its vast extent, and capability of improvement, render it an object well worthy of attention'.

He gives a careful account of the whole moor, its hills and rivers, pure spring water, bad roads (but with plenty of material at hand for making them 'firm and comfortable') and hilltop swamps with unlimited peat which would serve for household fuel or for burning lime, working iron or smelting ore. He mentions the vein of limestone running from east to west through the Forest, the presence of good slate and some copper and iron, and the regular sea-traffic from the northern ports to South Wales, where foundries were well established. He describes the small estate of Simonsbath, almost in the centre of the Forest – an enclosure of about 200 acres round Boevey's house and farm buildings – and the traditional handling there, by the Forester, of the agistment of 22 000 sheep – which he says, yields little profit to the owner. With fencing, cultivation and manuring, on much the same plan as had succeeded on Mendip, he thinks that 'what is now a barren waste might be made worth from 5 to 20 shillings an acre'. There is an echo of the warning given to Charles I, but this time, with reclamation seen as a national duty and a good long-term investment, it is more optimistic. 'A very large proportion of the whole needs but the spirit and the fortune of some one or more of our wealthy gentlemen in England, whose attention, if turned this way, sanctioned by the royal proprietor, would render the forest of Exmoor in a few years as fair a prospect as the surrounding country.'

Thinking so well of the possibilities, he concludes with detailed advice: 'Let there be a small town or village erected near the middle, suppose by Simonsbath House, which should form proper residences for artificers and husbandmen, to be employed in building farm-houses, and inclosing many a comfortable estate round them. From this centre town, or village, it would be easy to get a supply of provisions and all other necessaries, as a butcher, baker, shopkeeper etc. might be there settled. And till other houses or villages should be built, labourers, artificers and workmen might find lodgings, provisions etc. in the bordering parishes, many of which at this time have more labourers than they can well employ.'

Billingsley's report, suggesting what might be done, was written twenty years before the Acland lease expired, but it must have been carefullly studied by His Majesty's Commissioners when that time drew near. The Aclands had been wardens since 1767, when the seventh baronet, the first Sir Thomas, married the heiress of the Dykes, the wardens and Masters of Staghounds before that. Sir Thomas was a mighty hunter, drawing a very large field of enthusiasts from far and near, and dining and wining afterwards at Holnicote or Pixton, whichever was nearer, all those who were in at the death. (Each house had a silver dinner-service of five dozen plates, scratched by eager use as all those hungry trenchermen fell to.) The wardenship, the hunting, and the management of these two Dyke estates in Somerset gave the family forty years' close knowledge of Exmoor.

In 1808 the third Sir Thomas, tenth baronet, came of age (having inherited as a minor in 1794) and in 1809 or early 1810 he applied for his lease of the Forest to be renewed when it came to an end in 1814. An amalgamation of two government departments was in progress, and reply was delayed, but after a year or two the new Commissioners ordered a survey of the Forest, with special attention to the Navy's need of timber – the war was not yet over. Meanwhile, Sir Thomas wrote to the new department, offering to buy the whole Forest, unenclosed, if the government should think it more profitable to sell the freehold than to renew the lease.

Not until 1814 was the Commissioners' first report submitted to Parliament. Their surveyor had estimated that the extent of the Crown land was about 22 000 acres; he noted that the only trees growing on it were the thirty-seven round Simonsbath farmhouse, but he reckoned that some 9740 acres of the whole would, with simple drainage, grow ash, beech, sycamore, perhaps oak, and conifers. Their conclusion was that Parliament had three choices – to grant a new lease to Sir Thomas Acland, to sell the whole, either privately to him or by public auction, or to inclose and divide, retaining a large Crown allotment which could grow timber if required. The Commissioners disparaged the first, suspecting that there would be no improvement in productivity – perhaps they misconstrued the young baronet, whose energy, directed elsewhere, later made him 'The Great Sir Thomas'. They recommended the third choice, and Parliament adopted it, passed an Inclosure Act, and initiated a detailed study with plans for roads and quarries, and allotments to borderers who had Forest rights. The study was made, but by the time the final report went to Parliament in 1819 the Commissioners had realized that the tall trees fit for ship-building grew in the outer combes and on the slopes of the foothills, and few were likely to thrive in the salty sou'westerlies of the Forest, between 1000 and 1600 feet above sea-level. Besides, the war had ended. So their final decision had been to sell His Majesty's Allotment to the highest bidder, and it was put out to tender in the summer of 1818.

The second and third largest offers came from neighbours who knew the moor – Lord Fortescue to the west and Sir Thomas Dyke Acland to the east – but a farming depression after the war was hampering country landowners, and far the highest bidder was a stranger from Worcestershire, a very wealthy man from a family of successful ironmasters, a Mr John Knight. Money was the only criterion, so to him the Crown land was sold.

John Knight was fifty-five when his purchase was completed. He knew something of lowland farming and reclamation, nothing of the problems of hill country and Atlantic gales. He was another 'Sir Positive', cocksure, but whereas Boevey appointed the young farmer John Hill, from a few miles away, as his deputy, Knight would take no agent. Nor did he consult those who were reclaiming successfully on the Brendons. He thought to transform the whole area himself, to grow corn whatever the altitude, and to emulate the great Norfolk improvers of arable who had made the four-crop rotation famous. Any farming neighbour – John Thorne, for example, just outside his high southern boundary – could have warned him that wheat and barley would seldom succeed on these hills. A Wintershead farmer a century later put it shortly – 'Too near 'eaven, for one thing', and for another, 'nine months winter and three months damn' bad weather'. John Knight never learnt that, but obstinately repeated the attempt year after year.

The Crown Allotment which he bought was less than half of the Forest. It was centred on Simonsbath, its circumference pared down in concessions to borderers. Much the largest allocation was to Sir Thomas Acland, the last Warden, who was given more than 3000 acres to compensate for the Forest tithes. Knight acquired this from him immediately, at a price related to what he had paid for the Crown land, and over the next two decades he

145

bought out many other allotment-holders, until he owned more than three-quarters of the Forest, and also the whole manor of Brendon, including its common. Perhaps he was rather like Abraham Lincoln's farmer who said he wasn't greedy, he only wanted the land *adjoining* his own. Many Exmoor people, then and later, opined that he had very much more money than sense.

John Knight for twenty-two years, and then his eldest son Frederic for twice as long, tried to break and tame the Forest, and their story was told fully and sympathetically by the agriculturalist C. S. Orwin in *The Reclamation of Exmoor Forest*, in 1929. Orwin admired the whole venture, and wanted to rebut the criticism of those who, he said, 'failed to see the real achievement through the haze of costly experiment and misdirected effort'. But in the father's time, that haze was very dense.

He ignored Billingsley's recommendation to begin by making a village in the centre, round Simonsbath House (a licensed inn at that time, and still the only dwelling-house in the Forest). He had no plan to colonize the moor, and preferred to employ only unmarried men, who slept in makeshift dormitories in the farm buildings. Some lodged at Exford, which throve by selling supplies and services to the estate. Its north-country farmer-parson Joseph Relph rallied enough labour to metal the old Simonsbath 'road' as far as the parish border. A row of five cottages, including a carpenter's shop and a forge, was built at the instigation of Knight's steward Osmond Lock; the old inn at the bridge, The White Horse, was enlarged for travellers coming from up-country by Leland's road, and a new one, The Crown, was added.[13] So the village which Billingsley had suggested as the heart of the estate grew up outside it – five or six foot-slogging miles away. Knight's contribution was an inn on the way, The Gallon House or Red Deer, which he built and let. Simonsbath remained so lonely that his servants left for lack of company, and when, a generation later, his son was trying to let the new farms, some prospective tenants withdrew on arrival and others very soon afterwards. One of the Scottish shepherds who brought flocks down only stayed, he said later, because the single shilling in his pocket would not have taken him home.

The first work to be undertaken on the Forest was the actual enclosure, by a wall nearly 30 miles long surrounding the entire property. H. M. Commissioners had stipulated that this was to be done within three years of acquisition, and they had laid down exact specifications. On dry ground it was to be a stone-faced hedge-bank of standard width and height, with beech, birch, ash and quickset planted along the top and protected by frith[14] – exactly the traditional local type which Billingsley and Vancouver had described. On wet ground only a 6 foot bank of turf was required. Knight made his high southern boundary with beeches alone growing in the stone-faced banks – Billingsley had recommended them against salty winds, and this stretch looks down to the Taw estuary. In a boggy dip by Hoccombe Water he made the 6-foot turf bank. The rest of the long northern wall is stone-faced but entirely treeless (the stunted Hoar Oak shows the difficulty). It is high and strong and very impressive, marching across open moor and dipping into combes, mile after mile, as confidently as if Hadrian's legions had built it to divide Somerset from Devon.[15]

Before much reclamation could be done – it began at Cornham and Honeymead, with teams of six oxen to break the ground – firm roads were essential, to bring ploughs and harrows, carts and the indispensable lime. The Commissioners had indicated that new roads might well follow the old tracks and so, for the most part, they did.[16] Leland's road through the Forest marked the ways east and south, the most immediately important for labour and supplies; it had to be altered, for wheeled traffic, between the Barle and Blue Gate. The northward track over Brendon Common was made into a passable carriage-way for John Knight's journeys to and from Lynton, his base for the first ten years or more. The earliest lime-route from the coast was the old track from Lynmouth via Hoar Oak and Exe Head and down Limecombe. (Charles Whybrow suggested that the steep path up from Hoar Oak was improved at this time, to take the lime-butts.)[17] The westward route, turning north along the 'Liming Road' at Friendship Inn, was not made good until later, when Frederick Knight bargained with Challacombe parish council for a road from his boundary. Once that was in use, the tenant of Driver regularly took a three-horse waggon along it to fetch his lime from Combe Martin.

Having enclosed the estate, and improved the roads leading out of it, and begun to break the ground for better fertility, John Knight set out to find better stock. He went to Scotland – his first wife was a Scot - and bought Highland cattle, which fed well on the moor in summer and sold well at local markets, but could not support themselves in winter and were apt to go berserk. Frederic wrote that 'All were wild and some were wicked', and related how, in 1841, a bunch of twenty which the men were trying to drive to market 'started out in different directions across the country, tossed and gored everybody they met, and were shot in fields all over the country'. Eventually they were given up, and the familiar Red Devons returned. His local sheep – Exmoor Horns – were of poor quality, and he wanted to buy better but the neighbouring farmers were not selling. He tried Cheviots – later very successful – but he could not get good shepherds for them, and lamented that a great many of the animals were 'stolen, killed by dogs and disease, and lost by bad shepherds'. To counter these thefts, and the deer-poaching (by shepherds among others) he formed a guard of Irishmen, but, appointed as gamekeepers, they fought each other unless all came from the same district. He had used Irish labourers to build his wall – a stretch east of the Hoar Oak is still called 'Paddy's Dyke' – and to make Pinkery Pond and its abortive leat, for some purpose unrecorded and unknown. His second wife was Irish, and her brother Lord Headley helped with recruitment. He also sent Knight a herd of Westphalian pigs, which he had imported into Ireland, decided not to keep, and suggested would do well, wild, in the Brendon woods. They were lost without trace.

To Exmoor people using traditional methods in remote country which their families had known for generations, all this was bound to smack of Johnny-Come-Lately. When the stranger bought the Forest, he told the press that he planned to build 'a handsome residence' in the centre of his property. Foundations were laid, and high walls built, but that was all. The shell of it towered behind Boevey's house, but was never finished. It must have seemed characteristic – pretentious, unsuited to the moor, and abandoned like a spoilt child's toy. After ten years or so he left Lynton, to live in the seventeenth-century Simonsbath House, but only for seven years, and he was then in his mid-sixties. Next he moved to Jersey for his wife's health, and by 1840 the family was settled in Rome, where he spent the rest of his life. He handed over full control of the estate to Frederic.

At huge expense, over two decades, he had made the wall and the roads, and begun to develop two farms besides the Barton, and to mark out others. He had dammed the head of the Barle to form Pinkery Pond, with a leat which could not be used because it ran at the wrong level. He had made a deer-park near Simonsbath House and, the native red deer being very few, had stocked it with fallow deer which did so much damage that in the end the herd had to be destroyed. He had tried to 'improve' the wild ponies, producing good horses which could not fend for themselves. He had secured the mineral rights in principle but gone no further. In 1840 the alienation of another family fortune, which he had expected to inherit, altered both his own and his son's prospects. He had spent as though money were inexhaustible; Frederic would have to take much more care.

Perhaps if he had come to Exmoor younger, and settled at Simonsbath at once, John Knight would have learnt to respect local experience; or perhaps not. He did not quarrel with the neighbouring farmers and go to law with them, as Boevey did; he simply kept his distance. His background and his personality were against him. He had no sympathy with the slow West Saxons. If he had not tried to go so fast, perhaps in Exmoor phrase, 'twould

19. Charles Wesley (*J. Spilsbury, c. 1786*)

20. Porlock Weir (*Alfred Dawson, c. 1890*)

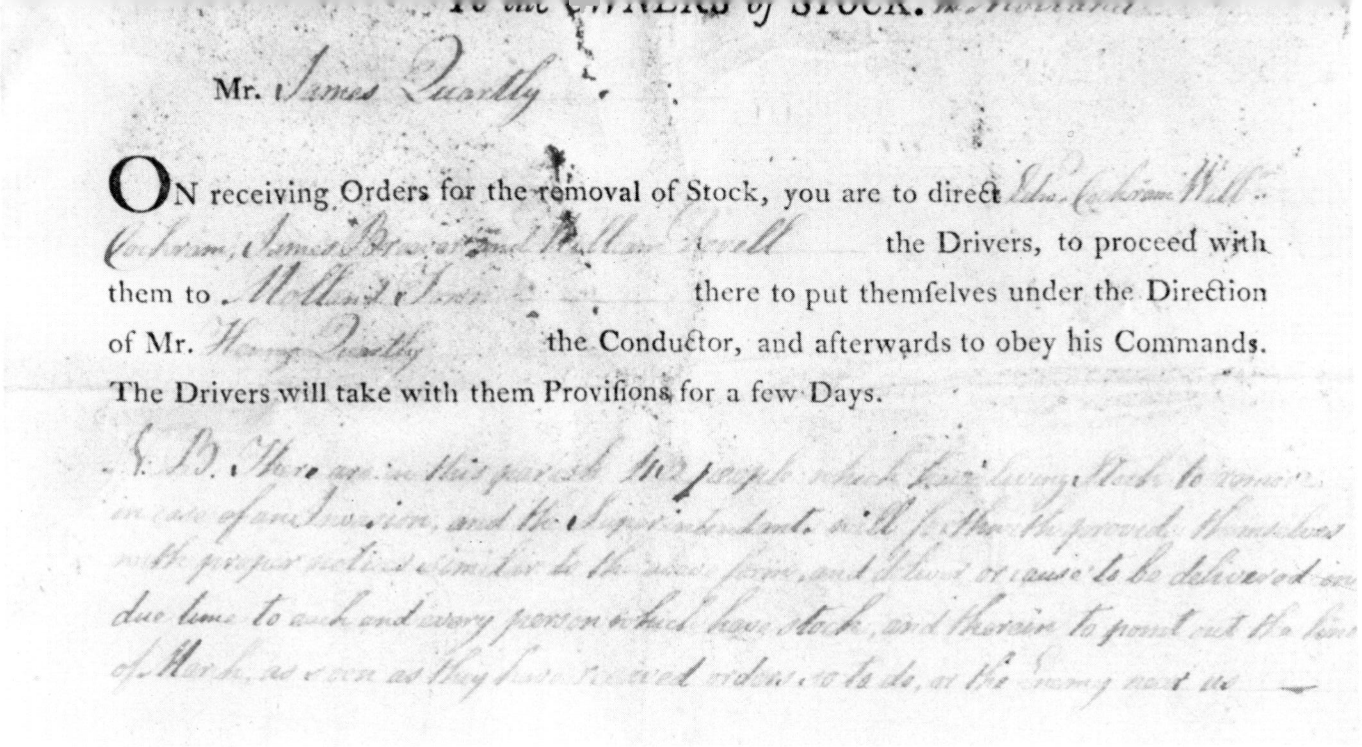
To the OWNERS of STOCK.

Mr. James Quartly

ON receiving Orders for the removal of Stock, you are to direct [illegible] Cochram [illegible] the Drivers, to proceed with them to Molland [illegible] there to put themselves under the Direction of Mr. Henry Quartly the Conductor, and afterwards to obey his Commands. The Drivers will take with them Provisions for a few Days.

21. Preparations against Buonaparte, Molland document

23. Samuel Taylor Coleridge *(Peter Vandyke, 1795)*

A true and perfect

Inventory of all & singular the Goods
Chattles & Creditts of John Hill of Weathypooles
late dec'd taken, prised & apprized the
29th Day of September by Edward
Laverous Joseph Strange & Hugh Winter
as followeth. 1695:

Impr: his wearing Apparrell
& money in purse ————————— £10 : 00 : 00

It: in Bedding & Bedsteds & furniture
to it ———————————————— 13 : 10 : 00

It: in Brass Pottes van ...
Brass ———————————————— 06 : 00 : 00

It: in pewter ————————————— 02 : 10 : 00

It: in Chests trunckes & boxes and
other Timber Stuffe ——————— 03 : 10 : 00

It: in Linnen ——————————— 02 : 00 : 00

It: in plate & Rings ———————— 05 : 00 : 00

It: in Chaires & Stooles Table boards
& formes ————————————— 02 : 06 : 08

It: in Sheep & fatt Soe's ————— 20 : 00 : 00

It: in horses and Colts ————— 10 : 00 : 00

It: one Chattle Lease for one Life — 30 : 00 : 00

It: things out of Sight out of minde
& not prized ——————————— 05 : 00 : 00

Edward Laverous ⎫
Joseph Strange ⎬ Sume is   110 : 01 : 08
Hugh Winter   ⎭

25. The wordly goods of John Hill, Deputy Warden,
at his death *(Somerset Record Office)*

LEFT: 24. The Manor Mill and Castle Inn, Porlock *(Early nineteenth
century, John Phelps)*

26. Withypool: second Methodist Chapel, built 1881 *(Sidney Perrin, 1974)*

27. The stell at Three Combes' Foot *(Ivan Durman, c. 1985)*

have all come by liddles'; but he was an ageing man, impatient to see his ambitions fulfilled, and he could not wait.

His son Frederic had a different start, and different obstacles, some very grave set-backs, but ultimately some success. He and his two brothers had grown up on the moor, rich, vigorous, high-spirited young men taking a full part in the hunting, fishing and shooting for which it was a paradise. From their father's large stud of thoroughbreds they and their guests were always well-mounted, and the opening meet of staghounds was regularly held at Simonsbath. They were at home on Exmoor, and the young heir was widely known.

When he took over the management, reclamation was not going well, funds were no longer unlimited, and the estate was not paying its way. It had been heavily mortgaged to finance the innovations and at one time the creditors threatened to take possession. A change of policy was overdue. Frederic Knight saw that one man alone would never be able to carry the whole experiment through, and he turned to tenant-farming, on twelve-year leases, at low initial rents as the tenants would have much of the labour of improving the ground. This went forward as fast as he could put up farmhouses and outbuildings, during the forties and fifties. He appointed a local agent, from Molland, who was not a success, then an able up-to-date agriculturist, Robert Smith, who had farmed in the East Midlands, and finally, local again, F. Loveband Smyth, from Lord Fortescue's Wistlandpound farm near Blackmoor Gate. But it proved difficult to find enduring tenants. Local farmers were not interested, and the low rents attracted men of small means from further away who did not know what conditions to expect; and much misery ensued.

A Scottish hill-farmer, Gerard Spooner, took the lease of Wintershead for a time. It is 1300 feet above sea-level, and he worked from his northern experience. He brought in Cheviots and Blackfaces, with Scottish shepherds and their dogs; he said his sheep would do well on the native grass - 'nought but powder and shot would kill them'. As he did not lamb until April, and the Cheviot ewes were good mothers, fewer lambs were lost. Frederic Knight took note, and some years afterwards he adopted the system with lasting success. A full century later, in Fortescue days, one might chance to see an immense flock of Cheviots, newly shorn and elegant, being shepherded back over Simonsbath bridge, up through the nearby gate in beech-dappled sunshine, and up past the woodland to graze on the hills again.

Other tenants did less well than Spooner. One after another failed, forfeited stock and gear in lieu of rent, and went away poorer than he had come. Some left debts all round, neighbours having helped as far as they could. Some flitted with all they could take away. One man, Groves of Pinkery, blew his brains out 'by the road side not far from his own front door'. Few lasted out their twelve years. The resultant problems for the landlord show clearly in Orwin's extracts from the copious Knight papers. After the publication of his book he was sent another record, preserved in another family, and R. J. Sellick printed long extracts from that at the end of his revised version of *The Reclamation of Exmoor Forest*, in 1970. It was written by William Hannam, a tenant who managed to hold Cornham for twelve years, and it lights up from ground level the troubles of the early farmers.

Hannam was a rather unstable young dairy-farmer who came to Exmoor in 1845 from the gentler country near Wincanton and hoped to continue dairying at Cornham. There was of course no local market for his milk. Like some of the other immigrants he made it into very good cheeses, which he sold at Barnstaple. He began to buy sheep, and lost heavily in the bad winter of 1853: 'I believe nearly half the lambs on the Forest died that winter'. He recalled, with a touch of vanity, that when he had typhus fever in 1847, 'Mr Knight was verey antios on my behalf'. He liked the landlord's civility, and hated the agent. In the end the difficulties were too many, he lost grip, and his grievances, real or imaginary, unbalanced his mind. He sank deeper and deeper into debt; the estate declined to renew his lease and recovered some of the unpaid rent by a forced sale of his stock and gear.

He knew the tenants who came and went, some of them rogues, some pitiful. The mention of Groves's suicide is his, with sadness for an invalid 'who ought to have been persuaded by someone that he was not a suitable person to occupy a farm on Exmoor'. He tells a dismal tale, spanning the most difficult years, and at the end, embittered, he quotes 'the old men' as saying 'that they should see it Exmoor again and as before a sheepwalk and the farm houses occupied by shepherds and herdsmen'.

Again Frederic Knight looked for other ways of making money out of his property. In tune with his time, and coming from a family of iron-masters, he began a search for mineral deposits under his land. There had been sporadic mining in the hills of West Somerset and North Devon since the Middle Ages at least. The royal silver and lead mines at Combe Martin were worked in the reign of Edward I, and helped to finance the French campaigns of Edward III and Henry V. In 1312 some of the King's miners were sent to search for silver at Dulverton and Brushford; it was mined there for a time in the eighteenth century, and later still Annie of the Bridge Inn at Dulverton used to treasure a teapot, and Brushford church a candlestick, made of local silver. An old mine at Molland had yielded some marcasite in 1729 and more than 500 tons of copper ore between 1826 and 1855. Wheal Eliza near Simonsbath may have been the site of iron-working in the sixteenth century, and in the parish of North Molton, neighbouring the Forest, copper and iron had been mined intermittently for centuries, sometimes on a considerable scale.

In the 1840s – when iron-mining on the Brendons was beginning – local interest in Wheal Eliza was revived. The Knights leased it to a small consortium, good iron ore was raised, and ten years later Frederic bought the lease back. Young Parson Thornton, installed by now as first incumbent of the new church at Simonsbath, enjoyed expeditions with his patron looking for traces of iron or copper on the moor. William Hannam said that in about 1850 the agent began searching for iron ore at Cornham, where he himself had often picked up large pieces on the surface. In 1855, relying on very favourable expert opinion, Frederic Knight leased the mineral rights to an important South Wales company, which should conduct the mining and pay him royalty and rent. But it was a long-drawn-out failure and bitter disappointment. They had all hoped for seams of metal, and found only pockets. The owner stubbornly refused to believe in the prospectors' regretful conclusions. He obtained £7000 from one company and £10 000 from another in payment for their withdrawal, and still went on trying to raise funds for a tramway over the moor to Porlock Weir, without which export would depend on pack-horses or carts. In 1865 he was obliged to admit defeat.

Exmoor had escaped a dreadful transformation. If the high hopes had been realized, there would have been mining settlements in the Barle valley at Cornham Ford and Wheal Eliza, and also up at Picked Stones, and over in one of the combes beside Hoar Oak Hill. There would have been hilltop workings at Blue Gate and Hangley Cleeve, where surface disturbances are still unsightly, and perhaps steeps of infertile scree, like the one in the Mole valley above Heasley Mill. Loaded trucks would have trundled from Warren to Porlock Weir, which would have become a smoky little port for the dispatch of ore to South Wales.

Over on the Brendon Hills, the work was much further developed and lasted longer. R. J. Sellick told its history in detail in his *West Somerset Mineral Railway and the Story of the Brendon Hills Iron Mines* (1962). For three decades a busy colony of miners worked on the long hill, and most of them lived there, with their families installed. The Welsh mining company conducting the enterprise built a village of sixty cottages for some 250 people at Brendon Hill, and a hamlet for another 100 or so at Gupworthy. The cottages were in grey terraces, sometimes mediaevally overcrowded. There were three churches – the Bible Christians built the Beulah chapel at the eastern road-fork, the Wesleyans used a stable loft, and the Church of England had a corrugated-iron mission building which was used as a school during the week. The Company (Ebbw Vale) planned for total abstinence. They built a Temperance Hotel, and a

Temperance Society and Band of Hope celebrated special occasions with teas, sports and bonfires. The nearest licensed inns were the older ones, at Raleigh's Cross in the east and Heathpoult Cross in the west.

The venture ended completely, for economic reasons. The machinery was taken away and the buildings were left to fall down. In 1890 Page, who loved the moor, described 'the gaunt chimneys, the ugly pumping-houses' still standing, in 'a landscape already rendered sufficiently dreary by the rows of ruinous cottages bordering the roadside'. Little can be seen now except a remnant of tramway down to the coast, one engine-house, the piers of a railway bridge which crossed the road, the footings of a few cottage walls, and the Beulah chapel, abandoned and then restored for the use of Methodists from a wider neighbourhood. Unshapely humps of upcast are grass-grown, rank weeds partly hide the fallen walls, but it is taking nature a long time to eliminate the traces of all that industry and the greedy hunger for iron.

Mining on Exmoor was always episodic – a few decades of production, and then closure – and, except indirectly, it was irrelevant to the age-old work of farming the difficult land. In the long run, it was helping to feed the foundries with ore for the machinery which was beginning to be important in the fields. More immediately, it meant a little modest prosperity for the nearest villages and farms. Though most of the miners were skilled immigrants, local men and boys began to learn, and they were needed from the beginning as builders, carpenters and blacksmiths. Pack-horses would be hired or bought from the farmers, and when roads improved, carts, draught-horses and carters were required. And the miners had to be fed; the farmers would sell them home-cured bacon, the farmer's wives providing eggs, milk, butter, cheese and perhaps an old hen for the pot. And they needed firewood or peat to boil the pot, and to warm the remote mining cottages in winter. These sales at the farmhouse door were easy income, missed when the mines closed. In a bad year, there were still the boats taking ore across the channel, and an Exmoor labourer might go and try his luck in the mines of South Wales.

So might a miscreant on the run, like William Burgess, the widower who lodged at Gallon House and killed his little daughter out on the moor. The grim tale was not one the neighbourhood could forget. The crime was an unsolved mystery for months, and the accounts given do not tally in every detail. The grandsons of two Withypool men who were reluctantly involved told me their families' version of what happened.

His grandfather was the village carpenter, and Burgess used often to drop into his workshop, where the little girl, who was always with him, would play happily with the curly wood-shavings while they talked. The other man worked with Burgess at the mines, and used to walk up over Braddimoor to a point in Gipsy Lane from which a track dropped to the recently abandoned Wheal Eliza. This point, the site of a big tip, was also on Burgess's way from Gallon House to the mine. A few days after he and the child had last been in the village, they chanced to meet him at that corner. The carpenter asked him why he was alone. 'What have you done with the little maid? You haven't buried her in the tip, have you?' It was said in rough jest, but as the man shuffled up an answer the look on his face was so odd that they rememberd it afterwards and became suspicious: 'Something wrong there.'

Wherever he had buried her, he disinterred the little body that night and threw it down the flooded shaft of the Eliza mine. Next morning he had disappeared. He was strongly suspected of murder, but there was no proof. The moor was searched for a grave, and at length the mine-shaft was drained and the poor child's remains were found. Burgess was believed to be working as a miner in Wales, and the police visited both Withypool men to ask whether they would recognize him. 'Goodness yes, of course!' So they were taken across to Swansea. All waited near the pithead as a shift ended; one batch of men after another came up, all strangers, and then – 'There he is!' The police told his former mate to go and speak to him, which he did, with the laconic greeting, 'Hullo, Bill!'

'Hullo, Willy!' exclaimed Burgess. 'What be you doin' here?'

'Oh, just comed to see how you was getting on.'

'Have they found the maid?'

'Aye.'

'Then 'tis all up.' The police came forward and arrested him, and he was hanged at Taunton early in 1859.

While the Simonsbath mines were petering out in the 1860s the new farms on the estate were at last beginning to do better. Frederic Knight had not neglected his reclamation and farming during the mining fever of the 1850s. He had had miles of hedge-banks built, topped with wind-resistant beech, and had planted trees in Birch Cleeve and round the new farmhouses. (There was a nursery for young trees at Ashott in Simonsbath, and huge quantities of beech nuts were bought for it.) The grey farmhouses stood solid on the south-facing slopes. Some of the highest, Wintershead and Horsen and Warren, typify the design the landlord approved: they had their shoulders to the bitter easterly and rain-sodden westerly winds, parlours and porch on the sunny side, great courtyards on the north, protected by shippon, stable and barn. This was the working side; the big warm kitchen, with cool dairy beyond, looked out on to the court, across a stone-lined gully, the path from the back door.

By the 1860s the Forest farming was more settled. In a sense 'the old men' were right; Exmoor was a sheep-walk again, but more heavily stocked; far more land had been drained, limed and cultivated for better pasture, and the Scottish sheep could winter on the moor. (At one time Blackfaces were settled on Hoar Oak Hill; this may be when the stone sheep-pen at the mouth of Long Chains Combe was built, with a little room in one corner for the shepherd.)

It was true, too, that shepherds and herdsmen were living in the farmhouses, but not in the desolate way the prophets of doom had meant. They had done well enough to take on tenancies. John Gourdie, the last of the shepherds to bring his flock down from Scotland, later farmed Wintershead. Warren and Picked Stones were tenanted by men who had begun as labourers on the estate, and understood the land. William Carter, an ox-boy in the early days at Honeymead, took over Crooked Post (nowadays called Litton's) reclaimed it, and bred the cattle he had known from boyhood, the Red Devons; later his son bought the farm, and then handed it on to a third generation.

Some of the holdings remained unlet, and there Frederic Knight pursued his own experiments. Steam-ploughing, with a Sutherland plough and a hook nicknamed 'the Duke of Sutherland's toothpick', pierced the iron pan on the hilltops. The coming of the Taunton–Barnstaple railway meant that Forest sheep, fattened for the big urban markets, need only be driven as far as South Molton, where they were slaughtered and sent away hanging in meat-vans. There were far more sheep on the hills, more cattle in summer and fewer ponies – the herd was reduced from some 400, mostly hybrid, to about forty brood mares, because ponies ate more than sheep and paid less.

Simonsbath was a village by now, with a church and a school, a new inn, a shop and a forge. As Billingsley had foreseen, this made the tenancies more attractive to enterprising young married men from the outer moor, who were ready to start up on their own. The good farming years of the 1860s and 1870s helped, and the pattern survived the two bad decades that followed. In those years, though, little new reclamation was done. The master of the estate was growing old, and in 1879 his only son died, at the age of twenty-seven. There would be no Knight heir, no dynasty. In order that at least it should remain a unit and be his until he died there, he sold the reversion of the property to Lord Fortescue and his son, in 1886 – the year in which, for quite other work, he was knighted. He lived on quietly for another eleven years, Simonsbath House his home, and then Simonsbath churchyard his burial place.

The eighty years of the two Knights' rule – a short time in the long history of the moor – had spanned the changes from oxen to horses and then to steam, from pack-horses and droving to railways, and almost from stage-coaches to private cars. They had tamed much of the Forest to make green fields round their thirteen farms, but much still rippled with tawny moor-grass, a wild haven for the deer and ponies, buzzards and curlew, in an open landscape continually varying between sunshine, mist and rain.

Meantime, the changes of these years were reaching the other forty parishes of the moor, in the purlieus and beyond, though less abruptly. Big landlords round the fringe, their working tenants, and the yeomen who owned smaller farms, steered varying courses as money allowed and experience and temperament directed. Turnpikes, machinery and railways altered the conditions for everybody, sooner or later, but the pattern was the old one – stock-farming with in-fields near the farms, limed if possible, and rough grazing up on the commons, the old manorial wastes. In the northern parishes that system still obtains, from Ilkerton ridge to Porlock Common.

Down in the Vale of Porlock there was arable as well, and fine corn crops were grown. Here the coming of the threshing-machine made trouble; as elsewhere, labourers thought there would be no more winter work for them with flails on the barn floor, so they rioted and wrecked the machines. A charred oak post behind the barn at Blackford is believed to have carried the shafting of a machine which the workmen burned down at night.[18] This was also country where forest trees could attain their full majesty. From the Iron Age until today, acorns have been renewing the oak-woods of Horner. Walnut trees grew so well near Bossington that they were used as live gateposts. Sir Thomas Acland, the tenth baronet – who might have owned the Forest – planted Selworthy, and the great ilex wood where the last spur of North Hill falls westward to the bay. During the second and third decades of the century he covered steep inhospitable slopes on his Holnicote estate with more than 50 000 trees. They obliterated little fields, probably always hungry ones, where some traces of old boundary walls survive. They still stand, changing with the seasons; woods on the hillsides, cornfields in the vale, heather moorland on the skyline – a rich and lovely landscape.

South-west of the Forest, in very different country, the outstanding change came in mid-century, with the enclosure of the commons. On the Bampfylde/Poltimore land, cultivation crept steadily uphill, field by geometrical field – across Span Common towards Eastern and Western Commons (Fyldon Ridge and Five Barrows) which were both left wild until recent years.

The Challacombe commons, close to Fortescue farms, were apportioned in 1862, and Shoulsbury Castle not until ten years after that. Parracombe Common was a late one, too. The track from Parracombe to Lynton passed over a great stretch of gorse and heather (this was where Hugh de Wichehalse had such trouble after choosing the wrong way from Blackmoor Gate). In 1859 the Lord Chief Justice, on holiday at Lynton, complained of the dangerous state of some of the 'roads'. Enclosure came three years later. Less than half a century after that J. F. Chanter, Rector of Parracombe, wrote, 'Now the moor can only be seen in the distance, the heather has disappeared, all has been fenced in, and wide roads have taken the place of the packhorse tracks'.

The loss of the commons was the cottagers' and small farmers' loss. For centuries they had had some limited ploughing rights, and were entitled to graze a few animals out on the common, and to cut peat or turf for fuel. More than two dozen cottages in Challacombe held these common rights. The commons formed much the greater part of the parish, so the apportionment in lieu of rights might be a couple of acres in a remote corner, too far away to be worth enclosing. A new pattern of life had to be devised.

When the old one was ending, the Dorset poet William Barnes caught the sadness and worry for the cottagers in an imaginary dialogue, 'The Common a-Took In'. Thomas meets John, carrying two of his geese to market. Yes, says John, he is getting rid of every goose and gosling he's got, and, worse still, is afraid he may have to sell his little cow. The common is to be enclosed, and they will have nowhere to run, in summer, while his orchard grass is growing for hay. He will not be able to fatten geese for gentle vo'ks to buy, nor feast his family on the giblets, nor sell the feathers and quills. He will lose his supply of furze and briars, and the dry cow-dung which the youngest children gather for fuel. Thomas sympathizes; 'Tis handy to live near a common' – but says he has heard that 'they' are making a habit of letting bits of ground out to the poor. John replies,

> 'Well, I do hope 'tis true, I'm sure'
> An' I do hope that they will do it here,
> Or I must goo to workhouse, I do fear.'

CHAPTER NINE

Plain living in harsh times

The cloth towns south of the moor, the fishing-ports and hamlets of the north coast and the villages and farms up on the moor itself were only gradually affected, some sooner and some later, and in different ways, by the changes with which nineteenth-century industrialism was transforming England. Sometimes, as with the inclosures, one man's meat was another man's poison.

The end of the Napoleonic Wars was good for the cloth trade; the price of wool fell sharply and foreign ports were open. This also suited ship-owners and sea-captains, and indirectly the wool-workers and ordinary seamen and their families. But lower payment for wool was a serious blow to the sheep-farmers in the hills, already struggling with exceptionally bad weather. A Corn Law protecting the arable farmer's pocket was driving bread up to starvation prices for the poor. Soldiers and sailors demobilized without pension trudged from parish to parish in search of work or charitable relief.

Later, the woollen industry of the South West was thrust out of the market by the northern mills, but there was spirited adaptation. Other uses were found for the fullers' water-wheels. Rag paper, needing fresh clear water, was made in Dulverton; so was some of the vast quantity of crêpe needed for Victorian deep mourning. Stage coaches on the new turnpikes brought in travellers and news and ideas faster than before. Then came the railway trains, able to bring in greater quantities of iron, much faster and more cheaply, so the more elaborate farm-machinery which farmers were beginning to want could be manufactured locally, and the experienced blacksmith had an important part to play in the new workshop. But it was a long time before steam replaced horses, and wood still served innumerable purposes on the farm or indoors. Farriers and carpenters and wheelwrights were still required. So were masons; late Georgian and early Victorian houses in the wool towns still witness to quiet good taste and money well spent.

On the coast, new ways came much more slowly. The Severn Sea was alive with ships, some sailing up and down with slates

157

from Cornwall or provisions from Bristol, others back and forth to South Wales, taking pit-props from the coastal woods and returning with coal and limestone. The ketches were run up the northern beaches at one high tide and unloaded before the next. Lynmouth traded like this until comparatively recent years; a print made in 1831 and a photograph taken just before 1930 show little change at the waterside except from pack-ponies to butt.[1] At one time the venerable smack *Looe*, which sailed for nearly 120 years, used to take a cargo of coal once a year to the sheltered cove at Glenthorne, where it was discharged between tides into carts which had been sent from Minehead the previous day; the carters and horses had rested overnight at Broomstreet before going down the steep and twisting private road to the beach. Further eastward, old account books tell of lime-ships lost by being overloaded with the raw stone, on the Welsh beaches, at low tide. When the water rose they could not be floated off.

Sheep and cattle were taken over from West Somerset to feed the miners and foundry-workers of South Wales. Brick went from Porlock Weir to Bristol and from Combwich to Ireland. Channel craft made long voyages as well as short. A little full-rigged ship, the *Lady Ebrington*, 400 tons, was built at Barnstaple in 1852 to carry emigrants to Australia – some of them in search of gold. For about a quarter of a century the tall ships brought in Australian wool; then, with steam-power first supplementing and after a time replacing sail, the importation of frozen meat from the 'new' countries began. In Porlock Vale, where farming and seafaring were closely linked, people were not slow to see where this would lead. When Captain Ridler brought home his first shipload of Australian mutton in 1882 he was pointed out in the market as the man who would ruin the hill-country. ('Only too true,' remarked his farmer son long afterwards, 'but he had to bring Mr Anderson's cargo!')

The sloops and ketches were invaluable carriers, for there was no turnpike along the coast, and until late in the century no railway anywhere near. The regular boat would take an extra load, by request. In the eighties a store-keeper from the fishing village of Minehead Quay used periodically to walk to Bristol, sleep there, and go round a warehouse early next morning choosing supplies for his shelves. Then he walked home, leaving his purchases to be sent after him by sea.

In 1890 the topographer Page, looking down from Cloutsham Ball, saw the sea 'covered with shipping'. There would be steamers as well as sail by then, but there was still no easier means of transport along the steep and dangerous Exmoor coast. Some ships ran on to the rocks and sank, and the rescue service became very important. It surpassed itself, in determination and ingenuity, at Lynmouth, where the fisherman had told Coleridge of their risky

158

endeavour to save a drowning boy. In 1819 this was the first place on the north coast to use the Manby mortar – invented in Yarmouth to fire a rescue line – but sometimes the steepness of the cliff made it useless. In 1868 the 800-ton *Home* ran aground off the Foreland, and the coastguard boat could not help. Captain Roe, J. P., organized volunteers into a chain of rescuers, ashore, steadying each other on the wet rocks, and they saved sixteen lives. One whom they could not save, 'Michael Devine of this parish', is buried in Countisbury churchyard, with other shipwrecked sailors, some commemorated, some nameless under simple mounds. The R.N.L.I. awarded Captain Roe a silver medal, and a church collection helped to provide the first Lynmouth lifeboat, the *Henry*.

Three decades later, on a tempestuous January night in 1899, came the almost incredible overland launch of the *Henry's* successor, the *Louisa* (*Lousia* to her own people). A nor'westerly gale was driving huge seas ashore, and a full-rigged iron ship, the *Forrest Hall*, was in distress in Porlock Bay. Lynmouth's was the nearest windward lifeboat, but like the nearest the other way, at Watchet, she could not possibly be got out of harbour in the teeth of such a storm. So coxswain and crew, with scores of helpers, and more than a dozen carthorses, set out at eight o'clock at night in rain and wind and black darkness to haul their boat on her heavy carriage up Countisbury Hill and along the ridge-road to Porlock, to launch from there. It took them several hours to reach Countisbury. Then, the gruelling climb achieved, many helpers, men and women, went back home, while after a rest at the Blue Ball (time-honoured signal of respite for small craft!) about twenty men went on. They knew the road, and had brought tools to batter down walls, gateposts or hedge-banks as necessary; they had to take the boat on skids along a mile of lane too narrow for her carriage, which was hauled over the open moor. With all drags working, all hands pulling back, they manoeuvred her down Porlock Hill, and at about six in the morning she put to sea with her crew of thirteen and went alongside the *Forrest Hall*. Working on the windward side, short-handed because some of the crew were lent to the crippled ship, they helped a tug to tow her across to Barry, and arrived at five o'clock in the wintry afternoon. There, exhausted, the men were treated with all the consideration they had earned, and in the morning they were peacefully towed back to Lynmouth.

Worlds away, in summer sunshine, happy parties of holiday-makers travelled by coach along this same road, through miles of honey-scented heather. They were not many yet, by modern reckoning; in 1890 Page wrote that on the almost treeless coast road there was very little traffic, except 'a carriage or two of folks on pleasure bent, or the gaily-painted coaches ... thickly packed with tourists, who are eager to know *which* is the Doone Valley, and whether they can see Oare Church.' Their numbers had been building up throughout the century; the taste for romantic scenery and the new fashion of sea-bathing led on to another innovation – family holidays at the seaside. As early as 1817 Madame d'Arblay, once the sparkling Fanny Burney, took her undergraduate son to Ilfracombe, where lodgings were cheap, to study undisturbed for his final examinations, but she deplored its popularity: 'the Multitude has warped what the Individual had enjoyed'.[2]

Lynmouth was attracting artists to 'the English Switzerland' in summer. The fishing-village became a 'resort' and Lynton grew with it. The herring shoals had deserted, but the visitors were good customers, and by the 1850s the villagers were attending seriously to this new seasonal trade. It was soon well organized. In summer a steamer went twice a week from Bideford to Bristol and back, anchoring off Lynmouth for small boats to ferry passengers aboard or ashore. 'Horse-buses' carried travellers to or from Barnstaple, connecting there with Tiverton and Plymouth coaches. In summer a coach left Lynton every day for Porlock, Minehead and Bridgwater; London-bound passengers changed at Minehead on to another coach for Taunton, where they never failed to catch the express train from Exeter. The return journey started after the arrival of the down-train, and the Lynton coach was home on the cobbles of Porter's Yard by half-past eight in the evening. It was a friendly affair; the last guard – in 1919 – used to blow on his horn 'Anchor's aweigh!' as they clattered out of town.

In 1898 the narrow-gauge railway from Barnstaple was opened, and a train would come puffing over Chelfham viaduct, over the hills to Blackmoor Gate, on above Woody Bay (where a rich stranger's plan to build a deep-water harbour failed)[3] and on to its terminus at Lynton. Local people crowded the trains merrily on market-days, and more sedately at other times – Bratton Fleming and Blackmoor Gate stations serving the families of the western moor. From Barnstaple the summer visitors travelled all the way – some 5000 of them, it seems, over the years. It was a very slow train, following a delectable route. There was no hurry. Parson Chanter of Parracombe used to scatter flower-seeds from the carriage window. Affectionate regulars mourned the closure of the line, in 1935, when motor-cars had prevailed.

Long before that the twin villages, aloft and alow, were linked by the pioneering work of a Lynmouth builder and engineer, Bob Jones. He designed the cliff-railway, the first of its kind – one carriage being pulled up from Lynmouth by the weight of the other coming down with its tank full of water from Lynton.[4] Later, between 1885 and 1890, he built it, when Sir George Newnes, the London publisher who had settled in Lynton, provided funds. It was and is still an irresistible attraction to visitors, and an alternative to the donkeys which had formerly carried them uphill.

Bob Jones also built the Foreland lighthouse. He took the materials in his own small boat from Lynmouth harbour to Countisbury Cove, and then up to the site by a temporary cliff-railway he had constructed for the purpose. His workmen walked there, arriving in time to begin the day's labour at half past seven in the morning. The result was so good that the Welsh commissioned him to build a lighthouse on their coast too. Staunch work, as always, for those in peril on the sea.

The moor itself was still remote, and little visited – still poor and difficult land, as it had always been. A cluster of names at Swincombe near Challacombe, used long after their meaning was forgotten, tells of Saxon farmers working against the odds; Yarbury Combe, Armeshead, and Woodbarrow Arms come from Old English *earm*, poor or wretched, and so does Airey field which the Huxtables who have farmed there for nearly two hundred years call 'Starvation field'. Yelland Cross, nearby, is the crossroads on *eald* land, old land, and the permanent pastures of Swincombe farm, before improvement, 'were like a pot-bound plant'. Challacombe itself means cold valley. But in this unpromising land, rising to 1500 feet above sea-level, sheep and cattle were bred and grazed, in bad times or good.

In the last decades of the nineteenth century the moorland villages were still almost mediaeval in character, and even in appearance. Thatched cottages huddled round the three pivots, ford and water-mill and church; by now perhaps a Nonconformist chapel had been added. Those who could afford to make their roofs more durable had slate brought from Treborough in the Brendons, or by sea from the Delabole quarries in Cornwall. Sometimes a slate-hung wall shielded the weather-side of a house – a protection still to be seen here and there, as at the school on the steep hillside of Exton, or the sturdy dwelling beside the church path in gale-swept Countisbury. Tall chimney-stacks, each nearly as high again as its cottage, were a defence against down-draught, and directed flying sparks further from the thatch. Bulges in the outer wall of the cottage show where the clay oven in the kitchen baked a good housewife's batch of loaves.

The villages contained many more cottages than they do now – tiny, for the most part, one room up and one down, and some of them served as workshops too. Surnames still familiar on the moor today had been appearing in the legal records for centuries – mediaeval names, mostly Saxon, distinguishing one neighbour from another by his occupation, John the Carter or Carpenter or Miller, Dick the Tanner or Hooper or Smith. These local trades were still important, in hill parishes which a bad winter might isolate for months on end.

There were industrious craftsmen, but machinery had not yet

reached the villages to standardize results. The cobbler's shoes might be square-toed and interchangeable, like Dr Johnson's or fitted to the peculiarities of the customer's feet, like Mr Penny's handiwork in *Under the Greenwood Tree*, but they would be very strong and kept carefully greased; rubber boots were not yet available. A John Milton of Withypool (related across two centuries to the poet) went to London by train from Dulverton to visit his sister-in-law, in a new suit made for him by Mr Tudball the village tailor, and a new pair of boots from the cobbler, Mr J. Quartley, who lived just across the road. Iron-shod and well-pleased, he clanked along a quiet Victorian street in London; but a Cockney called after him, 'My word, Mister, what a pair of boxes!' Mortified, he went to a shop and bought a ready-made urban pair.[5]

That John Milton was a mason, a hedger and a haulier. In the 1860s he carted down all the stone quarried on Withypool Hill for the fine new bridge over the Barle, so its Porlock builder arranged for him to be the first to drive across it. The whole village assembled to watch, and young and old remembered the occasion for the rest of their lives.

Mr Quartley the cobbler, better 'scholared' than his neighbours, did their legal business for them, and was nicknamed 'Torney-Mouse Quartley, to distinguish him from his less reputable brother Luke. Withypool had also a miller, of course, a baker, a blacksmith, and the carpenter in whose workshop Burgess's doomed child had played. Every farmer kept one black sheep in his flock for the women's stockings, and all the spinning was done by the witch, a clever woman of strong character. The peg-legged 'Gen'l'man Sweep', who being socially superior was 'allowed' to lie abed longer of a morning, lived up the Hawkridge road. A Mr Hayes, who owned a pair of donkeys, used to go out to the smaller or more distant farms to fetch their corn for grinding, and take the flour back.[6] There was a village shop, and the Royal Oak Inn stood, then as now, at the meeting of the Winsford and Exford lanes. The almshouses were close to the churchyard gate – no distance to carry the paupers who died there – and the children were taught, to the age of eleven, in a cottage just east of them which still stands, though they do not. There was no resident parson (he lived at Hawkridge), no real lord of the manor, and the nearest doctor was far away at Dulverton, but the village could meet all its everyday needs by its own labour. (Now, barely a century later, it has only one shop – doing duty also as post-office and petrol-station – hardly any craftsmen, cottages standing empty all winter, and the inn catering chiefly for holiday-makers all through the summer.)

Molland, even smaller now, had in 1893, among its population of 530, not only farmers but also two water-millers, three masons, two wheelwrights, three blacksmiths, two shoemakers, two tailors, a butcher, a shopkeeper, a grocer, and the host of the London

Inn. Clearly it was a busy parish, and it was scattered; there was the mining at Bremley, the important stock-farming of the Quartlys on the Throckmorton estate, and down in the valley the hamlet of Molland Bottreaux. At least one in six of the 530 were school-children; the parish school had been enlarged in 1883 to take 100 pupils, and the average attendance was eighty. (A schoolmaster is recorded, but no assistant.)

Traces or memories of other ancillary crafts remain, in the moorland villages – ancillary to the farming, for the most part. Most of them required wool, which was scarce on the higher hills, and might have to be brought a long way. A family of cartwrights at King's Brompton used to make waggons and putt-carts (butts) in great numbers, 'and very good they were', says a long-retired farmer who used them, 'well adapted to local needs'. The Parracombe wheelwright worked near the Holy Well, using its little stream to shrink a red-hot iron rim on to his wooden cartwheel; the big stone slab on which he rested the wheel is still there, beside the lane. Often the wheelwright was also the village carpenter, and he might branch out and become a mill-wright, building and repairing the wooden water-mills. A day-book kept by the Challacombe mill-wright, in the 1820s, shows him felling timber, sawing it, making a wheel – and a coffin – and travelling far around to dress worn millstones, or repair the mills, sometimes virtually rebuilding them.

Bark-strippers, especially in the coastal woodlands, pared oak-bark for the tanners; Lynmouth exported it to Wales, but kept back some for 'barking' the fishermen's ropes and sails (steeping them in a huge cauldron of water infused with the oak-parings; this proofed them against rot, and gave them their distinctive brown colour). From Porlock the bark was shipped in huge quantities to Cornwall – in one year, 1859, the Bolitho family paid £1650 for its supply. Ash was coppiced for building and for farm implements. Hazel was cut for hurdles, and willow or withy for baskets. Charcoal-burners lived in stone huts among the trees. In the steep woods of Culbone the ruins remained visible for a long time, and so did the charcoal-pits, the saw-pits where felled oaks were made ready for shipbuilding, and the tracks by which timber and charcoal were taken down to be shipped from Porlock Weir. In Dulverton (probably at Langaller) clog-makers arrived every autumn to cut alders – the trees which resisted water best, having grown in it. And all the time somebody had to make the gates, cider-barrels, firkins, and wide wooden hay-rakes.

Hedge-carpenters made some of the field-gates. A farm labourer might put his own flail together, with two strong sticks, a strip of cowhide, and a ring shaped from a ram's horn which had lain softening in a bog for a year. But it would take a good carpenter and experienced countryman to build the flood-gates needed where a boundary crossed a fast-rising stream, such as the pair spanning Farley Water at the gap in the Forest fence. These consisted of a row of vertical bars, spaced about six inches apart and held together by two strong cross-pieces, and they were suspended from a stout pole stretched from bank to bank. They hung down to summer water-level, and were heavy enough to keep cattle or sheep from straying, but when the stream became a torrent they swung upwards, floating but firm, while bushes or sticks were washed down harmlessly underneath them.

The villages supplied special skills, seasonal labour, rudimentary education, and such insurance against disaster as the community could afford. They were the hub; Sunday services in church or chapel, weddings and funerals, fairs or 'revels' drew the parish together. But they could not have lasted long without the constant work on the hill-farms, which depended ultimately, as it had always done, on proper care of the sheep.

Changes gradually reaching the farms were rather in *how* things were done than in what or why. Enclosure in the middle of the century enlarged holdings or added new ones, altering the landscape as more earth and stone banks, beech-topped, were made to divide the commons into fields. The Taunton–Barnstaple railway along the southern edge of the moor eased the marketing of sheep and cattle; they no longer had to be sold locally at buyers' prices, nor driven to the big up-country markets, but were taken to pens at the stations (at Molland, for instance, the home of the Champson Red Devons, or Dulverton, which eventually had a line to Exeter as well). There they were auctioned; dealers from the towns came by train to the sales and the animals they bought were trucked away by rail. Meanwhile, improved roads had enabled the richer landowners to bring in new heavy machinery, and had eased the carters' long journeys across the moor for lime, as yet the only fertilizer except dung.

In the middle and later decades of the nineteenth century lime-carts were far the commonest traffic on Exmoor roads. Carters would leave the farms early in the morning, in their horse-drawn butts, to fetch burnt lime from distant kilns. A few of these were inland; there were pockets of limestone, and at Exford and Challacombe the kilns were built near them. At Challacombe the soft rock of the quarry-mouth collapsed one day, and a young carter was trapped inside with his horse and butt. A small hole let in air and light, and he could have crawled out through it, but he had to wait and mind the horse while the fall was cleared from outside. A later and worse collapse, luckily at night, put an end to these workings. At Newland, Exford, any customer who transported a load of Welsh coal from Porlock Weir was entitled to a load of burnt lime, almost free, for his pains. Some farmers kept a man and cart simply to make this round journey every day, or in summer twice a day. The Newland lime-pit was very deep, and had been dug near a stream; one night a man who had been dismissed – unjustly, he thought – cut the stream-bank and flooded the pit; hence the large pond, still there, near the remains of the two kilns.

Winsford drew its supply of limestone from Watchet, where, it is related, the raw stone could be picked up on the beach. The coal to burn it was probably brought up from the harbour by the same route – Leland's road as far as Luckwell Bridge, then by a track south-westward to cross Thorne Lane (the ancient Harepath) for the new cart-road, which served Pinn's quarry as well. The kiln stood below a knoll at the foot of the quarry, and three larch-trees were planted on the hummock for shelter. But a sad tale is remembered there. A burner named Comer used to walk from Withypool each morning, two steep miles up and down by rough paths, and one day he fell into the kiln and was burnt to death. He was an experienced workman, unlikely to slip or stumble. The likelihood is that, resting at lunch-time, he lay, as burners often did, close to the lip of the kiln for warmth, and dozed and drowsily rolled in. The kiln was demolished long ago, but one larch still marks the place.

The need for lime to sweeten the newly broken waste land and commons was insatiable, and much of the raw stone came by sea from South Wales. The Exmoor 'lime-captains' who sailed the ketches across for it knew every nook and cranny of their own coast, and – like the smugglers – could run their cargo ashore wherever a bit of beach and a cliff-path gave the twofold approach they required. Kilns were built almost at the water's edge – as at Heddon's Mouth. Coal must have been brought too, so that the lime could be burnt at once and a more concentrated load carried uphill by the pack-ponies. Ruined kilns are dotted along the coast, though the heaviest trading was of course through the harbours. Even Lynmouth, where the limestone had to be unloaded on the beach between tides, carted up to the quay to be burnt, and then taken up one or other of the steep enclosing hills, imported enough to keep the limeworkers busy at its two kilns.

By and large, farmers east of the Forest fetched their Welsh lime from Porlock Weir, some of it by the old Limeway track south-eastward from Hawkcombe Head [7] and those west and centre from Combe Martin via Blackmoor Gate. The old ridgeway along Bratton Down became 'the Liming Road'. Where the Challacombe road leaves it, the old Friendship Inn, now a farmhouse, had – and still has – a little window through its eastern wall, at about shoulder-height from the road. This was the carters' bar; they could pay their pence and drain their tankards without letting go of the horses' reins.

It is a high and exposed corner. Once a young farmer returning home to Challacombe was caught there by a sudden snowstorm, and when he turned east into the blizzard he could see nothing at all. Drifts hid road and hedges alike. All he could do was to crouch in his butt for shelter and leave the horse to find the way home – which it did.

Another lonely inn, not built until after the sale of the Royal Forest in 1819, was the Acland Arms at Moles Chamber, where the Lynton–South Molton road (county boundary at that point) joined the tracks from Dulverton, Barnstaple and Porlock. It had a bad reputation, and its border position was attractive, it is believed, to smugglers, because of the easy escape from either county's police, but law-abiding carters young or old, returning with laden butts from the coast, used it too. They would need a pause and a drink on their day-long journey; they 'had just about time for supper and bed before starting out again,' said the grandson of one of them.

All the journeys began very early in the morning; from Challacombe it was at three o'clock, and, said my informant grimly, 'the carter had got to be there' – like poor Abel Whittle in *The Mayor of Casterbridge*. From near North Molton a farmer who brought his lime from Porlock liked his men to make the journey twice in one day, and rest the horses on the next, beginning with two trips on Monday. But that meant setting out before midnight on Sunday, and neighbours would be shocked. So to avoid scandal the carters muffled the wheels with sacks until they were clear of the village; the sound of horses' hooves would worry nobody – sleepy hearers would merely think someone was riding home late – but cart-wheels meant work. 'Working on the Sabbath! And he a chapel man too!' Discretion seemed the better part.[8]

The liming came nearly to a halt in the 1880s. Times were hard: first came a series of bad harvests, then the swamping of the meat market with frozen beef and mutton from overseas; and there was no longer a flourishing local cloth-trade requiring wool. Few hill-farmers could afford lime for more than their household corn and the horses' fodder. Old and new pastures were starved, and could feed less stock. The mines were failing too, and the miners' cramped little cottages, left empty, soon began to collapse. So did shepherds' cots, like the one near the foot of Long Chains Combe, and so did small, remote farmsteads like Radworthy in Swincombe, where Saxons had farmed an isolated patch of good ground before Domesday, and later field-boundaries still show clearly on the hillside.

There was significantly less demand for inns and alehouses on the old Forest – there were fewer people, and the vigorous temperance movements of the time may have been taking effect. The *Gallon House* which John Knight had built on the

Simonsbath–Exford road was used in Frederic's time by the Picked Stones miners, became a rogue's roost, and after one or two men had been killed in drunken fights lost its licence and became Red Deer farmhouse. The *Acland Arms* at the Moles Chamber crossroads lost its custom and its ill-fame and became a respectable farmhouse. The *Cork and Bottle*, alias Greenbarrow farm, on the Withypool Free Suitors' allocation of Forest land along the North Molton road, may not have been more than an unlicensed alehouse, convenient for travellers who had toiled up the hill from Withypool, but when the side-line was given up the livelier name lingered, especially among hunting-people who would prefer the more exact reference (Green Barrow itself is nearly a mile to the east). Then, like the *Acland Arms*, it was abandoned. The sign of it now, from the road, west of the modern cattle grid, is a length of stone wall interrupting the older roadside hedge, in front of a straggle of tall beeches. These grow out of old banks and enclose a small garden space, the low remnants of house walls, and a big deep pit. It was almost forgotten.[9]

The new difficulties were not peculiar to the sheep farmers in the hills. Corn-growing in the lowlands was similarly affected by huge imports of grain. (The Corn Laws had long been repealed, to bring down the ruinous cost of bread in the big industrial towns.) In the 1870s Sir Thomas Acland of Killerton, the eleventh baronet, active for agricultural progress, doubted whether farming could have any profitable future; he saw it heading for decline as cheap food poured in to the country. And as usual, the pinch was worst where the shoe was already tight.

All through the century the shadow of poverty was never far away, and the best hope for the indigent, if they were still young and strong, was to emigrate. Some managed to pay their own fare, travelling steerage. Some went with government support; for more than three decades from 1840, the Colonial Office was selecting labourers for the types of work most needed in Canada and Australia. The emigrant ships sailed from Plymouth, and must over the years have carried a great many passengers from the overcrowded Exmoor cottages and small farms: families recall, if only vaguely, that a great-uncle or distant cousin left for the New World and never came back – perhaps was not heard of again. Nowadays, descendants of the settlers, having done well, try to trace their origin. Some seek information from parish registers, or enquire in the columns of local papers. Some, on long-planned holidays in England, visit graveyards and question old people. When they succeed, everybody is pleased, but sometimes the uprooting was a generation too far back for the hearsay memory of humble families.

Molland has a poignant record. A grey slab out on the south wall of the church bears this inscription:

Erected
to the memory
and to record the disastrous death
of
Thomas and Sarah Pincombe
of this parish and their youthful
family of 6 sons and daughters,
all of whom perished by shipwreck
together with 187 of their fellow
passengers.

*The calamitous event happened on the Manacle rocks near the St.
Keverne coast of Cornwall on the night of the 3rd of May, 1855, within
6 hours after the lamented victims had left the harbour of Plymouth as
Emigrants on their voyage to Quebec.*

A happier tale has lately reached Challacombe, restoring a lost
link in the Huxtable family. In 1851 James Huxtable with his
second wife and his six children – the eldest a boy of thirteen,
the youngest a baby girl – set off for North America. He was one of
a family of eight – five of them boys – and was forty-two years old.
He bought a farm in Illinois, 12 miles from the riverside market
town Peoria, 'a handsome town, containing 14 000 inhabitants,
doubling its population every six years'. Five years later he wrote
home to a friend, Mr G. K. Cotton, who sent the letter to the
North Devon Journal for publication. Others would ponder his
testimony: 'I can truly say that I consider it very fortunate that
I came to America, as I could never have done for my family in
England what I can here; we have to work hard, but we enjoy
the fruits of our labours.' There were now three more children
(and there would be another six); the eldest sons, at eighteen
and sixteen, were 'strong and industrious lads', and except for
a little help at harvest-time and threshing, the family did all the
work; hiring labour was too expensive. The boys were growing
up as Americans; in the 1860s both fought, for the North, in the
Civil War.

It is a long practical letter, chiefly about land (very little manure
needed), crops, livestock and prices. More vivid detail comes
much later, from the distaff side. Charity Shoplin Huxtable,
youngest daughter of James's first wife, was four years old when
the family migrated in 1851, and she lived until 1932. Before she
died, her daughter May wrote down what she had heard from her
mother about the early days, and what Charity had learnt as a girl
from her father and step-mother. The grand-daughter writes that
James and Frances Huxtable and the six children 'came to America
from Plymouth, England, in the Spring of 1851. They came in a
sailing vessel which took five weeks to cross as the vessel was

168

blown from its course and was among the icebergs two weeks off the coast of Labrador. They landed at Quebec and sailed inland as far as Montreal, Canada. From there they went by stage to Peoria, Illinois.

'Later they bought 80 acres of timber land near Kickapoo, Illinois, then one of the sparsely settled sections of the state ... They lived in a red brick house which had a large fireplace. It was too late to plant crops and grandfather took up his trade as a cobbler in Kickapoo. They lived here six years. During this time, Mr Rudd, Uncle Robert Shambrook, Mr Ford, and others came from England. They built log cabins and rail fences, tilled the soil, and dug wells. The woods were full of wild flowers, and wild grape vines, which the children used for swings, hung from the trees.'

In 1858, she records, they moved from woodland to fertile prairie, near Benson. New immigrants with familiar Exmoor names – Tallyns and Hardings, Lees and Frys – settled near them. They held prayer-meetings in each other's homes until a Baptist church was built in 1862.

Another Nonconformist Challacombe family, the Piles, dispersed at about the end of the sixties, and two letters written in 1878 survive. By then, one son, John, was farming in Wisconsin, two, Philip and James, were in Australia, and their mother, at home, ninety-four years old, bedridden and poor and miserable, was trying to keep them all in touch, though on 2/6d a week from the Union she found it difficult to afford the postage. She wrote to thank Philip for 'a very welcome letter' which greatly rejoiced her soul as she had given up all hope of ever hearing from him again. She had just had a letter from John, too; he was 'doing very well indeed' in Wisconsin, and she gave Philip his address, hoping that he would write there; John had written to Australia but received no reply. She also hoped that Philip would write again to her soon, and would ask James to do so too.

Some nine months later John wrote to thank Philip for his welcome letter, and said he was also in correspondence with James. He enumerated his own family; two children had died, five were well and healthy, and 'all are members of the Methodist Church'. They had many neighbours from North Molton and other parts of North Devon, and he gave news of a Dallyn from Buscombe, his wife from Bratton, Richard Huxtable from Brayford, and William and John Gratton, living near him and doing well. In general, he said this was a good country for working people, and though finances were difficult at present, the chances of acquiring land further west were good.[10]

The letters from Philip and James, apparently not kept, might have shown the comparable Australian scene. A tiny indication appears in the comment of an eighteen-year-old midshipman from

Periton, near Minehead, writing home from Melbourne in 1863, and it echoes James Huxtable and John Pile in the United States. 'As to the advantages of leaving England to come here, I should imagine that when land is so cheap and good and the produce so valuable the persevering farmer with a little capital may do well.' Character would count. He reported, too, on the high pay of sailors in the coasting trade; 'Consequently the fine crew that my father saw sign articles at home have all left except four, to the sacrifice of their outward bound wages.'

Those who jumped ship had probably been schooled in smacks and ketches plying in the Bristol Channel; the chance of good pay for good seamanship, with a measure of independence, might be more attractive than life before the mast in a wool clipper. Similarly, men who had worked on Exmoor farms understood sheep, and would not arrive unskilled. The ranching throve. By the time that young midshipman from a sailing ship had become Captain Ridler, loading frozen mutton on to one of the first steamers in the trade, and bringing it into England duty-free, the emigrant families were fast outstripping the unprotected farmers at home.

During the second half of the nineteenth century a steady trickle of young farmers and labourers, alone or with their wives and children, left Exmoor for those distant underpopulated lands. It was a time of 'long families' – ten or twelve sons and daughters crowded into cottages since fallen down – and perhaps not only every parish in the hills but almost every family provided an emigrant or two, sooner or later. It is interesting that James Huxtable, in the prime of life, sailed for America just when Frederic Knight was trying to find tenants for his new farms, as yet undrained and untilled. The people of Challacombe lived alongside the Forest, and knew its bleak remoteness and sour soil. In spite of the wrench of leaving home for ever, hard work on virgin land in Illinois promised a better future, and the promise was soon fulfilled.

It must often have been the strongest and most adventurous of the younger sons who went overseas. If their father was a small farmer or an established craftsman the eldest might stay at home to help him, and ultimately take over. Other brothers would look for work as apprentice or seasonal labourers. They might leave school early – before they were twelve years old – because of the family's acute poverty, and go to earn a pittance in the mines, or – better in the long run – work on a farm, living in, paid little beyond their keep, but learning about land and stock. Some of these became tenants of small farms later on, and appreciative landlords let them pass on the tenancy to their sons.

There was hardship enough, without the personal sadness of

losing vigorous sons and brothers to the 'new' countries so far away. Some yeomen were having to sell up and become labourers; farmhands who had not left the land for the towns might be reduced to cracking stones for road-making. As they grew old and feeble, they and their wives lived in dread of the workhouse, where for administrative convenience they would have to live apart.

In 1901 and 1902 Henry Rider Haggard, writer and Norfolk farmer, busy also in colonial affairs, was very much worried by the depressed state of English agriculture, so he travelled twenty-six counties, Somerset and Devon among them, to make enquiries, and published his findings in a long book, *Rural England*. He had talked with farmers and landowners, auctioneers and tradesmen, here a rector, there a medical officer of health, and had recorded the conversations the same evening, almost verbatim, for fear of distorting them later on. He was told of the drift from the land, and crippling labour-shortage, but he tried in vain to get the opinions of farm-labourers; he found them shy and suspicious, and he ascribed this to their memory of very bad times.

All this may help to account for the demoralization in the lonelier parts of the moor in the last decades of the century. Drunkenness and violence, malice and fear, made a dark side such as Hardy knew in Dorset. The law was far away, and the unfenced county boundary which would deter either police force ran down lightly wooded combes or along misty ridges. The savage punishments did not prevent sheep-stealing. Withypool was notorious – though not unique –

> Steal the sheep and burn the wool
> Goes the bells of Withypool.

and the farmers were all in it, robbing each other but united against the law. When a policeman was sent from Dulverton 'the wild men of Withypool' flung him into the river and stoned him, and would accept nobody but the parish constable whom they themselves elected. So a poorer man caught thieving to feed his hungry family might be the scapegoat. He faced hanging or transportation, and it is said that the second fate was the more dreaded; the culprit might never have been more than a few miles from his own valley all his life, and would probably never see home again.

There were also the sleazy regulars. A tale is told of two brothers who took a stolen sheep to their secluded cot but were seen and recognized by two local men. One of the latter went to fetch the police, but the other, left on guard, saw a chance of enriching himself; he warned the thieves, and offered his help and silence at a high price. He helped them to bury the carcase indoors and escape, and duly swore to the police that nobody had left the

171

place, but he was not believed. The cottage was ransacked, then abandoned and never repaired, and for a long time reminded the neighbours of their unsavoury underworld and the men who might or might not have been sent to Botany Bay.

In village pubs, as at roadside alehouses, customers drowned their worries and their wits, fought and schemed and bullied and blundered. One night a powerful drunkard directed his gang to make a bonfire of his neighbour's gates and fences, and roared encouragement as the flames rose; but his followers were tired of his domination, and in the morning he found his own barriers gone and the other man's unharmed. The village relished it as practical justice.

The unscrupulous throve on the cautious silence of the rest. Everybody knew what was going on, but feared to annoy the rogues. Towards the end of the century an able-bodied and very lazy cottager in his forties declared himself ill and went to bed for seven years, drawing 3s.6d. a week of club money until it was all gone. Thereupon he 'recovered' and took work, until he had another idea. He insured his wife heavily, then killed her by continual cruelty and beating, and drew the money – £100 or perhaps £200, in sovereigns. Anxious to bury his bag of gold, he did not realize that he was incessantly watched. Somebody saw, and dug the money up. There was no sympathy for the man who had 'crashed the club', and was now deranged by his own loss. The thief bought a farm and did very well – and so did his descendants. My informant mused. 'They say ill-gotten gains never prosper, but I never knowed money thrive so good as that did. Well, he'd come by it badly, so in a sense ...'

Fear might lurk anywhere – fear of violence, of vengeance, of the supernatural, or of descent from poverty to destitution. Money was a kind of safety; obsessive greed for it might unleash rank cruelty, and the easiest victims were the women. One small farmer, a widower, married again, and his young second wife bore him several children. The grown-up sons and daughters of the first marriage, afraid for their inheritance, stripped and tarred and feathered their stepmother, and drove her naked through the village. This was in the 1870s or so.

Brutality was not new on the Forest, of course. In 1862 the bailiff said to a visitor, Henry Hall Dixon, 'Seventy years ago, Sir, there were only five men and a woman and a little girl on Exmoor, and my mother was that little girl. She drew beer at the Simonsbath public house. They were a rough lot of customers there, I promise you!' That was at Boevey's old house, thirty years before Exmoor proper, the Royal Forest, was sold. Graziers came there from all round the moor to pay their dues, or to buy ponies at the Warden's fair – held where the church now stands. Now and then, travellers went through on the main 'road' from Dunster to Barnstaple. Simonsbath was less than 10 miles from the coast, it was in no parish so had no constable, and three of the four tracks meeting there led away easily to the county boundary, north, west or south. The inn is credibly reported to have been much used by gangs of smugglers taking their contraband inland for sale; it would have been an ideal position for them during the Napoleonic Wars, until sale and inclosure of the Forest began to be mooted.

But the outbreaks of cruelty and greed in the later decades were different from the brandy-running of 'the fair trade'. A farmer told me he thought the callous wildness of his grandfather's day was a last fling, before better roads changed the times. In retrospect, perhaps, the significant thing was the lack of any control, legal or moral, over the known or suspected wrongdoers. An old social pattern, part Saxon, part feudal, was beginning to crumble. It was assailed from too many sides at once. Farming was hard-pressed, the cloth industry had collapsed, the sporadic mining was staffed largely by strangers from Cornwall and Wales, who had different ideas and spoke strange languages. So did the Irish labourers and Scottish shepherds with whom the Knights manned the Forest. The Irish must have been Catholics, however perfunctory; the Cornish and Welsh were determined Baptists, Methodists or Bible Christians, who helped to build the box-like grey chapels in hamlets and at crossroads, and maybe preached hell-fire sermons there themselves before most of them returned home. The Church of England was being discredited by some of its clergy – comfortable absentee rectors who were adjured by Bishop Phillpotts to 'reside or resign', and sporting parsons who preferred chasing foxes and deer to looking after their human flocks. There were fine exceptions. Parson Jack Russell, of Swimbridge and elsewhere in the foothills, hunted indefatigably all his long life and was none the less a simple and sincere parish priest, 'the best-loved man on Exmoor'. Young James Hannington, curate of Martinhoe in the early 1870s, agile explorer of barely accessible caves on the cliff-face, rode about the parishes in the north and west of the moor, preaching, and visiting invalids in remote cottages. Country people filled the little moorland churches when he was expected, and grieved when, only ten years later, as a missionary bishop, he was killed by African spearmen at the command of the King of Uganda. But the notorious Parson Froude of Knowstone and Molland, incumbent throughout the first half of the century, left a very different memory. He was malicious, cunning and lawless; his successor, who was a magistrate, said he had committed every crime in the calendar. His parishioners would see much and guess the rest.

Dark deeds there certainly were, in the bad times, and they made dramatic tales to be told on winter evenings, but the devil was not having it all his own way. In the Vale of Porlock, where soil and climate were kinder and hardship not so severe, good landlords, Aclands and Luttrells, were able to help tenants through the lean years. Around Dulverton, clergy and doctors – including Dr Palk Collyns, senior, of stag-hunting renown, and his son, Dr John – were doing what they could to succour the poor against the harshness of workhouse rules and the meagreness of 'outside relief'.[11] At the foot of the steep northern cliffs, everybody, or nearly everybody, turned out to the rescue when ships were driven on to the rocks and lives were in danger.

Up on the moor, honesty was not extinguished. Saxon kindliness and patience quietly survived – under a cloud, but ready to show again when the sun shone. A visitor noted it in the eighties, when poverty was biting hard. Richard Jefferies, naturalist and writer, was like W. H. Hudson, an intent and sympathetic observer of surroundings not quite his own. He walked on Exmoor as Hudson did in Wiltshire, making friends easily among obscure country men and women, and his *Red Deer* is as authentic as *A Shepherd's Life*. He emphasized the courtesy of Exmoor people, to each other as well as to visitors. There was always a greeting in the village street. On the road, 'every man, according to his station, nods his head or touches his hat, and no one passes another without saluting. Nor is it a superficial courtesy, but backed by a real willingness to oblige. If you are thirsty, you have only to knock at the nearest door, and according to your taste, you can partake of cider or milk; and it is ten to one you are asked to enter and spend half an hour in a pleasant gossip.' Strangers were uncommon, company was welcome, and time not over-exacting, and all this was still true half a century later in the 'hungry thirties', though a cup of tea might be offered rather than cider. Jefferies went on to describe shearing time as evidence of 'real goodwill under the outward politeness'. As of old, farmers and their sons visited each farm in turn; twenty or thirty would sit down in the barn to shear anything between 600 and 2000 sheep. It was one man's work to hand round cider and refreshment, 'and there was many a song at night'. He said that any farmer who would not help his neighbour at shearing would be accounted a churl 'but as a matter of fact, none ever do refuse'.

Courtesy, good will and endurance were not to be easily lost. They were rooted deep in a thousand years of pastoral life, in a landscape of long gentle ridges, sheltered combes and dancing streams, enchanting in fair weather, but in a hard winter full of peril for man and beast. Thinly populated, the whole moor was a neighbourhood; people were ready to help each other, knowing that they might at any time need serious help themselves. They shared enjoyment of the fixed high days and holidays, and drew steadiness from the work needed, year in and year out, to win food and livelihood from the soil. Nothing was transient.

CHAPTER TEN

Work and play

The hill-farmer's year begins after the big autumn sales of sheep and cattle, when the number of animal mouths to be fed during the lean months has been profitably reduced. The rams and ewes are mated, for lambing in March or April, and put back on the high pastures until serious winter threatens, round about Christmas. Meanwhile, in the shortening days, there is time to repair linhays,[1] gates, hedges and gear, after another year of wind and rain and hard use.

In the latter decades of the nineteenth century and the early part of the twentieth this age-old natural pattern was constricted, on and near the moor, by sharp poverty. Farmers could not afford to employ many labourers by the year; in autumn those who had helped in summer were laid off, and many of the younger men crossed to South Wales to work in the coal-mines during the winter. They did not think this a hardship; it was warm underground, and pay and lodgings were adequate. Some of them married Welsh girls and settled over there; some gradually saved enough money to rent a small Exmoor farm, a cheap one in the hills. The remote holdings were looked upon as the bottom rung of the farming ladder. Thrifty farm-hands began like this, and so did men who for years had lived only by rabbit-catching. At first they might take in sheep at 'half-crease' – providing the pasture, and keeping as payment half the lambs born. These were family farms, sons and daughters all sharing in the work. (Even as toddlers they had their *own* animals to look after with loving pride: it was customary when a baby was born to put aside for it a calf, a ewe-lamb, or a gosling, and the growing child would have all the offspring, kept comfortably near the farmhouse.) Not much cash was used or needed, except in autumn. The small weekly wages agreed at Lady Day were supplemented by perquisites – food in season, a daily pint of cider, grazing rights for an animal or two, or perhaps a small patch of ground where potatoes, the staple diet of the poor, would grow well. For bigger dealing, payment in kind was often the most convenient, as in much older times. Farm produce or young livestock would buy the skilled work of blacksmith or wheelwright, and the rate of exchange was calculated so exactly that it could be entered in the farm account book. (One such was found among old junk, but unfortunately thrown away, when the loft of a Knight farmhouse was being cleared out, within living memory.)

Established farms were almost self-supporting. The more sheltered fields grew turnips for winter-feed, and a little wheat for the household bread. The corn was threshed in autumn and winter – by flails on the floor of the barn, or later on, by the power of a horse, patiently turning a shaft in a round-house just outside the wall. These 'drums' were the machines which had provoked anxious riots in Porlock Vale in the early part of the century, but up on the moor even in the 1880s Page, walking the north-western ridges, said he heard everywhere the rhythmical 'thud-thud' of the flails, and nowhere any machinery. The grain was taken to the nearest mill in small quantities, perhaps a couple of sacks carried by pannier-pony – or on Mr Hayes's donkeys. An elderly widow, Barbara Reed, recalls what her father-in-law told her half a century ago, when she was a young wife at Knighton, a small north-facing farm in the valley of the Barle above Withypool. In his younger days, 'just a month's supply was ground at a time, as the flour wouldn't keep any longer than that, he said it went "pinded". When the harvest weather was good and the corn ripe and dry the bread made from it was lovely, but in a bad year, they did the best they could, but the bread would not rise and had a not very pleasant sweet taste, they had to eat it the same.'

An upland shepherd's life in Dorset or Wiltshire in the later nineteenth century is real to any reader of Hardy's *Far from the Madding Crowd* or Hudson's *A Shepherd's Life*, and it was very similar here. Gabriel Oak out lambing on a starry winter's night, or recognizing from the clamour of sheep-bells that something was amiss, or judging the nature of an approaching thunderstorm from the behaviour of the flock, might have been on Exmoor – except for the sheep-bells. So might Caleb Bawcombe, a good shepherd on terms of perfect understanding with his dogs, and interested in all the birds and small animals of the lonely downs. But Dorset and Wiltshire are not very high, and there is no mention in either book of severe snowstorms isolating farms and villages and transforming the landscape for weeks or months on end, as may happen in these hills.

Such winters as John Thorne of North Radworthy described in his diary do not come every year, but often enough to be present in every moorland farmer's mind as a grim possibility all through the coldest months. So defences have been evolved – high thick hedge-banks for shelter and guidance, stalwart bridges against the thaw, and, on the Forest only, the stells introduced by Frederic Knight's Scottish shepherds, who brought their flocks from similar stern weather on the Border. In the north, a stell was a ring-wall of stone, with an entrance, and was used for gathering the sheep at shearing time or for the sales. The word is akin to *stall*, and means a standing-place. But the characteristic Exmoor stells differ from ordinary sheep-pens and pounds. The surrounding wall was made in local fashion, a high bank of earth and stone, with trees planted along the top to provide additional shelter and to help send the blizzard eddying round the outside. When snow was imminent, any sheep too far from the in-fields were driven into one of the stells, where, protected from wind and deep drifts, they kept each other warm. The one in Long Combe under Tom's Hill is of thorn, now straggly; another at the head of Stellcombe, on the exposed moor north-west of Horsen, is square, and the biggest of the three; its crumbling banks are held together by the roots of close-set beeches. The best, now, is the ring at Three Combes Foot, beautifully placed where the three streams unite to form Chalk Water. Its beech trees, sheltered from distorting gales, have grown tall and shapely, and it has a narrow southern entrance towards the ruin of Larkbarrow farmhouse, less than a mile away, on the old Barnstaple–Porlock bridle-road. Slow-growing, the beeches would give little help at first, but when the stells were made, between 100 and 150 years ago, all three could be reached, without too much difficulty, from Knight farmhouses – Larkbarrow, Tom's Hill and Horsen. The shepherds would take fodder out if they possibly could.

The really bad snowstorms, sudden and unrelenting, are imprinted for ever in the memories of those who endured them. Vivid local anecdotes inform sons and grandsons which deep lane may fill with snow and freeze hard enough for a man with an unloaded cart to drive over it and see no hedges. They warn that it is dangerous to cross any open ground on foot during the storm, fatal to rest in the exhausting snow, vital to plunge on through it.

1891 was 'a remembered year', its winter very late, but long and terrible. The blizzard began on March 9th. Farmer Adams of Exford had just tilled his early spuds, his son Reg told me eighty years later. 'The snow comed in sudden, from the east, about four o'clock, and 'twas coming down like pepper. Father'd got two yowes had lambed early, down in the tunnel. 'E'd got a big chap called John working for 'n – big, tall, full-bearded – and 'e said to 'n, 'John, us'll go and get they in.' Twasn't but four little fields away. They went out, the snow was coming in, blinding of 'ee. 'E kept calling or saying things to John and 'e never answered a word – and when they got in, 'e found 'twas because John couldn't open 'is mouth, 'is moustache and beard was frozen together. Father used to tell how he got some boiling water, and kept wringing out the dishcloth, thawing the ice off till John could spake again.'

Either that or another blizzard caught an Exford farmer at Gallon House, on the Simonsbath road. He started home eastward, with his dog – called Tess, maybe – at his heels, but they were still two miles from home when a bend in the road brought them full into the blinding eye of the wind, and he decided he could not go on. There was a double hedge beside the road and he climbed up to spend the night on it. He settled comfortably, with the dog lying across his legs, the warmth of her body helping his, and fell asleep for a time, then, waking, realized that she was no longer with him. He could do nothing before daylight and tried to sleep again. Within an hour Tess was back; she had been home to feed her puppies, and returned to look after her master. In the morning they walked on to Exford together over the frozen snow.

On that March afternoon in 1891, when the blizzard came so suddenly two hours before sunset, Amos Cann, a young man who lived with his widowed mother at Greenlands near Exford, had gone to Porlock to sell two horses. Friends there urged him to stay the night, but he refused, knowing how his mother would worry until he was safely home. He insisted that he would be all right, and set off, on foot, and he had no dog. He nearly reached home by road; he had passed Alderman's Barrow but failed to strike the Greenlands track. Deep drifts, and exposure to the fierce cold, killed him. The snow lay deep for weeks, frozen hard in bright sunlight, and for seventeen days his body was hidden. His mother kept hoping that he had put up somewhere, was snowed in and could not send word. At last a slight thaw brought inescapable truth. 'She never really recovered,' said the ageing farmer who told me about it. 'And it was for her he did it – so that she wouldn't be worried.'

Spring that year, with the dry peppery snow covering everything, and probably whipped into changing drifts at the wind's whim, must have been calamitous for lambing. Nowadays, April is considered soon enough for that in the hills; a serious snowstorm then is unusual, though not unknown. Until very recently, lambs were all born out in the fields, and a sheep-farmer had to watch the weather like a sailor. Snow-buried ewes might survive, and even bear their lambs in a drift, but had to be found and freed before they starved. A wet spring might be equally harmful. Healthy thick coats keep the ewes warm, so long as they are dry, but the weight of sodden wool weakens them and makes a bad lambing year. The shepherd had time-honoured methods of helping nature. On a frosty night, going his round with a lantern every few hours, he might take a tired ewe and her new-born lamb to the barn, where bales of hay could make comforting little pens. If a difficult delivery failed, either ewe or lamb might die. Then, as now, if the ewe died, he would dress the orphan in the skin of a lamb which had died at birth, and patiently persuade the bereaved mother to take it as her own; relying on scent not sight she would sniff at it dubiously, and at length, with luck, allow it to feed. If there was no dead lamb to be skinned, the living one would be carried indoors, where the farmer's wife would pop it into a slow oven to get warm, then cherish it in the kitchen, feeding it by hand. She would teach it to drink from a bottle (rubber teats are still on sale in moorland village shops every spring) until it was strong enough to go out and nibble young grass with the others. It would remain a pet lamb, though, running in friendly expectation to anybody who walked across the field. These changelings, a joy to their proud rescuers, made up for all the trouble and mess which the housewife had accepted cheerfully in so good a cause.

A warm sunny spring, with good lambing, spread contentment all over the hill country. It was not only the farmer's pecuniary relief (though from very early times *pecus*, a flock, brought wealth – the fleece was golden). Nor was it only the satisfaction of a long task well concluded. The sight of young lambs at play on a sunlit hillside, while soft little white clouds moved across a blue sky, held timeless poetry. It proclaimed the renewal of life. All round the moor inquisitive lambs, hardly steady yet on their long legs, would run to their mothers for milk – tails wriggling in ecstasy, as they drank – then hurry back to absurd games with their companions while every ewe kept a wary eye on her own offspring.

For, as these matrons knew, there was danger, from which the farmer and his dog must guard them. Foxes, too, had their families in spring, and though a vixen with her cubs playing like kittens was also a pretty sight, the fox would now raid the in-bye as well as the hen runs to kill food for them, and his depredations had to be checked. 'Mommets' – a good Shakespearean word for scarecrows – were set up in mid-field, with lanterns hanging as though from their hands and lighted at dusk. Sometimes, if there was a breeze, this fooled the fox; sometimes not. Farmers might lie in wait with their guns, and perhaps bury the carcase discreetly in a thick wall where hounds would never detect it. Others snared them with wire, or used poisoned meat when their own animals were all shut up for the night. A few countrymen had the strange skill of 'whistling up the foxes', and one of these would always be welcome. By quiet arrangement he would go to the farm in the evening half-light, and walk slowly along under cover of a hedge until he was within earshot of the foxes' earth. Then – the farmer or his son standing by with gun loaded – he whistled in a way which brought either fox or vixen straight towards him. Afterwards, a different signal summoned its mate. If this could be done before the cubs were born, so much the better; but it saved the lambs on which they would have been fed.

In summer, work with the sheep was less exacting. Shearing and dipping were strenuous, and the sound of outraged bleating carried for miles between the hills. The flock was put out on the common or other rough pasture while the hay grew, and somebody had to ride round daily to see that all was well; he would take a bottle of disinfectant to treat wounds or sores. In early summer, if the weather was hot or heavy before the sheep were shorn, this patrolling became very important, for an animal tormented by parasites might lie on its back to roll, and be unable to get up unaided because of the weight of its fleece. Any country-bred passer-by would hurry to push it on to its side, until it could struggle to its feet and walk away in dudgeon, none the worse for the experience. But if it was left lying, its own efforts a failure, its courage gone, its legs sticking up motionless in the air, it would only live for a few hours – perhaps half a day – and birds of prey might attack it before it died.

Once the flock was shorn and dipped, that risk was over. Shearing would go forward smoothly if the weather was fine, but it might not be, and the wool must not get wet. The date was unalterable. On a given day, the same every year, just before or after midsummer, friends and relations would be due at a particular farm to help, and any different date would clash with somebody else's. So if a few days beforehand heavy clouds came bowling up from the south-west, the sheep had to be kept dry somehow or other. They would be shorn under cover in the barn, and the fleeces would be carried to the 'wool-chamber', the driest place available, at the far end of a loft or in the farmhouse itself, and stored there until a favourable time for selling. The days of wealth from wool were coming to an end, but it was still worth keeping back the wether lambs and putting them out on the hill to grow big and yield several more fleeces before they were sold at four or five years old as prime mutton. They would spend most of their lives 'out-over'. So a shepherd riding attentively along the ridges and combes remained a familiar figure all the year round.

Meanwhile, nearly all the other work done on the farm was for the well-being of the flock. Walls and hedges had to be made stock-proof. So had the field-gates and their coigns – the rounded ends of the hedge-banks on either side of the gap.[2] These were made of carefully chosen flat stones, like discs, placed one above the other in a column, a firm finish to the herring-bone walls. Abutting them might be a big standing-stone drilled with two holes as a gate-post; it was likely to be a prehistoric long-stone, uprooted from the moor and carried down on a sledge, or slung beneath a cart. Field-drains and neat little stone-built culverts had to be kept clear, since the merest pool of flood-water might be enough to drown a lamb. Shallow irrigation channels were dug

180

along the hillsides to provide an 'early bite' for the sheep and leave the lower pastures for hay. (Unfortunately the rabbits from far around enjoyed the early grass too, and once a farmer in the Vale of Porlock had all of his eaten in one night by wild geese pausing on migration.) Turnips were grown for winter feed, rush was cut to thatch the hay ricks. Hedges of beech, ash and hazel, properly relaid a length at a time, year by year, provided not only shelter, but also stakes for innumerable purposes, spar-gads (the pegs to keep the thatch in place) and a woodpile to supplement the peat-stack and keep the farmhouse warm.

The happiest and most sociable of these ancillary tasks, and always the most important, was making the hay which all the stock would need for winter keep. Machinery was just coming in to the more prosperous farms at the turn of the century, but hay was made entirely by hand on small remote ones until 1950 and after. And it had to be made while the sun shone, or at least during a series of rainless days. The cut grass lay out on the field until it was dry. Showers would damage it, prolonged rain could ruin the crop. So weather-lore was crucial. One farmer at least – and probably many others – kept a weather-book, a careful diary of the set of the wind, the phase of the moon, the sky at sunrise and sunset, and the shape and movement of the clouds. Any farm-hand or any cottager with an orchard to mow or a garden to till had a lifetime's practice in observing slight changes, good omens or bad. Nobody would fail to notice the gusty wind which ran along the ground lifting branches and showing the underside of leaves; many had a home-made barometer, a 'weather-bottle'; everybody knew when the moon would next be new or full, and anxiously hoped that with the spring tides for the sailor it would bring a fortnight's settled weather for the farmer. Nor would anyone sow or plant under a waning moon, and some would not put the rams to the ewes until it was waxing again. And after a wet St Swithun's day nobody would count on any harvest sunshine in the next six weeks.

If the weather seemed set fair when the grass was ready for mowing, the farmer and his sons and workmen would go to the hayfield as soon as the dew had vanished – early on an eastward or southward slope, miserably late if the farm land was 'back-sunded' (dropping steeply to the north). They cut with scythes, working aslant downhill, in echelon (Blackmore's 'like half a wedge of wildfowl') and on reaching the bottom walked up again, whetted their scythes, and went down mowing the next strip in the same way. Men from other farms might come to help in the evenings, for friendly company, and for the beer or cider which the farmer supplied to help things along. In fine weather the swathes were raked into long rows and left to dry; in a day or two, as the wilting grass lost weight, women and old men and children would toss and turn it, with picks or wooden rakes, until it was 'made'. In catchy weather it was pulled into heaps along the rows and carefully built into pooks (haycocks) so that the rain would run off the surface, and only a little be spoiled. On the first fine morning it would be spread out to dry, but if the afternoon 'turned away wet' it had all to be pooked again as fast as possible. When all was fit to be carried, the lines were 'spurred up' towards one end, and row by row the new sweet hay was pitched up with forks on to a waiting waggon – or, even as late as 1920 in Carhampton, a sledge – or directly on to a rick which was rising steadily in a corner of the field. Rick-building was skilled work – wintry gales and storms would find out any weaknesses, and a collapsed rick was a disgrace which could not be hidden. A tarpaulin was temporary protection until there was leisure for thatching. While the rick grew, helpers who had not enough muscle to pitch the hay were raking the remnants together, leaving a beautifully clean field for the 'after-grass'. If there was only a little hay, or some left over from the big rick, it might be made into 'round mows' – cylindrical to about shoulder-height, then narrowed into a cone. These, too, would be thatched, with skill that fascinated onlookers, only half a century ago.

Harvest-home, the thanksgiving for all crops, might be delayed by bad weather and a late corn-harvest. Meanwhile the autumn sales of cattle and sheep went forward, in one parish after another, and they were of crucial importance. Whether selling or buying or only watching, farmers would note the auction prices, study the quality and condition of other men's stock, and meet old friends and neighbours from miles around. But the best of all was Bampton Fair at the end of October, the great pony-sale of the year. That was an unforgettable treat for the whole family. And it was preceded by another annual event, relished even more heartily by the farmers who took part – the rounding-up of the wild ponies on the moor. In the sheep and cattle drifts of older times, Free Suitors summoned by the Forester had sometimes avoided an unwelcome duty by sending incompetent substitutes, but no vigorous commoner in later days would willingly miss the exhilaration of pony-gathering, the Saturday before Bampton Fair.

The foals were still running with their mothers and had never been handled. All had to be brought together in an enclosure where they could be parted, the foals being claimed by their owners and kept for sale, the mares put back to the wild. On Brendon Common the gathering would take a whole day, or sometimes more. Thirty or forty riders would spread out along the fringe and work up the combes to find the ponies. They drove them up to a broad ridge and then closed in on them in a great noose which gradually narrowed until the whole herd of

182

several hundred was steered into the customary yard or field. The mares had been driven before, the foals had not, but all thought they might be safer outside this ominous ring of riders. So the only way to keep them together was to take the whole thing at a gallop, leaving them no opportunity to break out. It meant some very rough going, and required experience and skill. The riders loved it. In 1941 an old man of eighty-four was looking forward to 'going after the ponies' for the seventy-first time.

At the end of the day's excitement came the memorable party at The Staghunters' or at Brendon Barton where the ponies were secure. The whole company assembled to eat and drink, talk and sing and play cards, far into the night, and went home early on Sunday morning in the happy expectation of the same again next year.

On the Monday, owners and prospective customers met at Brendon in The Staghunters' yard for the preliminary pony-sale, where many of the foals were bought and taken away, some of them for resale at Bampton on Thursday. That left two clear days for getting them all to the Fair. To drive a hundred ponies from Brendon right across the moor needed expert horsemanship. Journeys from Challacombe with about forty are remembered after two or three generations. The ponies, unshod, could trot peacefully along the lanes through Simonsbath and nearly to Exford, then southward to Comer's Gate. But between there and Dulverton stretched Winsford Hill, open moorland where the Acland ponies grazed, and if the herds mingled out there it would be very difficult to separate them. So the drovers behaved as in a pony-gathering – surrounded their animals and galloped them across, one rider ahead, one behind, and two at each side to head off any attempt at escape. After Mounsey Hill gate, lanes took them easily to Bampton, and a night's food and rest before the sale.

Bampton Fair dated from the twelfth century, when King Henry II gave it a charter, but it was only when Exmoor ceased to be a Royal Forest and there were no more pony-sales at Simonsbath that Bampton took over that trade. Horse and pony were all-important on the moor; until well into the nineteenth century there was no wheeled traffic to the hill-villages and farmsteads, because too few roads were fit for it. Oxen were ploughing and harrowing, but the hill-shepherd needed a pony. The farmer rode everywhere, and so did his womenfolk. James Hill of Newland bequeathed his Exmoor grey mare to his daughter in 1732; John Clarke took his bride home across the moor, on the pillion, in 1814; a mill-wright's sale-catalogue in 1852 mentions a side-saddle. To go to market, or down to the village shop, or to church or chapel, they had either to ride or walk. Rings for tethering the horses remained in use until a few decades ago, and stone upping-stocks for remounting can still be seen here and there. (One of them stands by the lane outside Skilgate churchyard.) Towards the end of the century a well-to-do farmer or tradesman might perhaps own a pony-trap for special occasions, and the weekly carrier's cart to the nearest market town would take passengers – reducing the fare for those willing to walk up the long hills. But all who could keep a pony habitually rode.

The farmer's sturdy little Exmoor would age at last, and his children, learning to ride (bareback, of course) needed quiet mounts if they were to help with the sheep or cattle. So, unless satisfied at Brendon pony-sale, everybody who wanted either a grown pony or an unbroken foal went off to Bampton Fair. The auctions were straightforward; buyers and sellers included the gypsies, always keen judges of horse-flesh, and knackers were present too, because there was a market for horse-meat. Horse-coping between man and man, or man and boy, demanded wary self-confidence, and some bad bargains were struck if ale or cider had been too strong. Until about the turn of the century, or later, behaviour might be very rough. Vendors drove their wild ponies up and down the street to show them off: residents barricaded their doors and windows. One pub was so filled with rogues every fair-day that no prudent countryman would enter it. But in the course of time pens were set up in a field and the auction was held there. The streets became the scene of a normal – though especially good and lively – fair, an outing for families from all over the moor. Amid the crowd, in the hubbub of shouting and neighing, the chaffering at food-stalls, the street music and the cries of excited children, were tricksters of every kind. Fortune-tellers were offering a rosy future, quack doctors selling cure-all pills, cant preachers selling salvation, and cheap-jacks crying any wares which indulgent parents or ardent young suitors might be persuaded to buy, on this great holiday of the year.[3]

Ponies were for work; for play, other and bigger horses were required, to carry young gentlemen or old across miles of moorland in pursuit of the deer, and hunters were not bought at Bampton Fair. Many came straight from private stables – at one time from the Knights' stud at Simonsbath – and they were a mark of social difference in the field.

Stag-hunting had been accounted the sport of kings, in olden days. It had lapsed and been restored at least twice, but in the late nineteenth century it was still 'the ancient art of venery', and still very largely class-based. For a long time only the rich man in his castle could afford to keep a pack of hounds, and when conditions became too difficult he had to give it up. So hunting stopped at the beginning of the Civil War, in 1642, when the royalist Sir

Hugh Pollard was Warden, and it was not revived for about a hundred years: the Puritans of Cromwell's government frowned on other people's pleasures, and after the Restoration Boevey the half-Dutch Londoner retained the wardenship, and he took no interest in the chase. At length, in the middle of the eighteenth century, Sir Thomas Dyke Acland, the seventh baronet, inheriting from his wife's uncle Edward Dyke, became Warden and Master of Staghounds, and began the astonishing period, rather larger than life, which his son the second Sir Thomas continued in the same style.

Both men, immensely enthusiastic and generous, attracted a huge following from far and wide. The elder had kennels at Holnicote and Pixton, and it was he who gave dinner on silver plates to followers who lasted out the day. (One morning in the early autumn of 1759 a field of some 1500 assembled – more than 500 on horseback, about 1000 on foot. But it was a 70-mile run, which surely must have thinned out the 500 long before dinner-time?) One of the sporting parsons, the Rev. John Boyce of Hawkridge and Withypool, who seldom missed a day's run, kept a diary for many years, during the reign of the second Sir Thomas. He spoke of this Master's fury if sheep were killed – 'Sir Thomas *ordered* the Huntsman to *Hang Himself* and the whole pack'. He described, too, a run from Holnicote via Alderman's Barrow and Cheriton to Hillsford Bridge; His Honour's horse went lame at Alderman's Barrow and gave out at Cheriton, so he ran the rest of the way from there to be present at the finish.

But when this baronet died, the French Revolution was raging, and the long wars against France had begun. The later Aclands were not hunting men. War brought financial strains, active young men joined the army and navy, and there were over-many changes of Master. A subscription pack was tried, but the arrangement did not last. In 1825 the hounds were sold to Germany. Since wild deer were not protected by the vicious Game Laws, a great many were now killed either for the pot or in defence of root-crops and corn. The herds dwindled, and one way and another hunting was in the doldrums for another thirty years – more than fifty in all. In 1855 it was re-established, largely through the persistent efforts of Dr Charles Palk-Collyns of Dulverton, with a subscription pack, and a new Master, Mr Fenwick Bissett, invited from 'away', and during his long tenure there was a complete change of attitude.

The big landlords in the wooded fringes of the moor had always valued the wild deer for their grace and beauty, as well as enjoying the chase and the venison. But in the unrest of the first half of the nineteenth century, the time of machine-wrecking and sheep-stealing and ferocious 'justice', and the 'hungry forties' when corn-harvests were failing, Exmoor farmers had no affection for these wasteful feeders, destroyers of far more than they ate, and villagers shared their hostility when stags and hinds came quietly down at night and raided garden-plots.

Richard Jefferies recorded the change. In the middle of the century, he said, the deer were almost extinct. Hill-farmers and local people were shooting them openly, and when a great plundering stag was slain his body would be paraded triumphantly through the village in a cart. After a while the farmers became more surreptitious, packing the venison into the salter as soon as possible. By the time Jefferies wrote, in 1884, it was very rare, he said, to hear of any deer being shot or poached. 'So greatly has popular opinion changed during the last seven and twenty years on Exmoor that at the present day were a man to shoot a stag he would be utterly sent to Coventry. No one would speak or deal with him or acknowledge his existence. He would be utterly cut off from society of every class, not only the upper but the lower classes being equally imbued with the sporting feeling.'

The deer did as much harm as ever, to apples and corn, turnips and saplings, and Jefferies affirmed that 'without the goodwill of the farmers stag-hunting could not last a single season'. Consequently they were wooed to share in the excitement. Landlords expected tenants to allow the hunt to cross their farms, and compensation was paid for deer-damage. A farmer would inform the harbourer if a stag was lying up in one of his coverts,[4] and would be consulted by the huntsman about access and viewpoints. Local people, gentle or simple, would attend a meet near home; in the woods and pastures of their own parish they might make a good guess at where the roused stag would run, and, sharp-eyed, be the first to view him. Many a farmer at work in his fields would keep a saddled pony tethered near at hand, and would mount and follow if hounds came his way. Other links were forged; farmers' wives walked the hound-puppies, and shows, race-meetings, and point-to-points were social events which all could enjoy. It helped to harmonize, if no more, the 'two nations' of Victorian England.

The lords and their kin, who might have high Roman noses or Norman names, mediaeval titles or Tudor mansions, had known their Saxon commoners for a very long time. They were the Masters of Staghounds, while the tenantry provided hunt-servants – significant appellations, not resented. Together they depended on the woodcraft and wiles of a good huntsman to make the most of the day. The followers, from manor or cottage – or indeed, from local rectory or surgery or lawyer's office – were there for various reasons. For the real enthusiasts the fascination lay in watching huntsman and hounds at work, the tufters[5] seeking out the warrantable stag located by the harbourer, separating it from the rest, and driving it out on to the moor where pack and field could take up the chase. There was also the exhilaration of a good gallop over the hills on a good horse, the stimulating touch of danger, the companionship at covert-side, and the absorbing reconstruction afterwards; the tales were told for years – tales in which the stag was almost the hero, certainly the noble foe. It was a glorious anachronism.

A curious building, Simonsbath Tower – known sometimes as the Round House, sometimes ironically as Simonsbath Castle – may be connected with a different means of killing deer. It stands alone in a field west of the road up to Preyway Head from Simonsbath House. It is cylindrical, some five paces in diameter; it has no roof now, and its wall, made of small flakes of sandstone laid horizontally, is 10 feet high at its tallest, but crumbling at the upper edge. It has a neat sham-Gothic doorway on the eastern side. This is only 6 ft 2 in. high at its apex; a single-slab doorstep leads in to a slightly raised floor, and the wall is pierced at irregular intervals by a few small oblong holes, probably structural. Assuming that the building was roofed, it would have been dark and damp, and until the road-banks were made, in 1928 or thereabout, it would have been fully exposed to the east wind, at 1300 feet above sea-level. Though circular, it was clearly not a round-house in the local farming sense, and it certainly cannot have been intended for comfort or amenity.

No firm record of its date or purpose seems to survive. The 'Gothic' building-style indicates the Knights rather than Boevey, and being inside the Forest it must have been put up for one or the other. (One local anecdote ascribes it to Frederic Knight.) Exmoor people have puzzled for years over its purpose, without finding a convincing explanation. Two generations back an archaeological team from up-country searched the surroundings and found only a bullet, about a gunshot to the north. Then a few years ago came the first authentic clue from local knowledge. An octogenarian in Lynton described how, as a stripling, he set out to walk to Simonsbath, over Lyn Down, and by the track from Hoar Oak to Exe Head and Dure Down, and lost his way near Exe Head in thick mist. He went on down the southern slope, guessing his direction, and then suddenly, to his great relief, saw 'the old shooting-tower' in front of him. This would have been within a decade or two of Frederic Knight's death, before memories faded.

John Knight had made a deer-park from Blue Gate to Preyway, and stocked it with the destructive fallow deer which in Frederic's time had all to be shot. One field to the east of the tower a distinctive wall runs roughly parallel with the road, at the steep edge of Ashcombe, for 150 paces; its present height varies between 4 and 6 feet, but thirty or forty years ago it was 9 feet high, and buttressed on the eastern side. Instead of the traditional herring-bone or vertical stone-work, devised for the rain to run down and away, this short stretch was made as the tower was, with thin slabs of shale laid horizontally. The likeness suggests that they were built at the same time, and by the same masons, for a particular purpose.

Was the tower a butt or hide from which the Knights and their friends, one or two at a time, could shoot the fallow deer for meat, and gradually exterminate the herd? Ernest Mold, who picked up the 'shooting tower' clue in Lynton, has lately added two others, one from field-work and the other from Orwin's book. He points out (in the *Exmoor Review, 1990*) that the doorway looks straight towards the gate at the southern end of the wall, and that a man standing back a couple of feet in the dark building would have a wide view, but would himself be invisible except from very near. For deer coming uphill from the combe the 9-foot wall would be too high to jump, and they would head, or perhaps be quietly headed, for the gap at the southern end. They would come on unsuspectingly towards the tower, and the hidden marksman could wait for a sure kill. Orwin noted that at Wolverley, the Knights' family home in the Midlands, 'there were some good heads of Exmoor fallow-deer ... each with the bullet-hole in the centre of the forehead'. It is a very persuasive hypothesis. The mediaeval kings and lords waiting with their barbed arrows for driven deer would feel quite at home.

The sport of active young men from poorer homes was wrestling. It was very popular when Vancouver wrote his survey of Devon in the early 1800s, and he described how the bouts were arranged. A purse of six to ten guineas was made, and a day fixed; the site chosen was usually near a big village or market town, and the ring, 15–20 yards across, was marked out by stakes and a single rope. To win, a contestant must toss or throw down five adversaries in a knock-out tournament. 'Above the waistband' no holds were barred. Each contest might last ten to fifteen minutes; much strength and skill were deployed, and meanwhile the wrestlers' shins were often streaming with blood from the kicks 'which on no account are ever permitted to be given above the knee'. (This was the Cornish style; elsewhere in England kicking was forbidden, and in the Lake District the competitors took their shoes off and fought in their socks.) More than a century after Vancouver wrote, the Rev. Walter Joyce described from his knowledge of the Brendons how the kicking began the match. The two men stood with outstretched arms, grasping each other's shoulders. They wore special boots, wide-toed and heavy, and they had tossed for the first kick. 'At the signal the first kicker launched his blow on the enemy with the force of a football player, and the second, if he had strength enough, kicked back in return, and finally the two closed in for a fierce struggle to place the vanquished on his back. It was in all points a brutal fight excepting that fists were not used.' Vancouver said that the fight generally began between two and three in the afternoon, and the competitors were so well matched that the winner might not be declared until after midnight, 'in which case the ring is properly lighted, and the same precautions continued during the whole time to secure fair, and prevent foul play'. There were three umpires, and no appeal.

But if it ended earlier in the evening, and local patriotism was inflamed, there might be outbreaks of violence with no umpire. It is recorded that after a fight at Exford the whole company would repair to the bar of the White Horse, near the bridge, and twice a Withypool winner, William Hawkins (an old man remembering, in the 1920s) was very nearly thrown into the river by the loser's angry friends. On one occasion he broke free, and when a group of Withypool men came along his persecutors melted away. On the other, he said, he was only saved by a man called Steer (of Exford?) pulling him back over the parapet by his legs, and threatening to report the roughs if they did not stop.

The sport continued, in spite of these untoward incidents, and the champions were proud of their scars. In Parracombe an old man of ninety-two who died in the late 1960s recalled, in conversation with his doctor, his grandfather's exploits: 'When I was a boy, Granfer used to say, "Feel my shins". And when I felt his shins they was all jagged. "Ah", says Granfer, "that were from wrestling, down in Cornwall. Us used to go to Cornwall to wrestle, now and then. But us all used to go together, in a bunch, on our ponies. 'Tweren't safe else, in they days." '

In the eighteenth and well into the nineteenth century most parishes held – as before the Reformation – an annual 'Revel' to celebrate the feast day of their patron saint. In their heyday the Revels began with a church service and might last a week, and wrestling was the chief amusement. Perhaps the Church was trying to moderate the sport by annexing it. The 'purse' raised by subscription began to be used to buy prizes; in Countisbury church, in the early part of the nineteenth century, the silver spoons to be wrestled for were hung in front of the gallery at morning service on Revel Sunday. (In some parishes, winners proudly wore the spoons in their hatbands after the day's event.) At Knowstone and Exton, said Joyce, 'wrestling of the most brutal order was the game of the feast', and the prize, a beaver-skin top-hat, was placed on the altar to be seen by all during the afternoon service. Sometimes the parson won it. The Rev. John Froude of Knowstone may indeed have taken pleasure in kicking his parishioners' shins.

Later in the century most of the Revels came to an end – some because wrestlers, by pre-arranging the results, disillusioned the subscribers, and some because the clergy thought the Sunday merry-making kept people away from church. Some were continued, or revived, and held on a weekday linked with the saint's day; the Revel became a fair, with pony-races (silver spoons for prizes) and the kind of country competitions which were familiar at 'club-walking'. The strongest men tried who could carry the blacksmith's anvil furthest. The most agile competed to catch a wether which had been parted from the flock; his rear had been shaved and then greased, and offered no handhold when he was set free and made his best speed back to the moor. There were shooting-galleries, swings, dancing and sweet-stalls. (In the 1870s a labourer called William Spurrier, who lived in a tumbledown cottage in Parracombe, used to go round to fairs and revels selling sweets and gingerbreads.) It was all great fun for young and old.

The Holywell Revel in the parish of North Molton may have an extremely long past, perhaps reaching back to pagan worship of the well. Its waters were still visited by invalids at the Revel on Ascension Day, almost until the First World War – the last occasion was in 1912. Though the spring is a long way from any house, a Holywell Chapel of Ease was licensed in the fourteenth century. Why?

Descriptions in 1877 and 1884 emphasized the holy well, not the revel. The North Devon Handbook of 1877 spoke of it as neglected: the well, about 20 inches deep and flagged at the bottom, had in past times always been cleaned out before Holy Thursday, but was no longer kept in such good repair, though a few invalids still came. The water was believed to be most efficacious in the early morning, and accordingly some visitors used to arrive the previous evening in the hope of having the first dip of the water at daybreak, either to drink it as a cure, or to bathe sore eyes. (Blindwells were not uncommon; one gave its name to a farm only two or three miles from Holywell.) An old woman used to attend the spring on Ascension Day: sufferers were expected to throw silver money into the well, and in the evening she carefully scooped it out in 'a long-handled bowl made for the purpose'. (Would not most of the coins have been the pretty little 'drippenny bits' which used to be put in Christmas puddings for luck? From the poor or infirm threepence would be a considerable offering.)

The decline seems to have been arrested. In 1884 the *North Devon Herald* reported that, 'On Thursday, last, Ascension Day, this celebrated well was as usual visited by suffering mortals with various diseases. One lady came from Tiverton...' A century later a few old people in North Molton still remembered a little about the well and the Revel. One told me that his mother and her friends used to carry up teapots and bring some of the precious water home. Another, Mr George Smith, a nonagenarian in 1981, spoke chiefly about the Revel, the annual village outing: children, if they were lucky, would ride up in Mr Lethaby's donkey-cart; Mr Lethaby, a shoemaker, who lived near the bridge, took his parties round by the lanes and into the fair-ground from the far side. Asked about the elusive tradition of a chapel, Mr Smith remembered none in his day, but then, rummaging in the back of his mind, recalled reading in an old book (which proved to be White's *Gazetteer*) that North Molton had once had three episcopal chapels, one of them at Holywell. In the 1960s Norman Annett, then schoolmaster of the village and an active explorer of its history, wrote that in the nineteenth century an old chapel had stood about 100 yards downstream from the well, a small, single-roomed building in which services for pilgrims were held. He searched that area but found nothing conclusive. He had also been told that the Revel had been held near this, 'in the only flat field below the spring'. But in the 1980s Arthur Bray of Millbrook farm, which includes the stream and the surrounding fields, offered practical evidence for both sites being not downstream but uphill on the left bank.

The hillside immediately across from the well is called Revels Field. Now subdivided, it was previously one large enclosure, steep near the foot but then levelling into a plateau, very suitable for races and all the fun of the fair, with easy access for carts at the far side, somewhere between Balls Cross and Kensal Cross. (Perhaps it should be explained that Balls Cross is neither dance-floor nor religious monument, but the lane-crossing for the farms of Wester, Middle and Easter Ball, in the parish of Twitchen, and a Ball is a rounded hill.)

Farmer Bray had lived nearly all his life at Millbrook, his father's farm. As a boy he had worked in those fields with an old labourer who had known them for a great many years before that, and used to tell him, while they sat under a hedge to eat their lunch, of changes he had seen. He had said something about a former chapel, and had pointed out to the boy what he believed to be the remains of a small rectangular platform in the grass. He had never heard tell of any cottage or shed there. When Arthur grew older, and inherited the farm, he investigated the well. The spring was blocked but he cleared it, and the water, running free, tasted delicious. He pondered over the stone rectangle for years, and was inclined to think it had been some sort of shrine. In 1981 he and his wife led me round the whole site on a fine summer evening.

The spring would have been difficult to find without help – it is close to a hedge-bank and was half-hidden by tall grasses. But there was no doubt about the cold clear water welling up, and then running downhill to join the main rivulet in a marshy pool a few yards away. Another hedge-bank borders that stream on the other side, along the lower edge of Revels Field, and there are traces as of a former way through it. Up in the nearest corner of the field I was shown the little platform, about eight paces by four, intermittently defined by almost buried boulders, apparently the footings of four walls. The roof they supported would have been thatched. Looking back from there directly towards the well it was easy to see the alteration in the hedge-bank. For a few yards the style of walling was different, and the trees were noticeably younger. A gap like a gateway had been filled in, perhaps with fallen stones from the chapel walls. The farmer's careful guess at the age of this new piece was 'about seventy years – certainly not less than fifty nor more than a hundred'. This would match the known date of the last Revel, 1912.

If, then, this isolated ruin near the well was a pilgrims' chapel, surely it must also have been the Holywell Chapel of Ease licensed in the fourteenth century, for pilgrim congregations, since there was no manor-farm to justify it? Belief in the sanctity of the spring must therefore have been older than that, and presumably inspired the building of this little stone chapel, or maybe a yet simpler one, of timber, before it. But when? The Church had accepted it, with its Saxon name (pronounced with a short 'o', as in holiday). Had St Augustine's followers incorporated into Christianity a cult which they could not eradicate? It is not unlikely. He told his missionaries to consecrate everything they could.

The Celts who preceded and outlasted the Romans in Britain worshipped their water-goddess Anu so persistently that when, a conquest later, Pope Gregory's missionaries came to convert the heathen Saxons, they found the old belief still very strong. St Augustine was worried by its tenacity and referred the matter to the Pope, who replied that he should simply dedicate Anu's wells to St Anne, mother of the Virgin. (The oldest church in Buxton Spa is St Anne's, and St Anne's Well there had been known to the Romans by the Celtic name *Arnemetia*.)[6] Others were consecrated, as Lady Wells, to the Virgin Mary, others again to St Catherine or St Agnes – keeping the sense of a female deity – or, with a different suitability, to St John the Baptist. Some of the springs certainly had mineral and perhaps medicinal qualities, and any good they did was attributed to the benevolence of the patron saint.

North Molton holy well is no longer regarded, the chapel has almost disappeared, and the revels are ended. But reverence for springing water as a source of life is primaeval, and the housewives filling their teapots only two or three generations ago may have been the last humble devotees in a line stretching back two or three thousand years.

There were other pleasures, home-made and untrammelled by

professionalism. Martinhoe and Parracombe met for an annual 'football' match; it was played across country, with a goal in each parish, an unrestricted number of players, and no particular rules. At Dulverton the Pixton estate parties were held in a barn, and the dancers trod so vigorously on the earthen floor that the thud of their feet brought the worms up, and they had to stop. Young people from lonely farmhouses found the fun of village dances worth a walk or ride of 10 or 12 miles; after dancing for hours to a fiddler's tunes they set off back across the moor on foot or on horseback, a cheerful group bent on seeing all the girls safely home.

There was no lack of fiddlers while the 'choir' played every Sunday in the musicians' gallery in church. Thomas Hardy's father, in the Dorset village of Stinsford, had played there since his own youth, and taught his little boy the violin as soon as he was big enough to hold it. The son, growing up, delighted in playing the old tunes for the old dances, all over the countryside, and caught the enjoyment of it all in lilting poems. Then, in *Under the Greenwood Tree*, he commemorated the 'choirs' of his father's time, and the sadness when they were disbanded in favour of a harmonium or American organ. It happened everywhere. In St Petrock's above Parracombe the gallery of box-pews is unaltered, though a harmonium was installed (with Miss Helena Crocombe as chief player) before the new building down in the village became the parish church, in 1878. At one end of the musicians' pews a larger box with a lowered floor provided extra room for the player of the bass-viol. In Withypool, aspiring instrumentalists had queued up for admission to the choir; they had practised regularly, waiting for somebody to die. The organ came, and the parishioners were disgusted; it was 'like a drumble-drane in a jar'. The dismissed performers nursed a grievance. A farmer told me that his grandmother never went to church afterwards, 'or hardly ever'. Her relations had been slighted and services were not the same. A link between church and village had been broken.

Singing remained a shared pleasure, especially carol-singing. Some Exmoor parishes had carols of their own, pitched low so that ageing voices could manage them on a cold winter evening. But by the end of the century that too was less cohesive. Some time in the 1880s the Withypool choir was split by a quarrel about sheep-stealing, and shortly before Christmas it broke up – a sad disappointment in the village. A simple episode lodged itself in a boy's memory and survived.

Fred Reed was eleven, and was working for an old couple called Thorne at South Hill, then a very small holding on the right bank of the Barle. He lived in, by way of wages, and remained there all through Christmas. As the day drew near the elders were moody and restless. Mr Thorne had been a carol-singer for upwards of sixty years and thoroughly disapproved of this unneighbourly conduct. On Christmas Eve they sat gloomily by the fire until, after a time, Mrs Thorne went out to the dairy. Then the old man rose quickly, took some papers from a cupboard, picked up his lantern and slipped quietly out of the house. He walked up the lane as far as the road bordering the moor, and then returned, singing a little to warm up his voice and feel a bit Christmassy.

Back at the farmhouse he quavered a snatch of a carol, and knocked on the door, which was opened at once. 'Good evening, Mrs Thorne. A merry Christmas to 'ee!' She had known him a long time: 'Good evening to 'ee all,' she replied, warm-heartedly. He set up his lantern, unfolded the sheet of music – though of course he knew all the carols by heart – announced the first, and went through the proper number, while she, in the doorway, listened and smiled and nodded appreciatively to right and left. Next, she invited the whole choir in to bite and sup, brought out the home-brewed and the mince-pies, and gravely welcomed 'them', each by name. He, as gravely, thanked her on behalf of all. The two kept up the charade for a time, then he said 'they' must be going, as they had yet to sing at Blackmoorland and Batsham. More thanks, and cordial goodbyes, and he picked up music and lantern and led his shadowy company away into the night.... He returned 'alone' and husband and wife talked contentedly about the singing, then settled down to enjoy Christmas.

They had been born soon after Waterloo, long before Queen Victoria inherited the crown, and this was the decade of her Golden Jubilee. They would preserve their world if they could. The boy, watching with an eleven-year-old's lofty contempt, thought them crazy; he was impatient for the eating to begin.

The Thornes had no children, the farm changed hands more than once, and they were almost forgotten. Some forty years later Farmer Fred Reed of Knighton, two miles upstream, happened to hear a story of winter sheep-stealing in the bad old days, and it reminded him of that Christmas-time. Looking back, he recognized the old couple's spirit, and the childlike sincerity behind their pretence, and he described the little scene to his son, adding from a sympathetic imagination the details which he could not have seen himself. He died, and nobody remembered the Thornes until in 1950 the son, Harry, farming Knighton in his turn, chanced to see their name in a faded parish record, recalled the tale, and told it to me.

CHAPTER ELEVEN

'Houses rise and fall'

At the end of the eighteenth century Exton was described as 'one of those high parishes near Exmoor that teaches its inhabitants the virtues of industry and frugality from a necessity of nature'. The necessity did not diminish in any of the hill parishes in the following generations. The nineteenth century was full of uncertainties – enclosures and emigration, doubtful mining ventures, extreme poverty, and the drift from the country to the towns – and it left more ruined buildings than perhaps any other time since the Black Death. And while the plague-stricken hamlets of the fourteenth century were deserted and then avoided, for fear of infection, so that the old walls tumbled only slowly, industry and frugality hastened the more recent decay. Smallholders or villagers, not afraid of hard work, would remove as much stone as they could to repair cowsheds or build new linhays or walls. It was as though even the houses were restless.

Some had been inadequately built, of poor stone, and could not be expected to last long in rain and wind. The most ephemeral, of course, were those contrived under Squatters' Rights. If between sunset and sunrise a landless man, working on common land with the help of family or friends, could erect something with four walls and a roof, and – all-important – 'a chimbley smoking', and could call four witnesses, he was entitled to keep it. The hearth made it a home; details could come later. One of the last to be built like this was in Withypool, on a corner of moorland beside the Hawkridge road; until lately a few elderly men knew of it from old hearsay, but any trace of it on the ground had long since vanished. At Challacombe in the 1850s, on a boundary up against Pixy Rocks, one Joe Nicholls tried to give himself longer by beginning in foggy weather and using a rock face as one wall, but the mist cleared and he was stopped. It was probably his last bid for independence; later his name was on the poor-house roll.

He would not have had an easy time in his eyrie if he had completed it. Not far away the Saxon farm of Radworthy in Swincombe was failing. Its last inhabitant, John Harris, moved away to a cottage in the village in the 1860s, leaving the walls to crumble and the beeches of the garden hedge to grow into fine tall trees. He was not the only farmer to be forced out by 'financial cramp'. Yeomen sold up and became labourers. Tenancies fell vacant, and cottages were deserted: the hill-farming could no longer sustain them. The sheepfold high up in Long Chains Combe, where Frederic Knight's shepherd had lodged in a little dry-stone room at the corner of his sheep pen, was no longer needed. (That had been stoutly built against the weather; it still stands up well, and the hearth could be distinguished not very long ago. There was plenty of stone for building – possibly including the remains of a Bronze age village further up the hillside[1] – but it would be difficult to cart the stone to farm-land for reuse.) Some of the water-mills ceased work, but their great wheels were seldom wasted: they were taken away and used elsewhere. (One which drove farm machinery at the Glebe in Challacombe was not required there when the rector stopped farming, and it was moved to Lower Hole in Brayford. Not long ago its owners relinquished it to Hudley Mill, Charles, where it is now used to generate electricity.) Many lime-kilns were pulled down. As the years went by, some of the forges closed. At Folly, on the West Lyn, low banks among overgrown beeches are the remains of a school in which, towards the end of the century, sixteen children from outlying farms were taught the three Rs. When it fell down, none of its stone was left lying about.

Some small buildings on the former Royal Forest, put up long after 1819, were gone within a century or so. They had outlived their purpose, and as dwellings they were too remote. Mines which had been opened in mid-century were closed after a few decades, and the miners dispersed. Ruins and records of the mining cottages at Cornham and on the Brendons suggest that they were no loss to the moor – mean little terraces, cramped and overcrowded, grey and dismal in the rain.

The Bampfylde copper and iron workings in the valley of the Mole or Nymet above Heasley Mill were much older, though often closed and reopened. Ore from there went down to Barnstaple in 1729, and some was extracted from the Florence mine on the other side of the hill more than a century before that. When the Bampfylde closed, late in the 1800s, some thirty to forty cottages were left empty and were pulled down; Lord Poltimore invited his farmer-tenants to help themselves to stone or timber to repair the buildings they rented from him. Woodland and scrub, especially the quick-growing hazels which gave the hamlet its name, now veil the hillside workings and the ruins of a few small houses. One of these, down by the stream, is reputed to have been the temporary home of a Captain of Mines. All overgrown now, it had a little garden, where a generation ago children used to gather very luscious 'wild' strawberries, and where strangers are

196

28. Simonsbath Tower, in the 1970s *(A. Phillips)*

29. Simonsbath buttressed wall, in the 1970s *(A. Phillips)*

ABOVE: 30. The Lynton–Minehead coach on Porlock Hill

BELOW: 31. Heasley cloth mill, c. 1885

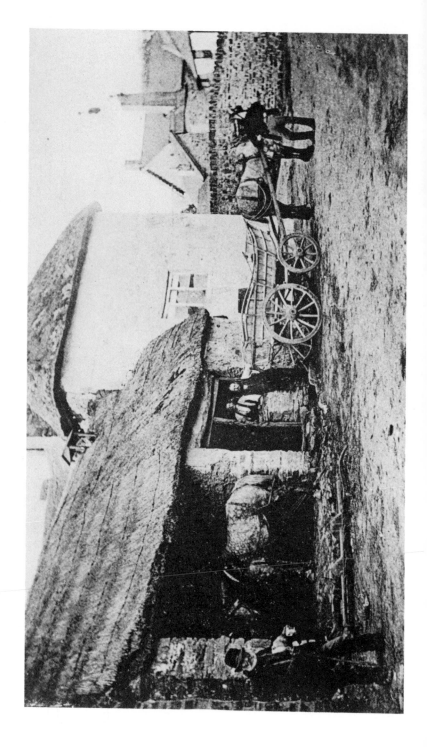

33. A Hawkridge farmhouse, 1895 *(Lithograph by Robert Bevan)*

Bevan (1865–1925) was an English art student in Paris in Van Gogh's time, and subsequently worked at lithography at Pont-Aven in Brittany among Gauguin's disciples. He then spent three or four years in Hawkridge, for the landscape and the hunting.

LEFT: 32. North Molton forge, c. 1890

35. Ernest Bevin in 1920 *(Press Association)*

LEFT: 34. Unloading coal at Lynmouth, c. 1928 *(Anon.)*

36. The Barle at Lanacre Bridge (*A. Phillips*)

still delighted to find lilies of the valley, and do not guess how they came there.[2]

For centuries Heasley village had been busy with cloth-making. A grist-mill recorded in 1669 was adapted, probably in the late eighteenth century; a huge oblong workshop, four storeys high and well-proportioned, was built to abut on it and run westward over what is now 'the green', and over part of the road beyond. It dwarfed the 'big house' as well as the cottages, and must have contained a great many looms.[3]

But in the middle of the nineteenth century the trade was ending, and at some time between 1851 and 1861 the woollen mill was closed. For a time it became a dormitory for the miners. When the mining ended too, it was entirely demolished; no trace of it is visible, and hardly any memory of it remains. But a picture-postcard has survived, and the chapel in the background dates that to the dormitory phase. The water-mill, no longer needed for fulling, reverted to its original purpose, and for a time it ground local crops of grain. Then it stood empty for a time, its gearing idle; now it is being adapted to make a dwelling.

In spite of the decay of so many buildings in the hard times of the nineteenth century, some new ones – farmhouses, rectories, Nonconformist chapels – were sound and have lasted. But far and away the most elaborate and expensive, an extravaganza like an eighteenth-century 'Folly', a flamboyant Victorian incongruity, visible for miles, was the Music Room at Woolhanger near Chapman Barrows, and by 1988 that was hardly more than a skeleton.

In 1889 Sir Henry Carew, ninth baronet in one of the big Devon families, and at that time only nineteen years old, married a young woman who had inherited Woolhanger Manor. He – or they – loved good music, especially if it was played on an organ, so he had a large octagonal concert-hall built, in the 1890s, close to their moorland farmhouse. One of its eight sides held a recessed platform, where he installed an excellent organ built in Bristol (no 'drumble-drane in a jar' for him!), and its bellows were powered by a water-mill out in the yard. The hall, domed inside and crowned by a rectangular lantern, is said to have been acoustically perfect. Now and then strains from Beethoven or Haydn used to float right over the moor as far as Brendon Two Gates – ethereal music, mysterious to any stranger riding across the bare hills at dusk.

Inside as well as out, the place is an architectural curiosity, gutted now but still impressive by virtue of its designer's brash self-confidence. He mixed his styles freely. The music room is an irregular octagon, imitating inaccurately the classical shape which eighteenth-century society enjoyed. It is approached through a long hall, the width of an empty eighth side, opposite the organ platform on a north–south axis. East and west, each middle wall of three contains a massive fireplace (for which Bath stone was fetched from Barnstaple by Sir Henry's carter). Each is surmounted by an immense carving of the Carew coat of arms, crest and proud Horatian motto.[4] The duplication is oppressive, but they give it something of the air of a Tudor banqueting-hall. Each of the walls flanking the identical fireplaces contains a tall square-headed window-frame, divided by stone mullions into three rows of four lights, the upper two rows 'Gothick', the lowest of well-proportioned upright rectangles. They are all vacant now, but once each of the sixteen along the highest level enclosed a small medallion-portrait, in stained glass, of a famous writer or composer – eight of each, selected by Sir Henry and hand-painted for him in Birmingham.[5] The lower windows were plain. The lantern was surrounded by small squares of glass, dark red, blue, green or clear, soberly Victorian, some of them still in place in 1988.

When the young owner wanted to hear his splendid organ really well played he sent his carriage down the rough lanes to bring out a renowned Barnstaple organist, Dr Edwards. It does not seem to be known who else enjoyed the recitals. There was room for a large audience, but these concerts at the turn of the century are just beyond living memory.

The whole thing was superb in its extraordinary way. It was a late-Victorian version of an eighteenth-century pavilion for music at the lakeside in a great man's ornamental grounds. The misfortune – or mistake –was its complete irrelevance to the moor. When the musical baronet sold up and went away, after only about fifteen years, its day was over.

A Mr (later Captain) Slater who bought it from him in 1907 was a keen fox-hunter; he sold the organ and domesticated the octagon. (The organ went to Yorkshire, and is likely to have been seen and heard for many years in the former Baptist Church at Hebden Bridge.) In 1939 the building was requisitioned for the forces, so the captain, long retired, moved away. When, a few years later, the War Office decided not to use it after all, he was not inclined to move back, and let it to Pickford's for the storage of furniture from bombed houses in Exeter and Plymouth. After the war he sold it to a couple who gave a great ball there for their daughter's coming of age. The guests were received in the first hall (by then a billiard-room) and went on down into the octagon to dance. One of them told me about it forty years later. Looking back, she was still thrilled: 'Fires blazing in both hearths – the orchestra playing on the platform – lots of people – all the ladies in long dresses – oh, it was lovely!' She was hardly twenty, and had grown up on a farm in the dingy war years when everything was rationed, clothes and dress-materials along with the rest. No wonder the party was unforgettable.

When buildings of special interest were listed for government protection, the criterion for any dated between 1840 and 1914 was 'definite quality and character'. The Music Room was excluded, having, perhaps, more character than quality. So when, about 1980, a stranger who had bought it thought it expendable, he could not be restrained. The water-wheel which had powered the organ had long been grinding farm corn. Now the lead was stripped from the roof and sold, and any saleable plaster-work was torn down. The stained glass musicians and writers went to Sotheby's. Finally the floor-boards were ripped up, and a farmer bought them to make good strong pig sties. The roof leaked, but remained; a swarm of wild bees came in through the empty window-frames and settled in the lantern; their honey used to run down to the floor. Then they deserted too. In 1989 its future came in question again. Anything might happen. 'Houses live and die.'

Entirely different, though equally eccentric, is the little Georgian poor-house at Ducombe Wells in the parish of Countisbury. Its exact date is uncertain, but it was standing in 1819, and one very much like it was built at Buckland Brewer, near Bideford, in the 1790s, to house four families, living independently without a warden. The design is ingenious – a cruciform building with a central chimney; each family had a separate wing, and all would be kept warm by the fire they shared. Ducombe had a second storey, attics with windows – one bedroom for each family? Whoever planned it, this little haven must have been built by local masons using the local material, and it is perfectly in harmony with its surroundings. So when the parish poor-houses were replaced by the dreaded urban 'Union Houses', it was not abandoned.[6] It is now a private house, lonely as a hermitage.

Shut away among the wooded hills it would have seemed to townsmen and their wives unbearably isolated. But it was built for country people, to whom the living silence was home. The setting was a proper Exmoor combe, with a lively little stream, trees dappling the ground and changing with the seasons, wild flowers and song-birds everywhere. A pauper who sat quietly on a fallen tree-trunk might be visited by an inquisitive hind or fox, might notice the ripple of a weasel's long back as he ran across the path, watch a buzzard planing overhead, or if nothing else, count on the company of a friendly robin. He – or she – would not feel quite so poor.

CHAPTER TWELVE

The women's part

The first two decades of the present century are a time not yet quite out of mind. The parents and grandparents of Exmoor people now in middle age had long and uncluttered memories, and would recall scraps of their own experience, or repeat what they had heard from their elders, with every detail vivid and exact. Men who survived the carnage of the Kaiser's war served on the home front in Hitler's, and some of them lived to see a third generation take the reins – or, by now, the wheel. It is not so very long ago.

In this nearer view, the women at work in farms and cottages can be distinguished at last. Of all those wives and daughters in all those 'long families' since before the Conquest, hardly a name, hardly a personality, is known. Grace Howe, finding the fugitive Major Wade in desperate need, stepped into history, but others who hid Monmouth's men were thankful to escape the spotlight. Mistress Joan Hill, the widow who ruled Newland, could not sign her name but ensured that her voice carried past her death. A few strong-minded women, in one century and another, were credited with magical powers; they frightened men as well as women, and their names have lasted, encrusted with sinister anecdotes. But most remained anonymous. Their endless hard work was taken for granted, and so, perhaps was family affection, but at the end mourners might stand by an unmarked earthen grave, because a memorial headstone would have cost too much. And some women, helpless victims in bad marriages, were kept silent by fear. In a remote farmhouse early in this century, one spoke for many: an elderly wife, newly widowed, stood at the dead man's bedside, looked down at him and said laconically, 'Well, you've been a bad husband to me.'

Life was much lonelier for the women than for the men. Farmers or their sons might go to buy or sell stock at a distant farm, or in the village or the nearest market-town, and some of them drank far too much, there or at home. A tale is told of a farmer who frequently slept in the churchyard, winter or summer, if he was too unsteady at closing-time to go any further. One morning when he was not yet home his wife turned on the tap of every barrel of beer or cider in the house, and let the liquor run down through the courtyard. The postman arrived, and saw the pigs and chickens reeling about drunkenly. But her device did the poor woman no good; her husband came home, beat her furiously, and bought a fresh supply of somebody else's home-brewed. Another wife was advised by friends to grease the stairs against her hard-drinking husband who staggered home late at night; he would have to sleep where he fell, while she stayed safe in bed.

The women hardly ever went far from home – they had not the time. Yet they held everything together; and a wife with ten or twelve growing children to be fed and clothed, and no housekeeping money except what she could earn by marketing her butter and eggs, was far too busy to repine. And usually too sturdy. Some had help from a girl living in, working for her keep and not much more, but many relied on the older children to look after the younger ones, to feed the chickens and geese and shut them up at night, and gather in the eggs, making sure they traced any hen who had 'stolen her nest'. Elder brothers and sisters would have to milk two or three cows each before they left for school in the morning, and milk again and feed the calves, and bring in firewood or peat, when they came home. In summer the boys might be needed for outdoor jobs, while the girls, in the kitchen, sliced beans or stripped redcurrants or peeled potatoes. And all the while, almost unconsciously, they were learning.

Very young they recognized every hand-reared lamb and every calf; before long they would be shown where deer were breaking through the hedges, or where badgers were breeding. Soon they would know dog-fox from vixen, as well as rabbit from hare. By the time they left school, at twelve years old, they were familiar enough with hill-farming to play a useful part in a life which was absorbing and endlessly varied, in surroundings they knew and loved. The farmer's wife had been brought up in the same way, and had all this to offset the remoteness. If she had no children, or they had grown up and gone away, her life was lonelier and harder, and good neighbours a few miles away were a very great boon.

At home, the old-fashioned farm kitchen was the heart of the house, unchanged for centuries (because money was not readily spent on any indoor comfort). It was the living-room, and friends and neighbours would troop into it after helping with shearing or haymaking, corn-harvest or threshing, and crowd the benches at the refectory table which stretched along one wall. The shearing-party was the best, when the wool-harvest was safely home; the men who had been working hard all day were feasted, and the fun went on, with drink and song and dancing, far into the night. As in Shakespeare's day, success depended on the warmth of the welcome, and on the generous preparations made. The table would be spread with good farm produce – home-cured ham, home-brewed cider, home-baked bread, butter and clotted cream fresh from the dairy, blackberry jam or whortleberry tart, cakes and buns made with new-laid eggs.

Food might be cooked in a crock on a trivet or 'brandiss'[1] on the great open hearth, or in one of the heavy pots which, like the kettles, hung from chimney-crooks as fire-blackened as they. For special feast-days a joint would be roasted 'to a turn' on the revolving spit. The fire was always kept burning; a huge log, the 'back-stick', would last a week and then be replaced. The chimney went straight up, very wide, to a view of the sky. On winter evenings snowflakes or hailstones might come down, and sizzle for a moment on the glowing logs, but the chimney-corner was where the family gathered, in high wooden settles against the draught, for fireside talk and old tales until it was time to light a candle and climb a narrow staircase, or perhaps a ladder, on the way to bed.

The farmer's wife took pride in her kitchen. Muddy boots had to be well wiped on the layers of dry bracken in the porch, sodden coats must be left in the back-house (the scullery) to drip. The stone floor was regularly sanded; the sand, trodden in, 'filed the dirt out', and when it was swept away the floor was cleaner than if it had been scrubbed. Then the housewife took a piece of white hearth-stone and made a pattern, all round the edge of the room, of 'squiggles, holes and squares, against witchcraft and all that'. My informant rememberd his mother doing that – 'as everybody else did' – until about 1930.

Much of the rough work was done in the back-house, to which – for lack of pipes and taps – pails full of beautifully soft water were carried in from the well. Here stood the copper, the wash-tub, and the mangle. Every Monday morning somebody had to pump up gallons of water and gather sticks to burn in the grate under the copper, and much hard work with brush and scrubbing-board was needed to clean the men's clothes, stiffened by farmyard grease and mud. Or there might be a huge cauldron, or boiler, hanging from the crooks over the hearth, and the washing would be stirred in that with a long stick. Later, the copper or boiler would heat fresh water for a luxurious hot bath in a tin tub in front of the fire. In a large family this treat might come only once a week; the luckiest had their turn on Saturday night, ready for worship and sociability next day.

Separate from kitchen and back-house, but not far away, was the dairy, cool and spotlessly clean. A low shelf of large slates along one wall rested on upright slabs of slate or columns of brick, like a miniature clapper-bridge, and on this stood the big pans full of clotted cream cooling. The churn was here too, of course, and that entailed further fear of the witch: if she had been slighted or rebuffed and afterwards no amount of churning would turn the milk to butter, that was believed to be her wicked revenge.

Outside the back door, chickens and geese foraged, and a companionable pig was encouraged to come for kitchen waste, a friendly word and a little back-scratching. Contentment would fatten him. Hens too old to lay were cooked and eaten, geese were pampered for sale at Michaelmas or Christmas, and when the pig was killed a flurry of work followed, to store the larder against winter. The bacon meat was packed into big salters or trundles; the hams were cured in a separate one, with honey and cider and saltpetre, and then hung from big meat-hooks embedded in the kitchen ceiling, to be smoked whenever a down-draught checked the fire. Part of the pig was made into sausages or brawn; the fat was melted down for lard; intestines, fried like crackling, became the chitterlings, a great delicacy – they would be stored in a steyn (a crockery jar) for winter treats. Nothing was wasted.

All this had been going on for longer than anyone could remember. Brass chimney-crooks and milk pans, copper boilers, salters and trendles were bequeathed as valuables in the Newland wills of the seventeenth and eighteenth centuries. In 1852 Richard Huxtable of Challacombe Mill, retiring and selling off farm-stock, mill gear (including a cast-iron wheel) and household goods, offered at auction 'Iron Pot and Boilers; 2 Brass Kettles; Milk Scalder; a Copper Tea Kettle … Salters & Trundles … 2 Cheese Presses'. Most of these implements were familiar in farmhouses until the 1930s and 1940s, though they are museum-pieces now.

It was rare to kill a saleable bullock or full-grown wether for family eating, though sometimes a lamb might be shared among neighbours. But there was always plenty of wild meat to be had by snaring, trapping or shooting. Rabbits abounded, a hare would feed a large family, and when Forest Law had become obsolete, a stag was fair game. Young pigeons or rooks made tasty pies (so did lambs' tails, newly docked with a sharp knife – which hurt the animal less than the modern rubber-ring). Far more fish came up, before we polluted our rivers and estuaries. Salmon and trout caught by age-old methods, innocent of rod or line, would vary the farmer's and labourer's diet. ('Be careful at that corner. One day Dad was fishing there and the bank gave way and he rolled in.') There was a persistent feeling that this was no theft, since fish came and went at will and nobody had reared them. In Withypool and Hawkridge the old liberty for Free Suitors to fish the Barle in their parishes seems to have lasted into the nineteenth century as an unwritten licence for farmers and commoners to help themselves. Elsewhere, the poacher gave friends or neighbours a generous share of his salmon, and everyone was happy.

Still more important were the bees. From time immemorial until only a few generations ago, any housewife on the moor depended on honey to sweeten her cookery and to delight her sticky-fingered children. Sometimes she made it into metheglin, a Welsh version of mead, the immensely ancient honey 'wine'. (Saxons feasted on that in their mead-halls, but it was drunk long before their day. Nearly all Indo-European languages had the same word for it, so Neolithic people must have been brewing it before they dispersed from their home near the Black Sea, many thousand years ago.) Perhaps on Exmoor in the Bronze Age observant boys were still tracking wild bees to their hive, and bringing the full comb back to the family hearth.

Wild honey remained a bonus, like mushrooms, right through the ages, though shepherds had become wise bee-masters in Mediterranean lands long before Virgil wrote his charming Fourth Georgic about their lore, and that was more than half a century before the Roman conquest of Britain. If the craft was not known here by then (though it may have been) the colonists would certainly have introduced it, and it would have spread from their lowland villas up to the Britons, whose hills must have been alive with wild bees when the heather was in flower. Virgil's beehives were made of hollow bark or woven withies lined with mud and leaves, the doorway narrow to keep out winter draughts. Later, the Exmoor 'skips' (or skeps) were warmer. In the Vale of Porlock they were made of wheaten reed, carefully prepared; in the hills, where wheat did not grow easily, ropes of oaten straw, called thumb-beans,[2] were coiled into a dome; a long bramble stripped of its thorns sewed the coils together, and the shape echoed the human dwellings of prehistoric times.

In Tudor or Stuart manor-houses in the foothills, where a big household needed the honey, walled bee-gardens were stocked with enticing flowers; here and there a row of bee-boles can still be seen - arched niches in a sheltered south-facing wall, where the skeps could stand in summer. In the hills a small orchard might be enclosed, in the sunniest corner of a sloping field, to serve the same purpose. Barbara Reed, again recalling her Knighton father-in-law's reminiscences, describes the cottagers as good bee-keepers. 'They made the straw skips or hives themselves and at the end of the summer killed all the bees in the older hives and took the honey from them, leaving the new swarms. They would follow one of their swarms miles to claim it and bring it home. I expect you have heard the old adage,

204

A swarm of bees in May is worth a load of hay,
A swarm of bees in June is worth a silver spoon,
A swarm of bees in July isn't worth a fly.

The May swarm would make enough honey to keep themselves during the winter. The June swarm might need a little help. But the July swarm would be useless unless you were prepared to feed them completely.'

She goes on to speak of her husband's grandmother, who was ninety-six when she died in 1933, and how she had contrived to feed a young family with her husband away in the Welsh mines each winter. The honey was a great help. It was all kept to be used at home, to sweeten puddings and cakes, rhubarb from the garden or whortleberries from the moor, or 'lovely apple-dumplings for tea on winter nights'. (The apples came from Porlock.) Then again, 'Harry's Gran would take a bowl and go round the fields and hedges any time of the year and pick you a salad, she called it a 'salet'. She would wash it and chop it up and sprinkle it with honey and vinegar and it was a delicious addition to cold rabbit pie.'

In summer and autumn, when the wild fruits and then the nuts ripened, picking was a pleasure as well as good housewifery. Vegetables, currants and gooseberries grew well in farm or cottage gardens, and a good husband would see to it that his wife never had to buy. But in April, 'the hungry month', there was much cooking of young nettles, both for the family and for the farmyard animals. Harry's father recalled, too, a year when the potato crop failed, from blight, 'but he managed to buy a hundredweight of lentils, which kept them going all the winter. Gran soaked them and steamed them until tender and served them with salt and pepper and a nut of butter. As he said, "they were lovely and filled our bellies".'

They 'managed', and were proud of it. Exmoor had made them frugal and hard-working, neighbourliness was a lifeline, and most people had relations not far away who would not let them starve. With home-grown food, and turf or wood fires, they were unlikely to be as hard hit in bad times as their contemporaries in the towns.

For the housewife in a small farm or a cottage, with little ready money, clothing the whole family was probably more difficult than feeding them all. A fleece kept back at shearing-time could be spun and knitted up into warm jerseys – so could shreds of wool gathered from brambles and gorse. When an ox was sold to the butcher the hide might be reserved, taken to the tanner (perhaps with some fresh oak-bark) and then kept until it was time for the village cobbler or tailor to make it into boots or gaiters, jerkins or breeches. The last must have been treasured for years, being so weather-proof and tough. James Hill of Newland, in 1810, bequeathed all his clothes *except* his new buff breeches to a young tenant. Rather later, a labourer in Withypool was nicknamed 'Old Buff-back' – did the mockers rather envy him an ancient leather jacket?

On Sundays or market-days the men would dress in strong woollen cloth, locally woven and expected to last half a lifetime. For working days on the farm, well-worn corduroy was protected by old sacks tied round the waist as aprons or slung over the shoulders against the rain. Clothing for husbands and sons, who had to work hard out of doors in any weather, had first claim on scarce cash and on the attention of the women, who would sew shirts for them, knit thick socks and pull-overs, and patch and mend again and again.

Next came the need to dress the children adequately when they were attending the village school and must not disgrace their mothers. In long families the outgrown dresses or jackets of the eldest were passed down to the next and then the next sister or brother, until, almost threadbare, they could only be worn at home and about the farm, where the poorer children went barefoot to save shoe-leather.

The mothers, seldom leaving the farm, could wear very old clothes under coarse aprons, and go slipshod on their stone floors. Out of doors, looking after the poultry and helping with lambing or hay-making, they too, would wear a sack round waist or shoulders. For corn-harvest, in the shortening days and chancy weather of August and September, when there was no time for a long lunch-break, the farmer's wife would put on a better dress and go out to the corn-field with a big basket of food for the men reaping and making the stooks or 'stitches'. Summer frocks many seasons old were to be seen in field or village; summers were short, and durability mattered more than fashion. Any self-respecting woman felt bound to wear a hat to church or market, and milliners throve (North Molton had eleven in 1850) but one hat for winter and one for summer would serve a farmer's or a cottager's wife for years and years.

Daughters grew up, mothers and maiden aunts grew old, within this long-established pattern. They had as yet hardly any legal standing, and they wrote very little except in rare letters to sons or daughters overseas. But the talk of grandmothers may still offer glimpses of the simpler world of their childhood.

Mist, like snow, is always dangerous on Exmoor. One day it reminded a farmer's widow in her eighties of a frightening experience when she was five years old, living at Tippacott in the parish of Brendon. She and a companion called Will,

206

two years her senior, had gone out on a summer afternoon to gather whortleberries. They wandered and wandered, she said, until they were on Badgworthy Hill, far out on the open moor, and then the mist came down. They were completely lost, and ran on and on in panic, following sheep-paths, crashing through woodland and crossing streams, with no idea where they were, until it was almost dark. Then suddenly they reached the corner of the lane above Malmsmead; 'I knows where we'm to!' she cried (and the relief still rang in her voice as she told the tale, all those years later). So she proudly led Will home.

The corner of a steep lane leading up out of Twitchen near Molland revived old sadness for another grandmother, because it was where as a girl she last saw one of her brothers. He had walked away up the lane to go to Barnstaple and join an emigrant ship bound for Canada. She had waved goodbye from their cottage home across the valley until, at that corner, he turned out of sight. He never came back.

When girls left the village school, most of them helped at home or went 'into service', in farmhouses or manors, or perhaps less happily in small local shops or inns, where harsh employers might grudge every penny and every free half-hour to the girls who worked from early morning until far into a summer's night to make them more profit. Marriage was the dream of release.

The neighbourhood was thinly populated but the moor was wide. Club-walking revels, market-days or distant fairs and dances brought young people together. Not many married away from the moor; a girl might move only a few miles, and keep house within easy reach of former friends. A young wife 'from away' might, if she was lucky, find herself drawn into a great web of friendly relations, and family gatherings would be uproarious fun.

But wedlock was not for all. At a small farmhouse, once only a cottage, beside the 'road' across the Chains from Barbrook to South Molton, very old thatch was taken down in this century, and in it, where the unlined roof sloped down towards an attic bedroom floor, workmen found a letter hidden. After four generations, the girl who had treasured it and the young man who had written it could both be identified. 'He lived at Simonsbath, and he was to have married a maid here, but he broke his word. They used to meet at Woodbarrow Gate. The letter was old and dry and crumbled but you could still read it.'

Old men or women who could no longer get about used to have their beds brought downstairs so that they could see and hear all that went on. The cottages on Minehead Quay were below road level, and in stormy weather the occupants had to fix boards across their doorsteps to keep the sea out. One day, when floods rose suddenly, the vicar hurried down to the Quay, where one of his parishioners, a fisherman's elderly daughter, lived alone, bedridden, on the ground floor. He found her radiant. She lay trailing her hand in the salt water lapping round her bed, looked up at him, and said, in deep contentment, 'I never thought I should feel the tide again.'

If the bread-winner fell sick there was no income, though on the farms his family would continue his work; and the doctor had to be paid (in theory, though many made no charge where they saw real hardship). Relief in cash came from the mutual insurance societies, chiefly the village 'club'. All cottage families paid a penny a week into the club fund, and could draw 3s.6d. a week in emergency. The chest was kept by a trusted member – in Withypool the treasurer at one time was 'Torney Mouse Quartley the cobbler – and even in the worst times, an old man recalled, the money was never stolen. It belonged to them all, and anyone might need it; when the ne'er-do-well labourer feigned illness for seven years and 'crashed the bank', the liability was honoured though resentment was strong.

The sense of shared responsibility was fostered by the annual 'club-walking'. On a summer's day, all the villagers put on their best clothes and joined in procession. Even in Withypool, remote and self-supporting then ('Exford was like a foreign country') there were two bands playing. Each man decked a staff with sprigs and flowers and a prize was awarded for the best. The club banner was carried aloft, and they all trooped to church for a service; then they had tea on the green, and the sports began – wrestling, carrying the anvil, catching the greasy wether. The whole parish was on holiday.

In the small towns there were other insurance societies – 'Buffaloes' or Foresters, a little like the mediaeval trade-guilds. In South Molton, adept at festivities, they all celebrated together on May 29th, Oak-apple Day; Cock notes that 'men and women (for women also had their separate societies) gaily dressed, carrying posies of flowers, having answered their respective roll-calls marched in procession to the Parish Church'. That is not the first record of separate friendly societies for the women; Coleridge's friend Tom Poole encouraged one in Nether Stowey at about the time of Trafalgar. But villages on the moor would not be able to afford more than their one club, and that paid benefit only for the bread-winner, not for the bread-maker or her children. And out on the farms it was on her shoulders that the weight of any illness in the family naturally fell.

She would not reckon she had time to be ill herself, but the long families testify to her frequent pregnancies, and there were miscarriages too. Sometimes a farmer's young son had to help his father bury a still-born baby brother or sister. When food was scarce the mother was likely to deny herself and sap her strength. A row of tomb-stones near Hawkridge church door tells a tragic tale of the closing years of the nineteenth century, when wool-prices were ruinously low, and some farmers sold little or none of their clip. As everywhere, undernourishment lowered the resistance of children to disease. In the Bawden family one daughter, Matilda, aged fifteen, died on May 1st, 1897. Bessie, her sister, who was eighteen, presumably helped to nurse her through the last stages of consumption, and herself died on September 11th. Their brother, John, aged thirteen, survived only until November 23rd, and at the end of December the thrice-bereaved mother bore a baby daughter who died, six weeks old, on February 8th, 1898.

It was in no way the doctors' fault. Four or five decades were to pass before modern knowledge enabled them to lessen the ravages of tuberculosis, and of other illnesses against which a hundred years ago they could do next to nothing. Perhaps they were not actually blamed; tragedy on that scale tended to be regarded as an act of God, or even, brutally, as a judgement. But some people in lonely places wondered whether it was worth the trouble and expense of a visit (the panel system was not introduced until 1911). A man who dropped an axe on his big toe, cutting it off, 'didn't believe in doctors'; he had been a sailor, put boiling pitch on the wound, and kept the toe; the flesh shrivelled, while the nail remained full-size, and he always carried it in his pocket as an interesting exhibit. A rogue who had always had enough money was guiltily afraid of his doctor, whom he had not paid for years. He feared a recommendation to Dulverton workhouse, which had such a bad reputation and such a high death-rate that when he could no longer look after himself, and had antagonized all his relations and neighbours, he shammed mad, was certified, and died in the asylum instead. Ignorance and fear and meanness must very often have made the patient's life more miserable and the doctor's task much harder than either need have been.

The wives put their heads together; at least they could help one another. They would walk miles to take a sick neighbour a basket of good food and comforting delicacies, and talk over symptoms with her and consider what might be done. Various natural remedies were available. Somebody who understood herbs might have gathered and dried them, like chamomile, to make an infusion in time of need, or the water of particular springs might help, if somebody would go out to the hillside and fill a jug for the invalid. There were pockets of mineral all over the moor; whether the water really had medicinal properties, or was good only because of its purity, experience recommended it. One child's recurrent complaint always yielded to a north-flowing spring on Brightworthy; a dying man in West Anstey insisted on being brought a drink from a special spring, marked

209

by a big quartz boulder, in a woodland combe he knew. The water of Coulsworthy spring near Combe Martin was bottled and advertised and became famous – Lord Kitchener, it is said, would not move without it, and had a bottle for breakfast wherever he might be. And there were, of course, any number of holy wells, many of them dedicated to women saints, from whom special sympathy might be expected.

If springs and simples failed, and 3s.6d a week from the club would not pay the doctor's fee as well as maintaining the family, there remained the supernatural. That might be enlisted through religion ('I prayed so hard God couldn't *not* listen') or through recourse to the local 'wise woman' or a man practising as 'white witch'. Some of these had powers of healing, even at a distance, and not only through the sufferer's credulity, for they sometimes cured farm animals too. Educated people, respecting their gift, might send for the witch-doctor, who succeeded when the vet had failed. This happened well within living memory, but was not much talked about. Rather longer ago, Richard Jefferies wrote, in *Red Deer*, of a prevalent and very strong dislike of opening a barrow or disturbing an old battlefield, and went on to record the mysterious curing of cattle, and how the country people both revered and feared the wise woman of the hamlet, and her dramatic invocations on their behalf. Belief in these things, he said, was shared with the labouring classes by many well-to-do people, but all were completely silent to strangers. So humble people thought it worth consulting the witch, alarming though she might be, with her incomprehensible patter, her authoritative manner, and a crock of toads in the corner of her kitchen. If they suspected that the ailment was due to a neighbour's ill-wishing, perhaps with pins and waxen image, the wise woman might be willing to neutralize that with stronger charms. It meant playing with fear.

As time went on there was less need for these alternatives. Pulling against nineteenth-century misery and greed was an opposing force of altruism, and this was reaching out to the hill-country from the fringes. The best of the doctors and clergy were concerned about patients or parishioners in distant farmhouses and cottages, and rode out to them in almost any weather. They had tried, in Dulverton especially, to soften the harsh rulings of stubborn Union Guardians as to workhouse conditions and 'outside relief'. Then, in the last quarter of the century, Cottage Hospitals became centres of far kinder care for the sick and poor.

Annual reports of the one at Lynton survive, from its foundation in 1874 until 1939, and happily the tale has been retold.[3] The hospital was set up in a cottage which had four rooms, two upstairs and two down, and it began with only four beds. It was intended for the poor of Lynton and seven neighbouring parishes, when an ailment could not be properly treated at home. (Infectious and incurable diseases were excluded, and so, at first, was childbirth.) Maintenance depended on voluntary subscribers, with a small charge to patients at the discretion of the medical officer, and this precarious income was supplemented by a variety of gifts in kind. Housewives sent the produce of garden and dairy, old bedclothes and hearth-rugs, a patchwork quilt and even a kitchen clock. It was their hospital, with nurse and servant needing to be paid; typically, the women had little money to offer, but could, and did, help to keep the patients well-fed and warm. The menfolk, it should be added, provided firewood and rabbits, and staffed the 'ambulance corps'.

The Lynton ambulance was very important. It was horse-drawn (until 1928) and the journeys by steep lanes or open tracks were necessarily slow, but it was always on call. To summon it the caller had only to send a telegram to Mr Saxon, Lynton. 'Only', but it might be miles from the scene of illness or accident to the nearest post-office. The whole procedure might take a long time, but the ambulance corps would not fail to bring the patient to the cottage hospital, where the doctor would be ready to do his best.

Patients were discharged as soon as possible, to make room for others. Most Exmoor people died, as they had lived, at home, in the parish where they were known. The slow tolling of the passing bell, which even the poorest families strained to afford, would inform their neighbours. In Withypool the sexton used to toll first the age of the person who had died, so that men or women out in the fields, knowing who had been poorly, could listen and count and interpret.

Then at length friends and relations would gather from all over the moor, and fill a quiet little church in the hills in farewell to a companion they had known since childhood. After the burial they went home to the saddened household, where the women had a good meal ready for them, and talk ranging back over the years rounded off a day of remembrance which would itself be long remembered.

211

CHAPTER THIRTEEN

Two world wars

Nationally, the thirteen years between Queen Victoria's death and the beginning of what used to be called 'The Great War' were immensely varied. Three contrasting strands all differed from anything on Exmoor. Sophisticated Edwardian society, liberated from mourning crêpe, glittered at court and at Sandringham, in fashionable London houses and stately country mansions. Coming-out balls and theatre-parties, salons, concerts, exhibitions, race-meetings, tennis, cricket, boating and field-sports diversified the year for those who had grown rich in the old Queen's reign. Meanwhile, people crowded in the grey industrial and mining towns were learning to demand a share of the cake; the Labour Party was a crucial innovation. And differently again, women were asking for a voice in public affairs, a vote if no more. The pioneers were intelligent women from comfortable families; some of them demonstrated violently and were imprisoned and set free and imprisoned again. In 1914 they postponed their lesser struggle for the greater, but women's war-work up and down the country had clinched their argument by 1918.[1]

The Edwardians were not much troubled by foreboding. As time went on a few thoughtful people, on Exmoor as elsewhere, saw danger looming beyond the Rhine, but for the majority it was hardly conceivable. There had been no major war since Waterloo, and the Empire had displayed all its power and glory at Queen Victoria's Diamond Jubilee in 1897. The splendour had drawn even from Rudyard Kipling a powerful warning against too much pride – 'Lest we forget, lest we forget'. But it was Germany, not Britain, which, 'drunk with sight of power', was to plunge the world into a terrible four years' war. Huge contingents from the Dominions, sons and grandsons of emigrants, would come back to fight beside their cousins. By the end, the collapse of four continental despotisms – Turkish, Czarist, Habsburg and finally German – would have changed the face of Europe. But as yet all that lay hidden. In Exmoor villages the celebration of sixty years of the Queen's reign may have meant little beyond local merry-making, the erection of Cuzzicombe Post,[2] and an issue

212

of Jubilee mugs to the children. The old lady was an honoured fixture, remote and well-nigh immortal. But there came a January day in 1901, when the Parracombe postman, passing through a farmyard, called to children playing there, 'Tell your mother that Her Gracious Majesty is dead.' At least one of them never forgot his measured and impressive tones.

King Edward's accession must have been almost a personal pleasure to many simple people on the moor. They had known him as heir when he was the guest of honour at a meet of stag-hounds on Hawkcombe Head in 1879 and something between ten and fifteen thousand people, mounted or in carriages or on foot, had gathered there to see 'Mr Purnce'. He had ridden his horse into what is still called 'the Prince of Wales's bog'. He had asked Nicholas Snow of Oare to point out to him the 'Doone Valley'. And he had invited Jack Russell to preach at Sandringham, where the hunting parson's homely talk – 'Yes, me dear', to Princess Alexandra – had delighted the whole company. Trifling memories of him lasted on and on; sixty years later, a farmer's wife in the Forest was offering guests a dish of potatoes sliced in the frying-pan with the old-fashioned angular knife, 'same as King Edward liked them for breakfast'.

Trains were beginning to bring more visitors. Stag-hunters came from up-country to stay in the big houses. Solitary fishermen returned year after year to remote inns beside the Exe or Barle, caught or failed to catch trout or salmon by day, and came home in the evening to blazing fires and generous meals, and talk in the bar with countrymen who knew all the deep pools and shallows. Antiquaries from nearby parishes were looking at churches or prehistoric monuments and writing down what they learnt of local history or obsolescent customs. And year after year the learned lawyer MacDermot rode about, increasing his knowledge of the Forest. Later, he lived at Lillycombe on the old boundary, and was a solemn visitor at local farmhouses – so solemn that one high-spirited little girl could not resist tiptoeing up behind his chair and sticking a postage-stamp on his bald head. In those days of few cars and no tarmac, strangers who moved along the lanes at a country pace were welcomed as friends, and never forgotten.

There were also workaday visitors 'from away', to be sized up and relished. An eccentric carrier, a poetic pedlar, a horse-coping gypsy, a 'chowder' hawking crockery, or the itinerant sand-sellers – regarded as socially superior, like Withypool's 'gen'leman sweep' – they were all key people in some small event in the yearly cycle. The nineteenth-century reddlemen with their donkeys no longer came round – by now, farmers bought reddle in the market-towns – but they were remembered as alarming apparitions, rough men with their faces, hands and clothing all ruddy with the dye.[3] A child's memory of being chased over Withypool Common by two or three of them who wanted him to drop the lunch he was carrying to his father was indelible. East of Exford, near Larcombe Pound, at the intersection of the ancient Harepath and the mediaeval Bridgwater–Barnstaple road,[4] a field enclosed from Kitnor Heath is still called Asses' Piece, because a reddleman from Bristol always turned his donkeys in there. (The pound itself, built conveniently near the crossways, was also useful to sheep-rustlers. Once a farmer missing some of his freshly dyed sheep went to the pound to look for them, and found the red wool shorn and left there, the sheep all gone.)

Such trifles were richly told and appreciatively heard. The elders were passing on the flavour of life as it had been. Their tales were different from the neatly pointed anecdotes of townsmen. The country manner was slow and ruminative, steeped in a sense of character and place. Warm burring speech enveloped any oddities of gender or tense, and simple local phrases – 'so gray as a badger', or 'laughing like a pixy' – might be set in rolling cadences. Many of the narrators could hardly read, but every Sunday they heard the resounding English of King James's Bible and the prayer-book of King Edward VI.

A good sermon might be the treat of the week. When Parson Jack Russell returned from Sandringham his parishioners asked him to preach them the sermon he had given before the Prince and Princess, and he agreed to do so. They packed the church, and were greatly disappointed when the sermon proved to be nothing high-flown, but one they had heard from him 'scores of times'. (The churchwarden protested; the parson replied that it was the same gospel for high and low.)

A visiting clergyman doing duty for the Rector of Hawkridge and Withypool took the morning service at Hawkridge and rode over to the daughter church in the afternoon, thinking to repeat his sermon. He took a short cut over the fields from the parsonage at Tarr Steps, and on approaching the road he was startled to see the entire Hawkridge congregation trooping along to Withypool, still dressed for church-going. Hastily he composed a different sermon as he rode. He was not very pleased with it but hoped it would do. It was not a success. Afterwards he learned that the Hawkridge people had enjoyed the morning sermon so much that they had walked the two or three miles up and down hill to hear it again.

Church and chapel people, divided by history and temperament, went their different ways, but all found an eloquent homily a welcome mental and spiritual tonic in a life of ceaseless physical labour. Extremes of deprivation opened a way for extremist sects, with powerful revivalist preachers tramping from village to village. Such, in 1912 or so, were the 'Goers', who assembled 200 converts beside the Barle at Withypool for what was long known irreverently as 'the Great Dipping'. It was baptism by total immersion, conducted from a field on the left bank, a little upstream from the bridge. The preachers were drawing many women into their flock, some of them fear-ridden and over-credulous wives, and by confusion with the Mormons it was believed – wrongly – that they would be instructed to leave home and 'Go' with the missionaries. So husbands and families, fearing desertion, gathered on the opposite banks to keep careful watch. Among them was a lusty mocker whose tremulous wife wished to join the sect. He did not restrain her, but walked down to the river too, to make sure of keeping her. He took their little boy of nine or ten with him, and some forty years later this son described the scene to me.

It had made a great impression. There was no sound from the unbelievers across the water, though they had all come to scoff. On the opposite side, the 200 converts were manifestly rapt and exalted; they wore white baptismal robes, the preachers held each of them under water during a short prayer or pronouncement, then they stood drenched on the bank, shivering but saved, until the whole ceremony was over. It took several hours. Details stayed in the child's memory – the women's draggled wet hair, a short man who lost his footing while he was being dipped, and especially the river pouring down in muddy spate, under a clear sky. This contradiction, which seemed a portent, was part of the story in the village for a very long time. 'The river ran *brown*!' (That occurs only rarely, after a bad cloudburst on the Chains. It was repeated in 1952.)

At Exford, two or three miles away, no river baptism took place. Stag-hunters rode out with whips, prevented any assembly, and drove the preachers away. The Withypool 'dipping' recalls the seventeenth century and Bunyan's religious agonies, and Exford was still not past the eighteenth century, when squire and parson set the hounds on John Wesley at North Tawton. Yet it was nearly 1914, and after 1918 either episode would seem unthinkable.

1914 – and in Lord Grey's sad words, the lights were going out all over Europe. The Kaiser broke the treaty guaranteeing Belgian neutrality – 'a scrap of paper', he called it – and his army swept through towards Paris, which Germans had besieged and occupied only four decades earlier. Older French people had grim memories of that. Britain honoured her alliance and declared war. Optimists everywhere expected it to be over within a few months, but in less time than that it had become very bad.

'Gott strafe England' was now one of the German slogans. In Kent and Essex the Flanders guns could be heard; zeppelins appeared in the sky, and the Channel had to be continually swept clear of enemy mines to let the food ships through. Exmoor was free of these ominous sights and sounds, but subject, of course, to the call-up of men and the demand for more and more food to be grown. At first the need for soldiers was paramount. The British Expeditionary Force – 'the first hundred thousand', the 'old contemptibles'[5] – crossed to France in time to help save Paris from the rapid German onslaught in the first weeks of war; but by the spring of 1915 it was plain that far more troops would be needed. Huge glaring posters of Kitchener spread his appeal for volunteers, and recruiting groups toured villages and small towns. But it was not enough, and in 1916 conscription was introduced. Trench warfare in deep mud, together with shell-shock and poison gas, was continually thinning the ranks, and young shepherds and carters from Exmoor were being killed or maimed with the rest.

Meanwhile, German submarines were sinking ships laden with the imported food on which this country had come to depend. (They infested the Western Approaches, and penetrated the Bristol Channel; a ship was torpedoed off Woody Bay, and U-Boats slipped into Heddon's Mouth for water; local people saw the German sailors washing themselves on the beach.) At the end of April 1917 there was only enough food for six weeks left in store. The danger of being starved into submission had not been properly foreseen, and many skilled countrymen had been called up. 'Substitutes', unfit for military service, were provided, but a piano-tuner sent to the arable Vale of Porlock could not be very much help. Horses, even the cart-horses essential for farm-work, had been requisitioned and sent to the Front. Orders came for more and more hill land to be ploughed, and much of it, high sour pasture, was quite incapable of growing an adequate crop of corn. Short of man-power and horse-power, farmers and their families had to do the best they could, and in these conditions there was hardly a cordial welcome for agitators from the towns who came urging labourers to strike for

> Eight hours' work and eight hours' play,
> Eight hours' sleep and eight bob a day.

Farmers' sons left school before they were twelve, to help their fathers. Wives and daughters worked harder than ever. The Women's Institute movement, newly introduced from Canada and soon to contribute enormously to the national larder, had not yet reached these hills, but many hard winters had schooled Exmoor housewives in preserving all kinds of food. They bottled, pickled, dried, salted. Older women could knit socks and mittens and Balaclavas for the men wintering in the trenches, and children could gather sphagnum for dressing soldiers' wounds, and whortleberries to dye the serge for sailors' uniforms.

Then, suddenly, it all ended. The German army yielded, the

Kaiser abdicated and the armistice was signed. Relief was boundless. The killing was over, and peace was expected. But the huge loss of lives was felt all over the kingdom. Even in the smallest Exmoor villages a Roll of Honour tells who left the tiny community and did not return, and their number is hard to believe. Some churches – Exton and West Anstey among them – list also those who served, risked their lives with the others, yet came safe home. In parishes where the fortunate and the mourners all knew each other, the rejoicing would be sadly muted.

Peace, so longed for, soon brought other troubles. Countless returning soldiers could find no work. Poverty and hardship, industrial unrest and economic depression led into the 'hungry thirties'. Groups of unemployed Welsh miners sang, unforgettably, in smart London streets, to earn rather than beg the alms of passers-by. There were 'hunger marches', culminating in 1935 in the one from Jarrow, which was joined by sympathizers all along the way to London; about a quarter of a million more were waiting for them in Hyde Park. There was no government response; but they had called the attention of well-fed southerners to the desperate needs of the industrial North East.

In the countryside things were grey rather than black. Imports of meat and corn undermined home farming again, and arable reverted to pasture, which needed fewer hands. Prices slumped, wages were very low, and the drift to towns was renewed; but the country poor, with a strip of fertile garden and probably a pig and some chickens, were better off than urban slum-dwellers in back-to-back terraces or cramped houses with a scrap of sour soil under perpetually falling soot.

On Exmoor, there was little change as yet in the old pattern of life. Lack of money meant lack of farm machinery; there were few cars, few buses, no electricity and not enough skilled labour. So man and horse and dog still worked together in familiar ways. Roads were improved, partly to provide employment. More than 200 Welshmen tramped from Cardiff to Dulverton hoping for a share in this work. Some fourteen of those selected made the new road from Coppleham Cross through Winsford to Exford, and thence to Simonsbath and Brendon Two Gates. They metalled the surface, built hedge-banks for shelter, and bridges across the streams. They could do about a yard a day; it took years.

The poorest were set to crack stones by the wayside. To minimize quarrying they were allowed to use any ancient stone visible above the ground, and Bronze Age landmarks disappeared for ever into a new road surface.[6] Old rotting gates to the commons were replaced, to keep stock from straying. For a carter these were no great obstacle; he could climb down, open the gate, call his horse through, and tell it to wait while he closed the hasp. Children from the nearest cottages soon found that motorists, lacking that friendly one-horse power, were glad to give them a copper or two to save themselves inconvenience.

On farms and in villages there was no room for extravagance, but time and energy could take the place of money. People walked long distances, as John Milton had gone afoot from Withypool to Dulverton, in his new boots, to catch the London train, and as the store-keeper from Minehead Quay had trudged to Bristol, and back next day. A builder's labourer working on farm repairs near Exford pushed his tools from Dulverton in a wheel-barrow. A Quaker from the south of the Forest walked to Barnstaple every Sunday for Meeting, always going a little out of his way to drink from North Molton's holy well in the fields. Another man walked from Picked Stones near Simonsbath to Taunton and back, on a summer's day; he confessed that the last few miles homeward had been very hard work. Wives trod hill-paths and stony lanes down to the village and carried home a week's groceries. And small farmers who could keep only one riding-pony had recourse to the old method known in the Midlands as 'ride and tie'. A father and son from South Hill farm in Withypool – where old Mr Thorne had sung the choir's carols – used to go like that to Porlock market. One would set out on foot; the other would do a few more jobs about the farm and then follow on the pony, ride a mile or two past the walker, tie the animal to a lone tree and walk the next agreed distance himself - and so on, all the way.

Economy could take harsh forms. Some employers were generous to their work-people, but some felt no responsibility for their welfare in hard times; there were boys and girls 'living in', working beyond their childish strength, underfed and stunted. Poverty had gone on too long, and everywhere 'a hungry father begets a puny child.' Wiry little men and women of the inter-war years had their brief schooling before the days of free meals and milk; but they were no fools.

In spite of road-making and stone-cracking, there were still the really destitute, the tramps, who in mild weather would rather doss down in a double hedge than in the Union houses. There were also gypsy tribes encamped for years at Scob Hill, Gypsy Lane, Molland Moor Gate, and Brendon Two Gates (where they exacted a 'voluntary' toll). Some of these lived in style: at Comer's Gate the grandmother would drive her pony-trap into the camp, swinging it round from the road in a fine wide curve, then descend and give the reins to a man or boy waiting to unharness the horse. Others made and sold clothes-pegs, decorative lace, or leather thongs to tie heavy country boots; they bought rabbit-skins or anything else the housewife had to spare. They nearly always had plenty of money, but, like the far needier tramps, might

218

help themselves to a chicken or duck if its owners had been careless. Suspicion kept the villainous man-traps in existence; an apple-grower in Porlock hung his in a shed and gave neighbours to understand that he set it regularly. Whenever he showed it to anyone, there was always fresh grass and earth on it; nobody knew whether this was spoof or not, but his orchard was never robbed.

Farmers were paid very little for beef or mutton. In the higher hills lambs sold for only a few shillings; the lime-starved pastures could not fatten them. Then, in 1937, a 50 per cent liming subsidy was a great relief. Old quarries and kilns were reopened, old skills retrieved, and gradually the arable and some of the better leys were refertilized. Meanwhile many farmers had gone over from meat to milk production. When a firm from the Torridge valley began collecting milk from Challacombe, in the 1930s, nearly every farmer in the parish jumped at the chance to sell. Though the payment offered, in summer, was only 5d. or 6d. a gallon, that was more profitable than other dairy work.

Remoter farmers could not sell their milk except locally, but it was rich milk from Red Devon cows, and made excellent butter and cream. The farmer's wife went down to market with her husband in their pony-trap, taking butter always, cream only in summer when visitors were about. Later, after 1945, the Milk Marketing Board collected by lorry from everywhere; some of the stands for the churns, small platforms of wood or concrete, survive, rotted or overgrown, where farm lanes meet a public road. They represented changing times; the demand was by then for quantity, to nourish the whole nation's children, and the Red Devons, so long a lovely characteristic of the moor, gave place to herds of black and white Friesians, aliens up from the lowlands, which yielded far more gallons of far thinner milk.

Perhaps in the 'hungry thirties' the tradition of frugality and hard work was clearest in small farms and cottages. Farmhouses might be like the old longhouses, one room thick, with a cowshed at the lower end, and upstairs no corridor, but bedrooms opening one from another. (The parents slept in the outermost, at the stair-head: 'Lock up your daughters'.) Cottages were tiny, with one room downstairs and an attic bedroom above, and a ladder, because there was no space for a staircase. Here the long families of ten or twelve children might be reared; the youngsters all slept in one bed, boys at one end and girls at the other, 'feet to feet'. There was no money for repairs; a sick woman might lie tilted, one leg of her bed having gone through a hole in the floor. Often the privies – at the bottom of the garden – were draughty contrivances perched high over a stream; some were two-seaters, for mother and child; a bent skewer and a staple would serve adequately for door-fastening. But the cloamen oven in the kitchen made lovely bread, and between the bedroom ceiling and the thatch, a hole carefully left in the gable-end, as in a barn, let the owls fly out at dusk, to forage for their ravenous young. It was pleasant to hear them returning, stump, stump, along the rafters, while the chicks hissed with greedy excitement.

Cottagers might use the village bakery; at Knowstone it was close to the churchyard, so they could leave their Sunday dinners with the baker on their way to morning service, and afterwards, for a penny or two, pick them up piping hot. The village tailors, sitting cross-legged on their kitchen tables, would make a good suit for less than £3. Even hamlets had parish gardens – strips which would grow a row of beans and some cabbages. (They show behind the houses, in the old photograph of Heasley cloth-mill, no. 31.) Exton had a field called 'Poors' Allotment'. Some owners of woodland let cottagers gather sticks from a specified area; where the 'new road' runs down from North to South Molton, three pieces of the Poltimore woods are still named as they were assigned – to the Parker, the Vicarage, and, nearest to the village, the Poorvolken.[7]

If the 'poor folk' were active and enterprising, there were plenty of small jobs by which they could earn a little money. At haymaking young and old helped for the sake of the company and hearty meals. Afterwards the rick-thatchers needed spar-gads, cut and bent indoors on winter evenings, and long strong hay-ropes, which the women and girls made with a revolving wooden tool like a small three-runged ladder. Rabbits were caught, and sold to pay the rent. They were insatiable nibblers, which had to be kept under, and their meat was tasty. (In the food-rationing of the Second World War Exmoor's nightly rabbit-train to Taunton went loaded for the cities from all the parishes along the south of the moor.) Rabbit-skins and mole-skins were valuable, too. Youngsters would peg out the mole-skins on a board to dry, then pack them flat, in piles; rabbit-skins were turned inside out – the furry insides stuffed with paper – then hung to dry, and finally tied in bundles like faggots of wood. When geese or chickens were plucked every feather was saved, to be sold for bedding and cushions. The whortleberries, far more plentiful then than now, sold well, though gathering took time. School holidays were arranged for the weeks when they would be ripe. Gypsies and pedlars picked too. In the twenties most of the fruit was sold to dealers; the chief of these in South Molton reckoned that half a ton a day might be brought in to him, and he also used to drive his trap out to Molland Moor Gate to take provisions to the gypsies and bring their 'whorts' back. He boxed them, and despatched them by train next morning – mainly to the mining districts of Yorkshire and Wales, because pies filled with them would keep moist even down in the pits.

Money and man-power being scarce, women and girls, whose labour cost less, did much of the farm-work; they might even have to turn the handle of a heavy wheel all day to drive the clippers with which the men were shearing. But their status was improving. They had stayed at school until they were fourteen, and after 1928 they all had the vote from the age of twenty-one. The Women's Institutes were educating them in practical democracy. Farmers' wives had begun to take in holiday visitors, for the sake of ready cash. Often these were townswomen who earned their own living: they came from quite different experience and brought glimpses of new possibilities. For these were the decades of the 'two million surplus women', the young widows, and girls whom the men killed in Flanders might have married, and who had to fend for themselves. They staffed the social services – cheaply – for a generation, and some of them were branching out into professions which had once been exclusively masculine. The atmosphere was changing; even on Exmoor, the younger women had rather more independence than their mothers had known, and would claim new opportunities for their daughters.

In spite of the hardships, men and women who were boys and girls at that time recalled, half a century later, what *fun* they had, and mused whether their grandchildren, for whom everything was so much easier, enjoyed life as much. Perhaps this was only the nostalgia of the elderly for their distant high-spirited youth – or were the simpler pleasures really more satisfying?

Each village was its own little world, and most of the children would belong to it all their lives and never forget the schooldays they shared. Parties of eight or nine boys and girls from neighbouring farms might go down together to the village school, two or three miles away by the lanes and field-paths – racing or dawdling, looking for birds' nests, noticing tadpoles or minnows, eating blackberries or picking a bunch of flowers for teacher. A former pupil from Knowstone school, beside the churchyard, remembers the delights of snow: the children would trample in the drifts to get their feet thoroughly wet, so that their socks would be hung to dry on the railing of the big black cast-iron stove in the schoolroom, while they sat round warming their toes and drinking mugs of hot cocoa.

Some of them would go on to secondary school, extending the moorland friendships further. Two girls from Simonsbath, farmers' daughters, were sent as *termly* boarders to Barnstaple because it was so far away. Somebody would drive them in the pony-trap to Blackmoor Gate, where they climbed into the slow good-tempered train from Lynton – 'So slow, we used to say we could pick flowers on the way!' Others, from Challacombe, went daily by school car to Bratton Fleming, and thence on to Barnstaple

Grammar School by that same train. For education was prized. In many families this was only the second or third generation of 'scholards', and parents who had left for work at eleven or twelve years old saw the value of the change. A labourer's daughter born about 1900 told me she thought her mother could write just about enough to sign her name, and her father had had only a fortnight's schooling before he had to leave and earn his keep. Her grandmother was one of the last to be bound apprentice; after that, she said, 'education came in'.

Some had been lucky enough to be taught the three Rs by teachers whose natural skill outweighed their lack of training. One such amateur was John Barrow, cobbler and parish clerk of Challacombe, who was described as 'Isaac' in A. G. Bradley's *Exmoor Memories*. He ran his school in the old mill-house, and on Sundays directed the church music; he and his sons formed the choir, and he introduced the tunes on his flute. His eccentricity fascinated the party of young gentlemen staying at the rectory for Latin coaching, but later, when the state took over village schooling, and a hand-organ in the church superseded his flute, one of them, the young Bradley, was touched by the elder man's two-fold demotion, and used to visit him to have a shoe mended or take lessons on the flute. By then – towards 1880 – John Barrow had quietly established himself as a mathematics tutor for farm-lads who had left school. Farmers sent them along, paying him a few pence a week to give them a grasp of practical geometry and arithmetic. One pupil, John Dallyn, kept the exercise book he filled in 1890, when he was sixteen, and his family treasure it. Long sums work out the amount of slating required for a hipped roof of given measurements, or the quantity of seed for a field of very irregular shape. Today's schoolboys, with their micro-chip pocket calculators, might blench at the rows and rows of neatly handwritten figures.

Growing older, boys and girls might retain a taste for practical jokes, which could be enjoyed in retrospect for years.[8] They found – had to find – most of their pleasure in their work. Companionship was important, and so was the glow of satisfaction in work well done, with the right tools. These were hand-made, and looked after very carefully, to last a long time. The scythe blade must be properly set, and kept sharp – perhaps by being hung in an apple tree all winter. ('It was the rust that did it, but the apple tree got the credit.') Driving his cart along a lane, a man might notice a branch in the hedge which was just the right shape for a trowel-handle he needed, and stop and cut it. People would remember appreciatively for years who made the firkin or bellows or wooden yoke and milking-pail they were using every day. A carter would take great pride in the turn-out of his horses – supple leather, shining brass. A village would be proud of an outstanding craftsman – at Hawkridge a carpenter, blacksmiths at Exford and Brendon. It all helped to knit the moorland community together.

So did the post-round. Between the wars, and until at least 1945, this was often a woman's job. Some did it on pony-back, some on foot: Mary Hooper of Withypool, wiry and wizened, trudged it for so many years, from one remote farm to another, that when she retired the village reckoned she had walked far enough to encircle the globe. Later, when the load of printed matter became heavier, the task reverted to men. At distant farmhouses they would drink a cup of tea and oblige the giver in some little way. Granny Quick of Willingford was short-sighted, so the kindly postman always threaded a supply of needles for her. Further north-west, the bringer of mail also delivered the neighbours' news: he had, of course, read everybody's postcards, and he would unwrap somebody's local newspaper for the household to skim through, then wrap it up again unharmed.

The moor was a neighbourhood. A farmer from the foothills said you would take your bit of lunch with you on a downward journey, but if you were going 'up over' you need never carry food.

The Second World War was no surprise. Internationally, the 1930s were ominous and tragic, and for a long time the question was not whether war would come, but when. After corn-harvest in 1939 Stalin made a pact with Hitler at Poland's expense, as shameful as the Munich agreement of the previous year, in which Chamberlain and Daladier had sacrificed Czechoslovakia. A day or two later the German army marched on Poland, and the phoney peace ended.

Ruthless war from the air was expected, and would overleap the English Channel, so long our defensive moat. Orders were proclaimed and enforced at once for the blacking-out of the whole island every night; all windows were to be darkened completely, and car-lamps, torches and lanterns were to be made very dim. (Poachers and rabbit-trappers on the moor found it difficult to take this last injunction seriously, until the bombs began to fall.)[9] Within the first few days thousands of town-children were despatched to country billets, carrying gas-masks and a little hand-luggage, and train after train from London came packed with them to the stations on the outskirts of Exmoor. Villagers and farmers' wives with long families had promised to take in two or three more school-children with their own. (When, by some mistake in the thronged London terminals, train-loads of mothers with babies arrived too, they presented a new difficulty, but it was met.)

The 1917 threat from submarines to the ships bringing food was not forgotten. Ration cards were issued. Farm-work was classified as 'work of national importance', a reserved occupation from which men were not to be called to the colours. The first seven months were uncomfortable but uneventful, 'the phoney war'. A British Expeditionary Force in northern France was bored with inactivity, and at home large numbers of recruits spent that icy winter in training, while munition workers built up a supply of arms for them.

Then, in April 1940, Hitler launched his *Blitzkrieg*, his 'lightning war', with terrible success.[10] By the end of June he had conquered Norway, neutralized Denmark, overrun Holland and Belgium and Luxembourg, and made himself master of France. The B.E.F. had been trapped, but reached the dunes and beaches of Dunkirk, where, under hostile aircraft, an impromptu fleet of little boats from all the south-east coasts of England, yacht or fishing-smack or even dinghy, plied back and forth over a calm sunlit sea to help the Navy take them off. Most of the soldiers got home, though all their equipment had to be left behind. Almost unarmed, we stood alone against the dictators. Hitler expected us to give in.

But the years of appeasement were over. When the 'lightning' onslaught began, against Norway, Parliament had finally turned against the Men of Munich, and Chamberlain had had to resign, Churchill, an old Liberal, was leading a strong and united coalition government with resolute energy, which, like his clarion speeches, transformed the moral climate and heartened the nation through all that summer's tragic news and imminent peril of invasion.

The first need was defence, against an enemy who might come by sea or by air, and the latter was a new danger. When the Spanish Armada came up the Channel in 1588 a chain of beacons flashed the news overland, but fires now would provide a flare-path across England for German pilots, so church bells became the signal instead: they were not to be rung for any reason at all except an actual landing. When Buonaparte might have invaded, in 1804 or 1805, evacuation and 'scorched earth' were planned, as in the order preserved at Molland; it was recognized as vital that civilians should travel through the fields and leave the roads clear for the soldiers. In 1940, refugees ahead of the advancing German army crowded the roads of north-eastern France, blocked them against defending troops and were mercilessly harassed by the Luftwaffe. So in England the instructions were that active civilians must stay where they were. If they had no firearms they were to improvise; housewives were advised to throw milk-bottles as hand-grenades – like the South Molton butcher's wife with her rams' horns in 1642.

Concrete obstacles were embedded in the wider beaches, where a landing might be attempted. Pill-boxes, like small Martello towers, were built, camouflaged, and equipped as strong-points, their guns commanding the coast or making a second line of defence between the south-west peninsula and the rest of England

– for, as in 1804, invasion might begin in the western counties. A few of the pill-boxes can still be seen; there is one, for instance, at Raleigh's Cross. To make things more difficult for an invader all signposts were removed. Train-passengers depended on the station-master calling out where they were. Every parish church and village post office quietly became anonymous.

Up on the moor the Home Guard was patrolling. A generation later, entertainers made popular fun of 'Dad's Army', but in mid-May 1940, while the Western Front was collapsing, the new national government's appeal for 'Local Defence Volunteers' was deadly serious, and so was the nation's response – 250 000 enrolments in the first 24 hours. These first L.D.V.s, later to be called the Home Guard, included veterans from 1914–18, seventeen-year-olds too young for call-up, and a huge number of men in reserved occupations who had no military training whatever. Only a few had firearms, and there was as yet no uniform, but they had to begin at once, in pairs or fours, a dawn-watch against paratroops. They were to *delay* attackers if they possibly could. Before long there were night patrols too, on horseback over the Exmoor hills. The only enemies they captured, in fact, were the crews of crashed aircraft; but in the summer months of 1940 nobody knew that in September Hitler's attempt at invasion would be foiled by the R.A.F. in the Battle of Britain, and that after the gruesome and unremitting bombing of London in the winter and spring he would postpone it indefinitely, and – like Napoleon – march east instead.

The concept of the L.D.V., hastily formed in time of great danger, was masterly, because *local*. Volunteers were guarding their own parishes, and on Exmoor this meant that they knew each other and everybody else. ('Halt! Who goes there?' and a young male voice answered from the darkness, 'Only me and Muriel!') They also knew every hump and hollow in the ground, every thorn-bush or gorse-patch. This did not alter the horrible question of who might be hiding there, fully armed; but they had nothing to learn about *esprit de corps*.

Farmers and labourers, village craftsmen or shop-keepers, some of whom had never been more than 20 miles from home, were caught up suddenly to play a part in what Churchill rightly declared to be Britain's finest hour, and they rose to the occasion. They were trained as they went along, with expeditions to capture Dulverton station (the only junction) or to defend Porlock beach, where the Danes used to land in Saxon times. But it bore hard on some of the old simplicities. A visiting instructor at an early meeting was asked, 'What if 'e come when I'm in baid?' and – more difficult to answer convincingly – 'What if 'e come when we'm lambin'?' Soon afterwards, though, they were riding their ponies over the moor on wet, dark and windy nights – 'Do King

Jarge *know* we'm doin' this for 'en?' and the cheerful answer was 'Noo! The old bugger's vaast aslape in baid!' (At this period a Cabinet Minister privileged to cross the grounds of Buckingham Palace on his way to Whitehall found the King putting in a little rifle-practice in the garden. He and his family would all be staying at home throughout the London blitz, not sleeping very sound.)

When aeroplanes, ours or theirs, tumbled down from the Exmoor sky, the nearest witness might be somebody less martial than the L.D.V.s were becoming. Hurley[11] vouches for the story of a farm-hand hurrying along a field-path at dawn and stopped by a German airman who wanted to surrender to him. 'No,' he replied, 'I can't be bothered wi' 'ee. I be late vor me work as 'tis.' There is also a sad tale, not widely told, of an old shepherd for whom adjustment was too difficult. He was up near a ridge, in misty weather, when a plane crashed in the next pasture uphill. He climbed the hedge to have a look, and saw the R.A.F. pilot lying, not quite motionless, near the wreck. The flock was not threatened, so he climbed back. When the coroner asked why he had not tried to save the airman's life, he said, "Twouldn't 'a' bin no use. 'E'd got no business flyin' in the sky, an' if they'd patched 'en up 'e'd only 'a' done it again.' (As the Battle of Britain pilots did, again and again.) The court saw that the old man, alone all day in the hills, year after year, had not yet fully entered this century, and nobody had the heart to condemn him. 'Twouldn't 'a' bin no use.

As the danger of invasion lessened, in the second year of the war, the need for more home-grown food increased. Germany controlled the entire southern coast of the English Channel, Ireland was neutral and said to be peppered with German agents: the convoys of food-ships and oil-tankers were in constant danger, and losses were heavy. So the War Agricultural Committees were appointed to intensify farm production, everybody with a bit of garden was adjured to 'Dig for Victory', and pig-clubs turned kitchen and garden waste into good meat.

The Exmoor 'War Ags' had a difficult task, trying to ensure that every acre was used to full advantage. They began by surveying the land – like Billingsley and Vancouver during the Napoleonic wars, but in much closer detail. Soil-testing showed very serious lime-deficiency, which had to be remedied before much else could be done. At first they recommended ploughing the hill-pastures for corn, but after one or two harvests the weather put an end to that, and the new fields were resown with grass. Subsidies for hill-ewes and then for hill-cattle encouraged farmers to lime the high ground and carry more stock. Meanwhile, in the grain shortage, they were required to grow more potatoes, and were inclined to demur. ('Four fields they wanted, and that wasn't 'taty land', and 'Oh, I wish you chaps was in *baid*! If you tell me you want a truck-load, or two truck-load, or dree truck-load, you shall have 'em; but I bain't goin' to plant they there!')

Those whose War Ag visitor had farmed Exmoor hill-country counted themselves lucky – he knew what could be done and what could not. Some, comparative strangers, made mistakes with a high hand. They were not popular; they had full power to evict any farmer who could not or would not improve his land and output; a number were dispossessed, and the War Ag farmed in his stead or found a co-operative tenant. It was a grim wartime necessity, like many others; but the Committees' work was well done. With farmers and skilled labourers working at full stretch, a huge increase was achieved.

Exmoor had helped in the defence of the realm, and it was sheltering great numbers of town-children (some had gone home during the phoney war, but a new flood had come, refugees from the London blitz, in the autumn of 1940). It was also sending an unprecedented quantity of food away, and a steady supply of foxglove for medicine and sphagnum for dressing wounds. Now came the preparations for attack. More and more soldiers arrived, gunners and tank-crews, British and then American, to be trained on the wild land for their part in piercing the armed walls of Hitler's *Festung Europa* – the fortress of Europe which he had boasted would be German for a thousand years.

In 1942 North Hill, the coastal ridge running from Minehead to Selworthy Beacon, became very important. It is claimed that nearly every tank-crew sent overseas had been trained there. The hill was cleared of stock, two abandoned farmhouses became gunnery targets, and a military road was built from end to end, with concrete turning-places for the tanks. (This was kept after the war as the 'Scenic Road'.) Another centre for tank exercises was Withypool Hill. Americans were there for a long time; one of their tanks was stuck in the marshy stream-bed above Portford Bridge for months; their camp site on Waterhouse Green had a large concrete hearth which, grassed over now, should still show in a drought. A commoner using his right to cut peat near Brightworthy Barrow mused on the contrast between his occupation, as old as any on the moor, and the cavorting of mechanical monsters nearby.

Exmoor distances were useful for long-range gunnery training. Two Knight farms in the Forest, Tom's Hill and Larkbarrow, were requisitioned as targets, to be fired at from Winsford Hill, Fyldon Ridge, Cheriton Ridge, Woolhanger. They were shot to ruins, with live ammunition; shell-craters dotted the moor, and unexploded shells buried themselves deep. Frank Glanville, the postman who walked his 20-mile round from Porlock throughout the war, and wrote as 'Afghan', recorded, in the *Exmoor Review*, 1972, that the learners 'managed to shoot many of the larger stags'. He remembered seeing a jeep on the road 'with an enormous pair of antlers fixed to the bonnet', and 'jeeps driving deer across the moor towards rougher ground where men with guns were hidden'. It was the modern equivalent, again, of mediaeval hunting with bow and arrow. Our own troops, Glanville continued, as well as the Americans, varied their army diet with venison, trout and game-birds – as, of course, farmers had always done when they could. It is unlikely that anybody grudged them this further Exmoor contribution to victory. Fierce fighting lay ahead of them.

One evening early in 1944 a G.I. on a crowded London tube-train remarked to his mate, 'If one more American comes on this island, it'll sink!' By the end of May the weight of men and armaments concentrated in southern England might, on that reckoning, have tilted it into the sea. British and American servicemen were all poised waiting for the unknown date when they would be taken to an undisclosed destination (the Normandy beaches). Thousands more Americans had come to Dulverton in troop-trains and were encamped on Exmoor and the Brendons. Then about a week before D-day another special train arrived, well-equipped as a comfortable temporary base, and out of it stepped the Supreme Commander of the whole vast enterprise, General Eisenhower. He shook hands with the station-master and said he would like to stay a few days. He had come to inspect and encourage the troops, and a powerful car took him from camp to camp. Afterwards, with a day or two in hand, he prolonged his visit, was lent a good Exmoor pony and went riding by himself. Complete secrecy was impossible, but golden silence was maintained – everybody had learnt discretion by then – and he rode as a friendly stranger. At Worth farmhouse, between Hawkridge and Withypool, he stopped to ask whether there was any chance of a cup of coffee; the schoolgirl daughter who answered his knock recognized him from newspaper photographs, and ran to tell her mother 'General Eisenhower's at the door!' She was not believed – 'Don't be so silly!' Coffee was scarce; perhaps they gave him tea from their ration. He enjoyed his short time on Exmoor, in the lull before the storm.

From June 6th there were Allied troops in France, as well as the 'Desert Rats' conquering Italy, and Russians pressing hard from the east. But the Germans were not easily defeated, and modern weaponry inflicted terrible casualties. It was another eleven months before a tired Britain celebrated V.E. (Victory in Europe) in May 1945. There were two days of holiday; not a leisurely week of rejoicing like South Molton's in 1814, but two days of immense relief, sobered by the knowledge that the Far Eastern war against fanatical Japanese was not yet over. That lasted another three months – until two atom bombs ended the war but wrenched the future awry.

We had waged a total war, and won it without becoming totalitarian, though under an Emergency Act the government had authority to direct everybody's energy and skill according to the national need. When Churchill became Prime Minister in the cataclysmic May of 1940 he at once chose as Minister of Labour and National Service, to wield this immense power, a man of grasp and steadfastness to match his own, a Trades Union leader of long experience, Ernest Bevin, born some sixty years before in the Exmoor village of Winsford. It quickly proved to be a brilliant choice, and in the autumn Bevin became a member of the inner War Cabinet, where he was Churchill's unshakeable supporter. The understanding between these two men was invaluable. One a descendant of Marlborough, born in the ducal palace of Blenheim, and one the illegitimate son of a pugnacious countryman and an almost penniless village widow, they worked closely together to shape eventual victory, and it was tacitly agreed in that coalition cabinet that they stood head and shoulders above the rest for sheer bull-dog courage. So a Labour member of it told me, early in 1945. One of his Conservative colleagues described Bevin as 'a diamond lying on a vast heap of coke', and perhaps that outlook helped to convince Attlee and Bevin that the Coalition could not continue after the defeat of Hitler.

They gauged common opinion correctly. When the government was dissolved, for the general election, the great national leader suddenly dwindled, between one speech and the next, into the Conservative Party's candidate, and the country, gratefully honouring the former, utterly repudiated the latter; the memory of the 1930s was too strong. Labour had a landslide victory, and a wise elder statesman from one of the exiled foreign governments in London told his friends when he reached home, 'The English are a wonderful people. They can have a revolution by voting for it.'

So Attlee formed a government, and on the King's advice as well as his own judgement appointed Ernest Bevin as Foreign Secretary. Exmoor villagers, knowing perfectly well who his father was, approved. They had watched his career with amused pleasure, noting that physically he was the image of that shrewd, capable and overpowering man (though he also inherited kindlier qualities from Mercy Bevin, his frail, hard-working, chapel-going mother). One of the older people of Withypool chuckled: 'Nobody never got the better of his Dad and the Russians won't get the better of he!' And they didn't. A few months later Londoners were enjoying an anecdote about a diplomatic meeting at which a smooth, well-educated Russian bureaucrat, an *apparatchik*, began to pontificate about the will of the proletariat. Ernie banged his fist on the table: 'Don't you talk like that to me! I'm a son of the proletariat, and I *know*!'

The 'Dockers' K.C.' of Bristol had become the pre-war T.U.C.

organizer, then the wartime Minister of Labour controlling the whole nation's energies, and then the post-war Foreign Secretary and chief architect of N.A.T.O. Exmoor has never had a son of comparable stature. When Churchill wanted to recommend him for a Companionship of Honour in 1945 he declined, saying he had done his job in the interests of the nation, as had thousands of others, and did not desire special honours. But when he died, in 1951, his ashes were laid in Westminster Abbey.

CHAPTER FOURTEEN

Yesterday ending

Peace-time conditions were slow to return. Rationing went on for a long time, partly because Britain, like the United States, was sending food to continental allies freed at last from Nazi rule. London and the other bomb-damaged cities were soldiering on, shabby and dusty, and their ruins and razed areas would take years to rebuild. For tired civilians and demobilized servicemen Exmoor, little known to outsiders, was Arcadia. The soft hill air was so clean, the moor so lovely under blue sky, with cloud-shadows moving across from the west, and quick shallow streams showing every pebble and minnow under the sunlit ripple. It was an enchanting harmony of earth, air and water. The quiet was seldom broken by any but natural sounds. The food was fresh and good. The people were as courteous as when Jefferies knew them, always ready to welcome friendly strangers; their life was tranquilly following the age-old pattern – shepherds on ponies, haymaking by hand, corn-harvest worryingly late as grey clouds gathered for rain.

Less obvious to summer visitors – though they *were* visitors, not tourists, in those days, and could look more closely – was the underlying dereliction. The farms were badly run down: the soil was impoverished, and farmhouses needed money spent on them. Things were a little better than in the thirties – the farmer and his family had rather more to eat and rather less financial anxiety. But out in the fields the banks were crumbling, and wooden gates, rain-soaked and rotting, veiled by delicate grey-green lichen, were lashed to decrepit hanging-posts with wire or frayed string. Gaps in the hedges were stopped with old bedsteads, sheds and barns were roofed with torn and rusty corrugated iron. building materials were strictly rationed, a ready-made gate or a sheet of galvanized iron was virtually unobtainable; a farmer could buy a little cement, but not nearly as much as he needed.

Change came later here than in other parts of England. Soon, about five years after the end of the war, it would catapult the hill-country from yesterday into today, about four centuries in a decade or two. Legislation in 1951, providing generous grants for modernization, and more liming subsidies, put the Exmoor farmers back on their feet. The landscape altered. Bigger and bigger farm machinery meant the widening of gateways and the removal of hedges between small fields, so that tillage became easier, though stock had less shelter. Lorries bringing farm supplies and tankers fetching milk directly from the mechanized 'milking parlours' required wider lanes, and the drivers wanted open corners, 'vision-splays' for safer speed. So more old hedge-banks came down, and post and wire fences took their place. Concrete and breeze-block ousted stone. Barns like aeroplane hangers dominated the slopes. Cars multiplied, and so did motor-coaches; hedges were clipped low for them, and ferny hedgerows shorn, and with that cover gone they glinted for miles. The moor was being tamed – 'bitted and bridled', said an old hand. But subsidies and grants, motorization, electricity and telephones were making life immeasurably easier for its people, both on the land and indoors. And the welfare state was removing some of the anxieties of illness and old age, and giving the young a better start in life. The transformation was so thorough and quick that those young, forty years older now, can hardly believe how their parents had to toil on and make do.

In the pause just after the war, while yesterday was drawing to a close, old ways and relics of older were everywhere to be seen – some of them almost for the last time. About the farm stood hayricks and round mows, storing the winter feed where it would be needed. Barns and shippons surrounded and sheltered the farmyards, with more hay in their tallets, or lofts; it had been tossed loose through the upper doorway from a wain below, the horse waiting patiently while the men worked from the top of the load. There were linhays standing alone in valleys, a precaution against snowstorms; they had hay in the loft and standing-room for sheep or cattle below. Most of the round-houses had been stripped of the gearing by which a horse, circling for hours, had once provided power for threshing or cider-making, but they still stood, and would hold any half-discarded implement which might yet come in handy; 'Oh, put it in the round-house!' Sheep still wintered out of doors, and lambed in the small fields near home. A cowman at Broford always used, for a sick animal, a very old stone shed with a splayed window, a narrow slit broadening inward through the thick wall, as in a Norman castle; it let in air but not rain, and for years his cows always recovered better there than in a smart new shippon built for their health and comfort. (This mediaeval style can still be seen in Tudor barns and cowsheds, here and there – at Cheriton and Brendon, for example.) And there were still men about who could heal an ailing cow when standard veterinary practices failed; 'laughing away the ringworm' actually worked.[1]

But a labourer's old widow picked out the greatest difference between then and now; 'I often wonder what our dear ones would say if they came back.' She was thinking only of her husband. 'D'you know what he'd say? "Mother," he'd say, "whatever's become of the horses?"' That was in the 1970s. In 1950 they were still doing nearly all the farm-work – ploughing, harrowing, dragging loaded carts uphill or through deep mud – and had to be fed, watered and harnessed before the day's work began. Another survivor, looking back to a time before farm-hands drove heavy machinery up and down the fields, said, 'You could *talk* to a horse.' (And you could see and hear the small animals and birds, without frightening them away; not having to protect yourself with ear-guards against noise.) Only a few farms have horse-ponds now – a joy to the ducks. Stones laid edgewise across the surface of a hump-backed bridge once gave the great beasts foothold, but now the passage of tractors has worn them flat. Almost the only reminder of all that good service is the row of horse-brasses which a farmer's wife keeps bright and shining to decorate her kitchen or parlour.

Indoors there was little change yet. Electricity did not reach the villages until the middle of the 1950s. Dinner might be cooked on a stove heated by portable gas, but more probably on a well-trusted iron range or a still older open fire, burning wood or peat. Oil-lamps and candles lit the dark evenings. Water might come from a local reservoir – delicious hill-water, unmedicated – or perhaps from the well across the yard. When Monday's washing had been dried, out in the wind or slowly in the back-house, it was pressed by flat-irons heated one after another at the fire. So the housewife's labours were not much less than before, though once in a while, when the petrol ration allowed, her husband might drive her to town for prudent shopping. On ordinary days a battery wireless set might enliven her kitchen work.

Tiny villages in large parishes were still the centre of social life: the towns were too far away. At church or chapel, at a hospitable forge, or in any post office which was also the shop, people gathered and exchanged news and civilities. Nobody would be ill for long without neighbours hearing of it and going to offer help. Careful plans were made for the next whist-drive or village hop, Christmas party or harvest supper. By moonlight, or with a torch or a lantern, young and old could go along to the parish hall for their home-made entertainment, unsophisticated and genial. A few hundred yards further, past the last cottage, the walker would be out on the road over the hills; there was no barrier – not even a cattle-grid – between the village and the moor. The wild ponies knew this too, and at dusk on an autumn evening would come padding softly down to nibble a meal from cottage gardens or appetizing hedgerows.

Most of the prehistoric and mediaeval roads were still in use; some had been 'made', with gravel or tarmac, some remained their old selves, white or sandy red or peaty brown. The ancient boundary road along Fyldon ridge and on past Kinsford Cross was not modernized until after the great flooding of all the rivers in 1952, when Lynmouth was laid waste. (The relief fund, oversubscribed, was used partly for this work.) Commons were open to the road; cars had not yet made fences necessary for the safety of the sheep. Corners were still blind; a bollaster – a big smooth boulder – might protect a house or barn wall from carts turning too sharply; the market town of South Molton has inconspicuous ones in its streets; a rough one can be seen at Yard Gate, where a long lane from North Molton joins the road which once brought flocks southward off the Forest. Best of all, the beeches in hedge-banks were left to grow for about fifteen years before being relaid, and their boughs overarching the lanes made dappled tunnels, lined with moss and small ferns. A few red squirrels still inhabited them. Near villages, wisps of hay or wool hung from the twigs when a loaded wagon had lumbered along.

Animals calmly took precedence on all the roads. It might be the dairy-herd of golden Guernseys going down Fore Street in Dulverton from their afternoon milking. It might be a flock of sheep halted near Honeymead, having walked from Exford, their young shepherd standing beside them, looking down in amused compassion at his dog, which had covered far more miles than the flock had and lay stretched out in the dust, 'She'm nearly tired, I reckon.' The clip-clop of hooves might mean hunters trotting uphill, or a pony carrying a farmer and his sack of flour home from the mill. (I last saw this in 1950, when the corn had been ground at Twitchen. A few years later that farmer's son did the journey by Land-Rover.)

About once in a decade, then as now, deep snow would obliterate all roads and most hedges, fill the lanes, and hide buildings under the drifts. The first months of 1947 – 'the bad winter' everywhere – were very bad indeed on Exmoor. From the end of January to the beginning of March, roads were impassable, villages cut off, farms isolated. Rationing was not yet over so housewives had not the reserves of yeast and flour and salted meat which formerly they had always built up in autumn. There were no helicopters yet. Groups of men with sledges set out from the hungry villages, hoping to meet the road-men working towards them with snow-ploughs and scoops, and they managed to bring home food to be fairly shared. When a road was cleared for a mile or two, between towering walls of snow and ice, another blizzard would fill it again.

The modern difference is only that relief comes more easily by air. Drifts and bitter frost are killers, as ever, and an immense amount of snow can fall, unexpectedly, in only a few hours – as in 1891 when it buried Amos Cann. Not long ago, a farmer left his Land-Rover in shelter after a sudden heavy snowstorm and took a short cut home across his own fields, but he could not see his house until he trod on its roof-ridge. The same thing happened to a doctor and his ambulance driver picking their way at night from the road to a cottage in the white expanse. Help of this kind had improved beyond recognition, of course; in the 1640s rescuers going into the Forest from High Bray had abandoned a man who was frozen to the ground, and seemed bound to die; not far away, in the bad frost of 1985, when a girl was found lying unconscious in the snow, a telephone call brought the Lynton ambulance driver with his stretcher; he had to cut steps in the ice to carry her down to the road, but her life was saved.

Such dire cold, feared every year, comes only like a seventh wave at sea. Far more typical are the days or weeks when soft clouds of moisture lie along the ridges and the sun, if it comes through, illumines silvery droplets on all the seeded grasses and sets them sparkling in rainbow colours when the thin stems quiver. This is proper Exmoor weather, quiet and secret. Out on the moor a walker moves from one tiny sphere into another. Delicate little flowers, milkwort and tormentil and bedstraw, grow close against the dry ground; bog cotton, sphagnum moss and bog asphodel warn of bad going. A snipe may rise, a hind may loom through the mist a few yards away, and there is no other sound to be heard. In yesterday's last years, when labourers still went afoot to their work, perhaps it was they who saw most, and were best attuned to the poetry of it all. After years of noticing much and saying little, cottagers would now and then reveal their sympathies. When the Barle had been 'bitted and bridled' after the 1952 flood, and rose high again in storm, talk in Withypool village shop next morning was about the river 'crying all night – oh, how it was crying!' Everybody had heard it. When the Americans landed a man on the moon, a gentle old widow said, '*Poor* moon! It wasn't *put*, not for going on.' Nearer home, when workmen had ripped up hedge-banks for a 'vision-splay', and exposed a clutch of new unsightly buildings on the skyline, and I had stopped to look with distaste at the harm done, a farm-hand whom I did not know said quietly from a gateway, 'They'm spoilin' of it, bain't 'em?'

So yesterday ended, in the 1950s. The long-delayed change came very fast, and continuity was threatened. New people took the land, with new money, new houses made in suburban styles with alien materials, new machinery and methods, new ideas. Many farmers and labourers who had known the hill country and its subtleties all their lives, whose forebears had maintained it for centuries, who had the moor in their blood as sailors have the sea, had to step aside or be pushed aside. Their tools, the heirlooms of the poor, became 'bygones' in local museums.[2] But other young men and women of good Exmoor stock learnt the new ways of doing their ancestors' work, and throve.

We cannot 'call back yesterday, bid time return', and perhaps few would wish to: change was due. Today and yesterday alike are of mingled yarn, good and ill together. Moorland not tamed to feed the towns is now a revelation and delight to town children brought camping. Commercial exploitation is a new danger; the National Park is a new defence.

It is such a small and intimate moor, very vulnerable and perpetually encroached upon. Ugly new buildings may become outmoded and collapse, in a century or two, but piecemeal destruction is insidious and irreparable. Even the herring-bone earthen banks, the coigns beside field-gates, or small slate culverts taking flood water away, were made by hand with loving care. Like the old stone houses and cob cottages, they carry steadiness from the past towards an uncertain future:

> 'Tread softly, softly,
> Oh men coming in.'

NOTES

Chapter 1: The King's deer

1. Forest still meant outland when Shakespeare wrote *As You Like It*. Orlando, in the Forest of Arden, apologizes for his rough manner, born of desperation – 'yet am I inland bred,
                    And know some nurture'.
   Later, Rosalind's educated speech threatens to betray her disguise as a native of the forest, and she hastens to explain that she was taught by 'an old religious uncle ... who was in his youth an inland man'. Spanish still keeps the word *forestero* for a stranger, an outsider.

2. There is a theory – unprovable, alas! – that the dragon ships, monsters with high beaked prows and shields along their sides like scales, roaring up the beaches to bring fire and slaughter, explain the dedication of churches along this flat stretch of coast to the great dragon-slayers, St Michael and St George. At Minehead and Dunster, for instance, the saints were well placed to see the invaders long before they reached the shore.

3. This identification was suggested by Stephen Morland and kindly communicated to me by David Bromwich, Local History Librarian in Taunton Castle. Hawkridge is not named in Domesday Book, but one entry (46.2 in the Thorn edition) says that Robert de Auberville had a virgate of land which Dodo held freely before 1066. It had then been added to the King's Manor of Dulverton, but by 1088 was restored to its old status as thane-land.

4. *Purpresture* was an illegal enclosure or encroachment on the King's land.
   Assart meant clearing trees and undergrowth with a view to ploughing.
   Vert was the greenery which might provide either cover or food for the deer.
   Chiminage was a toll to be paid for passing through the Forest.
   Pannage was the pasturing of swine.

5. *Suitors at Large and Free Suitors.* A summary may help to clarify the difference. A suit was a feudal duty. The Free Suitors of Withypool and Hawkridge, being direct tenants of the Warden and sub-tenants of the King, had fuller duties and compensatory freedoms, as described in subsequent paragraphs of this chapter; the Suitors at Large were independent borderers, with lighter duties and slighter privileges – for instance, when the Free Suitors perambulated the whole Forest with the Warden or his representative, the Suitors at Large rode only their own borders, in their own interest.

6. The thirteenth-century spelling is *Donekesbroch*. The Danes had nothing to do with the stream, which is named after the little dunnock or hedge-sparrow – nobody knows why.

7. If it was the same John; but the 'chaplain' of the second reference may have been a lay helper or locum tenens.

8. John Livingston Lowes, in his *Geoffrey Chaucer*, 1934, Ch. 2, explained the Windsor link with Sir Peter Courtenay, which Dr Krauss had recently shown. MacDermot, in Ch. 5 of his *History of the Forest of Exmoor*, gives the legal details of Sir Peter's tenure, under the Mortimers, of the wardenship of four Somerset forests, Petherton, Neroche, Mendip and Exmoor – Selwood being no longer part of the group. It is not clear whether he kept the forests in his own hands, but certainly Geoffrey Chaucer had the custody of the North Petherton estate, which always included Withypool and Hawkridge. Five years after his death another Chaucer, Thomas, followed Sir Peter as temporary warden; he may or may not have been the poet's son.

9. Further detail in *Ancient Exmoor*, H. Eardley-Wilmot, Exmoor Press 1983.

10. Meare-stones, or merestones; the word meant boundary-stones, or land-marks, in various Teutonic languages; the Latin equivalent was *murus*, a wall.

11. This information was extracted from the records by Norman Annett, for his unpublished work on North Molton.

12. T. H. Cooper, in his guide to Lynton and neighbouring parishes, transcribed the Brendon subsidy list. Robert de Whitering paid 12d.; there was also a Roger de Whitefield, who paid only two-thirds as much, and richer men, one from Countisbury and one from Brightworthy; this suggests that Whitefield might have come from the farm of that name in the parish of High Bray, or from Whitefield Barton in Challacombe. I know of no White Ring now; but did five white stones once stand in a ring on Windwhistle? Was Deddycombe on Robert de Whitering's land?

Chapter 2: The farmer's sheep

1. In the last return of the North Molton Parish Waywardens to South Molton Highway District. Norman Annett, *North Molton and its people* (see Note 3, Chapter 6).

2. For a fuller account see *Leland's Road and a Telling-house*, S.W. Exmoor, H. Eardley-Wilmot in *Devon and Cornwall Notes and Queries*, Autumn 1981.

3. The two gates were hung parallel on a single post, so that a wind opening one would close the other, and the stock would find it very difficult to get through.

4. *Cob.* William Chapple, a late eighteenth-century agriculturalist in Devon (see Note 1, Chapter 7) describes this method of building. 'In the Parts where Building Stone is scarce, we have Country Masons who value themselves on their Skill in making Mud-Walls, or as we call them, Cob-Walls; which if well perform'd, and supported by a sufficient Foundation of Stone-Work, are very lasting, and the Houses thus built, dryer and warmer than others. The Cob, as 'tis call'd, is a Composition of Earth and Straw, wet up somewhat like Morter, well beaten and trodden together; and after a Wall made therewith is rais'd to a certain Height, it is

allow'd some Time to settle before more is laid on. When any such Walls are pulled down to be re-built, they commonly make fresh Cob with other Earth; the Value of the old as a Manure for Land, sufficiently compensating the Cost of the new.'

5.   Ernest Mold, 'Doone Valley', in *Exmoor Review*, 1986.

6.   Hoskins calls them *truckamucks*, and in his *Devon* quotes a description of them by the Rev. S. Baring-Gould of Lew Trenchard as 'a sort of cart' but in fact 'nothing but two young trees, and the roots dragged, and the tops were fastened to the horse'. For the heaviest weights, four trees were used, and on steep hills oxen rather than horses.

Chapter 3:   Early roads

1.   This may be the origin of the report to MacDermot in 1910 or so of a telling-house near Span Head, since one of the two or three places so named is only a short distance away. If the Ordnance Surveyors in 1809 and the recent study of the sunken road near Yard Down, discussed in Chapter 2, were approximately right, MacDermot's informant was mistaken.

2.   *Severn* may be an Indo-European word for *western*, like the Greek zephyr, the west wind. *Locri epizephyrii* was a colony the Corinthians founded in the sixth century B.C. in southern Italy, almost due west of them across the Ionian sea. In Britain, Mendip lead was used before the Romans came, and prehistoric travellers from Old Sarum would catch their first far-off glimpse of the western sea as they climbed a flank of Mendip, perhaps 'mighty hill', and neared the end of their journey. If their name for river and estuary was *Severn*, the Romans, quick to follow the old road and develop the lead, lost the sense of western in their version, *Sabrina*, of the native word they heard. (Conquerors very often adopt local names for hills and rivers, and *b* is a standard variant of *f* or *v*.)

3.   *Cross* as a place-name almost invariably means, on Exmoor, a crossroads, which may be the meeting of three, four or five ways. When there were very few landmarks, the crossways were important reference points. They were often named after the nearest farm (Spire Cross, Stone Cross) and sometimes after a great landowner; Raleigh's Cross, marking the way down to Nettlecombe, had a memorial cross as well. Strangers are confused, expecting stone monuments, like the preaching-crosses in so many churchyards. The mistake is not new; it appears on the 'Map of Exmoor', a pictorial diagram made to help Boevey in his litigation in 1675. This stylized blend of fact and fancy illustrates Kinsford and Coles crosses with the Christian symbol. It is printed as frontispiece to MacDermot's *History of Exmoor*.

(The Ordnance Surveyors, less skilled at language than at trigonometry, sometimes mishear. Results like *Fanny*'s Cross for the nearby farm of *Venhayes* provide the neighbours with tolerant amusement.)

4.   Robert Dunning, *A History of Somerset* (Phillimore, 1983), amplified by personal communication.

5.   Since this paragraph was written, a quite different suggestion has

been made. A local amateur, Mr Jeffrey Samuel, noticed that the cross askew resembled the oldest form of St Bridget's Cross, an X in the middle of an encircled space (as carved on a stone at Cooscroneen in County Cork). That is thought to be a prehistoric emblem, adopted for St Bridget who had formerly been the Celtic goddess Brig. At Culbone (where the arms of the X reach right to the circumference) the same observer noted that the shaft outside the wheel is rougher work, and not perfectly aligned with the spoke from which it extends. His opinion that it was not cut by the same hand is endorsed by professional archaeologists working on a Royal Commission survey. They think the two parts both man-made, but not contemporary. The difference in date cannot be gauged, but it seems possible that a pagan symbol ritually linked with the nearby row was at some time deliberately Christianized. This would explain the slant.

6.   Chadwyck Healey, quoting this from the accounts which the bailiff, John Godde, kept for the widowed Lady Harrington of Porlock, remarks on the rarity of a road strong enough for a loaded wagon at that date. J. K. Ridler suggests that there may have been a Roman military road here, through *Stratford* and Brandish *Street*, for the defence of Porlock against raiders from Wales.

7.   *Chet* is from a Celtic word for a wood, as in Welsh *coed*. The Anglo-Saxon settlers were no linguists; in Buckinghamshire, since *chet* meant nothing to them, they added their own description and coined the repetitive name *Chetwode*. Trees may always have grown easily in the steep little cleeve of Chetsford Water. Apparently Saxon newcomers took *chet* for the name of the stream not the spinney, and called the crossing the *ford of the Chet*.

8.   *Summerway*. From his long and thorough local knowledge, J. K. Ridler tells me that he has always thought this to be the road up from Wheddon Cross. Brendon Hill farm and all above it was open moorland until the Inclosure Award for Cutcombe and Exton about 1797, and the Cutcombe stock would have been driven up there for summering. He agrees that the summer Harepath would be the steep track down to Bushel Bridge, the Cutcombe route being used only when the river was too high for fording. Our 'Summerway' was in that case the Winterway of the ancients.

9.   Grundy, 'Ancient Highways of Somerset', *Archaeological Journal*, Vol. XCVI and Whybrow, *Antiquary's Exmoor*, 1970 and 1977.

10. The nineteenth-century farm name Driver may preserve a hint of this. In the seventeenth century Drye and Dryslade are recorded three times as lying in the south-west of the Forest; 'a waye leading from Brayford to Drye' entered at Moles Chamber and must have been the old bridle-path. By the eighteenth century the Forest books were calling the grazing areas Dryslade and Dreford or Dryford; perhaps when the Knight farm was carved out the name Driver was a protest against the idea of a dry ford.

   Slade is Saxon and means valley; *dru* and *dry* are variants on a widespread Indo-European word for tree, especially oak tree. (The Greek wood-nymphs were dryads.) In the *Exmoor Review*, 1983 I suggested that Dryslade was that part of the Barle valley, perhaps wooded in prehistoric times (Dry being the older part of the hybrid word). On reading the article, Mr J. K. Ridler kindly drew my attention to a passage in Snell's *A Book of Exmoor*, 1903, describing the writer's visit to Driver to see the bog-oak which Farmer A. Kingdon was finding in deep peat on his hillside. Snell was shown the dark roots still plentiful where a stream from the Chains cut the surface, and he had no doubt that they were evidence of ancient forest.

11. 'La Rode' is a puzzle. Road Castle has been suggested, Road Hill might be rather better, but neither is entirely convincing. This is an obscure piece of the mediaeval boundary. In 1279 the landmark was spelt 'la Roode' – but why feminine?

12. Page, an observant topographer, had no doubt in 1890 about what he called a 'British trackway' leading from Combwich over the Quantocks and Brendons. He said that on the right of the road from Nether to Over Stowey it was traceable against the hedge for the length of one field. It was lower than the field and had the appearance of a hollow way, about 8 feet wide.

13. *Nymet* comes from an Indo-European root *nim*, for sanctity, often associated with water. Two Nymet rivers flow into the Taw, one which the Saxons renamed Mole, through misunderstanding *Molton*, (*tun* on the *bare* hilltop) and one passing Bury under the common Saxon river-name Yeo, meaning *water*. The Romans would know them by the native prehistoric name (which survives in Saxon and Norman villages on both rivers – King's, Queen's and Bishop's Nympton, once Nymet Bishop, in the fertile Mole valley, and near the source of the Yeo, Norman estates like Nymet Tracey and Nymet Rowland). The army camp, or 'station' called *Nemeto statio*, is more likely to have been this one overlooking the Nymet at Bury than the next one westward on the Taw at North Tawton, as formerly assumed.

14. Draper's Way is still the local name. The draper was William Thorne, also itinerant grocer and preacher, a tireless worker for Methodism who regularly travelled the hill villages, on foot, from 1814 to 1860. (N. Allen, *Churches and Chapels of Exmoor*: Cutcombe, Exmoor Press, 1974.)

15. The crossroads is named, as usual, from the nearest farm, and Chibbet appears to mean plover, and to have nothing to do with a gibbet.

Chapter 4: The Reformation and the New World

1. Chadwyck Healey, relating this, quotes a statute from Henry VIII's reign decreeing that 'Butts be made in every city, town or place, by the inhabitants ... according to the law of ancient time' and that the inhabitants must maintain the butts, and use them regularly for practice with long bows, on holidays and at other convenient times.

2. The Rhenish tower was destroyed in the 1952 flood, but rebuilt; the fire-basket was swept out to sea but later recovered.

3. Drake and Raleigh, south Devon men, had links with Exmoor.

Nettlecombe, north of the Brendons, had passed by marriage from Raleighs to Trevelyans, but the friends of both families would go down to the great house from Raleigh's Cross on the Harepath. Francis Drake rode to Combe Sydenham, nearby, to woo his second wife, and a young Trevelyan sailed with him for a time.

4. Information kindly supplied by Dr Alison Grant of Instow, who adds that these were very probably the five ships reported in Barnstaple as having crossed the bar to sail to Plymouth.

5. The prangstaff or sprangstaff was a military staff, like a pitchfork with straight prongs. Its length varied from three to four yards or more. It was obviously advantageous to have a longer one than your opponent had. Witnesses in these cases always estimated the length.

6. Noel Allen gives the tale in full in *Churches and Chapels of Exmoor* (Exmoor Press, 1974).

Chapter 5:   Divided loyalties

1. See the full article, 'Priest on Exmoor', by Berta Lawrence, in *Exmoor Review, 1984*.

2. J. Cock, telling this story in his *Records of the Borough of South Molton* (1893), recalled the site of the Angel Inn, at what had later become No. 8 Broad Street. He remembered the inn-sign, an angel painted on a huge board.

3. The old market cross, or 'High Cross', was taken down in 1794.

4. In the British Museum the hoard is called the *Thorndon* collection, as it was in the Numismatic Chronicle for 1897 in which coin experts recorded it in detail. Locally the farm is known as *Thornham*, and that name is on the O.S. 1:1250 and 1:25 000 maps, while the 1:50 000 O.S. tourist map gives *Thorndon*.

5. Until well into the present century a farm-hand's straw hat for weekdays might have little left except the brim which shaded face and neck.

6. At one time the letter was in the possession of the Rev. Michael Etherington of Withypool; he wrote about it in the *New English Review*, September 1946.

7. W. MacDonald Wigfield was told this family tradition by a direct descendant of Nathaniel's elder brother. (See his book *The Monmouth Rebellion: a social history*, Moonraker Press, 1980.)

8. Quoted by T. H. Cooper from *Western Martyrology*.

9. Country people living at Bridgeball are certain that Wade was shot in their garden. He might, indeed, have escaped downstream, and made for the small farmstead because Philip and Grace Howe were both across at Farley. His own account, carefully minimal, is that he was taken coming out of Birch's house. That might have been deliberate inexactitude, to protect his protectors. Three hundred years cover less than five lifetimes; memories in lonely places are long, and high drama had suddenly enwrapped simple people. They would hand down the details they knew as carefully as the Wade family treasured the story of the information concealed in a laundered shirt.

Chapter 6:   The poor man at his gate

1. Tucking was the western word for fulling. The fuller was called a tucker.
2. The stapler was the merchant, sending his wool to the staples, or markets, such as Barnstaple.
3. Norman Annett's work on *North Molton and its people* is available in photocopied typescript in local libraries.
4. The notebook is fully transcribed in Norman Annett's book.
5. The poor were near famine that year at Elworthy, Chipstable and Wiveliscombe (Robert Dunning, *A History of Somerset*) and there was serious hardship nationally after so much disastrous weather (J. R. Green, *A Short History of the English People*, 1892.)
6. Identified by Nicholas Orme, who described it in the Somerset Archaeological and Natural History Society's *Proceedings*, Vol. 128, 1984.
7. Though the song is set in the seventeenth and eighteenth centuries, it was adapted from a true story, told in Fuller's *Worthies*, of Simon Aleyn, vicar of Bray in Berkshire from 1540 to 1588. J. H. Bettye, in *Church and Parish* (1987), recalls Fuller's account. When somebody accused Aleyn of being 'a turncoat and an unconstant changeling' he replied, 'Not so, for I always kept my principle, which is this, to live and die the vicar of Bray.'
8. But that, if true, may be only part of the reason. By the eighteenth century families were settling along the East Lyn valley, and Cheriton was a long way away. The parish reported to the Bishop of Exeter that the old building on the western ridge was very frail, and too small for their congregation. The Chichester family gave the new site. (See Dr Vernon Hall's leaflet in the church.)
9. By an antiquarian parson, the Rev. Henry Ayre.
10. A photograph of this can be seen in the Rose Ash parish booklet, by the Rev. Christopher Tull.
11. Upping-stocks were mounting-blocks, also called leaping-stocks.

Chapter 7:   The coast and the wars

For fuller information on eighteenth- and nineteenth-century coastal traffic see: *No Gallant Ship*, Michael Bouquet, 1959; *The Cruel Coast of North Devon*, Michael Nix, 1982; and, with other works by Grahame Farr, his microstudy *Ships and Harbours of Exmoor*, 1970. His valuable survey of north Devon smuggling, complementing Chadwyck Healey's pages about the west Somerset ports, is unpublished, but is now in the Grahame Farr Collection held by the North Devon Maritime Museum, which has kindly given me information from it.

1. William Chapple edited and annotated, in the 1770s, Risdon's *Survey of Devon*, written in or about 1630. Both specifically excluded Exmoor, as lying chiefly in Somerset. The problems would not be quite the same, but in a long and moving passage, characteristically humane, Chapple lamented the grave deterioration in the circumstances of 'the daily labourers in husbandry' since Risdon wrote, and said that the change, even within the last thirty

or forty years, had been very perceptible. (The book was reprinted by Porcupine, Barnstaple, in 1970.)

2.   In *A Devon Family* (Phillimore, 1981), Lady Anne Acland tells the story of this spirited pair. When the Tory husband was badly wounded at Saratoga and taken prisoner, his Whig wife, a relation of Charles James Fox, persuaded the English general, Burgoyne, to let her go through the American lines to nurse him. She went down the Hudson River at night, in a small boat flying a large white flag, and took a note from Burgoyne to the American general, Gates, who was chivalrously indignant that any note should have been thought necessary.

3.   Some, too, kept sturdily clear. An old friend told me that his grandfather, who lived near Porlock, was approached one day by a man who said that if he looked in his row of kidney-beans at the bottom of the garden he would find something interesting – meaning a keg of spirit. The householder left him in no doubt what would happen if it was not removed immediately. (This was probably in the 1830s.)

4.   W. H. Thornton, *Reminiscences and reflections of an old West Country Clergyman*, Torquay, 1897. At Countisbury he was much in the company of the Hallidays of Glenthorne, and 'Brandy Path, as we called it' would of course be the name used by the family not by the smugglers!

5.   This was the only link between Watchet and the poem. A local claim that the imaginary ship sailed from there underrates Coleridge's grasp of seamanship. As she dropped down channel to the western horizon her sailors would lose sight first of the *lowest* landmark,'the kirk', then of the hill, and finally even of the lighthouse top. At Watchet the church of St Decuman is up on the hill, the lighthouse down at the waterside.

6.   See Hazlitt's essay *My first acquaintance with poets* for a description of the sermon Coleridge preached at Wem in Shropshire in 1797, shortly before their walk from Nether Stowey to Lynton.

7.   Page, quoting from Murray's *Handbook to Wilts, Dorset and Somerset*, 1882.

8.   The five guns on the quay formerly stood on a patch of ground on the east bank of the river, now called 'The Manor'. An old lady whose parents owned trading-ketches in Lynmouth at the beginning of the present century remembers that in 1914 the Council thought the guns might attract German fire, and had them taken away. There were enemy ships off Lynmouth in both world wars, so perhaps this was prudent.

9.   *General Wilson's Journal*, edited by Antony Brett-James (William Kimber, 1964) shows his impatience with Kutuzov. Tolstoy answers his accusations in *War and Peace*, Book XV, Ch. 4.

Chapter 8:   Continuity and change

1.   I am grateful to Jack and George Huxtable for this and much other information about their father's and grandfather's recollections, as well as their own. Jack lent me many pages of his manuscript

notes; George wrote about the ox ploughing and droving in *The Western Morning News*, 24th March 1983.

2. *A Tour of Cornwall*, by the Rev. Richard Warner.
3. This information is from a footnote to Billingsley's *Survey*, probably contributed by one of his local helpers, the Rev. Urwin Clark of Monksilver.
4. Susan Gates (now Baker), 1987; extract from work then in preparation, *Survival of the Fittest – the natural history of the Exmoor ponies.*
5. All these were shown to me in 1987 by Miss Joy Etherington, formerly of Newland; she has since given them to the Somerset Record Office which kindly provided the photograph (no. 25).
6. *Brass crooks* were hooks for hanging pots and kettles over the open fire in the kitchen. Out of doors, *wooden crooks* replaced panniers on either side of the pack-pony's saddle, for awkward loads.
7. The *drawer* was probably the undersheet, but the word is obsolete.
8. The 'Exmore gray mare' intrigues the specialists; the ponies are never gray in our sense; what colour was she?
9. This will has so many archaic or dialect terms that I try to gloss them all together.
   Beaufet – common eighteenth-century English spelling of buffet, the French for sideboard.
   Tack – horse's harness, or bridle and saddle.
   Mobs – mob-caps, with either two rows of lace or only one.
   Holland – linen, either brown or bleached.
   Table-board – board to rest on trestles, not table with legs.
   Salter – cask in which the pork was salted down; made either of wood or cloam (see below).
   Trendle – also a tub for storing meat; alternatively called *trundle*, in an 1852 sale list, and in later speech *trunnel*.
   Clome, cloam – clay. *Cloamen* – made of clay; pottery.
10. *Buff* (or buff-skin) *breeches* were leather ones, usually of ox-hide.
11. This chapel was superseded in 1881 by a bigger one, simple and dignified; a drawing of it appears in Noel Allen's *Churches and Chapels of Exmoor* (Exmoor Press, 1974). Since then it has been turned into a private house.
12. *Four Men of Somerset* collects four essays submitted for a competition held by the Somerset Archaeological and Natural History Society in 1984, and was published privately in 1985. One is an article by J. K. Ridler on Richard Locke.
13. Ibid. Article by M. Freeman-Archer on Joseph Relph and the Exford development.
14. *Frith* – virtually brushwood.
15. But on the boundary with Oare it changed direction suspiciously. MacDermot deduced that Oare had stolen a chunk of Forest land before the wall was built, in about 1820. Day and Masters' map, made a generation earlier, in 1782, shows a dotted boundary line going nearly straight across westward from Black Barrow through Stowford Bottom to join Badgworthy Water near Long Combe barrows. This does not tally with the Inclosure Map of 1819. (MacDermot thought Long Combe barrow or barrows had

disappeared, but in 1977 one and a half remained; the half was broken up, seemingly by a misaimed shell in gunnery training during the Second World War.)

16. Obliged to enclose, the buyer of the Forest was also required to leave the through-roads open. Hence the well-known gates in the wall, Kinsford, Moles Chamber and Saddle Gate, Brendon and Honeymead Two Gates. Another admitted an old track from Cheriton to Exe Head, and the two longstone gateposts can still be seen, built into the wall and drilled for hinges, to the east of the Hoar Oak; the gateway has been filled. The path is still firm, except for a wide wash-out on the Forest side, probably dating from the 1952 flood.

17. In his second and fuller edition of *Antiquary's Exmoor* (1977). It is not in the earlier one, of 1970.

18. *A Selworthy Notebook*, 1983, by J. K. Ridler, formerly of Blackford Farm.

Chapter 9: Plain living in harsh times

1. See illustrations 22 and 34. Welsh coal is being unloaded from the ketch in the photograph, to be hauled up to Lynton coal-merchants by cliff-railway. (A Lynmouth boatman, Bob Jones the younger, grandson of the builder of the railway and his successor in operating it, recognized, in 1989, the ketch *Enid*, her skipper, a Chichester, on deck, his mate Reggie Williams guiding the basket down, and the man in the butt, Ned Carey, at other times a coach-driver, ready to take charge of it.)

2. Quoted from Mme d'Arblay's letters by Lois Lamplugh, in her *Ilfracombe* (Phillimore, 1984).

3. A North Molton farmer told me a little about this; his father, living at Parracombe at that time, had worked at building the jetty, which was never finished, but can still be seen. The rich man 'from away' had come with big ideas, saw that the little bay was good and deep, and set a great many men to work. All the timber was taken up from Parracombe by horse and cart. They used to *canter* the horses uphill – horses were trained for that work. If the power was not enough they would add more horses, and more, and change them half way through the day. It was all so expensive that the stranger had to give up.

4. The counter-balance system had been known in canal construction early in the century, and the Grand Western Canal, built in 1838, made good use of it. But Bob Jones was the first to apply it as a practical help to seaside residents and visitors.

5. His grandson, Fred Milton of Weatherslade, recounted this in the *Exmoor Review*, 1968.

6. Mr Hayes was a resourceful man, and his donkeys were docile. On one occasion he arrived at a farmhouse when only the mistress was at home, and two sacks, though ready filled, were in the kitchen, and too heavy for him to lift alone. Permission asked and given, he took his donkeys indoors to the load, and told one and then the other to lie down. This enabled him to *roll* a sack across each

animal's back. They got to their feet and went off loaded to the mill as usual.

One of his sons became a Metropolitan policeman and saved Queen Victoria's life by his alacrity. He was in the cordon guarding her way to the House of Lords to open parliament, an armed man pushed forward beside him to assassinate her, and he grabbed him and snatched away his weapon. He was called to the Palace to be thanked and rewarded.

7. 'Afghan', A. F. Glanville, Porlock postman, afoot, for many years, recorded in a brief note in the *Exmoor Review*, 1969 (p.41), 'The old Limeway track on Bromham Plain also conceals lime stones, which possibly dropped off horse and donkey panniers.'

8. The Sunday taboo was difficult in such an unreliable climate. A farmer was not supposed to cut or carry hay, but it was permissible to harvest corn because Christ's disciples plucked ripe ears, rubbed off the husks and ate the grain, as they walked through a cornfield on the Sabbath.

9. The building can only date from after the Inclosure of the Forest, so it did not concern MacDermot. Orwin was writing only of the land John Knight bought, and this piece, outside His Majesty's allotment, had not been available to him. I heard of it from a retired hunt-servant as *The Cork and Bottle*, went to look, and accepted it as an inn or alehouse, of which there were vague memories in Withypool and North Molton. I knew nothing about Greenbarrow Farm until the publication of Roger Burton's *The Heritage of Exmoor* in 1989, from which it is clear that the buildings were identical.

10. All these letters were kindly lent to me by the Huxtables of Swincombe, Challacombe.

11. For details of their efforts, and those of other doctors and clergy, see Jack Hurley's *Rattle his Bones* (Exmoor Press, 1974). The guardians do not show to advantage.

Chapter 10:   Work and play

1. Linhays were sheds of various sizes, for many uses; distinct from the shippons which were cow-sheds with milking stalls.

2. Coigns and old gateposts are now vanishing fast, as gateways are widened to let big farm-machinery through. The traditional word *coigns* is of course the French *coin*, or corner, and the architect's *quoin*, pronounced *koin*.

3. Bampton Fair closed for the last time in 1987.

4. The harbourer is the man responsible for finding a 'warrantable' stag (an appropriate one for hunting) and, at the meet, informing the Master where it is harbouring – lying up for the day in a covert.

5. The tufters are three or four couple of experienced and trusted older hounds used to rouse the stag from the covert; the rest of the pack is not laid on until he has broken away into the open. These terms are defined and the whole process simply and clearly explained by E. R. Lloyd in his *The Wild Red Deer of Exmoor* (Exmoor Press, 1975).

6. *Nemet* or *nymet* meant holy. See Note 13, Chapter 3.

Chapter 11: Houses rise and fall

1. A group of stone rings like the footings of up to a dozen small Bronze Age houses and short lines which might have been the walls of their enclosures, was found by Arthur Phillips in 1980, when he was Warden of the Field Studies Centre at Pinkery. Several archaeologists, a geologist, and others who knew the moor well were convinced that it was not outcrop. For various reasons excavation proved impracticable at that time, but the traces are still there. I described them more fully in *Ancient Exmoor* (Exmoor Press, 1983) on p.56.

2. Another Captain of Mines, a German of the name of Klingender, locally nicknamed 'Old Cullender', was Lord Poltimore's tenant for a time in the spacious Georgian residence which is now Heasley House Hotel. He had reopened the Bampfylde mine in the 1880s, stored large quantities of ore, hoping the price would rise, and when it fell instead he was ruined and could not pay the wages he owed. For the fortunes of the nineteenth-century mining in Devon parishes south of the forest see J. M. Slader's *Days of Renown* (West Country Publications, 1965).

3. In 1835 the Higher Mole Mills in South Molton and the Heasley Mills (plural) together kept 200 looms working. (A. H. Slee: article in *Transactions of the Devonshire Association*, 1938.)

4. The motto is *Nil conscire sibi* – To know nothing against oneself.

5. An article by Ruth Brindle in Rosemary Lauder's *Anthology for North Devon* (published in 1983 but now out of print) names the writers and musicians: Tennyson, Spenser, Scott, Chaucer, Dickens, Shakespeare, Milton and Raleigh; Haydn, Gounod, Mozart, Beethoven, Purcell, Handel, Bach, Mendelssohn. It has also a good photograph of the interior taken in 1981, before the harm was done. In the *Exmoor Review*, 1990, there is a photograph of the exterior, taken by John Crisford in 1988.

6. The local charities run by the vestries had been neighbourly, but a heavy load on the resources of small parishes. So the Unions formed in the 1830s to spread the cost deliberately made their institutions uninviting.

Chapter 12: The women's part

1. The brandiss, or trivet, was used within living memory. Its three iron legs supported an iron plate on which the crock stood. Perhaps it was a little more versatile than the ancient Greek tripods, big cauldrons on three long legs, listed and drawn on the storekeepers' inventories of Nestor's palace at Pylos, but the principle was the same. The tripods must have been made of bronze; the palace was contemporary with Agamemnon's Mycenae, in the high civilization before iron-armed invaders swept down from the north.

2. The oaten straw was rolled into ropes, called *thumb-beans* because the maker began by twisting the straw round his thumb. Finished, the rope would be 7 or 8 feet long, and was used to tie oat-straw in bundles, for keeping.

3. See *Lynton Cottage Hospital, 1876–1981*, E. T. Mold, 1981. (Booklet privately printed, available at the hospital.)

Chapter 13: Two world wars

1. In 1918 women over thirty were given the suffrage; full electoral equality came with 'the flapper vote' in 1928.
2. The original Cuzzicombe (or Cussacombe) post, put up for Queen Victoria, rotted gradually in the wet winds. The present one is a replacement celebrating her great-great-granddaughter's Silver Jubilee in 1977.
3. The red dye, later bought from an ironmonger, was put on the ram's breast, so that it rubbed off on the ewe's rump, showing which had been served. It was not put all over the sheep, because of the importance of keeping the wool clean. A few weeks before shearing the sheep were washed in a stream, dammed to provide a deep enough pool. Sheepwash is a common name for farm or field or to indicate a moorland site where this work was done.
4. Roads E and 4, in Chapter 3.
5. The Kaiser was said to have referred to Britain's 'contemptible little army'. The survivors of the B.E.F. claimed the nickname with pride.
6. The men were paid by the yard for the broken stone they could lay beside the line of the road-to-be. A farmer recalled, twenty years later, that 'hundreds and hundreds of loads' were taken from Brightworthy Barrow. He thought there had been 'a sort of stone rampart round it', and wondered whether there had not been a stone approach as well, 'because they took such a terrible lot of stone to the road'.
7. Miscalled *Portvolken* on the O.S. maps – losing the meaning.
8. A tale of this kind was told by a member of a lively family from Dorset, who found his Devon neighbours rather slow. One evening, passing a very poor cottage on the moor where a man lived alone, he noticed that a hole in a window-pane had been stopped up with the crown of a top-hat. Dorset could not resist poking it in. Devon, blaming the wind, got out of bed and put it back. Before long it was pushed in again. Now Devon became suspicious; he replaced the hat again but waited near the window and *saw* the third attempt. He seized a great club and rushed out, barefoot and in his nightshirt. Dorset fled, Devon gave chase. They ran a long way but Dorset could not shake him off – until he came to a big bramble-patch and, safe in breeches and boots, leapt into the middle of it. Devon did not follow.
9. Things change very slowly. Salmon-poaching by torchlight, with spears, had long added zest to life and food to the larder. In 1610, as MacDermot reports, a group of Withypool men was charged with poaching near Lanacre Bridge. One carried the fish, and 'the reed to maintain the fire' and two stabbed at the shadowy form lying in a pool beside the bank.
   At almost the same spot, in 1940 or soon afterwards, a similar enterprise drew down a German bomb. A raider returning to France from Bristol mistook the light for a house imperfectly

blacked out. The poachers were unhurt, but the Withypool bomb-story was told and retold for years.

10. The word *blitzkrieg* provided the colloquial *blitz* for the bombing raids on London throughout the following winter. In its small way the abbreviation helped to belittle and defy the loud-mouthed dictator – rather like the *old contemptibles* in 1914.

11. Jack Hurley, *Exmoor in Wartime*, Exmoor Press, 1978.

Chapter 14: Yesterday ending

1. In the summer of 1981 a retired farmer, Stan Bawden, told me of an episode some thirty years earlier. His cows had 'the ringworms'. A vet who was credited with special powers was at the farm about some routine matter, after which Stan said to him, 'They tell me you can laugh away the ringworms.'
Vet: 'Do *you* believe I can?'
Stan: 'I don't know, but if you can I wish you would.'
So the vet told Stan to wait outside while he went into the shippon where the cows were. Stan could not resist looking through a knot-hole in the wooden door, and there was the vet, 'all alone, and laughing his head off'. He himself was laughing at the memory, all those years later. The cows recovered.

2. There are good local museums round the fringes of the moor, and a little further away. Kitchen and farm gear of many kinds can be seen at Allerford, Lynton, South Molton and Tiverton. South Molton has also a cider-press, a blacksmith's enormous bellows and an old fire-engine. Lynton adds things used by fishermen and coastal traders, including an oyster-plough. Allerford shows a gutter-plough and a schoolroom, and Arlington, in its stables, a collection of carriages, carts and farm-machinery which was drawn by horses.

SELECTIVE INDEX

Cranmer, Archbishop 63
Cromwell, Oliver 19, 42, 63, 71-80
  passim, 99, 100
Cromwell, Richard 77
Cromwell, Thomas 63, 103
Crook, Capt. Unton 77-8
Crooked Post *See* Withypool Cross
Crooked Post Farm 154
Crowcombe 48
Culbone 40, 98, 103, 118-19
  Cist 18, 40
  Hill stone row 18, 40
  Wheeled-cross stone 40
  Wood 119, 163
Customs officers and smugglers
  155-20
Cutcombe 13, 31, 37, 46, 142
Cuzzicombe Post 212

Dallyn, John 222
Danesbrook 9, 17, 28, 47
Dartmoor 36, 62, 123, 124
Day & Masters 26, 44, 49, 50, 53
Deddycombe 40
  Cot 18
Defoe, Daniel 91, 100, 101
Dennicombe, John 92
Dodo 3
Doniford 43
  Stream 48
Doones 84-5
Dorchester 41, 88
Drake, Sir Francis 61, 62
Draper's Way *See* Steart Lane
Driver Farm 26, 27, 46, 53, 147
Ducombe Wells 199
Dulverton 150, 157, 162, 163, 174, 218
  Cloth industry 91
  Early roads 48, 49, 57
  Forest boundary 5, 11, 12, 13, 20
  Railway 225, 228
  Workhouse 209, 210
Dunkery 31, 37, 44, 49, 62
  Gate 32, 45
Dunster 20, 80, 103
  Castle 6, 13, 73, 74, 75, 91, 98, 101
  Cloth industry 64
  Early roads 25, 41, 46, 54, 56, 83
  Yarn-market 91
Duredon 54
Dure Down 187
Dyer, David & Thomas 20
Dyke family 144

East India Company 95, 114
East Worlington 74, 80, 123
Edbrooke, John 29, 82

Richard 20, 82
Robert 82
Edgerley Stone 15, 52
Edward
  the Confessor 3
  I 5, 150
  II 6
  III 6, 18, 60, 150
  VI 29, 63, 64, 65, 69
  VII 213
Eggesford 48, 102
Eisenhower, General 228
Elizabeth I 30, 62, 65
Elworthy Barrows 44, 45, 46, 48
Emmetts 54
Ernesbarrow 47
Everard, R. G. 42
Exe, River
  from Exe Head 27, 36, 39, 50, 53, 57
  Through Exe Cleeve 39
  To Exford, Exton & Brushford, *q.v.*
Exeter 49, 78, 96, 164, 198
Exford 64, 192, 215
  Forest boundary 9, 12, 13, 20, 82
  Roads 44-55 *passim*
  Snow 177, 178
Exton 63, 75, 161, 189, 195, 217, 220
  Commons 142
  Part of royal manor 3, 7, 9, 13

Faggus, Tom 84-5, 106
Fairfax, General 71, 73, 74, 77, 87
Farley Farm 88, 89, 90
  Water 103, 164
Fiddington 48
Fielding, Henry 97, 105-106
Filleigh 108
Fifstones *See* Five Stones
Five Barrows 36, 37, 54, 155
Five Stones 15, 17-18, 40
Florence mine 196
Foreland 110, 113, 118, 159, 161
Folly 196
Forest Eyre 8, 11, 13
Forest Pounds 24, 93, 94
Fortescues 18, 145, 149, 154
Fortescue, farms 156
Four Oak Cross 54
Foxtwitchen 141
Fray, Henry 20
Free Suitors 7, 8, 19, 23, 24, 29, 35,
  137
Friendship Inn 147, 165
Frost, George 124
  Richard 123
Froude, Rev. John 173-4, 189
Fry family (of Wilsham) 112-13

257